6/16

THE OTHER CATHOLICS

Archbishop Richard Gundrey with new bishops (*left to right*) Patsy
Grubbs, Kera Hamilton, and Diana Phipps, Richmond, Va., October 16, 2005.
Courtesy of Daniel Dangaran.

The
OTHER
Catholics

Remaking America's Largest Religion

JULIE BYRNE

COLUMBIA UNIVERSITY PRESS

NEW YORK

Columbia University Press
Publishers Since 1893
New York   Chichester, West Sussex
cup.columbia.edu
Copyright © 2016 Columbia University Press

The author expresses appreciation to the Schoff Fund at the University Seminars at Columbia University for their help in publication. The ideas presented have benefited from discussions in the University Seminar on Religion in America.

Library of Congress Cataloging-in-Publication Data
Names: Byrne, Julie, 1968– author.
Title: The other Catholics : remaking America's largest religion / Julie Byrne.
Description: New York : Columbia University Press, 2016. | Includes
    bibliographical references and index.
Identifiers: LCCN 2015044785 | ISBN 9780231166768 (cloth : alk. paper) |
    ISBN 9780231541701 (e-book)
Subjects: LCSH: Independent Catholic churches—United States. | Catholic
    Church—United States—History—21st century.
Classification: LCC BX4794.2.U6 B97 2016 | DDC 284/.8—dc23
LC record available at http://lccn.loc.gov/2015044785

Printed in the United States of America

c 10 9 8 7 6 5 4 3 2 1

Cover design: Jordan Wannemacher
Cover image: Courtesy of Susan Collins

For Glenton

◆ ◆ ◆

She will hold the position of preeminence. I will hold the position of Patriarch, which will have second place to her.
—Herman Spruit, founder of the Catholic Apostolic Church
of Antioch–Malabar Rite, announcing the elevation of Meri Spruit
to presiding matriarch in April 1990

CONTENTS

ILLUSTRATIONS

◆ ◆ ◆

ACKNOWLEDGMENTS

◆ ◆ ◆

WORKING ON THIS book for many years, I benefited from the help of numerous people and institutions, and indeed could not have finished without them.

First and foremost I thank the independent Catholic women and men who welcomed a stranger into their midst and shared their lives with me. With these interactions unfolded the story and substance of the whole book. Above all I am grateful to Archbishop Richard Gundrey, who saw the possibilities of our meeting from the start and unfailingly supported my work. I am thankful to Bishops Alan Kemp and Mark Elliott Newman for continuing to support me and answer questions after Gundrey's tenure. I witness all of the amazing independent Catholic interviewees, correspondents, and survey respondents from the African Orthodox Church, the American Catholic Church, Ascension Alliance, the Catholic Apostolic Church in North America, the Church of Antioch, the Community of the Incarnation–Kansas City, the Ecumenical Catholic Communion, the Imani Temple, the Liberal Catholic Church, the White-Robed Monks of St. Benedict, and several other jurisdictions. Often interviews spilled over into dinners, drinks, other hospitalities, and new friendships. I am honored and forever changed to have met their acquaintance.

Thank you to many colleagues and institutions whose material assistance and intellectual vibrancy contributed to this book. At Hofstra University, Dean Bernard Firestone, Provost Herman Berliner, and President Stuart Rabinowitz lent steady support, not least in the form of special leaves, student aides, course reductions, and summer grants. My Department of Religion colleagues Balbinder Bhogal, Ann Burlein, Warren Frisina, Sophie Hawkins, Hussein Rashid, Santiago Slabodsky, and John Teehan are readers, collaborators, and friends. During early years of research I taught at Texas Christian University and Duke University. There, too, I found invaluable support from administrators and colleagues. I feel tremendous gratitude to have taught and learned from graduate and undergraduate students at TCU, Duke, and Hofstra. Special thanks go to Francesca Antonacci and Daria Perrone, students at Hofstra who transcribed all interviews, turning them from digital sound files into searchable Word documents. At all three institutions, I am grateful for the support of department administrators, especially Joanne Herlihy at Hofstra. At all three institutions, I thank the special collections librarians and interlibrary loan specialists who tracked down obscure items wherever they might be. In the same measure I am grateful for the help of staff at the following libraries and archives: the University of California at Santa Barbara, the University of Notre Dame, the Library of Congress, the Society of St. Joseph of the Sacred Heart (Josephites), the Episcopal Diocese of Fond-du-Lac, the Science of Mind Archives, and the Imani Temple. The Aaron Warner Publication Fund of the University Seminars at Columbia University underwrote the cost of professional indexing.

I also thank those who generously invited me to "workshop" parts of this book in seminars, presentations, and essays and thereby helped make it better: the American religion colloquia at Princeton University and Columbia University; the Duke Center for Late Ancient Studies conference "Late Antiquity Made New"; the North American Religions Section and the Roman Catholic Studies Group of the American Academy of Religion; the journal American Catholic Studies; the Center for American Religion at Indiana University–Purdue University at Indianapolis; and the Smithsonian Institute.

Far-flung scholars of religion are fellow travelers in thought and life who have consulted on this book over time. They include Catherine Albanese,

Emma Anderson, Scott Appleby, Yaakov Ariel, Craig Atwood, Randall Balmer, Courtney Bender, Kalman Bland, Kate Bowler, Matthew Butler, Joel Carpenter, Bill Cavanaugh, Tshepo Masango Chéry, Elizabeth Clark, Stephanie Cobb, Elesha Coffman, Andrew Cole, Timothy Daniels, William D'Antonio, George Demacopoulos, Michele Dillon, Markus Dressler, Robert Ellwood, Kumiko Endo, Jeannine Hill Fletcher, Paul Froese, Terry Godlove, Henry Goldschmidt, Rich Houseal, Andrew Jacobs, PJ Johnston, David Kaufman, Kathleen Kautzer, Amy Koehlinger, Nadia Lahutsky, Rick Lischer, Katie Lofton, James McCartin, Sean McCloud, Gordon Melton, Bruce Mullin, Lynn Neal, Ann Neumann, Mark Noll, Abraham Nussbaum, Michael Pasquier, Jill Peterfeso, David Powell, Leonard Primiano, Elizabeth Pritchard, Jacob Remes, Sue Ridgely, Jalane Schmidt, Chad Seales, Phillip Luke Sinitiere, Kyle Smith, Josef Sorett, Kathleen Sprows Cummings, Rodney Stark, David Steinmetz, Ann Taves, Magda Teter, Terrence Tilley, Ludger Viefhues-Bailey, Jan Visser, Grant Wacker, David Watt, Isaac Weiner, Judith Weisenfeld, Jeff Wilson, Lauren Winner, Phyllis Zagano, David Zercher, and the entirety of the fun and brilliant American Catholic Studies Reading Group, convened by Marian Ronan and meeting across three states. I appreciate the particularly careful and critical feedback provided by Jessica Delgado, Charles Parker, John Plummer, Stephen Prothero, Thomas Rzeznik, Nathan Schneider, John Seitz, Maureen Tilley, Thomas Tweed, David Yamane, and two rounds of anonymous Columbia University Press readers. All went above and beyond to help me improve the book.

Others who gave assistance at critical junctures include James Abbott, Alan Bailin, Theresa Billiel, Weston Blelock, Randy Calvo, Tobe Carey, Sandy Dijkstra, John Douglass, Roger Fawcett, Ed Fields, James Ishmael Ford, Christine Hall, Thomas Hickey, James Konicki, Carol Lauderdale, Peter Levenda, Paul McMahon, Jean McManus, Anthony Mikovsky, Nina Paul, Matthew Payne, Mark Peddigrew, Michael Ruk, James Saad, Lisa Spar, Rhazes Spell, Gregory Tillett, and David Woolwine. I am a huge fan of the scholars within independent Catholicism, several of whom assisted me in countless ways, including Tim Cravens, Rob Angus Jones, Lewis Keizer, John Mabry, John Plummer (again), Gregory Singleton, Peter-Ben Smit, Jack Sweeley, Alexis Tancibok, and Serge Theriault.

A few who helped me with this book died during the time of its completion. I am so fortunate to have met them. They are Peter Hogan, archivist at the Josephite archives in Baltimore, Maryland; Daryl Schmidt, friend, mentor and chair at TCU; Leah Flowers, my Texas lifesaver; Uly Gooch, Episcopal priest and Gentle Shepherd pastor; Jack Pischner and Becky Taylor, interviewees and Sophia seminarians; Bishop Connie Poggiani, Mother Millicent Mountjoy, Mother Virginia Essene, Dick Lemieux, and Trudi Willcox Wood; and Meri Spruit, interviewee and matriarch emerita of the Church of Antioch.

Despite much consultation with these transcendent minds, my lesser powers have resulted in an imperfect book. All its mistakes are mine alone.

I got to know the marvelous crew at Columbia University Press when they published my first book, *O God of Players: The Story of the Immaculata Mighty Macs* (2003). I am pleased again to work with editor Wendy Lochner and the whole team.

Family, friends, consultants on religion, and supporters of book writing—there is no distinction! I am awed to run in your circles, and I love you. Glenton DeLeon-Job, and Dylan and Aadan; Donald Byrne and Pam Neill; Michelle Morgan and family; Monica Byrne; Mary Byrne and Mark Rogers; Clare Byrne and Stefan Jacobs; Donald and LaKaisha Byrne, and Niko and Laxmi; Arminta Foushee; Whit Andrews; Cindy Kirby and Lee Steck; Everett Harper; Judy Dodd; Marian Ronan and Keith Russell; Jenn Henton; Phil Byrne and family; Sue and Ed Felty and family; Ajantha Subramanian and Vince Brown and family; Cassandra Marshall; Richard Tietjen; Greg Tietjen and Donna Snyder; Ellie and Eddie Mer and family; Jolie Olcott and Russell Lacy; Karen Hardwick, John Hardwick and family; LaKeesha and Mike Walrond and family; Laura and Joel Wysong and family; Jon Rubenstein, Karin Swann-Rubenstein, and family; John Spann; Frances and Alan Wiener and family; Edna Rodríguez, Brent Plate, and family; the Bartholomews of Trinidad; the Songuis of Brooklyn; the LaCroix of Queens; and all my mind-sparking, soul-salving neighbors in Bed-Stuy and East New York.

My mother graduated in the first Marquette University class that accepted women for the MA in Theology. She also failed to land a job as Director of Religious Education at a Roman Catholic parish after she answered truthfully an interview question about her stance on artificial birth control. My father left Roman Catholic seminary training in 1962 and became a pioneer in the use of folklore and oral history in the study of American religion. My sisters make art in song, dance, prose, and poems at the intersection of Catholicism and everything else, and my brother builds pine coffins for green burial, monk-style. My grandmother on one side was a Trinity College class president who married a Protestant, had seven children, and wrote home ritual guides for Paulist Press. My great-uncle on the other side was the Roman Catholic archbishop of Dubuque, Iowa, who visited my childhood home but did not eat, since he was fasting "for the souls of wayward priests," my father said, "possibly his own." He had come to lay hands on my mother who was fast losing her eyesight, though charismatic healing is not the norm among Roman archbishops. I could go on. But this is enough to make the point: I know intimately that "other Catholics" come in all forms, not just in independent Catholicism. Thank you to all the "other Catholics."

THE OTHER CATHOLICS

INTRODUCTION

OTHER CATHOLICS

I KNEW INDEPENDENT Catholics were different. But when I attended the Church of Antioch annual Convocation in 2005 in Richmond, Virginia, I was still not prepared for its main event, a high mass featuring the consecration of three bishops.

Three *women* bishops.

Mother Patsy Grubbs hailed from Houston, where she worked as a spiritual counselor and held weekly healing services. She was married with children and grandchildren, one of whom lived with her full-time. Mother Diana Phipps, with her spouse Kathy Perry, had just opened a retreat center at their home in the Texas Hill Country. Together the couple traveled in their RV doing contract gigs as operating room nurses. Mother Kera Hamilton celebrated mass once a month for a fledgling parish of about forty people in the Philadelphia suburbs. She was divorced and worked as a medical transcriptionist. All three women were converts to Catholicism. All had found the Church of Antioch on winding paths through other religious groups. All had arrived in Richmond to take the next step in lives that seemed as much of a surprise to them as they were to me.[1]

With family and friends gathered, the mass commenced traditionally, using liturgy dating to early centuries of Christianity. But when each woman had a Bible cracked open and laid across her shoulders, when presiding

FIGURE 0.1 Priests (*front to back*) Patsy Grubbs, Diana Phipps, and Kera Hamilton processing before their consecration as bishops, Richmond, Va., October 16, 2005. Courtesy of Daniel Dangaran.

archbishop Richard Gundrey lovingly laid hands on heads, when he said, "Be filled with the Holy Spirit," and breathed upon anointed scalps, when each was given a ring and crozier, then fitted with the miter and sweetly fussed with to make sure the hair still looked good, somehow there was no avoiding the sense that this ancient ritual resounded afresh when performed on female bodies. By the end of the presentation of the episcopal insignia, the new bishops were in tears, and so was most of the church.[2]

Laughter rippled through the assembly too. Archbishop Richard Gundrey was reminding the women, "Don't let the ego get you . . . don't let those pointy hats and sticks get you!" They were shepherds, he said, for "sheep not of this fold." Their calling was not about fancy regalia, obedience to a superior, or even belief in Catholicism—they were to go beyond fidelity to any earthly entity. "A higher power moves through you," Archbishop Richard said, now choking up again. "That's where you come from."[3]

Of course, by some lights the ordination of women is no big shock. In the early twenty-first century, especially in North America and Europe, many Christian churches and other religious communities ordain women. But

Catholics do not. At least not most Catholics. Yet here—in this small Richmond parish of the Church of Antioch, one of many independent Catholic bodies in the United States—a Catholic congregation gathered to make women bishops. It was an event that the Church of Antioch had already witnessed over a dozen times since 1974.

Across the United States today, some independent Catholic churches ordain women and some do not. But in either case, numerous bodies of these "other Catholics" operate separately from the biggest groups usually associated with Catholicism—the Roman Catholic church headed by the pope, Orthodox churches recognized by the patriarch of Constantinople, and the Anglican Communion led by the archbishop of Canterbury. They are "independent Catholics"—a name many of them use for themselves, though few love the label. In America in the early millennium they number at least 250 "jurisdictions"—geographic areas headed by a bishop. They include thousands of ministries and up to a million adherents, while independent clergy additionally serve thousands of nonmembers. With their own histories and polities, independent Catholics decide things like eligibility for ordination as freestanding churches. They decide what Catholicism means in ways both similar to and different from the major communions.[4]

In short, not all Catholics are Roman Catholics.

INDEPENDENT CATHOLICISM

"Other Catholics" was the label used by the United States Bureau of the Census in 1890, when independent Catholics first seemed to warrant classification. In that Census, six US Catholic churches besides Rome were listed under the heading of "Other Catholics (6 bodies)." One of the six "Other Catholic" churches of 1890 would lead to the Church of Antioch. Another was a church formed to protest the Roman promulgation of the doctrine of papal infallibility. Yet another was the Polish National Catholic Church, probably the best known today. From 1890 to 1936, when it stopped tracking religious bodies, the Census would continue to count independent jurisdictions such as the Liberal Catholic Church and the African Orthodox Church.[5]

To tell the overall story of independent Catholicism, I wanted to look at one church as a primary example. So I spent ten years hanging out with Antioch Catholics. Archbishop Richard Gundrey and the three new bishops in Richmond were among my interviewees. I selected the Church of Antioch because it was an important and long-lasting group, connected to many other US independents and encompassing the American movement's variety, including mystical, metaphysical, esoteric, and eclectic threads. Through the Church of Antioch, you can see the continuity and distinctiveness of the whole.

However, no one church can tell it all. Independents differ widely, ranging from right to left on the political spectrum. On the right, traditionalist churches practice versions of Catholicism more conservative than Rome. These include the Society of St. Pius X, founded by Marcel Lefebvre, as well as the Mount St. Michael's community in Spokane, Washington, and actor Mel Gibson's church in Malibu, California, which made headlines when he directed the movie *The Passion of the Christ* in 2004. On the left stand groups such as the Church of Antioch, the Ecumenical Catholic Communion, and the White-Robed Monks of St. Benedict.[6]

I focus on the left-leaning side for two reasons. First, the liberal types are older. The independent phenomenon began as part of Catholic reform movements dating to the early modern period, two and a half centuries before the Roman Catholic church modernized during the Second Vatican Council of the early 1960s. In contrast, the traditionalist groups started after Vatican II and are a comparatively recent development. Second, left-leaning groups are poised ultimately to have a greater impact on the future. While traditionalists get more attention from US scholars and journalists, liberal independents synch with larger liberalizing trends and mingle with the big bodies of Catholicism and other religious communities. For reasons past and future, then, my story concentrates on churches like Antioch, with traditionalists making cameo appearances. In 2016, many left-leaning independents not only ordain women, but also perform same-sex marriages, open communion to all, and allow multiple religious affiliations, among other surprising things.[7]

Independent Catholics are surprising. Catholicism apart from Rome? Many people reading these words may be taken aback that "other Catholics" exist at all. Why doesn't anyone know about them? The short answer is that the Roman Catholic church is a behemoth of size and influence. Constituting a fifth of the US population, it is by far the single largest religious group in the country. Globally too the Roman communion holds sway, making up a sixth of the world's population and enjoying worldwide unity under the leadership of the pope. Still, that unity is not absolute. The surprise of independents has the potential to shift perspectives on the whole of Catholicism—including the Roman kind.[8]

In the decade I spent with the Church of Antioch, my own perspectives certainly changed. Here, I tell what I discovered. I found that independent Catholicism is deeply continuous with the family of Catholicisms, linked to many other American faiths, and crucial if we want to understand Catholicism and American religion as a whole. It is "other Catholicism" because it is institutionally separate from bigger churches. But it is also "other" because it harbors and tests that which is elsewhere disallowed—such as women's ordination. It is Catholicism's research lab. It is Catholicism's arts incubator. It is Catholicism's black sheep. In short, it is part of how modern Catholicism works. Through independents, then, one can see better the thoughts and unthinkables, centers and peripheries, flows and fault lines of Catholicism and American religion. This hidden-in-plain-sight story tends to startle most Catholics about their own tradition. But for everyone, independent Catholicism jostles ingrained assumptions about the American faith landscape.

INDEPENDENTS AT A GLANCE

As a group independents are tiny. In the United States in 2016 I estimate that they number about a million. By comparison, total numbers for other US faiths include Quakers at 87,000, Orthodox at 1.5 million, Muslims and Episcopalians both at 2.8 million, Mormons at 4.9 million, Jews at 5.9 million, Pentecostals at 11 million, and Catholics at 64 million. So, independents are tiny in comparison to Roman Catholics, but so are most other religious groups.[9]

In the late twentieth and early twenty-first centuries, independents are gaining attention. Media covered the Imani Temple of Washington, D.C., founded in 1989 by former Roman priest George Stallings to celebrate a new African-American Rite. Three notable parishes went independent in 1998, 2005, and 2008, respectively—Spiritus Christi (Rochester, New York), St. Stanislaus Kostka (St. Louis, Missouri), and Spirit of St. Stephen's (Minneapolis, Minnesota). In 2009 Pope Benedict XVI made overtures of reconciliation toward the above-mentioned traditionalist Society of St. Pius X. Around that same time, a few Roman Catholic communities vigiling against church closure ended up going independent, such as the Community of St. Peter (Cleveland, Ohio), Our Lady of Guadalupe (Trenton, New Jersey), and St. Bridget's (Indianapolis, Indiana). Starting in 2002 and garnering significant media attention, guerrilla ordinations by Roman Catholic Womenpriests launched dozens of new Catholic congregations. Womenpriests claim Roman identity but, like independents, they ordain outside Roman protocols. In addition, growing devotion in Mexico and the United States to *Santa Muerte*, or Holy Death, is associated with the independent Traditional Holy Catholic Apostolic Church and generates frequent news stories and popular culture notice, for example, in the critically acclaimed series *Breaking Bad*.[10]

Beyond the headlines, however, lies a little-known story of non-Roman Catholicism dating back several centuries. It started in the Netherlands in 1724, came to the United States in 1819, and continued proliferating to the present time. In the vast sweep of reform afoot in European early modern Catholicism, changes took one of four paths: the reform died, or it succeeded within Rome, or it left Rome and became Protestant, or it left Rome and remained Catholic. That last possibility has been the least recognized of the four.

But Anglicans and other reformers from the sixteenth century onward claimed Catholic identity apart from Rome. So did Orthodox Christians. Non–Roman Catholics might still acknowledge the bishop of Rome as *primus inter pares*—"first among equals" among bishops of the world. But they deny that he holds jurisdiction over other bishops. On the contrary, they teach that from ancient times, papal decisions were not to override conciliar resolutions, meaning those made in councils of Catholic bishops meeting together.

To leave Rome but remain Catholic—this was the shadow possibility within the Catholic Reformation that led to independent churches. In the Dutch city of Utrecht, influential Catholics had long tangled with Rome over issues of theology and authority. In 1724 they bypassed papal permissions to collaborate with Dominique-Marie Varlet, Rome's Bishop of Babylon, to consecrate a prelate for Utrecht. After the French Revolution, Catholic experimentation with new churches accelerated. These churches generally featured conciliar polity, ecumenical aims, and vernacular masses not only before the Second Vatican Council (1962–65), but also before the First Vatican Council (1869–70). After the American Revolution, numerous short-lived non–Roman Catholic churches rode waves of revolutionary spirit. In 1819, Catholics of Charleston, South Carolina, planned to connect with Utrecht and start an "Independent Catholick Church of the United States." After the First Vatican Council, Utrecht joined with Roman reformers opposed to the doctrine of papal infallibility to create the Union of Utrecht, also known as the Old Catholic churches. And in 1892, Frenchman Joseph René Vilatte became the first independent bishop in the United States, founding the American Catholic Church two years later. By the middle of the twentieth century, independents could be found not only in Europe and the United States, but also in Australia, Brazil, India, Mexico, the Philippines, and South Africa, among many other places.

But independents thrive especially in the United States. Their flavors of Catholicism cannot be accounted for by simple reference to American nationalism, pluralism, culture wars, and religious decentralization. Yet all of those play parts in the flourishing of the US independent scene. Almost every month a new church is born. Almost every month a church splinters—a sign of dysfunction or a sign of vitality, depending on how you look at it. Some claim inspiration from the Old Catholic tradition, while others emphasize Roman, Orthodox, or Anglican identity. They celebrate common progenitors, but keep reviving or experimenting with the faith, from traditionalist sedevacantists who coronate their own popes to radical communitarians who question ordination entirely.

As diverse as they are, however, almost all independent Catholics have a few things in common. They have bishops in apostolic succession. They celebrate seven sacraments. They revere the saints. And they hold that it is possible to be Catholic outside the big bodies. Independents often express the sentiment in an aphorism: "It's Catholicism without Rome." In an interview, Antioch deacon Roberto Foss of Los Angeles added that he needed to say little more: "Often that's mind-blowing enough." Mind-blowing to some, increasingly familiar to others, it is indeed a different take than the widespread US understanding that being Catholic implies formal communion with the pope.[11]

From the standpoint of official Roman Catholic theology, being Catholic certainly implies formal communion with the pope. As the Roman church's *Baltimore Catechism* phrased it for generations of workaday Roman Catholics, "Our Holy Father the Pope, the Bishop of Rome, is the Vicar of Christ on earth and the visible Head of the Church." In that case, independent Catholics are by definition schismatic Catholics—that is, not fully or properly Catholics at all. But that is a theological stance, one position among many about what counts as Catholic legitimacy. Like the Orthodox and Anglican communions, independents hold that the "Rome" in Roman Catholicism is not a crucial part of the tradition. They are doing Catholicism, they say, but not under the jurisdiction of the Roman pontiff.[12]

Meanwhile, though the official Vatican stance views independents as schismatics, Roman reaction varies from case to case. Sometimes Roman authorities ignore independents. Sometimes they treat them as just another religious group on the pluralistic faith landscape. Sometimes they incorporate changes that independents represent, even if centuries later. In a few cases Roman authorities admit the sacramental validity of other Catholic bodies. Occasionally they make ecumenical gestures, as the Vatican did toward the Old Catholic churches of Europe after Vatican II. Infrequently, Rome sets up protocols for reconciliation, as when Benedict XVI reached out to the St. Pius X bishops.

On the other hand, it is easy to find Roman Catholic outlets that mock independents as "fake" Catholics "playing church." US Roman bishops routinely say that independents are "not Catholic" and excommunicate them. (Independents routinely reply that they are not under the jurisdiction of Rome, so Rome cannot excommunicate them.) So the approach of Roman leaders, by turns dogmatic and pragmatic, is an angle of the story, too. Tiny independents are part of Catholicism—not least an ongoing factor in Roman Catholicism.

CLAIMING CATHOLICISM

The independent aphorism "Catholicism without Rome" made me think about what makes a church Catholic. Does Catholicism just mean following bishops, celebrating sacraments, and venerating saints? If members self-identify as Catholic, does that make them so? If a church ordains women and most Catholics do not, is it still Catholic? If an independent communicant were gay and married and Buddhist, could these "other" Catholicisms include . . . pretty much anything?

As I hung out with independents, I started to realize that in the twenty-first-century United States, a lot of people claim the word "Catholic," starting with Roman Catholics themselves. Since most Americans already associate Catholicism with Rome, Roman Catholics must defend the claim very little. Even within the Roman church, however, naming is thick with history and politics. The term "Roman Catholic" was actually coined by outsiders, in this case sixteenth-century Anglican divines who wanted to distinguish their Catholicism from that of Rome. Ever since, some Roman Catholics have considered use of the modifier "Roman" an unwarranted capitulation to the idea that there could be more than one Catholic church. In their view, one should just say "Catholic" with no modifier. This is the practice of the Vatican itself, whose popes almost always call the church simply "the Catholic Church," as in *The Catechism of the Catholic Church.*[13]

In the twentieth and twenty-first centuries, some Roman Catholic progressives have likewise left off the "Roman," but for different reasons. To many it seems inadequate to name the whole church for one city—Catholicism is global but "Roman" is parochial. Other Roman progressives emphasize the "completeness" of the church everywhere: the Catholic Church in Dubuque is as replete as the Catholic Church in Rome, they say, so again one should not call the whole church "Roman." Still other Roman progressives, however, want to keep the "Roman" for reasons somewhat akin to the Anglican divines: it ecumenically acknowledges that there are multiple Catholic churches.[14]

As for me, I decided to use "Roman Catholic" all the time, just for the sake of clarity. That decision enmeshes me in the politics of naming, I know. But writing about a cacophony of claims to Catholicism requires modifiers. Most "other Catholics" use modifiers, too, mostly for the same pragmatic reason. So do Eastern Catholics, members of twenty-two separate churches that are not "Roman" Catholic but still in full communion with the pope. To talk about the Byzantine Catholics, Maronite Catholics, and Melkite Greek Catholics of the Roman communion, one adds descriptors.

Outside Rome, not only Orthodox, Anglican, and independent churches but also several historic eastern bodies claim Catholicism—the non-Chalcedonian Syrian, Coptic, and Armenian churches. Numerous Protestants claim Catholicism, too, sometimes within big Protestant bodies and sometimes in small independent churches. Lutheran, Congregationalist, Methodist, and Baptist claimants go beyond general Christian affirmation of "small c" catholicism and assert "capital C" Catholic identity. To them and to all Catholics, the word is historically preeminent, theologically crucial, culturally prestigious, and sentimentally treasured. But because of overwhelming association with the Roman church, all Catholics outside Rome continually have to explain and defend Catholic identity.

Few groups agree on the essence or definition of Catholicism. They all repeat a well-known tautology of the faith, "Catholic means universal," but they do not agree on what universal means. The Nicene Creed's "marks of the church," formulated in the fourth century and still widely cited in Christian circles ("one, holy, catholic, and apostolic"), are likewise subject to wide interpretation. Institutional unity in the Roman pontiff is definitive only for those in the Roman communion. Even those who agree about the role of a pope do not agree about which pope, such as sedevacantists, whose popes teach that the Roman papacy departed from the true church at the time of Vatican II. Other common Catholic elements like sacramentalism and apostolic succession also mean different things.

As I started this research, the clamor of claimants was both confusing and clarifying. It was confusing because even as a scholar and teacher of US Catholicism, I, like so many others, had never really grasped that "other Catholics" exist. It was clarifying, however, because it made me see that for all the fascinating claims, the clamor is the story in itself. How and why do all these groups, from Romans to independents, understand themselves as Catholics? How do people and groups click and clash with one another to create and differentiate Catholicism? How do they mediate a vast Catholic heritage that itself had been produced and differentiated over centuries?

My questions started to turn away from assuming anything about Catholicism, and toward discovering how Catholics claim it. I stopped asking if independents are "really" Catholic. Or, for that matter, if Roman Catholics are. Instead, I just accepted Catholics as Catholics whenever they said they were Catholic. While self-identification may not suffice for all contexts, in this case there are no criteria of Catholicism I can use that are not already part of the claiming and contesting. Instead, I tell the story of the clamor. I ask how categorizations work, rather than what they mean.[15]

Of course, this approach is no mythical stance outside the fray. Defining Catholicism by self-description is itself a position. It is a position at odds with "One True Church" Catholics, who can be found among Roman, Orthodox, Anglican, and independent churches alike. It is a position also at odds with Catholics who rhetorically "include everyone," since as a scholar of religion I do not aim for inclusiveness but rather just hope to represent Catholicism in its full complexity. Still, the mere fact of my noticing independent Catholics and writing a book about them surely amounts to taking a position on their significance. So, no doubt about it: I am producing Catholicism, too. Like claimants, I am hammering stakes, marking boundaries, and creating meaning.

FIFTY YEARS OF THE CHURCH OF ANTIOCH

In this book, I tell a story of US independent Catholicism using the Church of Antioch as a prism onto the whole. Founded in 1959 by Dutch-born

Californian Herman Spruit, the Church of Antioch followed the lead of this meandering mystic and passionate prelate. Herman Spruit started as a Methodist minister, spent time in a metaphysical group called Religious Science, was ordained by a gnostic independent Catholic bishop, and finally started his own church. He came to see Catholicism as a sacramental tradition to be practiced with radical openness. To him, "Catholic means universal" mandated a faith literally for everyone, offered without restrictions of any kind.

Yet he struggled with limitations—his own and those of others—as well as what boundaries to establish for his church. In his view, Antioch was traditional because it practiced the sacraments and put Christ at the core: Herman Spruit named the church for the city where by tradition the label "Christian" was first used. But Christ was not the only path to the divine. The Antioch founder accordingly incorporated people and ideas from many other traditions. Whoever came to the church could take communion. Whoever joined the church could complete its seminary preparation and be ordained. Whoever was ordained could create his or her own mass, with traditional or eclectic elements.

It seems never to have occurred to Herman Spruit to exclude women from ministry, but not until he founded his own church did he become a public advocate for their ordination. At that time in the United States, no big Catholic bodies were ordaining women to the priesthood. Spruit became known throughout independent Catholicism for blazing this trail, catching heat from other leaders before they came around. By the mid-1970s, women's ordination was a mainstream topic, but a female bishop was still ahead of the curve. When Spruit consecrated Jennie Maiereder as a Catholic *bishop* in the spring of 1974, it was still a few months before the "Philadelphia Eleven" were ordained as the Anglican communion's first well-known female *priests*. Then Antioch stayed ahead of the curve. Herman's decision to tap his partner Archbishop Meri Spruit as successor meant that by 1990, Antioch's presiding bishop was a woman. It was nearly unprecedented. And it remains highly unusual, even in today's independent Catholic churches.

Herman Spruit's spiritual seeking imprinted a "seeker" character on the church and on the whole American movement. He symbolically gathered

FIGURE 0.2 New bishop Kera Hamilton giving a blessing, Richmond, Va., October 16, 2005. Courtesy of Daniel Dangaran.

in himself many Catholicisms by receiving a handful of consecrations from bishops in different apostolic lineages. He in turn consecrated dozens who started their own churches, adding to cycles of wild growth and sudden expiration that make independents very difficult to keep track of. Many Antioch-connected churches are liberal, eclectic, and metaphysical. But other offspring lean right, because Herman made friends on the conservative side as well. Meanwhile, Antioch itself had ups and downs. Leaders came and went. During and after the time of the Spruits, some bishops broke away to form new jurisdictions.

Still, when the church celebrated its fiftieth anniversary in 2009, its ranks included over sixty clerics with thirty charters for "churches or creative ministries" in thirteen states and five countries: Argentina, Australia, Canada, England, and the United States. Each chartered ministry in the United States was covered by Antioch's listing with the Internal Revenue Service as a tax-exempt nonprofit charitable organization. More aspiring clerics were enrolled in Sophia Divinity School, Antioch's distance-learning seminary.

The church held annual Convocations, generated newsletters, sponsored a listserv, and maintained a website, all headed by Archbishop Richard Gundrey at "Church Central" in Santa Fe, New Mexico. Antioch's easily countable members were a corps of clerics serving populations both inside and outside the church. But each cleric served dozens to hundreds of people in various ways. The whole penumbra was quite diverse, including men and women, gay and straight, married and solo, converts and cradle Catholics from a variety of ethnic and racial backgrounds.[16]

Antiochians even said that Catholics can practice other faiths. Archbishop Richard, brought up in the Episcopal Church and affiliated for fourteen years with Religious Science, explained how Catholicism could be so open. "Universal: for all people," he said. "Catholic to me, when I use that word, doesn't mean associated with a particular religion. All humanity is Catholic in that sense. Our doors are open to anyone who wants to come in here. You don't have to take a test. You don't have to adhere to a creed."[17]

As much as some Antiochians distinguish their Catholicism from the Roman kind, their biographies show overlap between the two churches. A few count themselves fully Roman as well as independent. Many are former Roman Catholic nuns, seminarians, priests, or monks. Others continue to work in Roman Catholic parishes, serve in Roman Catholic hospitals, attend Roman Catholic churches, or teach at Roman Catholic universities.

The crossover goes both ways. Progressive Roman Catholics invite independents to their gatherings and collaborate with them for common aims. Call to Action, the largest Roman progressive group, holds conferences with masses celebrated by independent women priests. Another conference of progressives saw Roman attendees pack a session led by an independent bishop called "How to Start an Alternative Catholic Community." More cross-fertilization happens when Roman pastors reach out to independent clergy to help meet the sacramental needs of parishioners outside the provisions of Roman canon law. An independent priest can do a combined bris-baptism, for example, or the wedding of a divorcée, where a Roman priest may not.[18]

Independents have deep and unabashed ties to Protestants, too. In the early twenty-first century, a handful of independent Catholic clerics serve as full-time pastors in Protestant churches. Others pursue ordination as Zen

Buddhist priests or take initiation in Vipassana, a Hindu tradition. Also among independents one discovers a Catholic component of metaphysicalism, that "third stream" of American religious history. Independents show up in accounts of gnostic revivals, Masonic organizations, New Thought, and the Theosophical Society, giving sanctuary to a Catholic esoteric tradition.[19]

CONTINUITY AND CREATIVITY

Participating in common Catholic patrimony, remixing it with other traditions, and harboring alternative practices, independent Catholicism serves as a catalyst, cavern, and clarifier of Catholicism and American religion as a whole. It is part of how modern Catholicism works. It illumines how all of US religion works.

Independents both continue and re-create Catholic traditions. Maintaining and modifying tradition at the same time are not unusual—all Catholics do that. But independents are particular in what they maintain and change. They keep four things common to all Catholic bodies: apostolic succession, seven sacraments, devotion to the saints (especially Mary, the mother of Jesus), and the word "Catholic" itself. What independents discard is unusual: visible unity, or the idea that the "one" church avowed in the Nicene Creed is or should be one real-world human institution. For them, oneness in the form of invisible unity works fine.

The idea of the "invisible church" is strongly associated with the sixteenth-century reformer John Calvin—who adapted it from the fourth-century bishop Augustine of Hippo—and indicates God's elect within the visible church, and theoretically outside of it. The invisible church is the real *ecclesia* of Christ, according to this theological tack, no matter the number of Christian institutions. While the Roman church claims identity as the one true church both visible *and* invisible, nineteenth-century Anglicans invented a Catholic endorsement of multiple institutions, namely, the "branch theory," which saw Rome, Constantinople, and Canterbury as three branches of one Catholic tree. Independents on the left-leaning side radicalize branch theory to include not just three churches but all Catholic churches—and sometimes just everybody. As Archbishop Richard said, Catholicism includes "all humanity." Independents on the right-leaning side might still say that the invisible church manifests only in their own tiny institution. Even with this exception, however, it is still true that for all independents, Catholic churches can be—perhaps should be—both one *and* multiple.

Independent Catholic history is deeply enmeshed with other histories, most notably those of the big communions and western metaphysicals. In turn, Catholics and metaphysicals cannot be fully understood without reference to independents. From the eighteenth century to the present, conversations between the big bodies and independent Catholics have affected all parties, whether those conversations were loud and public or muted and ghostly. In the United States, Protestant founders of metaphysical groups are known to have been fascinated with Catholicism, but few realize that the attraction was mutual, at least among independent Catholics. The triangulation illumines yet again what scholar Catherine Albanese calls an American religious "historiography of connection." Traditions that seem discrete often overlap and imitate one another. Independent Catholicism highlights the rich mixtures and porous boundaries that characterize all religious organizations in the United States.[20]

Yet independents are "other" in two ways. They are "other" in the plain sense of existing apart from the big bodies, as denoted in the Census in 1890. But independents are also "other" in the sense of playing the role of the "other" in modern Catholicism as a social field. Theorists use the term "other" in different ways, including to indicate marginalization and oppression. But I am more interested in those who describe the "other" as a spectral but dynamic element of social systems. In this usage, the "other" guards and exposes what is unusual, experimental, or forbidden. It transforms the forbidden and siphons it back into larger flows. In turn the "other" and the whole social field are continually changed and exchanged.[21]

Change in Catholicism happens all the time. It happens daily in the lives of the world's billion Catholics, who replicate Catholic traditions and institutions but also alter them, usually minutely but sometimes momentously. In modern times it seems that one characteristic way that Catholicism changes involves the founding (and fizzling) of independent churches, over and over. Why?

It would take another book to prove, but maybe contemporary independents function for modern Catholicism in the same way as religious orders functioned for late medieval and early modern Catholicism. In the late 1970s philosopher Michel Foucault argued that past lay movements and religious orders functioned as "counterconducts"—practices that jumble prescribed conduct of community, body, and spirit. "Clearly not absolutely external" to the community, Foucault wrote, counterconducts are "border-elements" that "have been continually re-utilized, re-implanted, and taken up again in one or another direction, . . . [including] by the Church itself."[22]

In 2000, sociologists Roger Finke and Patricia Wittberg suggested much the same: religious orders incubate new ideas, serving Catholicism like denominationalism serves Protestantism, but with the advantage of remaining within the fold. Maybe medieval counterconducts stayed within Roman bounds relatively easily. Maybe in modern Catholicism, experimental space became scarce, as Tridentine homogenization and a strengthening papacy tightened Roman institutional boundaries. Maybe this is why quantities of other Catholicisms erupted into modern existence. Another way to put it might be that after the Reformation, Catholicism turned out to display the same "church-sect" dynamism that H. Richard Niebuhr described in Protestantism, in which "sects" broke away from "churches" to create innumerable "denominations" of Protestantism. But since no one thought Catholicism had "denominations," no one noticed.[23]

In any case, while the first sense of independents as "other" distinguishes them from the rest of Catholicism, the second sense nestles them deep in Catholicism's center. All three parts of my description—that Antioch Catholics choose common and distinct markers of the tradition, blend in and out of other groups, and mark boundaries and possibilities of Catholicism at large—make independents both familiar and strange on the American religious landscape.

In some cases independents mimic or echo major bodies: Roman Catholicism or Religious Science, for example. In other cases, they assemble various influences to push Catholicism in new directions. In Atlanta in

1946, a young former Roman seminarian named George Hyde started a gay-friendly church—the first ever. In 1965 in San Francisco, musician Franzo King attended a John Coltrane concert and founded what became the St. John Coltrane African Orthodox Church, where mass is an improvisatory jam session. Antioch founder Herman Spruit consecrated a female bishop by 1974, and other US independents might have ordained and consecrated women even earlier.

In 1999, independent Catholicism gained its most famous priest ever, when Irish singer and songwriter Sinéad O'Connor was ordained. Early in her career, O'Connor performed on *Saturday Night Live* and—in an oft-mentioned and much-criticized moment—took the opportunity to tear up a photograph of Pope John Paul II. She said later that she intended to protest clerical sex abuse and its toleration by the Roman Catholic hierarchy. That was in 1992—ten years before the *Boston Globe* broke the story that led to international awareness. O'Connor remains in the Catholic vanguard. For a show in New York City in 2013, she wore her clerical collar, sang gospel, and dedicated one song to all the "female Catholic priests in this country."[24]

Independent Catholicism is not numerically stunning. But it is important in other ways. Stories of "other Catholics" have the potential to suddenly shift focus from an assumption of the Roman kind to surprise at Catholic variety. Dissent within the Roman church is interesting—after all, millions of US Roman Catholics dispute, do not know about, or do not care about official teachings. But you can see the flows and fissures of Catholicism more accurately when you include whole churches outside the major communions. There are American Catholics more rebellious than Call to Action, more diverse than bilingual parishes, more daring than Dignity, and more traditionalist than Opus Dei. Many Roman Catholics believe that women should be priests, but some independents *are* women priests. Many Roman Catholics accept other religious truths, but some independents hail the Buddha at mass. Many Roman Catholics question bishops' decisions, but independents question the idea that Catholicism is only real if your bishops are Vatican-approved.

As "other Catholics," independents pay a price. What they gain in creativity, mobility, and vibrancy, they lose in strength, stability, and status. They meet with some positive reaction, but also a lot of disparagement. In the course of my research, I frequently read or heard from outsiders—and sometimes from insiders too—a list of charges: independents are illegitimate, disorderly, dim, and ego-driven, or even perverse, criminal, and insane. The more self-conscious independents arrange their affairs to ward off such criticisms. Others shrug off respectability and reclaim insults as points of pride. They "play church" because Catholicism could use more playfulness. They are "thieves" who have "stolen a blessing," like Isaac's younger son Jacob. They are indeed the notorious *episcopi vagantes* of yore—"wandering bishops" who are wandering Catholicism into a bright new age.[25]

In the wider view, as scholars have often pointed out, similar accusations have been standard fare in religious polemics for millennia. Whether Christian versus Jew, Catholic versus Protestant, or Sunni versus Shi'a, the craziness and corruption of the religious "other" are constant themes. So I do not want to make too much of independents' persecution or detractors' charges. Every group has its defamers. Every group also has its egomaniacs, abusers, and criminals. I get no sense that independent Catholicism is proportionally more slandered or riddled with malefactors than any other group. Is there any serious content in the charges? Sure. But obviously what counts as legitimate Catholicism, what counts as Catholic order, and even what counts as smart or sane to imagine for the faith are precisely the issues at stake among various Catholic churches.

In this book, it is not my aim to endorse independents, whose various manifestations range from quite heavenly to very human. Nor is it my intent to evaluate the Roman church, the most important kind of Catholicism by far. Still, not all Catholics are Roman Catholics. As I narrate this "other" story, I do hope to make it harder for us to hear "Catholicism" without asking, "What kind?"

ARCHIVES AND INTERVIEWS

To tell this story of independent Catholicism, I used two major archives, over four hundred survey responses, forty-six interviews, ten years of field notes, and other primary and secondary sources.

The archives included, most importantly, the archives of the Church of Antioch. These are housed at the home of the current patriarch or matriarch. When I used them, they were in boxes in Archbishop Richard Gundrey's garage in Santa Fe. Archbishop Richard also has several binders labeled "Important Documents." And there is a CD of church archives, carefully wrought by Father Jack Sweeley, Father Spencer Wood, and his wife Trudi Willcox Wood to make sources digitally available to those working on church historical projects. Publishing ventures connected with the church include the Sophia Divinity School Press (Santa Fe, N.M.), Blue Dolphin Publishing (Nevada, Calif.), and Hermitage Desktop Publishing (Gig Harbor, Wash.). Sophia titles are available for purchase from the Church of Antioch. Blue Dolphin and Hermitage titles are available from their websites, from major booksellers like Amazon, and in a few cases from libraries.

I also used the J. Gordon Melton American Religions Collection at the University of California at Santa Barbara Library. This collection was assembled and donated by J. Gordon Melton, preeminent scholar of independent Catholicism and other lesser-known American religions, who continues to add documents as he completes editions of his *Encyclopedia of American Religions*. Without Melton's decades of networking among independents, gathering sources, and publishing research, the present book would not be possible. The Antioch archives and the Melton American Religions Collection include correspondence, newsletters, articles, liturgies, brochures, homilies, photographs, mementoes, holy cards, mass programs, unpublished memoirs, prescriptive literature, and seminary catalogs, among other items.[26]

I spent time with independent Catholics in several stints per year for ten years, mostly within the Church of Antioch. During visits, I observed and participated, took copious notes, and gathered church literature. I conducted forty-six unstructured life interviews, thirty-two in Antioch and fourteen in other churches. Almost always the interviews were taped and transcribed. Almost all were "on the record." There are a few cases where I anonymize interviewees, use pseudonyms, or omit identifying details, due to an interviewee's request or my own judgment.

It will be noticeable that I talked mostly to clergy and leaders, rarely to ordinary laity. I made that decision for this reason: except in a few Antioch traditional parishes, "laity" are usually not members per se, but rather have encountered independent clergy apart from a parish context. To introduce myself and others to the movement, I had to talk to those who know the most, and while nonmembers who make use of independent Catholic clergy are fascinating, they often do not know the most. I hope that future studies of independent Catholicism can focus on the experience of the laity. Meanwhile I trust that the present book affords a rare look at the "lived religion" of Catholic clergy.

To gather demographic and comparative data, I circulated among independents an online survey of fifty-eight questions. This means I polled a convenience sample, which is much less reliable than a statistically random sample. And any survey is limited as a tool of measuring and producing reality. Still it seemed worthwhile to gather this information and try to discern basic patterns. I got 407 responses.

For comparison, I analyzed my survey results in relation to published polls of US Roman Catholic groups, read their online material, and attended four conferences of Roman groups on the progressive side: two Call to Action annual gatherings, one national meeting of Intentional Eucharistic Communities, and one national joint meeting of the Federation of Christian Ministries, CORPUS, the Women's Ordination Conference, and Roman Catholic Womenpriests.

I also read hundreds of primary and secondary sources written by or about independent Catholics.

THE LONGER STORY

In the chapters ahead, the story of independent Catholicism comes to life in the past roots and contemporary activities of the Church of Antioch. I clustered the chapters thematically according to common Catholic traditions of "succession, sacraments, and saints." In chapter 1, I reflect on "observing" independents, writing about my own observations as well as those of others and independents themselves. In chapter 2, I tell the life stories of two independent Catholic forebears, Dominique-Marie Varlet and Joseph

René Vilatte, whose eighteenth- and nineteenth-century ventures birthed contemporary US independents, including Antioch Catholics. In chapter 3, I turn to the story of Antioch founder Herman Spruit and his partner Meri Spruit. In chapters 4, 5, and 6, I follow Archbishop Richard Gundrey and other leaders from Los Angeles to Philadelphia in their sacramental and saint-populated work. Along the way, I suggest that while Antiochians always do "succession, sacraments, and saints," they also rework those traditions and the meaning of Catholicism itself, like other independent churches that mark and test where Catholicism may go next. In conclusion, I look ahead to the future of Antioch and wonder how the story of independents alters our understanding of Catholicism and religion in America.

◆　◆　◆

The Convocation of the Church of Antioch of 2009 was held at a midwestern Roman Catholic retreat center. Attendees basked in the hospitality of retreat center staff, who rented space to Antioch while asking leaders not to publicize their location, lest there be trouble with the Roman hierarchy.

A Convocation field trip took us to a spot where, three hundred years earlier and merely miles away, independent Catholic forefather Varlet had worked to evangelize Tamaroa Indians on the banks of the Mississippi River. Also on the Convocation schedule were celebrations of two milestones. One was Antioch's fiftieth anniversary. The other was a historic election. For the first time, the church's bishops would elect their next presiding bishop, rather than having him or her appointed. Archbishop Richard had initiated the new process as another step toward the consensus-based governance that members decided fit best with their vision of Catholicism.

Between the locale, the history, the anniversary, and the election, the whole vibe was that the Church of Antioch—along with independent Catholicism as a whole—was on the cusp of something big. What would that something be? Some were optimistic: the church would grow and become a leader in ministry to a new age. Others were anxious: in transition the church was at risk, and if there were a new age, it would not be welcomed by all.

Archbishop Richard took a moderate stance. He felt pretty good about where they were going. He had reason. His day-in, day-out life for twenty-one years had been devoted to building a church, administering the sacraments, and telling the world about independent Catholicism. The historic and vibrant Convocation of 2009 seemed to foretell that all the hard work was paying off.[27]

PART I
CATHOLIC

◆ ◆ ◆

1

WEEPING AND WOO-WOO

OBSERVING INDEPENDENT CATHOLICISM
IN AMERICA

PRESIDING BISHOP OF the Church of Antioch and pastor of the parish in Santa Fe, Archbishop Richard Gundrey also ran a wedding ministry. He was among the busiest officiants in a popular "wedding city." Ceremonies often took place in the enchanting Loretto Chapel in downtown Santa Fe. The chapel was built by the Roman Catholic Sisters of Loretto in 1878, and its most famous feature was a helix-shaped "Miraculous Staircase," unsupported except at the top and bottom, constructed by a traveling carpenter who the sisters said must have been St. Joseph himself. Loretto was sold into private hands in 1971 and became a tourist destination, as well as the subject of a television movie called *The Staircase* in 1998. But by special arrangement it was also the site of Antioch's Sunday masses. On a typical weekend, Archbishop Richard said mass at Loretto and married two or three couples, there or at other venues.[1]

One May weekend Richard was set to marry a young man and woman at Pojoaque Pueblo, one of a cluster of pueblos near Santa Fe. The couple was Roman Catholic but didn't have time to go through their parish's required marriage course. The groom was shipping out to the Persian Gulf in a few days. Hearing of Archbishop Richard by word of mouth, they inquired about his services. Independent clerics often get requests like this, directly

FIGURE I.I Loretto Chapel, Santa Fe, N.M. Copyright © Ingrid Elizabeth,
LiveLaughRV.com.

from lay Roman Catholics who wished for Catholic sacraments without Roman regulations.

The wedding was held in a new adobe chapel, set next to the pueblo's massive resort-casino and an expanse of tawny-rose desert. In the chapel I sat toward the back. Family and friends in full finery packed the pews. Archbishop Richard looked marvelous himself, tall and handsome at seventy-four and vested colorfully. He waited until the bride and groom faced him. Then he introduced himself as he always did, slowly and resonantly: "Welcome to this blessed occasion. I am Father Richard Gundrey. I am a priest in the Catholic Apostolic Church of Antioch." When he said this back in Santa Fe, a city known for religious diversity, it caused little reaction. But outside of town, in this Roman Catholic crowd, there was a murmur. A man behind me shifted and grumbled loudly, "Antioch?!"[2]

Antioch, indeed. I hear versions of that reaction all the time. "Antioch Catholicism" and "independent Catholicism" make people do a double take. I understand. That was my own first reaction, too. But over the course of ten years with Antioch Catholics, I got used to conceptualizing "other Catholicism" alongside Roman Catholicism. I started to notice the frequent interaction. I realized how and why a whole churchful of Roman Catholics could find themselves at a wedding officiated by an independent Catholic priest. I saw that it was not a rare but relatively common occurrence. And once I saw, I could not un-see. In this chapter, I describe to you the process of seeing— observing independent Catholicism, choosing to look at Antioch in particular, and watching the flow between Antioch and other religious groups.

I especially observe Roman Catholic progressives as a "proximate other" to independents. The two groups are so close that disparity between them stands out all the more. What are the similarities and crossing points? Where are the boundaries? What do I see? What do others see? "Antioch?!" I didn't have a chance to talk to the man behind me at the Pojoaque Pueblo wedding, but he seemed to have doubts about the officiant and his church. But the young Roman Catholic couple at the altar—she in her wedding gown, he in his Navy whites—had decided that Archbishop Richard was just the man for their big day.[3]

INDEPENDENTS AND ROMANS

While the Pojoaque couple jumped to schedule an independent priest for a short-notice Catholic wedding, other Roman Catholics may find such an option unsettling. In almost all US Roman communities, leaders teach that Catholicism is one unified body under the pope and that institutional unity guarantees sacramental authenticity. Even Antiochians who are ex-Roman—about 64 percent—said that they, too, were initially skeptical of independent Catholicism. When seminarian Marian Bellus of Philadelphia first attended an Antioch mass, she said she felt anxious about doubting the unique authority of Rome. "I was a little afraid, like 'is a bolt of lightning going to come down and strike me?'" she said. "Because it's so ingrained, 'no one else has the sacraments.'"[4]

On the other hand, lay Roman Catholics may take independents completely in stride. Another woman attending mass on the same day I talked to

Marian Bellus was Cindy, Roman Catholic goddaughter of Mother JoEllen Werthman, priest at the Philadelphia-area Antioch church. Cindy and her family attended this independent Catholic mass once a month and went to their Roman parish the other three Sundays. She said it was "no big deal" to come to Antioch, "not even a concern at all." In a few months, Mother JoEllen would baptize the family's new baby.

Often a range of reaction can be seen even in one single Roman layperson. Following Archbishop Richard around Santa Fe on Holy Saturday in 2007, I attended the baptism of Bryan Flores, a thirty-something young man converting to Catholicism. Bryan was drawn to the faith through his Roman Catholic fiancée, but both of them balked at the Roman requirement to investigate his first marriage, which had ended in divorce. So, he would be baptized and later married in Loretto by Archbishop Richard. Attending the baptism in Richard's home chapel were Bryan's fiancée, her Roman Catholic mother, and her Baptist stepfather. The future in-laws would be Bryan's godparents. As everyone arrived, there were introductions and conversations. People were perusing Antioch literature and asking about the Kuan Yin statue in Richard's front yard. Then the baptism. It was a day of rare April snowfall and the mood was joyous.[5]

But after the baptism, the mother of the fiancée turned somber. Is this really Catholicism? she asked. The Roman Catholic church officially offers communion only to members in good standing. If the Church of Antioch says anyone can receive the Eucharist, is it really real? Yes, Archbishop Richard said. The church has valid sacraments, but practices open communion. Quaveringly, the mother explained more. Like the young couple, she too had a difficult history with the marriage norms of the Roman church. She had contracted this second marriage with her Baptist husband without annulling the first. In her priest's eyes, she said, she was an adulterer. She had not taken communion in her home parish for years. She looked close to tears.

Her daughter grasped her hand and said, Mom, you can take communion here. At our wedding. You can take communion *with Dad*. Her husband said, You can do it; it is okay. She looked at them sadly and considered. But then slowly shook her head. "I'm not ready for that," she said, adding that it just wouldn't feel right. Archbishop Richard said, "That's okay. You have to do what is right for you." She nodded and wiped her eyes. Later, Richard said he saw it all the time: Roman laypeople who are intrigued but not convinced—receptive to "other Catholics," but also faithful to Rome. This mother-of-the-bride gladly served as godparent in the Church of Antioch baptism. But she drew the line at taking communion there.

US Roman Catholic leaders' reactions equivocate, too. Unlike many workaday Catholics, leaders are usually aware of the existence of independents. There are conservative leaders for whom Catholicism apart from Rome makes no sense and independents are just "kooks." There are liberal leaders like journalists of the *National Catholic Reporter*, which covers independents with cautious optimism. Different bishops handle independents differently, too. At one end of the spectrum, they respond with excommunications, heresy trials, and (in at least one case) a lawsuit over use of the name "Catholic." At the other end of the spectrum, they coolly cede ground—as when Father John Hotchkin, executive director of the US church's Secretariat for Ecumenical and Interreligious Affairs, told a reporter, "The name Catholic is not copyrighted," or when Los Angeles archdiocese spokesperson Father Gregory Cairo told another reporter that "we just explain that [independent Catholics] are separate." Most reactions fall somewhere between the poles of litigious and latitudinarian.[6]

At higher levels of Roman authority, church councils responded to independents with similar variety. Documents such as *Unitatis redintegratio* of Vatican II, also known as the "Decree on Ecumenism," show ambivalence. *Unitatis* heralds the Orthodox and Anglican communions as especially close to Rome and signals the existence of additional churches "in which Catholic traditions and institutions in part continue to exist"—a line most scholars take to indicate Old Catholics of the Utrecht Union and a few others. But the same document also affirms that there is "one Church and one Church only," that ecumenism ultimately aims for the "authentic catholicity" of all within that single institution, and that no other churches "benefit fully from the means of salvation."[7]

Popes, too, take different tacks depending on the case. Benedict XVI made public gestures of reconciliation toward the traditionalist Society of St. Pius X (SSPX) as well as conservative Anglicans in 2009. In 2007, however, he anathematized all Catholic persons or groups that "attempted" ordinations of women, with a reminder that participation in such events incurred *latae sententiae*, or automatic excommunication. In 2010 Benedict XVI further put such "attempts" in the canonical category of "grave crimes." (Since the Vatican does not accept the idea that it is possible to ordain women, any such act is only an "attempt.") The statements in 2007 and 2010 were widely seen as prompted by the activities of Roman Catholic Women-priests. In just three years, then, the same pope who reached out to SSPX members pronounced harshly upon the Womenpriests.[8]

Excommunication—the ultimate ecclesiastical punishment within all versions of Catholicism—literally means being prohibited from receiving communion and amounts to spiritual banishment. An excommunicated person is barred from the sacrament considered in Catholicism to provide Jesus's Real Presence, bond believers, and aid salvation. Rome has levied excommunication on independents from the Imani Temple and Spiritus Christi to Womenpriests and St. Stanislaus Kostka. But most US independents do not draw explicit Vatican attention. They are too small and Rome is too big. Even in cases that do come to Vatican attention, most often its approach is to issue reminders about *latae sententiae*: if you say you are Catholic but depart from official Roman teachings, you in effect excommunicate yourself. That kind of passive excommunication often goes unenforced—except by conscientious Roman Catholic themselves, like the mother of the bride-to-be at the Antioch baptism. She probably could have found a sympathetic Roman priest to give her communion. But she took it upon herself not to receive the sacrament after her remarriage.

Excommunication by Rome, official or automatic, is experienced by Catholics inside and outside the Roman communion in different ways. Some are relieved or defiant after long struggles with the church. Others find it sorrowful, painful, or frightening. I encountered dozens of independents who had received official letters of excommunication or absorbed the implications of *latae sententiae* with seriousness. But for all "other Catholics," excommunication by Rome ultimately does not carry weight, spiritual or otherwise. They do not consider Rome their home jurisdiction. The godfather of US independent Catholicism, Joseph René Vilatte, stated the rationale when he was excommunicated by Rome for a second time in 1907. "That act of exclusion does not touch me," he wrote. "The Church of Rome arrogates itself a power of universal discipline over the other Churches, even those separate from her. I neither admit nor recognize that power." Some Catholics repudiate the whole idea of excommunication. "None of us really believes in excommunication," said Spiritus Christi priest Mary Ramerman. "It's a totally foreign concept to the Scripture, to Jesus."[9]

Regardless, excommunication by any Catholic body does not stop other Catholicisms from forming. On the contrary, Catholics repeatedly organize themselves outside of Rome, Constantinople, and Canterbury in fresh, minuscule manifestations. Excommunication arguably contributes to the proliferation, expelling members but also generating new alliances. In turn, those new groups sputter, cluster, or diffuse. SSPX Catholics drawing closer to Rome and Roman Catholic Womenpriests finding themselves repudiated are both part of Catholic cycles of relationship to other Catholics.

US INDEPENDENTS AMONG THEMSELVES

By this point, it is clear that "other Catholics" display considerable variety. Some date from early modern Catholicism, while others launched since the last US presidential election. Some rewrite the mass; others say the Latin mass. Some revere the pope; others elect their own popes. A few meet in cathedrals, while most sit on folding chairs in someone's living room. The majority of groups are tiny, but jurisdictions also include the Polish National Catholic Church with about twenty-five thousand US members and the SSPX, USA District, with between thirty and forty thousand members. With such variety, it will come as no surprise that the churches draw distinctions among themselves.[10]

Some consistent distinctions made by independents suggest a layered typology for the US scene. First, independent Catholics differ by the tradition with which they most identify: Roman, Orthodox, Anglican, Protestant, Old Catholic, or none of the above. So while many groups call themselves independent Catholic, some prefer names like Old Catholic, noncanonical

Orthodox, Continuing Anglican, or independent Lutheran. In addition, a lot of independents say they identify with no particular big church—they are "just independent Catholic." I borrow this phrase from Archbishop Richard, who told a radio show host in 2009: "We're not under the pope; we're just independent Catholic." On top of identification by type of Catholicism, groups run the gamut from left to right in terms of the US political spectrum and interpretations of Catholic tradition. Two Rome-identified independent jurisdictions may still be very different, with one full of Tridentine traditionalists and the other populated by "spirit of Vatican II" reformers. Finally, cutting across all of the above is another subgroup with strong metaphysical, mystical, esoteric, or eclectic orientations. The Church of Antioch is among these.[11]

There are many scholarly discussions of definitions of "metaphysics," "mysticism," and "esotericism." In this book I try to use terms mostly how Antioch leaders use them. Briefly, in their usage "metaphysics" is not the metaphysics of Roman tradition, that is, the neo-Aristotelian philosophy of being articulated by Thomas Aquinas and held as the foundation of natural law theology. Rather, Antiochian metaphysics follows the hermetic strain characterized by a worldview of correspondence between physical and metaphysical levels of reality—"as above, so below"—wherein each human being is a microcosm of the universe and the universe is consciousness writ large. "Mysticism" refers to practices of perceiving or being absorbed in ultimate unity behind apparent multiplicity. This absorption can happen individually and dramatically, as in visions or revelations, or it can happen in group settings or everyday activities, such as the mass or even just "peeling potatoes," as Antioch founder Herman Spruit once said. Finally, "esotericism" involves techniques of access or initiation to other levels of reality. These techniques include not only the sacraments of Catholicism but also rituals of gnosis and induction in eastern and western traditions.[12]

So independents categorize themselves by major tradition, political leaning, and mystical inclination. They also use the label "independent Catholic" in at least three different ways: as a generic name for all "other Catholics"; as a particular name for "just independent Catholics"; and as a historical designation for churches of past decades and centuries that did

Catholicism outside the big bodies. (The latter is less anachronistic than it may seem, since the phrase "independent Catholic" shows up in sources as early as the second decade of the nineteenth century.) In this book, I adopt all three senses of the phrase. I try to specify sense with context. But I do not try to homogenize my usage, or theirs.[13]

While "independent Catholic" is the most common way that contemporary independents identify themselves, almost no one loves the adjective "independent." Traditionalists like SSPX Catholics actively repudiate it. Old Catholic–identified churches in the United States often recoil at being grouped with independents, whom they see as overly liberal, motley, or opportunistic. Those working for Roman reform, such as the Womenpriests, consider themselves fully Roman and not part of the independent phenomenon. In turn, handfuls of "just independent" types opine that Old Catholics and traditionalists are too conservative, so, fine if they don't want to be "independent Catholic." And if Womenpriests reject the identification, well, that is annoying, but ultimately fine, too. Because even while using and defending the descriptor, "just independents" themselves still debate it. Some in Antioch say "independent Catholicism" is a contradiction in terms. How can a Catholic church be independent if the meaning of Catholic is universal? "I don't know that the two words follow," said Father Thomas David Siebert, pastor of the Richmond Church of Antioch, in an interview. "You know, Catholicism is Catholicism. We're all in it together." Bishop Michael Adams of the Antioch parish in Iowa wrote me in a similar vein: "None of us are independent."[14]

Occasionally they brainstorm new names: free Catholicism, alternative Catholicism, new Catholicism, neo-Catholicism, inclusive Catholicism, open Catholicism, progressive Catholicism, or contemporary Catholicism. The great classifier J. Gordon Melton divides Catholics between the western and eastern "liturgical traditions." Then there are nicknames, like "indie Catholics" or even just "indies." The most hip name was coined in Baltimore, where Antioch deacon Ted Feldmann and his associates call themselves Indy Cats.

Some don't love the "Catholic" part of "independent Catholic," either. Those who identify with Orthodoxy, Anglicanism, or Protestantism may say "Catholic" is too Rome-identified to define a varied movement. Almost everyone complains that it is exhausting to swim against the current of popular association of Rome with Catholicism. For both reasons, independent bishop-scholar John Plummer of Nashville, Tennessee, proposed a different name: the Independent Sacramental Movement. Abbreviated ISM, it gained a good measure of popularity. But for many, Independent Sacramental Movement is also a hassle to explain. "Catholic" signifies things a lot quicker.[15]

Naming among independent Catholics is in flux because the groups themselves are in flux. They sometimes mix across deep theological differences. For example, though US left-leaning and right-leaning independents stand far apart on many issues, they cross paths in the intimate gestures of Holy Orders, since traditionalist churches often gain bishops by reaching out to liberal prelates. In the early 1970s, Antioch founder and women's ordination pioneer Herman Spruit consecrated Walter Adams as bishop of the very conservative Anglican Episcopal Church of North America, part of the Continuing Anglican movement. The two men reportedly became good friends, "in spite of the fact," wrote independent Catholic bishop-scholar Lewis Keizer, "that Anglican Episcopalians would rather burn in Hell than ordain a woman!"[16]

Other left-right convergences unfolded over decades. In 1908, Arnold Harris Mathew was consecrated by the modernizing Utrecht Old Catholics to start a branch in England. By 1971, one of many bishops descended from Mathew was American sedevacantist Francis Schuckardt. As a sedevacantist, Schuckardt regarded Vatican II as so aberrational that it proved that recent Roman popes are impostors. The "seat of Peter" is "vacant"— *sede vacante*—and the true pope is in exile, someday to reveal himself to a faithful remnant. After consecration, Schuckardt moved his Tridentine Latin Rite Catholic Church to Spokane, Washington, to form the Mount St. Michael's community. It soon counted among the most prominent sedevacantist groups in the world. This ultratraditional Catholicism traces its first bishop, then, to the liberalizing Old Catholic church.[17]

Similar instances of surprising convergence repeat time and again. Independents call it ecumenism. Others see it as theological laxity or errant expansion. In any case, trying to secure boundary lines between independents is hopeless. Groups continually confound nomenclature and explode categories.

THE "GATEWAY" TRADITION
FOR SMALL-CHURCH CATHOLICISM

Almost all independents agree on the importance of succession, sacraments, saints, and the word "Catholic" itself. All are very traditional concepts. Apostolic succession in particular serves as a sort of "gateway" tradition authorizing other traditions. As such, it is a focus for "other Catholics," who often feel pressure to prove their authority and authenticity. It bears pausing on the issue of apostolic succession—and on points of history and theology that lie behind the way most independents practice it—to map some fault lines between small churches and big bodies.[18]

Across modern Catholicism, the principle of apostolic succession expresses the belief that Catholic bishops stand in an unbroken line of succession extending back to Jesus's twelve apostles. Consecrating new bishops, Catholic prelates pass on authority to teach, govern, confirm, and ordain. Ordaining new priests, they pass on authority to celebrate the sacraments, especially the Eucharist. Given the critical importance of apostolic succession, all Catholics maintain standards for proper ordination. But standards vary. Two major schools of thought trace to the differing sacramental theology of "Church Fathers" Cyprian of Carthage (d. 258) and Augustine of Hippo (d. 430).

Cyprian held that when heretical priests and bishops performed baptisms, they were null and must be redone. Deployed for modern issues, the "Cyprianic" view holds that authority to perform the sacraments inheres not in the clergy member himself or herself, but rather in the ongoing assent of the community to call this cleric for service. Ordination is therefore "relative" to the community—if a priest or bishop departs from the communion, his or her authority evaporates. Orthodox, Anglicans, and Old Catholics follow the Cyprianic model, and numbers of progressive Roman Catholics prefer it, too.[19]

Augustine, on the other hand, argued that baptisms performed outside church protocols were still valid, since sacramental power came from God and Christ. As long as the right words and physical matter were used and the priest wanted to do whatever the church wanted to do, the sacrament was valid. Since the early modern period, proponents elaborated this "Augustinian" model to make ordination "absolute"—ordination confers a spiritual mark on the priest himself or herself and cannot be repealed. This model elevates the power of the sacraments over the vagaries of human channels. The sacraments work in and of themselves—*ex opere operato*—regardless of celebrants' moral or canonical status. Rome and most independents follow this "indelible spiritual mark" line of thought. "Once a priest, always a priest," as the saying goes.[20]

Though both Cyprian and Augustine hoped to promote church unity, neither model prevented fragmentation. Institutional splintering started after the First Council of Ephesus in 431, when anathematized Nestorian Christians sought refuge in Persia and established the historic Church of the East. Many historians argue that separate churches existed even earlier, though they were deemed heretical by orthodox bishops. The eastern church practice of "relative ordination" practically means that when conflict develops, bishops stripped of authority can find another church or go "autocephalous," so that their authority is reestablished relative to a new "self-headed" church. After the Great Schism in 1054, the east featured a sprawling communion that frequently splintered and grafted parts. Bishops headed overlapping jurisdictions that veered in and out of communion with Constantinople, Rome, and other sees, often with practical considerations for survival in the face of hostile governments. The western church developed stronger centralized leadership in Rome, and some eastern churches joined. But according to the western practice of "absolute ordination," if bishops or priests leave the communion, they take the power to celebrate valid sacraments with them.[21]

Regardless of whether they ordain relatively or absolutely, however, in the modern era all Catholic churches use apostolic succession as a mark distinguishing Catholicism from Protestantism and authenticating Catholicism itself. Big and small bodies claim origins in one of the twelve apostles of Jesus, such as Peter, Andrew, or Thomas. Independents sometimes add as apostles Mary Magdalene or Joseph of Arimathea. Contemporary historical scholarship supports the idea of multiple Christian origins, but not of original apostolic succession. As religion scholar Ann Taves summarizes it, today historians "would argue that lines of succession . . . were retrospectively constructed, given the historical evidence that the role of the monarchial bishop emerged gradually over the course of the first two centuries of the common era." Especially in early modernity, polemics between Rome and the Church of England sharpened mutual claims to unbroken succession "in the construction and defense of . . . 'orthodoxy.'"[22]

This reconstructed and newly accented concept of apostolic succession remains standard in most official versions of Catholicism in the twenty-first century. Lots of present-day Catholics readily acknowledge the historical-critical take on succession, but still affirm it as Catholic tradition. "So [apostolic succession] is ultimately a myth," writes independent Catholic priest Jordan Stratford, "but a pragmatically transformative one." It links contemporary church authority back to Jesus himself. It represents the mystical oneness of the faith. It also legitimates a plethora of independents. Utrecht gained apostolic succession with help from Dominique-Marie Varlet, Rome's Bishop of Babylon, and hundreds of small churches descend from that line. Periodically other Roman prelates consecrated bishops apart from papal permission, including the aforementioned SSPX founder, Marcel Lefebvre. Other formerly Roman bishops who founded new bodies include Carlos Duarte Costa of Brazil (1945), Pierre Martin Ngô Đình Thục of Vietnam (1975), and Emmanuel Milingo of Zambia (2001).[23]

Following the Augustinian principle that the sacrament is bigger than the celebrant, Roman authorities may still consider rebel ordinations valid. They do not, however, consider those ordinations licit or regular. In Roman canon law all three qualities—validity, liceity, and regularity—govern the authenticity of sacraments. Illicitude means juridical illegality, like when a consecration takes place without papal sanction. Irregularity means that the technical form of the sacrament is somehow off—wrong words or wrong "matter," such as grape juice instead of wine. If a consecration is merely illicit, that alone does not affect validity. But if a consecration is also irregular, then in Rome's view validity is compromised. This is because sacramental regularity is taken to reveal correct spiritual intent, definitely a component of validity. The upshot is that the Vatican considers ordinations of men in big-body Orthodoxy and the Union of Utrecht to be valid but vexed, for not being in union with the pope. It accords the same status to some ordinations performed by its own rebel bishops, to assorted historic eastern churches, and to a few bishops of the national Chinese church not in communion with Rome. Regarding Anglicans and most independents, however, the Vatican views ordinations as also irregular, which cancels their validity.[24]

But independents offer other views, starting with the idea that there are other views. Sacramental regularity and validity, "like beauty," wrote British independent Catholic bishop Alan Bain, "lie in the eye of the beholder." Independents are well aware that by major jurisdictions' standards, their sacraments may be problematic. But they try not to worry about others' standards. Rome's rules for regularity, for example, included requiring that a consecrator intend to consecrate only for the church of Rome, that the ordination take place within a Roman sanctuary, and other things that ipso facto irregularize most non-Roman rituals. Instead, independents concentrate their energies on validity. Rome might not recognize it, but other Catholics often do. Validity is the property of sacraments with "the juice," so to speak. The sacraments work in and of themselves. Divine power trumps human rules. Without needing any big church's permission, independent bishops can pass on apostolic succession and independent priests are able to administer the sacraments. Basically, accenting and preserving validity makes small-church Catholicism possible.[25]

It also makes small-church Catholicism keyed on apostolic succession in a way that big-body Catholics tend to find unseemly. Roman Catholic progressives—those who populate Call to Action, the Women's Ordination Conference, and CORPUS, for example—share much in common with left-leaning independents. But they often balk at what they see as independent obsession with bishops and "lines." Hoping for a less clericalized path to the future, they interpret Vatican II documents to tilt from the Augustinian to the Cyprianic approach, locating ritual power less in the person of the priest and more in the church as a whole. As such, some "Vatican II Catholics" idealize relative ordination for a specific community, rather than absolute ordination as a conferral of inherent powers.

Roman progressives' criticism of absolute ordination takes aim at the official Roman position as well as independents. Some make fun of absolute ordination as "magic hands theology"—the idea that when a priest does rituals with his anointed hands, grace flows automatically, regardless of the larger church context. For Roman progressives, "magic hands theology" sums up all the clericalism, superstition, obfuscation, and sexism they wish to reform. A worthier way to make the world a better place, according to them, involves socially conscious living and social justice activism. So even though left-leaning independents actually carry out reforms that Roman progressives only dream of, it still looks to them like independents are going backward. Independents have women priests, married priests, and out-gay priests, but only by obsessing about a Holy Orders ever more "absolute," "magical," or "mechanistic." Instead, Roman progressives say, the future lies in ordinations conferred not by bishops but by whole congregations, as some progressive communities are already doing.[26]

The most radical Roman progressives consider doing away with a sacerdotal priesthood altogether. Ordain no one. Ordaining women or gay people changes nothing, they say, if the resulting clericalism just perpetuates hierarchies. "Ordination is subordination," theologian Elisabeth Schüssler-Fiorenza famously proclaimed at a Women's Ordination Conference (WOC) meeting in 1995. A dozen years earlier, like-minded WOC members had already founded Women-Church Convergence, which was feminist and "Catholic-rooted" but not keyed on women's ordination. In other Roman progressive circles, the Dutch Dominicans published a booklet in 2007 describing parishes in the Netherlands where lay people consecrate the Eucharist. The necessity of a sacerdotal priesthood, the Dominicans suggest, has already come to an end. American historian Garry Wills calls for similar reconsideration in his book *Why Priests?*, published in 2013, echoing theologian Hans Küng's work of the same title from 1972. The early church did not have priests, Wills writes, and contemporary Roman Catholics do not need them either. "We have each other."[27]

Given these liberating ideas and realities, Roman progressives wonder why in the world independents are so consumed with obsolete notions like apostolic succession and validity. In the *Journal of Feminist Studies in Religion*, scholar Marian Ronan expressed that very concern about Roman Catholic Womenpriests. The organization's "enormous emphasis" on apostolic succession "as a sign of legitimacy" is "troubling," she writes, "trading as it does on one of the more theologically vacuous and historically unsubstantiated aspects of the Roman Catholic ordination discourse." Many Roman progressives go further to say they care little about Vatican norms at all. At the national conference in 2009 of Intentional Eucharistic Communities—largely Roman Catholic progressives who meet in house churches—sociologist Michele Dillon presented results of a survey indicating that 70 percent of conference participants said "the institutional church is not important to them personally."[28]

Yet while Roman progressives may regard apostolic succession as vacuous and ignore the Vatican, they are still Roman. The bottom line, institutionally speaking, is that they have not left communion with the pope. In fact, Roman progressives often work extremely hard for the reform and thriving of a communion they love. As such, they are still part of a religious institution whose spiritual legitimacy and general clout are widely recognized. Perhaps Roman progressives can afford not to care about the Vatican. Perhaps they have what might be called "Catholic privilege"—the privilege of taking Catholic belonging for granted. With "Catholic privilege," there is no need to recite a bishop's apostolic lineage and no worries about valid ordination. Perhaps Roman progressives appreciate the Roman part of Roman Catholicism more than they think.

By contrast, independents do not have the luxury of indifference to traditional authorizations. But they are also not as obsessed as Roman progressives charge. Many actually do interrogate ordination and criticize clericalism quite a lot. And since independent history includes examples of almost everything, it certainly features a few who rejected apostolic succession altogether. In the 1980s, Archbishop Irene of the American Orthodox Catholic Church decided that her church would renounce the necessity of apostolic succession in order "to avoid the further creation of hierarchies." At least one Roman Catholic Womenpriests (RCWP) community went that way, too, ordaining one of its own by congregational laying-on of hands.

Throughout independent churches, as in Roman progressive liturgies, one finds parishioners joining priests to say Eucharistic prayers or joining the laying-on of hands for ordination.[29]

It is true that the overwhelming majority of independents do not consider doing away with the sacerdotal priesthood. They have other ways of juking tradition. Some with strong connections to Roman progressives, such as the RCWP and Bishop Jim Burch's Catholic Dioceses of One Spirit, allow that ordination may fade in the future but should be maintained now for continuity and legitimacy. Others, including those in the Church of Antioch, use the language of "balance"—Archbishop Richard Gundrey's favorite word— to uphold absolute ordination and affirm lay power at the same time. "There are reasons for formal ordinations," Archbishop Richard wrote the church, "but when [priests] are saying mass with our congregation gathered around the altar THERE IS NO POWER IN US THAT IS NOT IN ALL THOSE GATHERED ALSO." Others in Antioch take the concept of shared human priesthood and run with it: instead of ordaining no one, ordain everyone. "Everybody is a priest," said Bishop Diana Phipps. "The laying on of hands to heal, the laying on of hands to consecrate, to take mundane elements and make them God—we all have that ability." Certainly this echoes the characteristically Protestant concept of the "priesthood of all believers," translated into Roman terms at Vatican II as "the common priesthood of the faithful." Independent bishop-scholar John Plummer even suggests that the abundant ordinations of independents can be seen as a Catholic version of the Quaker move: not abolishing the clergy, but abolishing the laity.[30]

Even more radically, several independent churches uphold apostolic succession as a mystical endowment rather than an earthly ritual. Groups that claim succession directly from Jesus or the apostles include conservative groups such as the Catholic Apostolic Church (aka the Irvingites) and the Apostles of Infinite Love, as well as esoterics like Jules Doinel, who headed a late-nineteenth-century Cathar revival; Rudolf Steiner, early-twentieth-century founder of the Anthroposophical Society and the Christian Community; and Earl Blighton, founder in the mid-1960s of the Holy Order of MANS (aka HOOM), many of whose members joined big-body Orthodoxy by the turn of the millennium. For independents who are so inclined, these "inner priesthoods" easily resonate with worldviews that assume frequent esoteric interaction between humans and divine beings.[31]

Still, the broadest swath of independents practices a physical laying-on of hands and understands the priesthood to confer an "indelible spiritual mark." In other words, ordination does give you "magic hands." Far from shrinking from the accusation, many independents celebrate "magic hands theology" as a witness to religious mystery. Standing apart from Roman progressives' rather rationalized sacraments, independents see magicalism as a healthy corrective to modern disenchantment. Who is really sure that ritual action does not, as ritualists assume, change reality? Even if it doesn't, what is the charm of treating the priesthood unmagically, like another rotating assignment at the office? "Relative ordination," scholar-bishop John Plummer tweeted, "is no fun!"[32]

For independents, absolute ordination is part of the "fun" of Catholicism. It is also a helpfully robust stance when you are trying to tweak common traditions with very little money. Independent church members do lots of social justice activism as individuals, but as churches they have no collective funds for national lobbying campaigns or bus trips to climate marches. Instead, they concentrate limited resources on what I call "sacramental justice" issues—ordaining bodies other than celibate men, for example, and opening the sacraments to all. If social justice aims for an equitable society, sacramental justice demands equitable sacraments. Roman progressives have a bigger social justice footprint, but independents arguably do more for sacramental justice, because they "just do it." And the confidence to "just do it" comes from "magic hands theology," the experience of spiritual power inhering in priests and sacraments.

At Convocation in 2006, Archbishop Richard told the gathered leaders that their priesthood is potent and miracles are possible. "If you don't believe that," he said, "you're in the wrong church!" Antiochians dislike clericalism as much as other left-leaning Catholics. But, they argue, you can easily have absolute ordination and theological progressivism at the same time.[33]

OBSERVING INVISIBILITY

Despite interaction with big bodies over several centuries, independent Catholics are still invisible to most Americans. Roman, Episcopal, and Orthodox leaders know about independents. So do many scholars—I describe their work in a bibliographic essay on the publisher's web page for this book. Journalists' accounts of independents are now "broadcast to the nation with their cornflakes," as UK bishop Alan Bain wrote. Independents themselves produce reams of newsletters, information, and advertising, lately by means of electronic communications and social media sites. In 2016, to do an Internet search of "Catholicism" and *not* run into independents is positively challenging. So how is it that most Americans—even those very interested in religion—do not know they exist? Mostly I think it is about independents being small. But there are also a few other factors in play.[34]

The effective "branding" of Catholicism as Roman in the United States cannot be overstated. The church of Rome in America, like all religious institutions in the context of US voluntarism, developed as many ways as possible of influencing both members and nonmembers. With vast resources, foresightful steps, and historical luck, the Roman church was unusually successful in doing so. It generated hospitals and orphanages, sports teams and social clubs, parishes and schools, histories and pamphlets, media and lobbies. These enfold Rome's own and touch millions of others. Regarding independent Catholicism, as we have seen, Roman Catholic leaders speak with many voices. Yet they convey some basic points at all levels of influence. The Roman church is united in the pope and has unique authenticity. It is a special kind of Christianity and the only kind of Catholicism. Catholicism is identical with the Roman communion. Most people in the United States—not just Roman Catholics—get the message.

It is very hard for independents to convey alternative messages. In 2008, Archbishop Richard Gundrey told a Santa Fe talk show host about his efforts to inform the public that Antioch was *not* Roman Catholic. "I'm very strong on disclaimers," he said. "Every ad that I put out has that we are not affiliated with the Roman Catholic church. The sign out in the front says that. The flyer that you get when you walk in says [that]." Yet "no matter how much publicity you put out," Archbishop Richard said, people still assume Roman Catholicism. Occasionally he would see an "irate" person harrumph out of Loretto in the middle of mass, stage whispering, "This is not Roman Catholic!" "So," he sighed, "it's an education process that's going to go on for millenniums." Some independents go further than Archbishop Richard's disclaimers, making non-Romanness a positive selling point. Antioch's Gentle Shepherd parish in Richmond printed a brochure in 2005 that read, "Rome Has No Monopoly on Catholicism." Website mottos include "All of the sacraments. None of the guilt" and "Vatican-Free Catholics." But, independents lament, it is still virtually impossible to avoid being lumped in with Romans.[35]

Sometimes independents themselves contribute to the confusion. As much as they take care not to falsely advertise as Romans, they also insist on claiming Catholicism. They make distinctions, but profess kinship. An Antioch brochure available on Sundays at Loretto poses an imagined reader's question: "Are you telling me that there is more than one Catholic Church?" Answer: "NO! There is only one Catholic Church. However there are a fair number of Catholic 'denominations,' of which the Roman Catholic Church is only one, of course overwhelmingly the world's largest." Sometimes independent Catholics do not want to be seen as too different. Sometimes, then, they are complicit in blending their tiny numbers with the mass of Roman Catholics. Perhaps this also means that they are complicit in their invisibility.[36]

The ephemerality and complexity of independent Catholicism add to invisibility. After two centuries in the United States, members might still number just around a million. Ever groups rise and fade, start new churches, and poof into nothingness. Every month, some formerly active website is defunct, while three more sites announce new jurisdictions. It is impressive fluidity—or perpetual pandemonium. It defies "seeing" independents, much less studying them. As scholar Peter Levenda declares only half tongue in cheek, studying independents leads investigators into a "veritable labyrinth of madness, pleading for the comforting attentions of a hungry Minotaur." After years of struggling to keep various independent groups straight, I laugh and sympathize.[37]

There is one more reason why independents are all but invisible in the United States: they confound a picture of national identity drawn by sharp contrast between multiple Protestantisms and one Catholicism. From the time of the early republic, US nation-building rhetoric profiled Protestantism as free, democratic, diverse, and denominational, while Catholicism signified one disciplinary papal monolith. Protestantism and Catholicism are US fundament and foil, and the historical ideology of America is unintelligible without this opposition. Even today the cultural work of Catholicism in the American imagination—including among Roman Catholics—depends on its being one Church in contrast to multiple Protestant churches. Multiple Catholic churches, on the other hand, make no sense. "Other Catholics" destroy the productive tension. American nationalism, then, also helps hide independents.[38]

OBSERVING VISIBILITY

But maybe still the main reason why few know about independent Catholicism is that it tends not to get big. When it gets big, it splits. It functions by fragmenting. Independents are self-conscious of splitting and often agree with critics who call it dysfunctional. Scholars of religion, however, might call it dynamic. Like Protestants whose passionately conflicting readings of the Bible cause thousands of denominations to proliferate, perhaps independents are Catholics who care enough to split. In the decades surrounding the new millennium, there seem to be more splits and more fragments. Fragments grow into new jurisdictions and the numbers creep up. So does visibility.

It's just an educated guess. I cannot be sure about growth without definite numbers, and there are no definite numbers. "No one knows whether they are increasing or decreasing in number," journalist Jeff Diamant wrote in a *Washington Post* article in 2007. Still, impressions are not nothing. With highly fluid groups, often "largely impressionistic" guesses are all we have, as religion scholar Catherine Albanese puts it. Short of definite numbers, it is certain that there are currently more attention and regard for independents among fellow Catholics, other religious Americans, and media observers. That new respect seems important in its own right, since it may mean that independent Catholicism currently synchronizes with other components of the US faith landscape.[39]

Since the Second Vatican Council "other Catholics" have played a greater role within Roman Catholicism. After the council, traditionalists looked to various independent bishops to bequeath apostolic succession upon new anti-reform Catholic churches, while liberals looked to Utrecht as an example of how to push reform even further. In 1974, liberal theologian Hans Küng was quoted in *U.S. Catholic* saying it was "strange" that after Vatican II "so little attention has been paid so far to the Old Catholic Churches." Richard Mc-Brien in *Catholicism* (1994) and Garry Wills in *Papal Sins* (2000) mention the Old Catholic movement favorably, as does Küng again in *The Catholic Church: A Short History* (2001). The Old Catholic church "continues to be Catholic but is Rome-free," Küng writes. "This little bold and ecumenically open Old Catholic Church from the beginning anticipated reforms of the Second Vatican Council and recently has even gone beyond them with the ordination of women." Repeatedly articles in the *National Catholic Reporter* mention independents as harbingers of reform.[40]

It is not that droves of progressives leave Rome for independent churches. Some claim that is the case, such as journalist David Haldane in a *Los Angeles Times* article in 2006. "Fueled by the church's sexual abuse scandal and increasing demands for full participation by women, gays and others," Haldane writes, "the independent Catholic movement has gained momentum in the last several years," and its tiny percentage of US Catholicism "is growing rapidly . . . among those who reject the faith's conservative social teachings yet remain theologically Catholic." Actually, not so much. For one thing, independents are by no means all former Romans. Among my survey respondents, a quarter had never been Roman Catholic at all. For another thing, formerly Roman independents give all the same reasons for leaving Rome—an assortment of personal, pastoral, doctrinal, and liturgical reasons—as ex-Romans who do not join independent churches. More, surveys of those who *stay* in the Roman church feature the same criticisms. So, formerly Roman independents are not unique in their reflections on Catholicism's biggest communion. And it does not follow that those who share those reflections will become independent.[41]

But just because few Roman progressives actually join independent churches does not mean the two groups are not interacting. On the contrary, they are interacting much more.

Roman Catholic progressive organizations include groups from the long-established Call to Action and Women's Ordination Conference to the upstart "Occupy Catholics" and "Guerrilla Communion" movements. There are also CORPUS (for married priests), DignityUSA (for LGBTQ and allied Roman Catholics), and a dozen more. The Leadership Conference for Women Religious, representing 80 percent of US nuns, also lends a strong progressive voice. Lefty groups and individuals of the Roman church can get very radical. Liberal and liberationist theologians of the Americas offered new ideas and faced Vatican censure from the 1980s onward. Religious communities gave up canonical status to become more democratic or ecumenical, such as the Immaculate Heart Community in Los Angeles, California; Holy Wisdom Monastery in Madison, Wisconsin; and the Sisters for Christian Community. And the worst-kept secret in progressive Catholicism is that some women's religious orders ordain sisters as priests to celebrate the Eucharist within the community.

Edgy enough already, around the turn of the millennium US Roman progressives started collaborating with independents more frequently, apparently at a juncture of frustration with the slow pace of hoped-for changes in the Roman church. The collaboration seems primarily a pragmatic means to jump-start Roman reform on sacramental justice fronts, especially ordaining women and married men. Roman progressive interest in independent Catholic ways and means started at least as far back as 1984, when four Roman progressive groups joined forces to create the Ecumenical Catholic Diocese of America. Peter Brennan, a CORPUS stalwart from Long Island, New York, was tapped to lead them and be consecrated as an independent Catholic bishop. But the pace of crossover picked up in 1998 when the

Spiritus Christi community of Rochester, New York, broke away from the local Roman Catholic parish and established its own church. Immediately Spiritus Christi had the support of progressive groups such as Call to Action. A few years later Spiritus Christi sealed its break from Rome by enlisting independent bishop Peter Hickman of the Ecumenical Catholic Communion to ordain Mary Ramerman as a priest.[42]

The pace accelerated again when, in 2002, Roman Catholic Womenpriests ordained the "Danube Seven" on a boat in the Danube River in Germany. Immediately the Women's Ordination Conference endorsed the Womenpriests. Other progressive groups invited them to speak or celebrate mass. The Rochester Catholic Worker called long-time member Chava Redonnet as its priest, and Womenpriests ordained her in 2010. Maryknoll priest and School of the Americas Watch founder Roy Bourgeois gave the homily at a Womenpriests ordination mass in 2008, and Jesuit Bill Brennan concelebrated mass with a woman ordained by Womenpriests in 2012. These men were not the first US Roman Catholic clergy to publicly support women's ordination, but they were the first to affirm it actually happening apart from Rome's jurisdiction. Vatican disciplinary action meant that Bourgeois eventually had to leave the Maryknolls and Brennan, who died in 2014, was prohibited from celebrating the sacraments for the rest of his life.

But collusion continued. Like Roman Catholic Womenpriests, Hickman's Ecumenical Catholic Communion (ECC) became a favored partner for Roman progressives, starting with Hickman's role in Mary Ramerman's ordination. At a major conference of Roman progressive organizations held in Boston in 2008, a total of seven independent Catholic jurisdictions were represented on the program. But it was Hickman of the ECC who ran the standing-room-only workshop titled "How to Start Your Own Alternative Catholic Community." Soon CORPUS too collaborated with the ECC to form a new religious order called the Community of John XXIII. Working with ECC bishops, CORPUS can now supplement its mission of advocacy for married Roman priests with Catholic ordinations of married men and women.[43]

Despite cross-fertilization, Roman progressives remain ambivalent about independents. Like Bourgeois and Brennan, those directly subject to Vatican authority can face repercussions: the Roman retreat center staff who book space for independent gatherings, Roman monks who speak at their conferences, Roman priests and nuns who attend independent-officiated weddings of priests and nuns. In *The Underground Church*, sociologist Kathleen Kautzer writes that independent Catholic collaborations occasion the most contention of any protest strategy within Roman reform groups, which remain very loyal to Rome or at least very "deferential." If they do collaborate, they "describe their experimentation . . . not as an exit route," Kautzer writes, "but rather as an opportunity for redefining the terms and conditions of loyalty."[44]

Overlap between Roman and independent Catholics comes about in one other huge way: Roman laity seek out independent priests for the sacraments. This happens because the United States Roman church faces a critical shortage of priests at the same time as its members continuously trend more liberal and less committed, and cannot or will not meet Roman requirements to receive the sacraments. The confluence of factors means that while Romans stay Roman, they may choose to receive the sacraments from independent clergy. Perhaps a lesbian couple wants to have a new baby baptized. Or a single mom does not have time to take her child for required confirmation classes. Or an engaged pair wants to have a beach wedding, which for sacramental marriages is against Roman rules. People find independent priests through word of mouth or Internet searches. Some "indie" priests even get reviewed on sites like Yelp, such as the popular Robert Dittler, abbot-bishop of the White-Robed Monks. "I truly appreciated Father Dittler's willingness to give us the exact ceremony we wanted," wrote reviewer Cassandra S. on May 15, 2012. "He is a very interesting and spirited man, and we loved having him solemnize our marriage." Reviewer "keelynelson" admitted "that it is extremely awkward to Yelp a priest!" But, she continued, "I feel that most people looking into [the White-Robed Monks] are challenged to find a priest that will provide a Catholic ceremony in an outdoor setting. In that case, it is not a parish or lifetime commitment [to a church] you are looking for."[45]

Archbishop Richard got calls not only from Roman laypersons like Bryan Flores's fiancée and the Pojoaque Pueblo couple, but also from Roman priests. I was in Archbishop Richard's home office when his phone rang with a call from a local priest. Could he pass on Richard's information to a couple he knew? Good kids, just can't do it, he said. Sure, sure, Richard answered. There were in fact three local priests who regularly called Archbishop Richard in this way. "Now there are other . . . Roman Catholic priests in this area who would never do that," Richard said, "but these guys . . . [are] more liberal, more open."[46]

Hundreds of other independent priests have similar working relationships with Roman confreres. Some jurisdictions specifically structure themselves for the purpose of meeting the Catholic demand for sacraments. Dittler and the White-Robed Monks state plainly that they see no need for another independent Catholic *church*. Their monastery-in-the-world is instead a loose affiliation of ordained monks who provide the sacraments to all, sometimes by way of "off-the-radar" referrals from Roman priests. In this regard, independent jurisdictions function similarly to coalitions of married Roman priests that offer the sacraments without church approval, such as CORPUS, the Federation for Christian Ministries, and Celibacy Is The Issue, which runs a "Find a Priest" service, formerly called Rent-a-Priest.[47]

From a market viewpoint of the multitude of Catholics and Catholic sacramental occasions, it is arguable that the growing visibility of US independents in the early twenty-first century has to do not only with a crossroads in the Roman church, but also with filling a sacramental niche. Critics abhor this aspect of independent Catholicism as "entrepreneurial." Independents just call it pastoral. "They exist to offer the sacraments," writes independent bishop-scholar John Plummer, to "those who are unable or unwilling to request the services of mainstream clergy."[48]

Independents are also more visible in their work with other Catholics, Protestants, and Orthodox. They are big on intercommunion agreements, for example, which establish mutual recognition and sharing altars. The most significant intercommunion agreement in the independent world is the Bonn Agreement of 1931, forged between the Union of Utrecht and the Anglican church. Ever since then, Old Catholics of Europe consider the Episcopal Church in the United States as their own stateside presence. Eventually two other large churches joined the Utrecht-Anglican alliance: the

Philippine Independent Church and the Polish National Catholic Church (PNCC), though the PNCC withdrew in 2003 over objections to the ordination of women. Most US Old Catholics are not officially linked with the Episcopal Church and therefore not with Utrecht. But a few churches use the Episcopal channel. When St. Stanislaus Kostka in St. Louis parted ways with Rome, for example, it explored Old Catholicism by opening conversations with the Episcopal Diocese of Missouri.[49]

Independents cooperate with Protestants, too, including renting worship spaces, doing joint services, serving on ministerial boards, and joining ecumenical organizations such as the National Council of Churches. Sometimes Protestants who identify with Catholicism even invite independent Catholic priests on staff at their churches. Especially those with congregational polity, such as Unitarian-Universalist, United Church of Christ, Disciples of Christ, and Presbyterian Church USA churches, have the local freedom to make such hiring decisions. Some Protestants, like non-Roman Catholics, reach out to independent Catholic bishops to help form new churches that are simultaneously Protestant and Catholic, such as the Augustana Catholic Church or the New Methodist Conference.

This kind of "Protestant Catholicism" has a long history in the United States, from the transatlantic "High Church" movement in Anglicanism, to Evangelical Catholicism among Reformed leaders like Philip Schaff and John Nevin, to the "community church" movement that traces heritage to Joseph René Vilatte, to the Convergence Movement and Emergent Church of late-twentieth-century evangelicalism. Most dramatically, in 1979 Convergence leader Peter Gillquist and others from Campus Crusade for Christ founded the independent Evangelical Orthodox Church. Portions of that church went on to join big-body Orthodoxy.[50]

The latest US front of Catholic-Protestant-Orthodox blending is "the new monasticism," a broad reclamation of Christian contemplative practices by people inside and outside monasteries. Arguably the first "new monastics" were independents, who since the late nineteenth century founded new and unconventional religious orders. Now joining them are Protestant founders of alternative abbeys, virtual friaries, and intentional communities from Boston to Los Angeles, who occasionally reach out to independent Catholic bishops to ordain priests. One can find "monks in the world," "art monks," and "eco-ascetics" wandering in and out of "Protestant Catholic" and independent Catholic scenes. There is even a contemplative megachurch, the Church of Conscious Harmony in Austin, Texas. Antioch deacon Jeff Genung and his family number among its founding members.

Independents may still be little known, but with all the trends and cooperation, they are getting easier to see. I live in Brooklyn, New York, famously a "City of Churches" with at least two thousand houses of worship. It is no surprise that while writing this book, there were three independent churches within two miles of my building: St. Lucy's Old Roman Catholic Church on Kent Avenue, St. Leonard's on Putnam, and St. Michael's on Troy. The latter two are branches of the historic African Orthodox Church (AOC). Another branch of the AOC met for part of 2011 in Bedford-Stuyvesant's iconic Slave Theater on Fulton Street. But imagine my astonishment when I visited relatives in rural Goldston, North Carolina, population 2,003, and just yards from the sole village minimart saw a house with a sign that read: United Ecumenical Catholic Church. As it turned out, four of Goldston's 2,003 residents were independent priest Carl Matthews-Naylor, his partner, and two children. Within a short time I further discovered that Father Carl had left the United Ecumenical Catholics and joined the Church of Antioch. As part of Antioch's eastern diocese, he celebrated mass every Sunday in his home chapel. The only other churches within the approximately one square mile of Goldston proper are Protestant, one Baptist and one Methodist. The closest Roman church is St. Julia's in Siler City, sixteen miles away.[51]

That is just one anecdote, but I am not the only one with anecdotes. Once you have eyes for independent Catholics, you see them everywhere. Friends, family, and colleagues reported from all areas of the country. My father mailed me a newspaper clipping about Bill Hausen, a Pittsburgh priest who left Rome to start a church called Christ Hope. My sister stumbled into a Vermont café run by freelance Franciscans. A university dean recounted his time as a parishioner of Spiritus Christi. Colleagues from St. Louis wrote when the local synagogue hosted a Roman Catholic Womenpriests ordination and again when St. Stanislaus Kostka won the right to keep its church property. Some colleagues *are* independent Catholics who teach religious studies and theology at Roman Catholic institutions, including several An-tioch clergy.

With eyes to see, you can glimpse independent Catholicism in other very Roman places as well. In the classic autobiography *The Seven Storey Mountain*, a young and archorthodox Thomas Merton describes encoun-tering in the monastery an older independent Catholic bishop who had re-turned to Rome. Though Merton admits that the man seems quite merry, he says the apostate realized his venture with Old Catholicism was "obviously silly." Now doing penance, the man was "serving Mass every morning for some young Trappist priest who barely had the oils of his ordination dry on his hands." When Merton published those lines in 1948, his own days of questioning Roman vows and crossing lines between faiths lay well in the future.[52]

COUNTING INDEPENDENT CATHOLICS

Independents are getting more visible. But I am not sure they are growing, because I and others find it hard to count them accurately. To measure any segment of the American population with precision requires an extensive national survey, quite beyond the scope of my resources and capabilities. Existing US polls of religious identification offer no Catholic category other than Roman Catholic. Orthodox and Episcopalians are not counted as Catholics. Many independents, if asked to state their religion for a survey, would just say Catholic—another instance of how independents may con-tribute to their blending into Rome.

Only scholar J. Gordon Melton makes serious attempts to count indepen-dents. His successive editions of the *Encyclopedia of American Religions* rely on churches' self-reported numbers, as religionists often must. Self-reporting can skew numbers, but not in uniform ways: depending on the circumstance, religious bodies may inflate or deflate their estimates. Melton at least tries to verify numbers and notes when figures look very wrong. He also maintains equanimity in the face of independent churches' high rate of change, which means listings may be obsolete by the time they are published.

The most serious skew in counting independents, however, is less their transience and more their structure, often operating as corps of worker-priests who hold day jobs and do ministry outside traditional parish contexts. In any church like that, most actual members are clergy and leaders. The fact that official counts are so dense with clergy leads to caricatures that independent church folk do little but meet up to ordain one another. Rather, what they do most is meet up to serve people who are not independent Catholics at all.

For example, clerics in two locales of the Church of Antioch say Sunday mass at local drug recovery clinics. In Gig Harbor, Washington, Bishop Alan Kemp spends Sundays at a nearby clinic, while his full-time job is teaching college sociology. To the southwest in Gallup, New Mexico, Mother Linda Rounds-Nichols and her husband Deacon Phil Nichols celebrate Sunday mass in a hospital addictions unit. She is a retired public school teacher and he is a parole officer. Mother Linda, Deacon Phil, and Bishop Alan do not do "the Catholic service" at these facilities—they do the only service. Both officiate "interfaith masses" for ten or twenty attendees. No attendees are members of the Church of Antioch. Many are not Catholic or even religious. It is a new batch of people every week. So, how would one calculate the size of these ministries to compare them to the size of traditional parishes?[53]

Even in parish-like ministries, counting can be tricky. In Santa Fe, where the Loretto Chapel functions for most of the week as a tourist attraction, a portion of Sunday congregants is the downtown hotel crowd. When a tourist returns to the Antioch mass on the next trip or calls to schedule a wedding or a baptism, Archbishop Richard still does not consider that person an Antioch member. Attendance? He keeps scrupulous count. About fifty on an average Sunday, seventy-five to a hundred at Easter and Christmas. Baptism and marriage records? By the book, verifiable by any church or state that inquires. But membership? Richard doesn't pay attention. To the archbishop, membership means, "Show up and give money." That's it.[54]

So independent leaders count heads, but not always in ways that compare easily to other counts. Roman dioceses report as members everyone baptized in parishes within diocesan borders. Some religious groups count everyone on membership rolls. Others consider only tithers as members, but count attendees. Religious orders count only the professed as members, but separately may keep track of how many they serve. As it happens, asking "how many served" gets at the lay component of independent Catholicism better than queries about membership. So on my survey, I asked independent clergy that question. For 2011 and 2012, Antioch clergy estimated that they each served an average of twenty-seven people per week. That means that the Church of Antioch, with sixty clergy serving twenty-seven people per week, averaged serving 1,620 people per week. For the same time period in the Ecumenical Catholic Communion (ECC)—probably the most parish-oriented of early-twenty-first-century left-leaning independents—the average was seventy-three people. The ECC, with at least twenty-six clergy serving seventy-three people per week, averaged serving 1,898 per week.[55]

Despite the complications of counting, I did estimate the size of US independent Catholicism as a whole, not including "how many served." My guess—somewhere between a half-million and a million—represents consideration of several sources. First, I tallied up self-reported numbers for US independent Catholic, Anglican, and Orthodox groups listed in Melton's 2009 edition of the *Encyclopedia of American Religions (EAR)*. I judged his numbers on the conservative side. For example, where groups did not report membership, I counted them as having ten members per ministry; where groups listed no specific ministries, I counted them as having ten members in total. Second, I consulted the Association of Religion Data Archives website and the *Yearbook of American and Canadian Churches*, comparing numbers for independents with those listed in the latest *EAR*. Third, I took into account other reasonable published guesses in media articles, almost all putting the total around six hundred thousand. I did not count groups that did not yet appear in the *EAR*, since they were probably roughly balanced by listed groups that were already defunct.

That is how I came up with the estimate of half a million to a million. This guess is of course extremely loose and unverifiable. At its low end, maybe it misses some sizable new jurisdictions. At its high end, maybe it accidentally includes some laity served, rather than people who consider themselves members. Finally, however, the looseness is all right with me. For small institutions with high fluidity and much out-group activity, "guesstimating" comes with the territory.

SURVEYING INDEPENDENTS

Just as I cannot exactly enumerate independents, so I do not claim precision for my survey of a convenience sample. In all convenience samples, those who respond are usually those who care the most about the topic at hand, so there is a distorting "selection effect," as opposed to more representative numbers gleaned from a statistically random sample. The survey was anonymous, but many people spontaneously listed their names, phone numbers, and other identifying details, which could have subtly affected the freedom with which they answered sensitive questions. So my results are not representative and not fully anonymous. Still, in hopes of observing left-leaning independents from a number of angles—and having something to compare to much more thorough studies of Roman Catholics—I trust the survey serves as a blurry snapshot until others sharpen the picture.

The link to my Independent Catholicism Survey at SurveyMonkey.com was open from September 12, 2011, to August 12, 2012. I circulated the link as widely as I could among my targeted populations: the Church of Antioch, the Ecumenical Catholic Communion, and other mostly left-leaning types. Four hundred and seven people responded. Analyzing my results, I was careful to break out responses from different jurisdictions and distinguish between clergy and laity.

I also compared left-leaning independents to Roman Catholics, especially Roman progressives, as they appeared in state-of-the-art studies conducted by sociologists of Catholicism. Mostly I used polls conducted by teams led by William D'Antonio at the Catholic University of America, results of which were published in 2007 and 2013. I designed my survey so that questions replicated or closely approximated those on the D'Antonio team surveys whenever possible. If Roman progressives are a "proximate other" to independents, I wondered whether comparison of the two groups could

tease out hints of why two very similar populations choose different Catholicisms, apart from the vast differential of size and influence.[56]

My comparison—admittedly very rough—indeed suggests that left-
leaning independents and Roman Catholic progressives are very alike. Their
common liberal views mean they strongly endorse primacy of conscience,
wide religious truth, open sacraments, social justice, and participatory
church governance. The two groups also show demographic similarity
in age, class, race, and political orientation. Largely white with few black,
Hispanic, and Asian members, most are baby boomers or older, rank in
the middle classes, and vote overwhelmingly Democrat. Both groups are
extremely highly educated: 65 percent of Roman Catholic progressives
and 56 percent of these independents have graduate degrees, compared to
14 percent of Roman Catholics as a whole. And both groups rank among the
most pious and committed Catholics in the United States. While the total
Roman Catholic population says church is "the most or among the most
important" part of their lives at a rate of 37 percent, independents and progressive Romans share percentages in the range of 60 to 79 percent. While
the total Roman population attends weekly mass at a rate of 34 percent, independents and progressive Romans share rates of 64 to 86 percent. In other
words, both groups seem to consist of ardent Catholics who put church at
the center of their lives.[57]

On the other hand, comparison hints at differences in religious background. While about 90 percent of Roman progressives are born into the
Roman church, independents in my survey come from diverse faith origins.
They report growing up in *some* religious tradition at a rate of 92 percent,
but a comparatively low 72 percent name that birth tradition as Roman
Catholic (or Eastern Catholic within the Roman communion). Of Antioch
respondents, only two-thirds are former Romans. The other churches of origin are, in order of most frequently named, the Anglican Communion, the
Southern Baptist Convention, and unspecified evangelical Protestantism.
Other faiths of origin include everything from United Methodist and Mormon to Jewish and Taoist. Only one survey respondent, scion of a historic
African Orthodox family, indicated that he was actually born into independent Catholicism.[58]

Though I do not have comparable evidence for Roman Catholics, it is also notable that a slight majority of independent respondents list "other religious or spiritual traditions" with which they "identify." Respondents often explain further that they are actually practitioners, adepts, or ministers in other faiths. The most popular other tradition is Buddhism, with Zen Buddhism specified most frequently. Buddhism is cited at double the rate of the next closest tradition, which is Anglicanism, followed closely by Roman Catholicism, and then, by less than half again, Orthodox and Eastern Catholic churches. Other traditions mentioned in small proportions include everything from Jedi Realists and Jehovah's Witnesses to Santeria and Sikhism.

Though progressive Roman Catholic and left-leaning independents are generally middle-class and highly educated, there seem to be class and education differences. While 80 percent of Roman progressives report household incomes between $75,000 and $150,000, only 30 percent of independents say they are in that range. (The percentage for the general Roman population is 29 percent.) Though none of the surveys—mine or others—asks about the accreditation of universities from which respondents graduated, independents likely attend nontraditional graduate programs more often. Some Antiochians' degrees, for example, may be those offered by Sophia Divinity School, the church's distance-learning seminary, which, like all independent theological colleges in the United States, is not reviewed by major accrediting bodies. There are several dozen of these colleges and seminaries within independent Catholicism, as well as degrees earned by the old method of "reading for orders," that is, doing private study with a bishop. If there were a gap between progressive Roman Catholics and left-leaning independents in terms of mainstream academic credentialing, this would be no shock, given the much more mainstream status of Roman Catholicism in general.

In the new millennium, however, any gap of credentials may be narrowing. Independents have always attracted a few Roman priests and numbers of Roman, Orthodox, and Episcopal seminarians, as well as women and men professed in religious orders, all rigorously educated. Now independents also draw those who earn degrees at major universities, seminaries, or divinity schools. My colleagues around the country reported independent Catholic seminarians and PhD candidates in their classes at Harvard,

Vanderbilt, Notre Dame, Duke, the University of Iowa, Catholic University of America, Lutheran Theological Seminary, Garrett Evangelical Seminary, and New York Theological Seminary. A few jurisdictions are even requiring leaders to have accredited divinity degrees or Clinical Pastoral Education certification. Most churches of any size at least discuss it, though independents have mixed feelings about buying into conventional seminary education. The discussion itself, though, is another sign of growing interaction with the larger religious world.

Another demographic difference is that independents appear to include greater numbers than Roman Catholics of those who are "never married," divorced, remarried, or "living as married." In parallel there is a probable difference in self-description of gender identity and sexual orientation. The D'Antonio surveys of Roman Catholics do not ask these questions. But if Roman Catholic rates mirror expert guesses about rates in the US population, then 2 to 5 percent of Roman Catholic progressives are lesbian, gay, or bisexual, and 0.03 percent are transgender. Left-leaning independents on my survey, by contrast, identify as lesbian, gay, or bisexual in the range of 40 to 60 percent, and trans at about 1.5 percent. One can also infer that independents have fewer children. Not only are they more often single, gay, or trans, but also, since independent churches have minimal economic resources, most do not offer childcare during Mass, much less full-scale programs for children and youth. The greater proportion of lesbian, gay, bisexual, trans, and queer (LGBTQ) in independent Catholicism can more easily do without child-friendly options.[59]

With all the differences between left-leaning independents and progressive Roman Catholics, then, is this *the* difference? Even roughly compared, there is a huge delta between percentages of those identifying as LGBTQ versus "cis"—cissexual, meaning attracted to the opposite sex, or cisgender, meaning gender-identified the same as one's biological sex. So, is that it? Independent Catholicism is queer Catholicism?

Independent churches are nowhere near primarily for or about LGBTQ people and issues. But the idea of "other Catholicism" as queer Catholicism is intriguing, in the sense that "queer" can signify not only same-sex sexual preference and alternative gender identity, but also great expanses of

FIGURE I.2 Archbishop Richard Gundrey celebrating the marriage of Angelique
Neuman (*left*) and Jen Roper (*right*), Pojoaque Pueblo, N.M., October 11, 2013.
Copyright © *Albuquerque Journal, Mountain View Telegraph*, reprinted with
permission; permission does not imply endorsement.

"otherness." Among Christianities, Catholicism has always featured "other"
sexual paths, for example, a celibate priesthood and single-sex religious orders vowed to chastity. Religious orders are famous for harboring innovation and funneling it into the wider Catholic world. Perhaps independent
churches put a modern twist on sexually alternative communities that similarly "queer" Catholicism.[60]

More literally, though, left-leaning independent churches provide a
spiritual home for some Catholic gender and sexual minorities, especially
those who are out and noncelibate. Between that welcome and having open
sacraments—women and noncelibates can be priests—maybe independents' approach to gender and sexuality concerns is *the* contemporary difference between them and Roman progressives. Maybe cis Catholics who

disagree with official Roman stances can better afford to stay in that church and hold out for reform, while non-cis Catholics whose bodies and lives are directly and negatively affected seek out independent spaces. "We ordain women and married people, and we ordain homosexual people," as Archbishop Richard told Santa Fe radio show host Bob Ross. "We're not fighting about those issues."[61]

My survey is very limited. Future polls will tell us much more. But at the very least, results show the fruitfulness of comparing Catholics in and out of the big bodies. Surveying only Romans, one fails to get an accurate picture of all of Catholicism, including the Roman kind.

FOCUSING ON "JUST INDEPENDENTS"

If any independent churches were growing in the new millennium, it may be those with strong ties to Roman Catholic reform groups, such as the Ecumenical Catholic Communion and Roman Catholic Womenpriests. Along with sizable parishes that broke directly from Rome such as Spiritus Christi and St. Stanislaus Kostka, they are also the ones most in the news. So why in this book do I not focus on the fastest-growing, most newsworthy segment of independent Catholicism?

Two reasons. Because independent Catholicism always changes fast, the growth of any particular segment—and its overall importance—can also change rapidly. When Francis became pope in 2013, independent groups linked to Roman reform deflated somewhat, as Roman progressives gained new hope for change and felt less of an urge to collaborate. I do not want conclusions of a book bound to the latest news cycle.

More important in my decision, though, is that "just independent" churches best illumine the boundaries of Catholicism precisely because they have the fewest formal ties to the big bodies. With generations of autonomous bishops behind them, they take for granted the possibility of independent Catholicism. Especially those with an added mystical or esoteric bent show the confidence—or recklessness—to move the fastest and experiment the most. They have the loosest structures, the fuzziest boundaries, the wildest mixing, the sparkliest magic. They inspire. They scandalize. They climb high. They crash spectacularly. Through them, you can best see the "otherness" of the "other Catholic" phenomenon. After all, my argument that independents are part of modern Catholicism would be rather weak if it only pertains to the most Rome-like groups, fortifying a norm from which *other* "other Catholics" deviate.[62]

My generalizations may be disputed by Antiochians themselves, who are quite divided on whether to pursue mainstream respectability or keep a "wildcat church" reputation. At the very least, however, all Antiochians are proud of sheltering Catholics who don't fit elsewhere. Most embrace the "woo-woo," as they affectionately nickname the alternative spiritualities and uncanny phenomena that seem to swirl in church life. Antioch is "plenty woo-woo," seminarian Claire Vincent of Nashville, Tennessee, told me. "But that's ok with me, [because] I've been woo-woo . . . since I was a little kid." Wildcat and woo-woo, Antioch and other "just independent" mystical types play with others' epithets, all true and not true at the same time.[63]

FOCUSING ON ANTIOCH

In my initial explorations, the Catholic Apostolic Church of Antioch–Malabar Rite emerged as a good church on which to focus a study of "just independents." Antioch is not necessarily representative of "just independents," unless one understands singularity as representative, which is arguable. But Antioch does showcase the worker-priest structure, mystical orientation, and eclectic combinationism of the genre. Somewhat bigger than average—in 2008, Antioch reported seventy-five clergy and thirty-three chartered ministries in the United States—it is one of the older continually operating jurisdictions. It has extensive archives. It has influence and respect within the independent Catholic world, since founder Herman Spruit personally ordained many bishops of other churches.

It should also be said that I chose to study Antioch Catholics because they were willing to be studied. From the first time I met Archbishop Richard in May 2005, he was eager to talk about the church and share perspectives. An experienced business manager, Archbishop Richard knew free advertising when he saw it. Since the book would help me, too, in various creative, intellectual, and professional ways, I didn't resist the idea of helping Antioch, if the book had that result. Archbishop Richard and I were frank about this dimension of cooperation and responsibility. He wanted to get the word out. I wanted to write a good book. He felt an extra burden of leadership to shape a church that would hold up in the light of inquiry. I felt responsibility to tell the story with the same openness and generosity with which the church dealt with me.

Archbishop Richard relayed his understanding to the rest of the church. Not every last person liked what I was doing or participated when I asked. But, with credit to Archbishop Richard and all church members who opened their doors and lives to me, I experienced largely unambivalent support. As all ethnographers know, such reception cannot be taken for granted. Among other independents I usually found warm reception, but not always. No wonder. Plenty of published treatments of independents are ignorant, biased, hysterical, and scurrilous. So who is this Julie Byrne anyway? An outsider who specializes in "Catholic Studies," which conventionally covers only Roman Catholicism. With that thumbnail picture of me, Antioch's welcome of this outsider is all the more notable.

At that very first meeting, Archbishop Richard invited me to attend the Convocation in Richmond later that year. In total I attended eight Convocations from 2005 to 2015 and was always afforded a program slot to update attendees on the book. I was put on the Antioch mailing list and the church's private email listserv. Archbishop Richard sent me about a dozen church publications for free, though usually the church charged small amounts to cover reproduction costs. He tucked clippings or personal notes into material that came via the main mailing list. Church communications carried news and appreciations of my work and visits. When I presented work-in-progress at a Princeton University seminar in the fall of 2009, four Antioch leaders from Philadelphia and Baltimore traveled to support me and report back on the listserv. When I asked a few leaders for feedback on the design of my survey, they generously spent time to send impressions and ideas.[64]

Another major help was that the church sped up the organization of its archives for the sake of two ongoing book projects: mine, and that of Father Jack Sweeley, commissioned by Archbishop Richard to write the official church history. Uncatalogued in 2005, the archives consisted of forty-two boxes stacked in Archbishop Richard's Santa Fe garage. The church reverenced its history and had long planned to deal with the boxes. But when I told them I hoped to make use of the archives, leaders jumped on that huge project. Archbishop Richard asked Mother Linda Rounds-Nichols, who lived two hundred miles away in Gallup, New Mexico, to visit Santa Fe and catalogue the collection. Mother Linda's husband, Deacon Phil, was ever her companion in the work. By 2008, the boxes were still in Archbishop Richard's garage, but they were meticulously organized with an eleven-page typed index. When Mother Linda gave me a copy of the index, I dug in.

As I worked through the boxes, my host worked on Antioch business a few rooms away. Richard let me use his copy machine. He also let me use his stove and tea supplies for numerous caffeinated cups. He took me on tours of downtown Santa Fe, the pilgrimage site of Chimayó, and the Bishop's Lodge, the former private home of Jean-Baptiste Lamy, the Roman prelate made famous in Willa Cather's novel *Death Comes for the Archbishop*. We took lunch breaks together at McDonald's, or at the local diner where Richard had a tab, or at the restaurant he formerly managed, Tomasita's. Sometimes he paid, sometimes I paid, and sometimes we paid separately. Back at the house, when I found something in the archives particularly noteworthy, I would interrupt him to show the item and talk.[65]

Also furthering the archival project, Archbishop Richard selected, edited, and compiled three spiral-bound books of Herman Spruit's writings. I received these in the mail without asking. In one of these booklets, Archbishop Richard's editorial notes credit me with having discovered the document *The Conquest of the Rings* by Herman Spruit. Mother Linda really discovered it, but it was one of the documents I had shown him while working in his house. Archbishop Richard also sent me a copy of the Church Archives CD.[66]

I did not get everything I wanted. For example, I was not allowed to attend the bishops' meetings at Convocations or their yearly retreats. Also, Mother Linda told me she removed from the archives some materials deemed too private, likely concerning the inner lives of Herman Spruit and his partner Meri, since the archives contained their personal papers. It is possible that I was kept from seeing other sensitive material as well, perhaps having to do with difficult episodes or personnel matters. So, Antioch archivists shaped the story I am telling. But this is not unusual. Almost all archives undergo curating and censoring at one stage or another. Few religious groups allow unconditional access. And despite winnowing, the Antioch archives still contained much patently personal and sensitive material that I was totally free to see and use, and church members liberally related sensitive historical information, from stories of the Spruits to personality conflicts to past church splits. In the archives and in person, Antioch Catholics made themselves vulnerable to me.

That interaction was not one-way. I was vulnerable to them, too. I researched this book partly by the method that anthropologists and ethnographers call participant-observation. This means I not only observed the Church of Antioch in action, but also participated. Participation in the life of a community has a way of stripping away lingering illusions that research takes place from some omniscient, objective perspective. Instead, research happens amid everything—amid their lives and amid mine. So, I was affected by Antioch Catholics. I let myself be affected. I started research on independents with certain assumptions and ideas, and in the course of ten years I changed, partly because they changed me.

I gained a deeper appreciation for what some have called the "ethnography uncertainty principle." This somewhat tongue-in-cheek principle—riffing, of course, on the Heisenberg uncertainty principle in quantum physics—states that not only does observation change the observed and the observer, but it also is itself part and parcel of the whole scene. Therefore, anything that you "know" from observation of a scene remands to a state of fundamental uncertainty outside of it. In the case of me and the Church of Antioch, the ethnography uncertainty principle leads me to admit, and even embrace, the idea that knowledge is always a relationship. What I learn is only how it appears when I look, where I look, and because I look. I am one part of a constellation that made the church known to me in the limited and provisional ways that I describe in this book.[67]

But for you, my readers, to know something about independent Catholicism, you may have to go look for yourself. Antioch Catholics would like that—the idea that you have to experience them to know them, and that what you find will be both familiar and far out. Several Antioch members are no strangers to ethnography, having themselves conducted participant-observation research. More broadly, the church is full of people whose Catholicism features a God of boundless inscrutability, whose metaphysics posits a highly interconnected universe, and whose temperaments are notably comfortable with uncertainty. To Antiochians, it was inevitable that something would happen to me as I spent time around them. And if you spent time, something would happen to you, too.

In any case, I participated. Daily I followed events on the listserv. Between 2005 and 2009, I traveled to visit Antioch Catholics in eight US states. I stayed in leaders' homes when invited. I shadowed them and participated in all possible masses, weddings, healing services, meetings, and social events. At masses, I received communion and partook of prayers, responses, hymns, and blessings. When asked on three occasions, I read parts of the mass as a lector. I sometimes put small amounts of money in collection baskets. I sat in contemplation in about a half-dozen Centering Prayer sessions. I received a didgeridoo-blown "chakra clearing" from Father Daniel Dangaran, a Tarot reading from Bishop Patsy Grubbs, and an astrological reading from Mother Jenni Walker, all unsolicited but accepted. Some Antioch priests bless material items during mass, so in Santa Fe I put a rosary on the altar; in Olalla, Washington, a tiny stuffed bear; and in Tahlequah, Oklahoma, a bracelet. I was given as a gift an Orthodox-style prayer rope by a priest who makes them by hand, and a book by the spiritual teacher Osho by a seminarian who had lived at his ashram in India. I told several church members about scholarly books that I thought they might like. I rode with a carful of seminarians to Trader Joe's for snacks. I ate numerous meals and drank wine and talked late into the night. Behind a church I smoked cigarettes with a priest who was hiding because she was supposed to have quit. She razzed me because the only kind I had were clove-flavored. She tore off the filters.[68]

I did not accept every chance to participate. Regarding three direct requests in particular, I demurred because I thought that participation would result in a conflict of interest. One request was to create a syllabus on independent Catholicism for Sophia Divinity School. Another was to provide a quotation for a press release, and another was to blurb an Antioch priest's book. The requesters understood and graciously accepted my declines. In fact, everyone in the church seemed to understand that a published account would carry more weight if written by an outside scholar, who thus in their interest should remain outside. But obviously the lines are fuzzy. It is not as if being quoted in a low-circulation press release is definitely more of a conflict of interest than getting my rosary blessed.[69]

I cannot fully say how participation affected me. I wanted to experience whatever I could for the sake of giving a rich account, not to pin down what participation "really" meant. Still, three notable kinds of interaction with Antioch Catholics kept happening, almost every time I was with them.

First, they told me that I should be ordained. One priest told me that the Holy Spirit told her to tell me to read "The Hound of Heaven," a popular classic poem about being chased by God; a few years later, she asked me if I'd read that poem yet. John DiChiara, a seminarian from northern California, passed me at Convocation and tapped me on the shoulder: "When are you going to become a priest?" Most dramatically, during my interview with Father Daniel Dangaran, Richard's associate pastor in Santa Fe, he paused. "I'm sorry," he laughed. "You're an old, old high priestess and you cannot hide that anymore. You cannot. It's the cause of so much pain in your life that why, why go through that?" Then he said he could see me changing, and that I should just give in to the "strong priestly genetic" in me. There were others, too. Interestingly, they didn't say I should join the Church of Antioch or its particular priesthood—just that I should be a priest. And how significant is that? I do not know. All the speakers were priests or seminarians. Perhaps they say that to all the girls.[70]

Second, they prayed with me and for me. Across distance and up close, they prayed. Archbishop Richard gave me several spontaneous hands-on blessings, at his home and during mass, for my work to go well and for the divine to shine through me. I received several more blessings with laying-on of hands at the Santa Fe parish's Wednesday night healing services, and another in Bishop Patsy Grubbs's home in Houston, Texas. A priest in Arizona performed an elaborate ritual for me. Burning sage and inquiring about my life, she diagnosed my spirit as suffering from anger. In response I murmured that I didn't think I was a very angry person. Likely confirmed in her discernment, she went on to pray for my healing. These occasions were unsolicited but accepted. But another blessing I actually asked for. Right after Alan Kemp was consecrated a bishop in Loretto, I noticed a line of people making its way toward him. It is traditionally auspicious to receive a blessing from a new bishop. I just watched, until seminarian Jack Pischner found me. "Did you get your new bishop juice yet?" I laughed and said, "I'm going to." Jack motioned me to get in line, and I did. I knelt in front of Bishop Alan and he laid his hands on my head, praying for me and my work. I got my "new bishop juice."[71]

Third, spending time with Church of Antioch folks, I had frequent somatic responses. My field notes recorded that I sometimes got goose bumps —in the middle of an interview, during a healing service, or looking at a document in the archives. Another time, talking to a bishop, I felt tingly limbs and "micro-undulating inside," my field notes said. But by far the most frequent somatic manifestation was weeping. Not usually a teary person, at Antioch masses I found myself going through whole purse-packs of tissues. When the three women were consecrated in Richmond, I wept copiously. When Bishop Alan blessed me, I cried. When hands were laid on me in a Santa Fe healing service, hot tears flowed. Church members would turn to look at me, gently teasing, "We made you cry!"—or, as one person mischievously said, "Who's watching who now?!" Some took my wet eyes for evidence that I am indeed "called," in some fashion, for something. Regardless, they comforted a person in tears. They grabbed my hand or hugged me. Once, during the recessional hymn as he walked down the aisle, Archbishop Richard reached and with his fingertips brushed the tears from my cheek.[72]

Touch was a part of things—not only ritually but also affectionately. Already at the Richmond Convocation in 2005, my field notes included a side jot that I felt "unbearable" tenderness from the Antioch Catholics. But apparently I could bear it, because continually I touched and was touched. I affected and was affected. I was called to the priesthood and prayed for. I wept. I do not analyze why. Still, I describe my interaction with Antioch Catholics at some length, since it shows the radically particular nature of ethnographic research and the resulting account.[73]

◆　◆　◆

In this book, you get a peculiar take, my take, the effects of mutual observation and influence. Watching the Antioch Catholics changed my sight lines. Altered sight lines shifted categories. New categories rebuilt an entire frame of reference. Soon I was not just accounting for one tiny American church oddly calling itself Catholic. It was a bigger story, a bigger book. They changed the story. Or I did. Or we all did.

I had to go back to the beginning—before these Antioch Catholics, before contemporary American independents, before the first modern split in the Roman church. At the time of that split, the story already straddled Europe and the New World. Independent Catholicism did not start in the Americas. But the ecclesiastical fortunes of Dominique-Marie Varlet did.

PART II

SUCCESSION

◆ ◆ ◆

2
MISSION AND METAMORPHOSIS

NARRATING MODERN CATHOLIC HISTORY

IN EARLY 1713, a thirty-five-year-old priest named Dominique-Marie Varlet boarded a ship sailing from Port-Louis, France, to the Gulf Coast depot of Mobile, then the capital of the New France colony of Louisiana. After stops in Saint-Domingue and Cuba, Varlet disembarked in June of that year. It was the start of his new missionary career. Previously a scholar and pastor in France of the ancien régime, he left parish work to join the Paris Foreign Missions Society and train for an assignment such as this. With two other priests, Varlet planned to travel north to Cahokia, a village in Illinois country just south of the confluence of the Mississippi and Missouri rivers. There they would revive the defunct Sainte-Famille mission and evangelize the Tamaroa, a member tribe of the Illinois Confederacy.[1]

But this plan went quite awry. In Mobile Varlet fell ill with dysentery and almost died. A slow recovery and logistical problems delayed him for almost two years. Finally Varlet and his companions tagged along with a commercial expedition to Cahokia. Varlet had not been favorably impressed with Mobile, but seemed gratified to try to win souls among the Tamaroa. After another two years, Varlet traveled further north to Quebec. There he received word of an extraordinary appointment. Rome had named him the next bishop of Babylon.[2]

Years later, when Varlet was a bishop-in-exile in the Netherlands—and known throughout Europe as a hero or a heretic—he expressed nostalgia for Cahokia. "I still frequently miss the woods of America," he wrote to his sister in 1733. Varlet biographer Basil Guy speculates about those woods that "perhaps he secretly wished that he had never left them." A century later, it turned out that Varlet never really left—or at least, his legacy returned and never departed again. Hundreds of story lines of independent Catholicism branch from Varlet's single trajectory. Antioch Catholics, like many other independents, claim Varlet as their spiritual father.[3]

Historically speaking, I am less confident than independents in asserting linear progression from then to now. There are many independent origins, and Varlet's world of early modern Catholicism bears little resemblance to postmodern American independent churches. Back in the eighteenth century, Varlet could never have imagined an archbishop like Herman Spruit, who ordained women, including his own partner. And by 2009, when Antioch held its Convocation a few miles from Varlet's old mission grounds, participants would have found offensive their forebear's preoccupation with the conversion of Indians. Still, there is no question that after Varlet, new Catholic churches proliferated. There is also no question that Antioch has a deep past. Though American independents now reflect contemporary concerns, their churches are not "made in the USA."

When I started this project, I did not know about independents' long history. By the time I decided it was a critical component of the story, it was too late to travel to libraries in the Netherlands, France, Rome, Azerbaijan, and Sri Lanka. But I had recourse to others' research. Scholar-bishops wrote histories of independent Catholicism. Outside scholars analyzed modern Catholicism and key figures in independent history. Still others are starting the archival research that remains underdone. Gratefully I use their work to narrate a short version of the story here.

What follows, then, traces a lineage of western independent Catholicism that leads from Varlet to the Spruits. From the anxious landscape of early modern Europe to the restless experimentation of postwar California, novel Catholicisms kept popping up. They popped up so often, in fact, that one may consider independents a characteristic feature of modern Catholicism.

FRENCH CATHOLICISM IN THE ANCIEN RÉGIME

Varlet and other missionaries in New France rarely wrote home that village life was comfortable and safe. Yet compared to the turmoil of Catholicism and politics in the ancien régime, the colony could seem sedate. Under the "Sun King" Louis XIV (1638–1715), the French monarchy was at its height. Through persecution, it also helped generate the largest exile population of Europe. In 1685, the Sun King revoked the tolerating Edict of Nantes, and many Protestants and Jews fled the country. But near-total Catholicism by no means established a nation of religious peace.[4]

Louis XIV maintained tight relations with the papacy but resisted the increasing ultramontanism of the Holy See and Jesuit allies. Ultramontane means "beyond the mountains," that is, in Rome. Promoting papal powers, scholastic philosophy, intense devotionalism, and international standardization, ultramontanism aimed to lift the church above national vagaries. It did not, however, accord with the "Gallican" flavor of French Catholicism or the interests of the French king. In 1682, Louis XIV assembled the French clergy to draw up the famous Gallican Articles. The Articles declared the pope subordinate to the king in temporal matters and subordinate to episcopal councils in spiritual matters. Sounding a lot like the state-headed Church of England, which broke with Rome in 1534, these statements were immediately condemned by Pope Innocent XI. By 1693 the king himself had disavowed them. But the Articles still operated as a manifesto of widespread Gallicanism. Especially notable for conciliarism, Gallicans favored national councils rather than Roman popes as the norm for church decision-making.[5]

Though Louis XIV opposed ultramontanism, he helped the pope suppress a movement deemed threatening to both of them: a Catholic revival of Augustine associated with the Dutch theologian and bishop of Ypres Cornelius Jansen (1585–1638). When Jansen's *Augustinus* was published posthumously in 1640, it inspired a fervent pietism emphasizing the grace of God, penitential rigor, scriptural study, and "signs and wonders." While Catholic opponents charged that it was just Protestantism in disguise, the movement manifested in France in numerous forms, from the renunciant Solitaires' educational ministry to the dedicated women of the Port-Royal convents to whole dioceses that took on an Augustinian flavor. At first the movement was utopian and politically inept, but the king and the pope sensed a gathering critique of establishment powers, and Augustinians rose to the occasion. Jesuit theologians met them with defenses of the papacy and an ultramontane vision of the church. Thus commenced more than a century of battles between Jesuit and Augustinian partisans.

In 1653, Pope Innocent X's bull *Cum occasione* condemned five propositions attributed to Jansen. All Catholic clerics and religious were required to sign a formulary agreeing with this bull. French priests and bishops who refused were excommunicated, jailed, or exiled. Some Augustinian clerics signed in good conscience, they said, but only because the pope had not properly understood Jansen. This charge led to a rift over papal infallibility, another cause the Jesuits were championing. How could the pope be infallible, followers of Jansen asked, if he misread *Augustinus*? A few years after *Cum occasione*, Louis XIV forbade Augustinian epicenter Port-Royal-des-Champs to accept new novices. And in 1709, he ordered soldiers forcibly to remove holdout nuns and raze convent buildings. Backing up the destruction of the convent, Pope Clement XI's bull *Unigenitus* from 1713 condemned "Jansenism" as a heresy. The burning of Port-Royal and required oaths to *Unigenitus* were intended to crush this neo-Augustinian Catholicism once and for all.

But "Jansenism"—a term used by Augustine-inclined Catholics themselves around the turn of the eighteenth century—never really went away. The movement in France gained a reprieve in 1715 when the new acting ruler, the Duke of Orleans, released Jansenist prisoners from jail and invited exiles home. The movement's networks started to overlap with a number of other causes birthed in persecution, including "campaigns to expel the Jesuits, abolish the Inquisition, and soften penal codes against heresy." Jansenism migrated to Ireland, Italy, and other countries. Still anathematized by the Holy See, the "heresy" became increasingly mainstream in France in the 1720s and 1730s, less as a pietism of renunciants and more as the terrain of theological faculties, the radicalization of Gallican politics, and the counter-culture of the middle classes. It inspired popular offshoots in the apocalyptic Figurists and the ecstatic Convulsionnaires. And its new hotspot was Utrecht in the Netherlands, where, as we shall see, a dispute in 1702 over the city's Jansenist exiles led to the formation of a new Catholic church.[6]

By the 1760s, Jansenist, Gallican, and Enlightenment ideas together inspired other countries' resistance to ultramontanism and the formation of new churches, as seen in Febronianism in Germany, Josephinism in Austria, and the Synod of Pistoia in Italy. By the 1770s, Jansenists publicly advocated in favor of civil rights for "Protestants, Jews, and Negroes," while the offshoot Convulsionnaires morphed into radical communitarians with female priests and spiritual marriages. When Revolution came, France's diffusely Jansenist groups seemed awed by the upheavals that they had all but called for, including the establishment in 1790 of the Constitutional Church, a Catholic church separate from Rome and subordinate to the state. Historian Dale Van Kley famously argues that the spark of the French Revolution was the conflagration at Port-Royal a half-century earlier. Historian Brian Strayer adds that not only the assertions of the *philosophes* but also the oppression of the Jansenists tilted French sympathies toward revolutionary ideas.[7]

Indeed, recent scholarship describes Jansenism merging with the Catholic Enlightenment to such an extent that "we cannot define where one movement ends and the other begins," as historian Owen Chadwick puts it. Spanning the second half of the eighteenth century, the "Catholic Enlightenment was in dialogue with contemporary culture," writes historian Ulrich Lerner, "not only by developing new hermeneutical approaches to the Council of Trent or to Jansenist ideas, but also by implementing some of the core values of the overall European Enlightenment." Many Catholic intellectuals opposed radical Enlightenment ideas, Lerner says, but "actually fought for a moderate or conservative Enlightenment." In contemporary US Roman Catholicism, Jansenism is usually remembered—if remembered at all—as crypto-Calvinism or even as just Irish puritanism. Instead, Jansenism served as a hothouse for seeds of reform in modern Catholicism.[8]

Still other French Catholic groups of the ancien régime tested the fortresses of the king and the pope, including occult ritualists, renegade eremites, and the *philosophes* themselves. In 1678, the year of Dominique-Marie Varlet's birth, the discovery of a plot by some occultists to murder Louis XIV plunged Paris into turmoil and eventually resulted in thirty-six executions. In this so-called Affair of the Poisons, it is seen that occultism pervaded whole strata of Catholic clergy and faithful, who took for granted mainstream church life but repurposed its ritual power and hierarchical structure. Apolitical on their face, occultists' self-authorized rites and liturgical egalitarianism challenged establishment Catholicism. Priests offered the sacraments, but so might female initiates. Congregants sought the true church, but might participate in "amatory masses" to reverse original sin via ritual sex.[9]

Then there were the rebel hermits. Among them, Dominique-Marie Varlet's own father left his family to join a band of renunciants at Mont Valérien, a popular pilgrimage site west of Paris. Widely regarded as saintly by the populace, these freelance monks denounced church corruption and constituted "a living reproach to the ecclesiastical authorities of their time," as Varlet's biographer Basil Guy puts it. The Sun King's successor, great-grandson Louis XV, ordered the dispersal of the Mont Valérien hermits in 1729.[10]

Finally, French *philosophes* famous for espousing tolerance, disestablishment, and deism were critics of the Catholic church, but also nominal members of it. René Descartes (1596–1650), the "father of modern philosophy," who died a generation before the birth of Varlet (1678–1724), set the tone in critical reappraisals of theology, which he claimed were evidence of true Catholic devotion. In different ways, Gallicans, Jansenists, occultists, hermits, and *philosophes* were all Catholics renouncing the given institution and living the alternatives.

Such was the scene of early modern French Catholicism, rife with experiment and danger. The biography of Dominique-Marie Varlet takes distinct turns, but its backdrop is the commotion of the late ancien régime. His missions led him not only to America, but also to the Netherlands, Russia, and Persia. Along the way, he found himself catapulted between roles, from

Augustinian seminarian to ultramontane priest, from missionary vicar to bishop *in partibus*, from Jansenist maverick to exiled monk.

DOMINIQUE-MARIE VARLET

Varlet's father and mother were members of the lesser nobility in France, likely inclined toward Gallican and Augustinian flavors of Catholicism. When Varlet was in his late teens, his father's decampment for Mont Valérien marked one parent's rebellion against establishment Catholicism. The son did not run to follow his father. But he too seemed passionate and devout.

To study for the priesthood, Varlet entered the Oratorian seminary of St.-Magloire around 1702. A cradle of Augustinianism, St.-Magloire put Varlet in circulation with Jansenist luminaries. He was ordained in 1706 and that same year received a doctorate in theology from the Sorbonne. Then he joined the Priests of Calvary, the order associated with his father's Mont Valérien pilgrimage site, and ministered in Paris under the supervision of its Augustinian-inclined archbishop, Cardinal Louis-Antoine Noailles. But Varlet worked the ultramontane side, too, as did Noailles and many other clerics. For example, Varlet signed the formulary swearing to *Cum occasione*. Apparently he seemed orthodox enough, since he quickly gained a post as pastor of a suburban parish.[11]

That pastorate failed, however, possibly because Varlet's Augustinian ideas alienated parishioners. Or maybe he was just green and overzealous. In any case, soon Varlet exclaimed to Noailles that he might have better luck converting heathens. He vowed himself to *les oeuvres saintes abandonnées*—work with populations forgotten or cut off from church life—and turned to the Foreign Missions Society. Affiliated with the Holy See's Sacred Congregation for the Propagation of the Faith, also just called the Propaganda, the Society was founded to wrest control of Catholic evangelism away from patronage by the crowns of Spain and Portugal. It recruited hundreds of "secular" or diocesan priests like Varlet and dispatched them as missionaries. Sometimes they were sent to areas already assigned to "regular" priests, that is, members of orders such as the Jesuits or Dominicans.[12]

Varlet sailed for Mobile early in 1713, so he was not in Paris in September, when *Unigenitus* sparked the hottest intra-Catholic battles yet. By the summer of 1715, Varlet was saying mass for the Tamaroa in Sainte-Famille, a log-cabin church established by the Foreign Missions Society in 1699. But if Varlet thought he had escaped the French scene, familiar conflict preceded him. The bishop of Quebec officially supervised Sainte-Famille, but Jesuits had already worked the area for twenty-five years. Earlier seculars had been hounded by Jesuits, who had the advantage of knowing the Tamaroa language and generally adjusting their evangelism to accommodate Indian ways. Eventually Rome backed the Quebec bishop. But the Jesuits maintained a presence in Cahokia and also moved south to establish a rival mission at Kaskaskia, attracting Tamaroa to live with them. In 1702, a plague struck and Seminary missionary Marc Bergier used the occasion to preach against native medicine men before succumbing to the plague himself.

FIGURE 2.1 The Church of the Holy Family, Cahokia, Ill., built as the Sainte-Famille mission in 1699, headed by Dominique-Marie Varlet in 1715–17, and reconstructed in 1799, is today the oldest continuously operating Catholic church in the United States. Copyright © M gastn, Wikimedia/Creative Commons.

Some Kaskaskia Tamaroa were so disgusted that they returned to Cahokia to celebrate Bergier's death and desecrate Sainte-Famille.[13]

So when Varlet showed up in 1715, the mission was defunct and Jesuits were the only priests seen in Cahokia for eight years. Just as in France, it was Jansenists versus Jesuits, "white collars" versus "black robes." Still, Varlet threw himself into a cycle of farming, catechesis, and liturgy. When the Tamaroa decamped to their hunting grounds, Varlet went with them. He seemed to love the life of *les oeuvres saintes abandonnées*.[14]

After barely two years, however, Varlet's health again failed. In 1717, he traveled to Quebec to persuade Bishop Jean-Baptiste de Saint-Vallier to assign more missionaries to Cahokia. Varlet also described plans to shield the Tamaroa from the influence of lawless French settlers, of whom Jesuits were more tolerant. At this point Saint-Vallier appointed Varlet vicar-general for all of Illinois country, which covered everything from the Great Lakes to the Missouri River. But before Varlet had a chance to start his new job, word came of another precocious appointment. Rome had appointed him to the post of coadjutor bishop of Babylon, in Persia. As coadjutor, Varlet would assist the head bishop and then succeed him.[15]

The see of Babylon was a see *in partibus infidelium* or "in the land of unbelievers"—a sort of placeholder for a historic Roman Catholic diocese that no longer existed because of Muslim rule. Bishops *in partibus* administered disestablished churches, oversaw missionary efforts, and minded Rome's political and economic interests. At that time in Persia several thousand Armenian Catholics in weak communion with Rome lived under the relatively tolerant Shi'a Muslim Safavids. Other Armenians were Gregorian Christians. Minority Sunni, local Zoroastrians, Russian Jews, and Georgian Orthodox lived there, too, as did British Anglicans and Dutch Protestants of their respective East India Companies. Roman missionaries had little success converting Muslims, so they tried to evangelize other Catholics— mostly the Gregorians and the Orthodox. This caused great tension with those churches' patriarchs.[16]

As Varlet arrived in Paris to prepare for Persia, relations deteriorated between the Holy See and decriminalized Jansenists. Those who refused to sign *Unigenitus* had requested a church council to review that bull, whereupon Pope Clement XI excommunicated all who requested a council, whereupon they appealed their excommunication to a church council as well. Varlet's sympathies certainly lay with the seekers of appeal, or Appellants. But the pope still ran the church and Varlet was on the ultramontane track. On February 19, 1719, Varlet was consecrated as a bishop. No sooner had mass concluded than Varlet again received dramatic news. The bishop of Babylon had actually died over a year earlier. Now Varlet was not coadjutor but bishop in full. He needed to depart right away. He should take the long route to avoid war in Turkey. He was instructed to travel incognito. Likely this was for his protection. Outside Catholic countries, a Catholic bishop might encounter trouble.[17]

Historians agree on what happened next, but not on how or why. Varlet omitted one step of his preparations: visiting the papal nuncio to swear allegiance to *Unigenitus*. It is possible that Varlet did not know about the requirement, as he later claimed. Others speculated that the pressure of haste, the order to assume disguise, or Varlet's opposition to *Unigenitus*—conscious or unconscious—caused the omission. Regardless, failing to make this stop would haunt Varlet for the rest of his life. Sailing from Antwerp, Varlet's ship hit a storm and diverted to Amsterdam. And in Amsterdam the most agitated front of the Jansenist controversy in all of Europe awaited him.[18]

Varlet wrote later that his New World sojourn also made him unaware of the scene in Holland. It is unlikely, however, that he was a complete political ingénue. All well-informed Europeans knew the recent history of famous Jansenists in the United Provinces. Its Reformed government made Catholicism illegal and thus difficult to practice openly, but Jansenists found a home in the underground church, already resonant with Jansen's Augustinian sensibilities. Secular clergy and Jansenists together chafed at the presence of Jesuits, usually also Dutch but seen as interloping foreigners in a land the Holy See considered "The Holland Mission." While secular clerics saw themselves as continuing their homeland's pre-Reformation parish and diocesan ministry, Jesuits operated on the basis of the land's mission character. Seculars claimed all the rights of historic dioceses, including the right to elect bishops. Jesuits pointed out that missions did not have bishops, only apostolic vicars, so missionaries in the United Provinces were answerable only to their own superiors.[19]

By the late seventeenth century, conflict between Dutch Catholic seculars and regulars was endemic. Apostolic vicars bristled that Jesuits ran amok. Jesuits accused apostolic vicars of Jansenism. The real crisis commenced in 1688 when the Dutch clergy's elected vicar, Pieter Codde, refused orders from Rome to turn out Jansen sympathizers living in his jurisdiction. In 1702, Codde was deposed by the pope, who then appointed an apostolic vicar of his own choosing, Theodore de Cock. But some Dutch clergy refused to recognize de Cock. Especially in Utrecht, clerics kept following the deposed Codde. From the turn of the century, then, a rift developed between a small but influential group of secular clergy loyal to Codde and a larger group—the rest of the seculars plus Jesuits—that supported de Cock. Making matters more complicated, at this point the government of the United Provinces threw its weight behind Codde. It banished the pope's choice, de Cock, demanded to approve all future vicars in advance, and called for the wholesale ouster of the Jesuits. Codde and his allies certainly cultivated this government favor. So while de Cock and his successors now ran Roman church business remotely from Cologne, significant portions of the Dutch Catholic community ignored them.

When Codde died in 1710, his followers did not have recourse to a bishop's powers. As such, they could not ordain priests or confirm children. They asked the Holy See's permission to hold an episcopal election. Rome replied that their rightful leader was de Cock. So the Codde clergy took an unusual but, they believed, necessary step. To a sympathetic Irish bishop they secretly sent twelve candidates for priestly ordination. When the Holy See discovered the repopulation of pro-Codde ranks, it was predictably outraged. Across Europe, Catholics started to follow the low rumblings in the Low Countries. For Rome the Dutch scene was a minor smudge on the global picture. But to Catholics wary of ultramontanism, the defiant Dutch became a David-against-Goliath tale of inspiration—and sometimes imitation.

With new priests but still no bishop, Catholics in Utrecht now faced the impracticality of sending hundreds of children overseas for confirmation.

They really needed a bishop on site. That is when the newly consecrated Varlet blew into port in Amsterdam. The Utrecht Catholics quickly found him, anonymized travel or no. Within a few hours of Varlet's arrival on April 2, 1719, a well-connected pro-Codde cleric offered lodging at his home and harbor to say Palm Sunday mass. Within a few days, Varlet heard the favor he might perform for his new acquaintances: confirm their children.

By Varlet's own account, he initially refused. He told the Utrecht Catholics that the children could go abroad. They countered that the poor and orphaned could not. Still Varlet refused. But, waiting for a ship for several weeks, he found himself persuaded. Were not the innocent unconfirmed children an unexpected instance of *les oeuvres saintes abandonnées*? On April 19, 21, and 23, Varlet confirmed 604 persons of the Dutch Catholic church. Then he sailed for St. Petersburg. But those confirmation masses—which immediately became international news—were "never forgotten, or forgiven, by the Court of Rome." Conducted without Holy See permission, outside Varlet's own episcopal jurisdiction, and against Rome's appointed vicar, the confirmations put Varlet near the top of the list of disfavored notables and suspected Jansenists. What seemed "charity" and "duty" to him was "insubordination" and "irresponsibility" to Rome.[20]

Continuing south from St. Petersburg, Varlet only got as far as the Persian city of Shamakhi before war again interfered with his journey. It was November 1719, and the governing Safavid Empire was in its turbulent final days. Located in present-day Azerbaijan, Shamakhi lay just north of the encampment of the royal court-in-exile, so travelers holed up there in relative safety. Scottish sailor and author of *A New Account of the East Indies* Alexander Hamilton passed through at that time, as did consuls from Russia and France, who wrote letters about the "detain[ment] for many months at Shamakhi owing to the disturbed state of the country." Varlet used his time to meet with the Armenian bishop in town. Formally in communion with the pope, Bishop Isaiah wanted Varlet to help him forge stronger ties—and greater political leverage for his people. Apparently the Jesuits and Dominicans already posted in Safavid cities had not risen to that task.[21]

In the spring of 1720, a Jesuit priest arrived in Shamakhi and delivered to Varlet a letter from the bishop of Isfahan, Persia's capital. The letter informed

Varlet that he was under interdict by the Propaganda as of May 7, 1719—that is, within days of performing the Dutch confirmations. The interdict also cited Varlet's failure to swear to *Unigenitus*. His financial support was gone. He was not to exercise any episcopal functions. He was not to proceed to the episcopal residence in Hamadan. Surely Varlet was very disturbed at this news. But like the Utrecht Catholics, he felt he had taken illicit steps in good faith and would eventually be vindicated. Some of his correspondents even advised him to ignore the interdict, which they considered canonically weak. But Varlet reasoned that he would fail in any mission as long as Roman censure clouded his reputation. So he headed back to Europe.[22]

Perhaps Varlet was naive about his chances for successful redress. More likely, he simply could not have anticipated how his person suddenly served as proxy for the deepest struggles of early-eighteenth-century Catholicism. Even before Varlet reversed course, his brother bishop in Isfahan had installed Dominican friars at Hamadan and put them in charge of its affairs. Varlet biographer Guy wonders if the young bishop, promoted quickly but lacking strong ultramontane credentials, was simply too much of an upstart for the Jesuit-dominated Propaganda and Dominican allies to stomach.[23]

Varlet was at risk of imprisonment in Paris and soon became a permanent exile in the Netherlands. From there he wrote a series of tracts and appeals, often supported by fellow bishops and famous canonists. He became increasingly adamant that conscience would not permit him to do what Rome required for rehabilitation: accept *Unigenitus* and apologize for the confirmations. This stand effectively "closed the door on any such recourse as he or his friends might have desired or any such accommodation as could have been arranged," Guy writes.[24]

A NEW CATHOLIC CHURCH

Meanwhile, the Utrecht Catholics had gone forward with electing a bishop, Cornelius Steenoven. Duly they wrote Rome to approve the choice. Instead, the new pope, Benedict XIII, appointed another apostolic vicar. Utrecht Catholics then launched a sort of public relations campaign, broadcasting the predicament far and wide. Sympathetic tracts like Zeger Bernard Van Espen's *Dissertation on the Miserable Condition of the Church of Utrecht* created a sensation across Europe, arguing that if the Holy See did not give appropriate permissions, history and canon law were on the side of Utrecht going ahead by itself. "I can think of nothing," exclaimed the bishop of Boulogne, "except of *les affaires présentes de cette glorieuse Église d'Utrecht*."[25]

But the campaign and canonical arguments failed to persuade Rome to approve the election of Steenoven. The Utrecht Catholics approached Varlet again. "What will be your praise in the Catholic Church," they wrote him, "if you raise up a church that has almost fallen, a church which God has perhaps preserved free from certain new bondages and scandals, that when He shall renew His signs, . . . it may minister to the execution of His counsels?" This time it seemed Varlet acted not just from charity but also conviction. On October 15, 1724, the bishop of Babylon consecrated Cornelius Steenoven for the See of Utrecht.[26]

It had happened before and it would happen again: without permission a Roman bishop performed a consecration. Such acts were valid but illicit and usually soon inconsequential. But in this case, after years of contestation over papal authority, the unsanctioned episcopacy turned a page in the historical record. The new Catholic church created by Varlet, Steenoven, and the Utrecht community endured. It gave rise to a new adjective, "ultrajectine." Like ultramontane, the word "ultrajectine" has geographical connotations. Derived from *traiectum*, Latin for "ford," it is the old Roman Empire name for Utrecht.

After Varlet consecrated Steenoven, the Holy See excommunicated the Church of Utrecht. But in some eyes, the ultrajectines gained respect. Dozens of bishops wrote their congratulations. Numerous canonists sided with them. Anglicans and Orthodox noted that "the Rubicon was passed." Varlet became a minor celebrity. He continued writing on behalf of himself and the Appellants. He consecrated another bishop for Utrecht when Steenoven died, and then two more successors after that. More Appellants had arrived in the Netherlands, especially Carthusian and Orvalist monks who promptly put themselves under the jurisdiction of the Utrecht bishop. In a few years Varlet left his Amsterdam apartment to live with the Orvalists. He remained with these brothers for over a decade, enhancing his reputation for holiness. After a series of strokes, Varlet died on May 14, 1742. He was sixty-four.[27]

Perhaps Varlet only helped Augustinian causes by circumstance or self-interest. Perhaps he was artless and dreamy, tone deaf to politics, rapt with righteousness. He was a cause célèbre but never a leader of the new Catholic

FIGURE 2.2 Dominique-Marie Varlet. Photo courtesy of Museum Catherijneconvent, Utrecht, the Netherlands.

church he launched. He never imagined that the ultrajectine church would remain independent, much less seed hundreds of other non-Roman Catholicisms around the world for several centuries. Had he known, it likely would have disturbed his peaceful old age. Unintended though these consequences were, however, it was still radical of Varlet to embrace Utrecht. Merely sympathizing with the cause at that time "entailed great risk to body and soul," as Guy puts it. Varlet was also courageous for refusing repeated Holy See reconciling overtures that he considered unprincipled, though the refusals came at significant vocational and financial cost.[28]

So that is how Dominique-Marie Varlet helped start the first non-Roman Catholic church in the west since the commencement of Anglicanism in 1534. The Utrecht church has existed alongside the Roman church in the Netherlands ever since. It continually generated Catholic reforms. Future independents followed Utrecht's pattern of ordination by bishops in apostolic succession to secure valid sacraments. Modern Catholicism went forward as ideologically diverse but also as institutionally multiple. And while today's US independents are far removed from Varlet's concerns, they recognize themselves in him. They call him their founder, name him a saint, and celebrate his feast day. As one American independent website puts it: "Meet the Ultrajectines."[29]

After Varlet died, Utrecht Catholics continued their appeals, joining calls for a general council and keeping in touch with Rome unilaterally. By the later decades of the eighteenth century, however, they developed a distinctive conciliar Catholicism. In 1763 Utrecht held its own "Provisional Council," including not only bishops but also ten priests who could vote. Two priests were designated representatives of the laity.[30]

AN "INDEPENDENT CATHOLICK CHURCH OF THE UNITED STATES"

Varlet never returned to the "woods of America" recalled fondly in the letter to his sister. But North America had non-Roman Catholics before Varlet's descendants crossed the ocean. Anglicans settled in Virginia in 1607. In

1789 they formed the Protestant Episcopal Church, the queen of US Christianities for two centuries. Greek Orthodox colonists landed in Florida in 1768, and Russian Orthodox monks evangelized Alaska in 1794. In addition, small groups of US Roman and Eastern Catholics repeatedly broke ties with Rome, starting with the "Nugent Schism" at St. Peter's parish in New York in 1785.

Most historians of the Roman church, like its leaders, characterize breaks from Rome as "schisms." Schism can be a neutral and technical word, but in this literature it tends to carry an affect of dismay and disdain, and usually aspersions about originality, authenticity, and morality, too. So I decided not to use the word. Still, when I read against the grain of accounts of schisms, historians of the Roman church describe numerous US Catholic churches separated from Rome for shorter or longer periods of time. Among early historians, Peter Guilday in 1922 bemoaned that he was compelled to discuss eighteenth- and nineteenth-century schisms so often, if only because their repeated occurrence dominated the sources. The "Catholic laity were assuredly doing more and planning more for God's Church," he writes, "than the movements for independence from church authority with which the documents abound." In 1985, historian Jay Dolan writes frankly that "schism in the American Catholic Church had occurred throughout the nineteenth century" and calls the resultant groups "schismatic independent churches" or just "independent churches."[31]

Usually historians explain "independent churches" according to familiar tropes of American Catholic historiography, such as the "trustee controversy," "ethnic rivalries," or just "Old World" views. But details often link breakaway churches to European Catholic reform, such as that of the Church of Utrecht or the "constitutional clergy" of France. Writing about the famous Philadelphia breaches that embroiled the parishes of Holy Trinity (1797) and St. Mary's (1820) for years, Guilday ties participants to nationalism as well as Jansenism. Bishop of Baltimore John Carroll was warned in 1797 that the Philadelphia instigators were "turbulent men" who had "declared themselves independent" of the pope, with Guilday interpreting independence as continuous with "Jansenist or Gallican tenets." In 1820 the St. Mary's trustees backed their favored priest, William Hogan, with an open letter calling on American Catholics to join them in establishing an independent Catholic church.[32]

A year earlier, in 1819, trustees of the Catholic parish in Charleston, South Carolina, not only determined to separate from Rome, but also took the leap of suggesting to their desired priest that he travel to Utrecht for consecration as a bishop. Trustees appreciated the ultrajectine alternative. As articulated in a lengthy letter, Utrecht was a living, breathing example of a properly conciliarist Catholic church. The trustees cited support from conciliarists in France to Febronius in Germany to republicans in America. They aimed no less than to found an "Independent Catholick Church of the United States"—perhaps the first time that phrase was used for the American phenomenon. A flurry of Roman episcopal communication picked up the phrase. Seventy years later, historian John Gilmary Shea in the *American Catholic Quarterly Review* directly linked these southern "malcontents" to the "wretched Varlet" and the "pseudo-Archbishop of Utrecht." As the bishops and historians make clear, US Roman Catholic leaders knew of Utrecht. Lay trustees in Charleston not only knew of Utrecht, but also wanted to be like Utrecht.[33]

This US southern Catholic initiative had a huge impact on Holy See actions in America. The propositioned priest rejected the Utrecht idea, but news of the plan flashed across Europe. Within two years, hoping to prevent a Netherlands situation in the United States, the Holy See set up dioceses in both South Carolina and Virginia, rather than only in far-off Maryland. And in 1829, bishops gathered at the first Provincial Council in Baltimore to quash participatory governance of churches, even though the bishops officially supported American republican government. Historian Guilday concludes that a "real danger" was averted and calls the trustees "evil." "Had the Southern schismatics gained their objective, namely: the creation of an 'Independent Catholick Church of the United States,' subject directly to the Jansenist Archbishop of Utrecht," he writes, "the seamless garment of the American Church would undoubtedly have been rent for all time by these first rebels, and their followers, against episcopal authority."[34]

But the Holy See and bishops did not quell what came to be called "Independentism." William Hogan of Philadelphia soon inspired a lesser-known breakaway led by the "Hoganite" Father John Farnan in Brooklyn. Their common commitment seems to have been Irish nationalist conciliarism. Farnan and his "countrymen" ended affiliation with Rome in 1831, establishing what contemporaries called the "Independent Catholic Church" at the corner of Jay and York Streets near the Brooklyn waterfront. In 1835 Farnan published in Philadelphia's *Unites States Gazette* that he "award[ed] . . . the Bishop of Rome, no higher ecclesiastical powers than belong to every other bishop" and that his own church was "independent of the Roman Catholic bishop of New York and of the See of Rome."[35]

As in many cases, this "Independent Catholic Church" did not last long. In 1842 it became Assumption of the Blessed Virgin Mary parish within the Roman Catholic Diocese of New York. But US splits occasioned by "nationalists" and "ethnic" partisans with "Old World" loyalties—in other words, likely reform-minded Catholics with ultrajectine sympathies—were only getting started.

FROM VARLET TO VILATTE

Despite all reform impulses, Catholic history trended steadily in ultramontane directions. Historian Van Kley suggests that reformist councils like those at Utrecht, Pistoia, and Paris could only enact radical agenda precisely because they were powerless. There are several reasons why ultramontanism in the nineteenth century became increasingly compelling, starting with the French Revolution in 1789. Waves of antireligious sentiment, anticlerical violence, and church disestablishment convinced many Catholics to rally around the pope as the champion of tradition over modernity. But as time went on, ultramontanism proved supple in adjusting to new realities. The Holy See changed to accommodate non-Catholic governments, preferring the status quo to revolution, working to secure religious tolerance, and even arguing for the "social utility" of other Christianities, as opposed to secularism, indifferentism, and atheism. Closely linked to ultramontanism, the "Devotional Revolution" generated new observances such as the Immaculate Conception, which elevated Mary and the pope at the same time. To the "surprise and relief" of many Catholics, then—including ultramontanists themselves—the Roman church in the nineteenth century survived and even thrived.[36]

In the United States, ultramontanism was especially pervasive, since, as historian John McGreevy writes, "most Catholic institutions were founded as the ultramontane style crystallized" and missionaries to America, often refugees from revolution, "tended to have strong ultramontane sympathies." Even "Americanism"—the "updated version of Gallicanism" espoused by some US Catholic leaders in the latter half of the nineteenth century and condemned by the Vatican in 1898—was as much ultramontane as nationalist. While "Americanists" appreciated the possibilities of modern scholarship and positively preferred the liberal state, they too endorsed a "papal internationalism," completely assuming that, as historian Terence Fay writes, "loyalty to the spiritual and political leadership of the Holy See [was] the best way to reconstruct Catholic life, worship, and culture" after the French Revolution.[37]

But prospering ultramontanism did not utterly vanquish different versions of the faith. In fact, it arguably created them. Eighteenth-century confrontations with Rome opened space for nineteenth-century Catholic options, just as similar Enlightenment-era pressures produced liberal Protestantism and Reform Judaism. Scholars of Catholicism always discuss handfuls of Roman church republicans, liberals, and modernists from John Carroll to John Ireland, as well as their international influences from Lammenais to Lord Acton. All but unknown, however, are thousands of reformers who could be found starting and populating new Catholicisms.

In France, Bernard-Raymond Fabré-Palaprat revived the Knights Templar in 1804 and founded the Johannite Church several years later, while followers of the mystic Eugene Vintras formed the Church of Carmel in the 1840s. Both of these ecclesial bodies morphed, branched, and connected with independents, including French national church bishops. In England, Anglicanism thrummed with Catholic revival from the 1830s. Historically minded divines of the Tractarian Movement and the Oxford Movement reinstituted Catholic liturgy, theology, and monasticism, while others sought the reunification of Christianity in organizations such as the Order of Corporate Reunion. In Germany in 1844, priest Johannes Ronge left Rome in disgust with ultramontanism, especially what he considered the "superstition" and "fanaticism" of the new devotions. He helped found the "New Catholic" movement, led a liberal wing called the *Deutschkatholiken*, and then joined with like-minded Protestants to create the *Freireligiöse*. Many *Freireligiöse* joined the migrations in 1848, settling in Wisconsin and other US states. Rejection of Roman authority happened outside Europe, too. In southern India in the 1880s, when the Vatican tried to replace traditional *Padroado* leadership, Portuguese-speaking Indian Catholics and Syrian ecclesial sponsors teamed up to start a new church: the Independent Catholic Church of Ceylon, Goa, and India.[38]

Above these tiny ephemeral churches towered the Varlet-descended Church of Utrecht. It was known as the Old Catholic church after 1853, when Rome finally reestablished its episcopacy in the Netherlands and won many Dutch Catholics back to Rome. But Old Catholicism was rejuvenated after the First Vatican Council, when a number of German, Austrian, and Swiss priests and parishes reached out to Utrecht in common opposition to the promulgation of the dogma of papal infallibility. Together, they formed the Union of Utrecht and issued the Declaration of Utrecht in 1889. Soon there were Old Catholic churches in a half-dozen European countries, from Italy to England. They rejected not only infallibility but also other Romanisms, such as the Immaculate Conception, aural confession, and the *filioque* clause. They embraced the modernism, historicism, and ecumenicism that Pius IX's Syllabus of Errors (1864) condemned. They revived past traditions of conciliar governance, vernacular worship, and—though much more slowly—clerical marriage. Indeed, Old Catholics came to consider nothing doctrinally binding after the first seven ecumenical councils, which ended in 787 CE. It was another reason they were Old Catholics, they explained, since they took ancient conciliar traditions as the norm and opposed new ultramontane doctrines.

It is ironic, of course, that a modernist church claimed the adjective "old" and accused ultramontanes of innovation. But like other religious modernists, Old Catholics tried to sift for what was historically ancient as opposed to what was promulgated as eternal. In the German universities, two-thirds of history professors joined the Old Catholic church, "a disaster for the Roman Catholic study of history," historian Owen Chadwick writes. Their leading light was priest and professor Johann Ignaz von Döllinger. The work of Döllinger had inspired the thirteenth item on Pius IX's Syllabus, namely, the "error" of thinking that the "method and principles by which the old scholastic doctors cultivated theology are no longer suitable to the demands of our times and to the progress of the sciences." Döllinger was also the anonymous "Quirinus" who, with information from his friend Lord Acton, wrote critical reports about Vatican I that were published serially in Germany's leading political paper, the *Allgemeine Zeitung*. After being excommunicated by Rome for not accepting infallibility, Döllinger sojourned with the Old Catholic church and championed its potential for ecumenical work.[39]

Old Catholicism is large, stable, and enduring compared to other non-Roman groups. In 2011 the Union of Utrecht numbered approximately 64,500 Old Catholics in ten European countries, including the Czech Republic and Croatia. Partly the size and stability owe to its apostolic succession, unquestioned as valid even by Rome—notwithstanding early barbs such as in *Iampridem* (1886), in which Pope Leo XIII called Old Catholics "treacherous men who . . . spread new and perverse teachings and strove to attract to themselves unfortunate disciples deceived by fraud." In the late nineteenth and early twentieth centuries, Catholics on the reform spectrum could join the Old Catholic church or request help in the form of the ordination of priests and bishops. The Mariavite Catholic Church in Poland received episcopal orders from the Old Catholics in 1909. The Philippine Independent Church (founded in 1896) and Czechoslovak Hussite Church (founded 1919) were not directly linked to Old Catholicism until later, but both started with ultrajectine inspiration. By the 1880s, US churches of Czech, Polish, Italian, French, Belgian, Flemish, Hungarian, Slovak, and Lithuanian Catholics had repeatedly gone independent, sometimes with priests or bishops ordained by Old Catholics.[40]

The largest of these resulted in the Polish National Catholic Church (PNCC), founded in 1897 by Father Franciszek Hodur and based in Scranton, Pennsylvania. Utrecht consecrated Hodur as PNCC primate in 1907.

Often treated in US Catholic historiography as "just" an "ethnic" or "national" church, the early PNCC was an amazingly progressive community, incorporating Hodur's interests in Catholic reform, Universalism, and eastern religions. Early documents rejected original sin, espoused universal salvation, counted gospel proclamation as a sacrament, and possibly countenanced reincarnation. Hodur also championed women's rights and saw a future priesthood of both men and women. Over the next hundred years, the PNCC grew much more conservative. But in the early twenty-first century it continues to reject the concept of original sin and some activists are trying to realize Hodur's vision of women's ordination. The PNCC remains the biggest and most enduring American independent Catholic body, with approximately twenty-five thousand members.[41]

Hodur was not the first Utrecht-consecrated bishop in the United States, however. In 1897, Anton Kozlowski of All Saints in Chicago was consecrated in Berne, Switzerland, becoming the country's first Old Catholic bishop. And five years before that, in 1892, Joseph René Vilatte was consecrated by the aforementioned Independent Church of Ceylon, Goa, and India, making him the first independent Catholic bishop on American soil of any jurisdiction. Even more than Varlet, Vilatte would figure hugely in US independent Catholicism, including in the history of the Church of Antioch.

In the middle of the twentieth century, a Brazilian Roman bishop started another new Catholic church. Appointed Rome's bishop of Botucatu in 1924, Carlos Duarte Costa challenged Vatican policies and worked for political reform in Brazil. He was demoted to a merely honorary see in 1937. Then criticizing church and state collaboration with Nazi Germany and its allies, Duarte Costa was accused of communism and imprisoned in 1944, though soon released due to international pressure. The bishop then charged the Vatican with secreting Nazi war criminals to Brazil via the now-infamous "ratlines" and announced the formation of the Brazilian Catholic Apostolic Church. Duarte Costa's agenda reads like an ultrajectine primer: restore conciliar governance, reject papal infallibility, elect bishops by popular vote, allow clerical marriage, and say mass in the vernacular. Clergy are worker-priests who hold regular jobs. In the late 1940s the church was actively persecuted by the Rome-aligned Brazilian government, but it gained popular credibility. As of 2010, the Brazilian Catholic Apostolic Church was the second largest in the country, with 561,000 adherents. It also helped start national churches from the United States to Argentina to Zambia, totaling four million members worldwide. Upon the formation of the Zambian Catholic Apostolic National Church in 2007, archbishop-elect Luciano Mbewe told the press, "It should surprise no one to hear of yet another Catholic church."[42]

These multiple foundings challenge narratives of nineteenth- and twentieth-century modernity that reflexively pit Catholicism and nationalism against each other. Certainly the Roman church and nationalist movements sustain mutual aversion in many instances. But a minority of Catholics inside and outside Rome has rallied for new state formations as part of envisioning a renewed church. And nationalists, far from being always "anti-Catholic" or "anticlerical," repeatedly supported the formation of new Catholicisms. In numerous cases, the "anti-Catholicism" of nationalists may be more accurately described as anti-Romanism, rejecting a "particular (ultramontane, priest-ridden) *style* of Catholicism," writes historian Matthew Butler.[43]

This was the case, Butler says, in the formation of yet another modernizing Catholicism in 1925, namely, the revolution-era Mexican Catholic Apostolic Church. In Mexico, nationalists sought not "root and branch disenchantment," but Catholic reform and renewal through "free national churches" unfettered by papal dominion, Butler writes. The opposite of secularizing, this movement of "dissident or liberal Roman Catholic clergy and Catholic revolutionaries" took a deeply religious stance that "sprang from personal, patriotic, or canonical disillusionment with the discipline and claims of the Roman Catholic church."[44]

To be sure, revolutionary Catholics sometimes found themselves in debilitating relationships with sponsor governments—as Mexican national Catholics learned the hard way, as did the Constitutional Church in France, Old Catholics in Bismarckian Germany, the "red priests" of Russian Orthodoxy during Bolshevism, and the Chinese Catholic Patriotic Association bishops in contemporary China. Even so, Butler writes, Catholic involvement in nationalist movements suggests that "liberal Catholics and Old

Catholics—not just freemasons and Communards—were in the vanguard of the 'culture wars' against the ultramontane papacy in nineteenth-century Europe."[45]

To find this kind of nationalist Catholicism in the United States—affirming the nation-state to oppose a "particular (ultramontane, priest-ridden) *style* of Catholicism" but maintaining a liberal priesthood—one need look no further than dozens of churches whose names include "US," "North American," "American," "National," "Free," or "Independent," starting with Charleston's Revolution-inspired idea for an "Independent Catholick Church of America" in 1819. Eighty years later, Old Catholic bishop Anton Kozlowski celebrated the nation as a favorable climate for Catholicism. Contemporaneous with Americanists on the Roman side who operated fully within ultramontane parameters, Kozlowski and other independents promoted an ultrajectine Americanism linked to global Catholic reform. Kozlowski wished his parishioners unending "Spiritual independence, which you now regained here in the land of the free," he wrote in a pastoral letter in 1897. "May this noble independence remain with you as a perpetual blessing, so that you indeed rejoice in the liberty of the children of God."[46]

Twenty-first-century independents inherit many nationalistically labeled churches and start new ones, too. What they mean in invoking the nation-state differs from case to case. Some names reflect little more than geographic location within US borders. But others are chosen deliberately to maintain American-identified ideals and echo forebears' Americanism. Roman progressives are "always talking about starting an American Catholic church," independent Bishop Peter Hickman told a reporter in 1988, when he was affiliated with the American Catholic Church–Old Catholic. "Here we are."[47]

The life of Joseph René Vilatte, the first independent Catholic bishop in America, strikingly illustrates how the ascendancy of ultramontane Catholicism coincided with a proliferation of Catholic alternatives and eclectic combinations. Vilatte was born in France into La Petite Église, a Constitutional Catholic remnant. Raised Roman Catholic, he quit seminary in Quebec and got his first ministerial license from the Presbyterians. Then he joined an interdenominational project based in Montreal, started a

Wisconsin mission under an Episcopal bishop, and traveled to Utrecht for ordination as an Old Catholic priest. A few years later he was consecrated in India. In three decades of episcopacy, Vilatte's many ventures included bequeathing apostolic succession on esoteric Catholics, ordaining Anglican Benedictines, and inspiring a Mexican commune. In addition, he consecrated bishops for US independents of Polish, Italian, and West Indian heritage. In 1894 and again in 1915, Vilatte founded his own American Catholic Church. If Dominique-Marie Varlet was the progenitor of modern western independents, Joseph René Vilatte is their American godfather.

JOSEPH RENÉ VILATTE

When the Concordat of 1801 forged between Napoleon and Pius VII reseated Roman bishops in all French dioceses, it was a triumph for the Holy See and a final blow to the established-then-disestablished Constitutional Church. Yet thousands of priests and laypeople rejected the Concordat on Gallican principles and kept their allegiance to the now-exiled Constitutional bishops. When Napoleon fell in 1815 and most exiled bishops were reconciled with Rome, three still held out. These three, along with their constituencies, called themselves La Petite Église Anticoncordataire.[48]

But the little church's bishops slowly died out, having consecrated no more. Clergy passed away too, so laymen presided at mass and performed sacraments. That is why, if Joseph René Vilatte's baptism in 1854 took place in La Petite Église, he was likely baptized by a layman. The Christian Brothers in Paris suspected so. After Vilatte's parents died, he ended up in an orphanage of the Christian Brothers, where they promptly baptized him *sub conditione* or conditionally—that is, in case a possible prior sacrament was not valid in Rome's eyes.[49]

It is not known what Vilatte's personal take on Petite Église Catholicism was, but it is easy to imagine that this countercultural heritage had lasting effects. A far more palpable impact, however, came from personal experience with war. In 1870, the sixteen-year-old Vilatte enlisted to serve in the Franco-Prussian War. France suffered a major defeat that shortly gave way to a violent civil war, as the Communards of Paris tried to hold out against the national army. Though the national army routed the uprising, thousands on both sides were slaughtered or deported. Traumatized, Vilatte left for Canada. He found employment as a teacher at a Christian Brothers lumber camp mission in Gatineau, Quebec. Recalled to France for military draft, he instead went to Belgium and professed with the Christian Brothers.

Sometime in the late 1870s, Vilatte returned to Canada to study for the priesthood at the Holy Cross Brothers seminary in Montreal. One evening Vilatte took advantage of the intellectual life of Montreal to attend a public lecture by the famous ex–Roman priest Charles Chiniquy. Vilatte already knew of Chiniquy from his founding of temperance societies, including one at the lumber camp mission. Now Chiniquy was a Presbyterian minister who preached against Rome with stunts like consecrating hosts and then stomping on them, mocking priests' attributed sacerdotal powers and the doctrine of transubstantiation. Chiniquy's message startled Vilatte. But it also might have resonated with his Petite Église sensibilities. Vilatte was already finding his seminary courses "rabidly Romanist." By the time he left the lecture, Vilatte reported, his convictions about a Roman vocation were shaken. A few years later, he consulted Chiniquy and decided to pursue ordination by a different path.[50]

Chiniquy was well known for anti-Roman lectures and publications. He even originated the oft-repeated conspiracy theory that Jesuits were behind the assassination of Abraham Lincoln. But reading Chiniquy as a garden-variety Catholic-hater does not capture the complexity. For the better part of his life, Chiniquy served as pastor of St. Anne's, a parish in rural Kankakee, Illinois, which was part of the Roman Catholic Diocese of Chicago until 1858. At that time, St. Anne's went independent and called itself a "Christian Catholic" church—or as the *Montreal Witness* put it, "Neither Protestant nor Roman." That is only one hint that Chiniquy was part of transatlantic Catholic reform. His lectures targeted French immigrants alienated by ultramontanism in France and Canada—immigrants like Vilatte. At St. Anne's, practices included lay governance, vernacular mass, bible reading, and the citation of Augustine to justify everything. By 1863 St. Anne's was spiritually isolated and financially strapped, so Chiniquy and the church joined the Canada Presbytery. Yet when Vilatte met Chiniquy a decade later, the preacher was still conversant with Catholic reform in Europe and handily connected Vilatte to his contacts overseas.[51]

In 1884, Vilatte too was licensed as a Presbyterian minister. Through the French Canadian Mission Society, an interdenominational group aimed at converting French Catholics to Protestantism, he worked in Quebec, Massachusetts, and New York before traveling to St. Anne's to see Chiniquy's "Christian Catholic" church in action. Then Vilatte went to pastor Calvary Church in Wisconsin, an officially Presbyterian church populated by some former St. Anne's parishioners who had relocated to the Door peninsula. Vilatte found the peninsula inhabited by Illinois migrants, Menominee Indians, and Belgians who were assortedly nominal Romans, Petite Église devotees, or spiritualists. To gather as many as possible, Vilatte imagined a church like Chiniquy's. His "conviction," he wrote in *My Relations*, was "that neither Roman Catholicism nor Protestantism could satisfy the needs of these people who had already abandoned the Roman Church." But a "purified Catholic Church," he said, "would present the Gospel to the people as did the primitive Church, and exercise authority according to the Spirit of free America."[52]

Vilatte's Protestant ordination, however, would not pass muster on the Catholic-identified peninsula. Chiniquy put Vilatte in touch with Hyacinthe Loyson in Paris. Former provincial of the Carmelites and now luminary of French Catholic reform, "Père Hyacinthe" was so renowned a Roman apostate that the future saint Thérèse of Lisieux herself was praying for his repentance. Excommunicated by Rome in 1869 after he spoke out for church democratization, clerical marriage, and a limited papacy, Loyson worked closely with Döllinger and the Old Catholics. But most Old Catholics did not accept clerical marriage at that time. So Loyson, who had married in 1872, founded a new Gallican Catholic Church.[53]

For support Loyson turned to the Anglican church. Anglicans at the Lambeth Conference in 1878 had voted to help new Catholic churches on the continent by making bishops available for oversight and visitation. One of the bishops appointed to oversee Loyson's Gallican church was Arthur Cleveland Coxe, American bishop of the Protestant Episcopal Church (PEC), Anglicanism's stateside body. Coxe is best known to posterity as editor of the American edition of the *Ante-Nicene Fathers* series of texts, by which he hoped to "disarm Romanism" and send "honest and truth-loving" Catholics to "a reformed Catholicism such as was represented by . . . Döllinger and the 'Old Catholics,'" according to historian Elizabeth Clark. Such sentiments witnessed the crescendo of Catholic revival within Anglicanism, at least as strong in the United States as in Britain. Indeed, starting in 1877, PEC Catholics, including Coxe, pushed to establish the PEC as *the* Catholic church in America, before Roman power caught up to Roman growth. In successive General Conventions they proposed changing their institution's name from the "Protestant Episcopal Church" to the "American Catholic Church."[54]

It is no surprise, then, that when Loyson received a letter from Vilatte, he directed Vilatte to the PEC. Perhaps Vilatte could link with a PEC bishop just as Loyson had linked with Coxe. Nearest to Vilatte in Wisconsin was PEC prelate John Henry Hobart Brown, head of the newly created Diocese of Fond-du-Lac. Brown was not only strongly Catholic, but regarded Anglicanism as the one true church. While most of the PEC "Catholic party" subscribed to the "branch theory" that Orthodoxy, Romanism, and Anglicanism were triequal Catholic churches, to Brown the PEC was literally more Catholic than the pope. Rome, not the Church of England, had gone into schism and abandoned the apostolic faith. In remote Fond-du-Lac, Brown established the frontier of Anglo-Catholicism. He corresponded with European Old Catholics, built up Nashotah House seminary, and strategized how to evangelize Catholic immigrants. He even allowed his priests to use the Roman Rite rather than the Book of Common Prayer. In effect he was part of a small international vanguard practicing "an unofficial . . . and un-approved form of intercommunion between and among the Anglican, Episcopal and Swiss and (some) German Old Catholic churches," writes scholar Gerard O'Sullivan.[55]

So when Vilatte approached Brown to bring his Catholic ministry within the PEC, Brown jumped at the chance. He and Vilatte could build a Catholic alliance in the United States to mount the same challenge to stateside Romanism that reformers were attempting on the continent. Brown wrote to a fellow bishop that with Vilatte's help, "I hope to see these Belgians and their children not members of the Roman intrusion or schism in this country but loyally and firmly united to that branch of the Ancient Church which rightly exercises here Apostolic & Catholic authority." Vilatte commenced outreach to the Door peninsula populace. He prepared for ordination at Nashotah House. He recruited a few ex–Roman priests to help him. And in the summer of 1885, with the urging of Loyson and the approval of Brown, he traveled to Switzerland. There, Swiss Old Catholic bishop Edouard Herzog ordained Vilatte to the Old Catholic priesthood—the first priest so ordained for America.[56]

Not all Anglicans were so high on this frontier ecumenism, not even all in the Catholic party. Employing Roman and Old Catholic priests—did it not imply that Anglican ordination was not really Catholic? Worse, were Vilatte's missions "tricking Roman Catholics out of their papal allegiance by disguising Protestant Episcopalianism under the trappings of Old Catholicism?" asked a concerned PEC contemporary. Vilatte's parishioners packed his churches, funded new chapels, and voted at synods, so they hardly seem to have been inveigled. But when Brown applied to the PEC mission board to pay Vilatte's stipend, he was turned down. So Vilatte commenced fundraising tours. He had modest success. In three years, he established three Catholic missions, in Gardner, Duvall, and Walhain. In addition there was work with the Menominees.[57]

After Brown died in 1888, however, the relationship between Vilatte and the PEC frayed. The new bishop of Fond-du-Lac, Charles Grafton, was, if possible, a more passionate Catholicizer than Brown. He founded the first US Episcopal monastic orders, instituted weekly Eucharist, and forged alliance with other Catholics, even striking up a correspondence with the Benedictine arch-abbot of Monte Cassino. Under Grafton, Fond-du-Lac became the spikiest of all dioceses, credited later with tipping the whole PEC permanently in that direction. So Grafton certainly appreciated the Old Catholic work. But he was nervous that Vilatte was not formally bound to Fond-du-Lac. To remedy the situation, he persuaded Vilatte to legally transfer the mission properties to diocesan ownership, in exchange for financial support.[58]

At this point, the head of the Utrecht Union, Archbishop Johannes Heycamp, wrote his priest Vilatte that the whole PEC arrangement was unacceptable. Much less open to Anglicanism than Swiss bishop Herzog, Heycamp reminded Vilatte that Utrecht, like Rome, officially regarded the PEC as lacking valid apostolic succession. Vilatte should not be under "Protestant" bishops or "ever accept from them any religious service." Vilatte replied that sending priests abroad for ordination by the Old Catholics was too expensive for their small missions, so Utrecht should soon appoint its own bishop in the states, whether Vilatte himself or one of his priests. Heycamp responded positively to the possibility. In November 1889, a Wisconsin missions synod comprising clergy and laypeople convened and elected Vilatte as bishop. Early the next year, the synod incorporated itself as the Old Catholic Church of the Diocese of Wisconsin and published *A Sketch of the Belief of the Old Catholics*. In the preface, Vilatte wrote that they hoped to "demonstrate that we are as far removed from Protestantism on the one hand as we are from Romanism on the other: in word, that we are Catholics without any other qualification."[59]

Vilatte showed Grafton the letters from Utrecht. By September 1890, Vilatte and his parishioners felt compelled not to deal with the "Protestant" Grafton, even to the point of refusing confirmation at his hands. This caused terrific scenes. Grafton told Vilatte he had to go—and leave the missions to the Fond-du-Lac diocese. Vilatte responded by opening an unauthorized fourth mission in Green Bay.[60]

CATEGORIZING CATHOLICS

Vilatte became a fulcrum point not only in international wrangling between Anglicanism and Old Catholicism, but also in the categorization of Catholics in the United States. In the government's *Census of Religious Bodies* from 1890, Vilatte's four Wisconsin missions show up in a new category labeled "Other Catholics." The "Other Catholics," according to census analysts, comprise "6 bodies": Vilatte's Old Catholic missions (with 665 total members), two Orthodox churches (Greek and Russian), some Armenian and "Reformed Catholic" churches, and a "Uniate" church—Greek Catholics in communion with Rome. Together with the Roman church—and not including the PEC—they make up what census analysts call the "Catholic" "denominational family."[61]

Grafton and Heycamp—as well as Roman bishop of Green Bay Sebastian Messmer—would have sputtered at the notion of a "Catholic" "denominational family," if for different reasons. Census analysts, for their part, seem to be trying to make sense of new appearances of the name "Catholic." The Orthodox, Armenian, and "Uniate" bodies were ancient churches, but their growing presence in the United States led analysts to count them for the first time. The Old Catholic congregations under Vilatte seemed totally new. And then there were the "Reformed Catholics," who had "originated in the withdrawal of several priests and laymen from the Roman Catholic Church soon after the promulgation of the Decree of Papal Infallibility in 1870," analysts reported, with "the movement taking definite form in 1879, when organizations were formed in New York, Boston, and other cities." Leaders of these churches, like Chiniquy, tended to make news for anti-Roman preaching rather than works of Catholic reform.[62]

By the time of that census in 1890, the Roman church had solidified its status as *the* Catholic church in America. Given overwhelming Roman numbers, PEC ambitions to corner the US Catholic market already seemed quaint. By the time of a report on religious bodies in 1906, census analysts had deconstructed the "Catholic" "denominational family." Its component churches were put in other categories, declared extinct, or designated as singularities. The new "Polish National Church of America," for example, got its own category. Catholicism was Roman Catholicism. Orthodoxy was Orthodoxy. And "Other Catholics" were, as report authors put it, "unrelated." Explaining the new absence of the larger Catholic category, authors point to a "predilection of some of the constituent denominations to be considered unrelated bodies." This explanation does not specify *who* had the "predilection" to view "Other Catholics (6 bodies)" as "unrelated" to one another and to Rome. But I would guess the *who* included most Roman Catholics, most Protestants, and most Americans of all persuasions, except other Catholics themselves. In sixteen years, the cultural swirl associating Catholicism solely with Rome had quickened. And with that quickening, census analysts decided that while Protestants had denominations, Catholics did not.[63]

Still, the census in 1890 witnesses for the ages a surprising, if contained, public moment when US Catholicism was considered not one church but a "denominational family," when Vilatte's missions among "Other Catholics (6 bodies)" counted with Rome as just so many different versions of Catholicism. Historian Matthew Butler argues that Catholicism in Mexico "was *made* rather than born 'Roman,' which involved the gradual weeding out or exclusion of alternative, proto-national, Catholicisms." Do census reports of Catholicism witness a similar weeding-out in the United States?[64]

AMERICA'S FIRST INDEPENDENT CATHOLIC BISHOP

Archbishop Heycamp and the Old Catholic Congress in Cologne decided not to make Vilatte the first Old Catholic bishop in the United States after all. Likely they were prejudiced by PEC bishop Grafton's report that the missions were small and poor. Severed from the PEC and now rejected by Utrecht, Vilatte was at a loss. He wrote to the Russian Orthodox archbishop in San Francisco, Vladimir, as well as local Roman bishop Messmer, possibly because his mission congregations encouraged him to do so. Of each he inquired about joining the communion and being raised to the episcopacy. Messmer consulted with the Holy See's apostolic delegate to the United States, Francesco Satolli, and according to letters the two seem at odds about accommodating Vilatte in some way. Orthodox archbishop Vladimir agreed to start by being Vilatte's bishop.[65]

These moves incensed Grafton even more. He wrote to Vladimir and helped persuade him to drop Vilatte. This missive marked the beginning of what became a full-fledged defamation campaign. For the rest of his life, Grafton would send letters disparaging Vilatte around the world—to Colombo, London, Paris, Rome. PEC historian William Hogue says he cannot pinpoint "what really drove Grafton to his relentless harassment of Vilatte." Perhaps there was a conflict of temperament. Grafton seemed severe and ascetic, while Vilatte was gregarious and handsome, with a weakness for Cuban cigars. Regardless of reasons, however, "there is little doubt that [Grafton] did contribute mightily to the refusal of recognition," Hogue writes, "not only by the Anglican churches but by the European Old Catholics and by the Roman Church as well." Hogue even faults Grafton for "the cloud of suspected fraud and ecclesiastical illegitimacy" that has hovered over Vilatte's spiritual descendants to the present.[66]

As bishop-elect with no one to consecrate him, Vilatte brainstormed with his fellow priests, among them Bernard Harding. Harding had been an Oblate of Mary Immaculate in Ceylon—present-day Sri Lanka—where in 1888 he witnessed firsthand the origins of the aforementioned Independent Catholic Church of Ceylon, Goa, and India. About five thousand strong, this church in southern India formed in reaction to "Vaticanization," like kin in Europe and North America. To obtain apostolic succession its leaders approached the so-called St. Thomas Christians. Legendarily founded by Thomas the apostle, St. Thomas Christians really linked to Mesopotamia and Syria, whose mariners and missionaries carried Christianity to India as early as the fourth century. By the late nineteenth century some west Syrians made up the Syriac Orthodox Church led by Mar Ignatius Peter IV of Antioch, then near present-day Mardin, Turkey. It was Mar Ignatius Peter IV who gave his blessing for the consecration of the new Indian church's elected bishop, António Francisco Xavier Álvarez.[67]

On Harding's suggestion, Vilatte wrote to Álvarez, episcopally known as Mar Julius I. Soon he got a lavish reply. "We from the bottom of our hearts thank God that He has mercifully shown us the way out of the slavery of Rome; and we rejoice to see a large number of Christians making heroic efforts in the same direction as ourselves in the New World," the Indian bishop responded. "And we feel confident that the good God will deign to mercifully help these holy endeavors." So, in July 1891, Vilatte bought a third-class ticket and sailed for Colombo. A letter from Grafton preceded him, urging Mar Julius not to consecrate Vilatte. The Indian independents investigated the situation for months, while Vilatte remained in Ceylon. Finally, as Mar Julius later wrote to his and Vilatte's mutual friend Ignatius of Llanthony in Wales, "we found to our full satisfaction that Bishop Grafton was only trying to pay off a private grudge." So on May 29, 1892, Mar Julius and two concelebrants consecrated Vilatte as Mar Timotheos I in the lineage of the Antioch church.[68]

Back in the United States, word spread about the American independent Catholic bishop. Arthur Cleveland Coxe immediately took note, hoping that Vilatte's eastern orders could boost PEC Catholic credentials. Coxe congratulated Vilatte and proposed recognition by the PEC. He then wrote Grafton to the same effect, seemingly not aware of Grafton's hostility to Vilatte. Grafton agreed to have Coxe put his proposal on the agenda of the General Convention in 1892, but privately campaigned to dispute the validity of Vilatte's orders because of Syrian church links to "Jacobitism," considered a heresy by big bodies in the west. Debate at the General Convention was vigorous, but Grafton won. The PEC bishops resolved that Vilatte's consecration was null and void, partly due to its heterodox taint, and partly due to their rejecting the possibility of overlapping Catholic jurisdictions. In December 1893, Vilatte answered the PEC resolution in a pamphlet addressed to all bishops of the United States. Many found persuasive Vilatte's defense of his orders, as well as his point that in the United States, overlapping Catholic jurisdictions are ineludible. Even so, Vilatte's relationship with the PEC was done.[69]

But other connections soon materialized. In September 1893 Vilatte attended the World's Parliament of Religions in Chicago, the largest of auxiliary congresses held in conjunction with the vast World's Columbian Exposition. Twenty Roman Catholic speakers were on the official program. Vilatte, like leaders of many tiny groups, was not invited. So with fellow religious ignorables he set up an information booth at the Exposition. He talked to attendees and distributed literature on his new American Catholic Church. Within a few weeks, Polish Catholics in Detroit contacted him for episcopal assistance. After this, Vilatte was never again out of demand.[70]

But the path was difficult. Vilatte was fighting legal battles with Grafton over the old missions. One was purchased by Roman bishop Messmer, who invited French-speaking Norbertines from Berne Abbey in the Netherlands to combat what he regarded as the dangerous heresy of Old Catholicism. Meanwhile, Vilatte's new work was beset by financial instability. Even some fellow Utrecht-ordained priests chose Grafton's side, surely in part for the more attractive economic situation. By 1898, Vilatte was discouraged—and likely harrowingly poor. Somehow he scraped together enough for passage to Europe. For the better part of the year he would meet partisans of Catholic reform in England, France, Austria, Romania, Russia, and Italy—and of course raise more funds.[71]

In London Vilatte probably met Frederick George Lee, who—with Grafton—had started an Anglican Benedictine order, the Cowley Fathers. Lee had also cofounded the Order of Corporate Reunion, then engaged in a clandestine project to reordain hundreds of Anglican clergy with what it considered more valid eastern-derived orders, such as those of the Syrian churches. The ultimate aim was the reunion of all Catholic bodies and possibly all of Christianity. Vilatte, like many other Catholics and other Christians of the time, was deeply interested in Christian unity. This can seem odd, since he was actively creating more small Catholic bodies. But from their perspective, small bodies with ultrajectine theology were less of an impediment to unity than one pope who denied the legitimacy of all other Christianities. Reading newspaper reports of Vilatte's European activities, Grafton wrote across the Atlantic to denounce Vilatte in language so strong that the leading Anglican *Church Times* declined to print it, considering it libelous.[72]

Some of Vilatte's European contacts had considered joining the Roman church, and it is possible that they encouraged him to consider it, too. However it happened, Vilatte spent the whole year of 1899 in Rome, discussing terms of reunion with Vatican authorities. But talks ended in December with no agreement, and Vilatte immediately redoubled his efforts on behalf of Catholic reform. Clearly this was a more comfortable groove. For the rest of his life, Vilatte traveled between continental Europe, the British Isles, and North America. His activities consisted in equal parts raising the American Catholic Church, helping other new churches, and staving off poverty. Only in old age, in 1925, did Vilatte really return to Rome, grateful to find care in a Cistercian monastery near Versailles. But even then he corresponded with bishops and priests in other churches. After Vilatte's death of heart failure in 1929, his tombstone in Versailles read: "*1er Évêque, Église catholique-chrétienne, Canada & U.S.A.*"[73]

Vilatte's start as an Old Catholic priest for a "flock of farmers and fur trappers" in Wisconsin is unlikely. So is his reputation as the godfather of independent Catholicism, given his final resubmission to Rome. Yet in the twenty-first century, almost all observers agree that the French orphan-cum-archbishop is not only the first but also the most important independent Catholic bishop for the US scene. He is assigned feast days on liturgical calendars. There are namesake organizations such as the Vilatte Guild, the Vilatte Institute, and René Vilatte Press. Even relics of Vilatte occasionally surface for sale on eBay.[74]

Two particular areas of Vilatte's work constitute his legacy in the twenty-first century. First, he permanently linked independent Catholicism to western esotericism. Second, he originated lasting churches not only in the United States, but also in Mexico, the Caribbean, and Africa.

ESOTERIC CATHOLICISM

Leaving Rome at the end of 1899, Vilatte went again to Paris, a Belle Époque city alive with magic. As the public power of the Roman church receded, so did its ability to sideline practices of metaphysics and conjuration, and fin-de-siècle society saw a boom in esotericism of all kinds: chivalric, spiritualist, "Oriental," Masonic, Martinist, Theosophical, Swedenborgian. All attempted to make the new century intelligible by recovering lost practices or channeling new revelations. All appealed to people's yearning for religions of intense experience rather than traditional authority. All rhetoricized science and rationality as aids to worlds of wonder, not destroyers.[75]

In 1901, the secularizing French Third Republic passed the Associations laws, which tried to accommodate both religiosity and disestablishment by allowing churches and other collectives to register with the state as "cultural associations." In 1905, it implemented full *laïcité*, reversing the terms of the Concordat from 1801 to once again shutter and nationalize religious schools, abbeys, and churches. A sort of re-Revolutionary disaster for the Roman church, the Associations laws prompted a condemnation by Pope Pius X and street protests by French Roman Catholics. But the laws were a boon for other groups, since they could now gain recognition as *associations culturelles*. Old Catholics and other independents could apply for use of de-Romanized churches. So could any esoteric group.[76]

Vilatte was a key bridge between reform and esoteric Catholics. In Paris he hoped to research the Syrian roots of his Indian consecrators and dispel the "Jacobite" taint. To that end Vilatte stayed at Ligugé, a center of study headed by Syria scholar Dom Jean Parisot. Parisot promptly wrote a biography called *Mgr Vilatte, fondateur de l'Église vieille-catholique aux États-Unis d'Amérique*. He also got Vilatte interested in the chivalric fraternities, so that Vilatte revived and combined a few into the Order of the Crown of Thorns. Descended from medieval Catholic traditions such as territorial

FIGURE 2.3 Joseph René Vilatte, in a photograph first printed in a biography from 1899 by Jean Parisot. Photo courtesy of Alexis Tancibok.

abbeys and orders of knights, orders such as the Crown of Thorns were attractive to Vilatte and other reformers partly for their witness to Catholic authority of a decidedly non-ultramontane variety. Some revived orders mixed lay and cleric, men and women; some harbored esoteric theology or incorporated Freemasonry. The Order of the Crown of Thorns did all of the above. Parisot and Vilatte spent a few evenings with another visitor to Ligugé, the avant-garde novelist Jorge-Karl Huysmans. Infamous for his portrayal of the esoteric underground in the novel *Là-Bas* (1891), Huysmans had applied to become a Benedictine oblate. Later a friend of Huysmans would remark that Vilatte "looked like an American athlete" and, bless his memory, "his Havanas were excellent."[77]

Ligugé was an early indication that Vilatte was aware of and sympathetic to esoteric Catholicism. He seems not to have been much of a practitioner himself. When he returned to Paris again in 1906, it was to take advantage of the opportunity to start a new Gallican church, in the spirit of Loyson. With several French backers and assorted priests, Vilatte gained use of Holy Apostles church on rue Legendre and started l'Église catholique apostolique française. The venture itself did not succeed. But one of his priests, Louis-François Giraud, ended up transmitting a great chunk of Vilatte's legacy—his esoteric legacy. Like Vilatte, Giraud had family ties to the Petite Église. He joined the Cistercians, but recoiled at the promulgation of infallibility at the first Vatican Council and immersed himself in esotericism. A few years after Vilatte left France again, Giraud and other Crown of Thorns clerics reorganized Vilatte's church as l'Église catholique gallicane. By 1912, Giraud had been consecrated via another Vilatte bishop and was serving as church primate.[78]

In 1913, when Giraud consecrated yet another ex-Roman, Jean-Baptiste Bricaud, Vilatte's esoteric bequest went worldwide. Bricaud had managed to gather five major groups of esotericists, including the Ordo Templi Orientis of Theodor Reuss and the neo-Gnosticism of Jules Doinel. Doinel, a bishop who said he was mystically raised to the episcopate by Christ himself, founded l'Église gnostique to revive Catharism, a thirteenth-century Catholic dualism that was papally condemned and persecuted. According to the Cathar understanding of sexless spirits repeatedly reincarnated in female and male bodies, all humans were female and male in previous lifetimes, and all humans were composites of masculine and feminine now. Doinel therefore ordained and consecrated both men and women, hoping to mirror the gender balance of the gnostic universe. The first ordination of a sophia, as the female bishops were called, was of Marie Chauvel de Chauvigny in 1892. Doinel's consecrations in the mystical episcopacy merged with Vilatte's traditionally recognized line of apostolic succession when Doinel joined Bricaud. Many western esoterics continue to trace their heritage to the Bricaud nexus, partly because of the status conferred by succession from Vilatte.[79]

This brings up the question of why esotericists would want to maintain apostolic succession. After all, esotericists had shortcuts like mystical consecration! But the question problematically assumes a separation between Catholicism and esotericism. In fact, all of the above actors are Catholic. To them, esotericism is part of the Catholic faith, perhaps even its core. Its importance is hidden, lost, or persecuted, but that is only more evidence of its truth. Esotericists form new churches for Catholicism, not against it, though they are certainly in tension with Rome. "The heterodox churches," historian Joanne Pearson writes, work "beyond or behind orthodoxy, offering the potential for subversion [and] the chance to dream up new visions of society and religion."[80]

Doinel's new vision put sophias alongside bishops. Another vision manifested when Reuss's Ordo Templi Orientis became identified with Aleister Crowley's leadership of the British Isles chapter in the first decades of the twentieth century. Perhaps the most influential modern occultist, Crowley practiced a mash of Catholicism plus Egyptian, Indian, and Chinese traditions that resulted in, among much else, a new mass and a monastic experiment. Perhaps this seems strange for someone who was "virulently anti-Christian," Pearson writes. But Crowley laid fault "at the door of the Church rather than at the foot of the cross." His Gnostic Mass from 1913 aims to "represent . . . the original and true pre-Christian Christianity." Its celebrants are two priests, male and female, plus a deacon and two children. It ends with the consumption of the Eucharist and the words, "There is no part of me that is not of the Gods." The Gnostic Mass became Crowley's most popular work and remains the primary ritual of the Ordo Templi Orientis in the twenty-first century.[81]

Even more transgressively, in 1920 Crowley founded the Abbey of The-lema in Palermo, Sicily, named for the famous monastery in *The Life of Gargantua and of Pantagruel* by sixteenth-century ex-monk François Rabelais, a Catholic visionary in his own right. In Rabelais's fiction, one law governs the monastery: "Do what thou wilt." It is an adaptation of Augustine's "Love, and do what thou wilt," which Crowley further adapted in the Gnostic Mass. "Do what thou wilt shall be the whole of the Law," it intones. "Love is the law, love under will." At the real-life Palermo abbey, Thelemites aimed to overcome the false dualism of spirit and flesh through ritual sex. Sex was sacred and the sacred was sexy. Rituals likewise bridged the gap between clergy and laity. For this reason, apostolic succession inherited from Reuss (from Bricaud from Vilatte) gave way to a series of gnostic initiations, prob-ably involving sex acts then considered taboo, such as masturbation and anal sex. Still, to the present day the Ordo Templi Orientis considers apos-tolic succession a "valued part of the group's history."[82]

As many scholars note, historic accounts of ritual sex are notoriously dif-ficult to assess, given their origins in atmospheres of sensation, slander, and secrecy. But in modern esoteric Catholicism, masses of sacred sex are not unheard of and not always concealed. The Abbé Boullan—the Church of Carmel leader whom Huysmans fictionalized in *Là-Bas*—was pretty open about sex magic as a component of liturgy. So was Crowley. They and their followers wanted to transcend dualities and reverse the Fall. They also hoped to manifest the Divine Feminine as an experiment in "post-revolutionary socialist feminism," writes Pearson, however unevenly they lived its ideals. The esoteric churches godfathered by Vilatte, including the Ordo Templi Orientis, only gained in feminist importance over time, since they deeply influenced Gerald Gardner, the founder of modern Wicca, and with him decades of Wicca practitioners.[83]

NEW AMERICAN CATHOLICISMS

In addition to linking independents and esoterics, Vilatte helped start Catho-lic churches in the form of ordaining other bishops, about eight in his lifetime.

FIGURE 2.4 Sweetest Heart of Mary Roman Catholic Church in Detroit, Mich., briefly independent under the episcopal oversight of Joseph René Vilatte, 1893–94. Copyright © Nheyob, Wikimedia/Creative Commons.

Vilatte maintained honorary or mentoring relationships with these bishops, but he also let them go their own ways. Twice Vilatte successfully gathered a handful of communities into his own American Catholic Church—the entity envisioned from his booth at the World's Parliament of Religions.[84]

The Detroit Poles who contacted Vilatte after the Parliament were participants in what historians call "the Kolasinski affair." Led by former Roman priest Dominic Kolasinski, the independent parish Sweetest Heart of Mary—about four thousand souls—asked Vilatte to be their bishop. On December 24, 1893, Vilatte blessed the gorgeous new Sweetest Heart of Mary building at a huge Christmas Eve celebration. The relationship was short-lived; early the following year, the parish was accepted back into the Roman Catholic fold. Apostolic delegate Satolli—familiar with Vilatte's work in Wisconsin—had basically ordered the Detroit bishop to make peace with Kolasinski.[85]

While Vilatte and Kolasinski parted ways, Vilatte had come to the attention of other Poles. A Cleveland church headed by Anton Kolaszewski contacted him for episcopal oversight. After consecrating the Cleveland church in August 1894, Vilatte announced the formation of the American Catholic Church to a convention of eight thousand Polish independents from fourteen cities. The new church, Vilatte said, would comprise all nationalities and embody a Catholicism full of "liberty" and free of "despotism."[86]

Eventually the Poles voted to elect a Polish suffragan bishop to assist Vilatte. They picked Stephen Kaminski, pastor at Holy Mother of the Rosary in Buffalo, New York. But supporters of another priest, Anton Kozlowski of All Saints in Chicago, refused to accept that result. Kozlowski appealed to the Old Catholics to be consecrated, and in 1897 became the first Old Catholic bishop in the United States. Meanwhile Vilatte backed the Poles' majority vote for Kaminski and consecrated him in March 1898. After that, Kaminski took over day-to-day administration of the Polish Catholic churches. Vilatte was free for his journey to England, Rome, and the continent.[87]

Though Vilatte left Rome at the end of 1899, he returned to meet with Italian Catholic reformers. In May 1900 he unwittingly launched an Italian American independent church when he raised to the episcopate Paolo Miraglia-Gulotti. Called "a modern Savonarola," Miraglia-Gulotti was a well-connected preacher who hoped to start a church in Piacenza on the Old Catholic model. After the consecration, though, the Inquisition under Pope Leo XIII issued a bull of excommunication for both Vilatte and Miraglia-Gulotti. Vilatte sailed back to the Americas. Miraglia-Gulotti soon came west too. He joined Vilatte's American Catholic Church and established missions in New York, New Jersey, and West Virginia. Italian Catholics in Youngstown, Ohio, heard of Miraglia-Gulotti and sought him out for episcopal oversight. The Youngstown priest, Carmel Enrico Carfora, sojourned with the American Catholic Church for about a decade. Then Carfora launched his own jurisdiction, the North American Old Roman Catholic Church. At its peak in the 1930s, its numbers possibly reached fifty thousand, with about thirty bishops serving independent churches of different ethnic groups. In 1952, several dozen parishes left Carfora's jurisdiction and were accepted into Ukrainian Orthodoxy en masse.[88]

Both Carfora and Vilatte were interested in events south of the US border. Before the Mexican Revolution, the government was offering foreigners sizable land grants to encourage investment. Vilatte hoped that "colonies" would advance the cause of independent Catholicism, and in 1910 he obtained fifty thousand acres in the state of Chihuahua. With his priest Gildas Taylor, Vilatte traveled to Candelaria, Texas, crossed the border, and then left Taylor in charge. The energetic Taylor started an agricultural commune and named it Vilatteville. But no sooner had Vilatteville gathered a small group of settlers than the Mexican Revolution began to unfold. In 1911 a new governor of Chihuahua rescinded land grant programs and the borderlands commune disintegrated. Even so, Taylor stayed in Mexico, encouraged by a minority of liberal Catholics who wanted a national church on the model of the French Constitutional Church. When the revolutionary Mexican Catholic Apostolic Church was formed in 1925, its leader Joaquín Pérez traveled to Chicago to be consecrated by Carfora. Mexican Catholic Apostolic parishes sprouted in "several hundred communities," sometimes overflowing into Texas and California. Several remain active in the present.[89]

Vilatte left Mexico to reside in Chicago. He ordained one William Henry Francis Brothers, whom Vilatte knew from their mutual links to a Fond-du-Lac monastery founded by Grafton. Brothers was later consecrated and went on to start a nonethnic Orthodox church—one of several precocious attempts by US independents to indigenize eastern Christianity. But Brothers, aka "Father Francis," is better known for his pastorate in Woodstock,

New York, where in the 1960s his longtime pacifism, socialism, and feminism fit with the local counterculture and exposed hundreds to a different Catholicism, including his pal Bob Dylan. In Woodstock Father Francis fed and housed dozens for the vast music event of August 1969, earning him the nickname "the Hippie Priest." His successor still runs a used bike shop in town, where a photograph of Father Francis is prominently displayed.[90]

In 1915, Vilatte incorporated the American Catholic Church in the state of Illinois. The formal incorporation had partly to do with the appearance of an eminent convert. Frederick Ebenezer Lloyd had a distinguished career as an Anglican priest and missionary. He served as a member of the Illinois House of Representatives and, a few years after meeting Vilatte, "married a Peabody"—Philena Peabody, a widow whose family had fortunes in oil and real estate. Lloyd was impressed by Vilatte's reformed Catholicism and, with like-minded members of his Episcopal flock, set up St. David's on East 36th Street in Chicago as a mission of the American Catholic Church. Vilatte rightly saw in Lloyd an experienced administrator who could lead the ecclesia into the future. Consecrating Lloyd, he named him "first Bishop of the American Catholic Church." "The need for a Church both American and Catholic," Vilatte proclaimed, "and free from paparchy and all foreign domination, has been felt for many years by Christians of all the denominations." Lloyd took up the theme in his episcopacy, writing in the late 1920s that this new church was happily free of both Rome and Canterbury. "The Church of the future will be both Catholic and American," Lloyd proclaimed. "May God speed the day."[91]

But Vilatte was not done with America yet. His last consecration before retiring to France in 1925 launched what was the most successful independent Catholic jurisdiction other than the PNCC, namely, the African Orthodox Church (AOC). The first majority-black independent Catholic body, this church boasted thousands of members at its height in 1934. It spread to Canada, the West Indies, and South Africa. From there the AOC migrated to Kenya and Uganda. In Kenya the church played a significant role in that country's independence movement, making the AOC, as historian Richard Newman writes, "one of several links between black separatism in America and independence movements in Africa which remain largely unexamined."

In Uganda, the church joined Greek Orthodoxy under the patriarch of Alexandria, making it "the first major contemporary expression of Greek Orthodox missionary interest," Newman says, and "one of the most important religious bodies" in Africa. These African AOCs, unaffiliated with those in the United States since 1960, came to be understood as an early instance of African independent churches, which in general served "as entrees into white European Christianity and also as conservers of black African civilization and leadership."[92]

The founding of the African Orthodox Church in the States unfolded in the context of black nationalism and pan-Africanism. The early-twentieth-century United States counts among the most racially harrowing yet hopeful times in American history. Black citizens routinely faced racism, segregation, discrimination, and violence, while at the same time artists, activists, and religionists forged institutions aimed at change. Alongside the National Association for the Advancement of Colored People, the United Negro Improvement Association, and the Nation of Islam stood the African Orthodox Church (AOC). Its founder, George Alexander McGuire, emigrated from Antigua and became a PEC priest before he concluded that Episcopalians would not raise a black man to the status of bishop in full anytime soon.

Likely McGuire's realization came about while working under PEC bishop William Montgomery Brown in Arkansas, where McGuire served as Archdeacon for Colored Work from 1905 to 1909. Later in life, Bishop Brown was tried and convicted for heresy by the PEC on the basis of his book *Communism and Christianism* (1920), the cover of which proclaimed: "Banish Gods from Skies and Capitalism from Earth." "Bad Bishop Brown" later became an independent Catholic prelate himself and published a magazine called *Heresy*. But during McGuire's years in Arkansas, Brown believed that black men should be bishops in a totally separate Episcopal church. With the segregated way Brown ran his diocese and the glass-ceilinged success McGuire experienced, it is possible that McGuire agreed, if for different reasons. By 1918, he joined Marcus Garvey's United Negro Improvement Association (UNIA). In the UNIA—a black nationalist organization with over a hundred thousand members by 1920—McGuire served as official chaplain and became "one of Garvey's most able lieutenants," Newman writes.[93]

But, Newman continues, McGuire "was always a churchman before he was a Negro nationalist." He soon had the idea to start a church led by black men in apostolic succession. Full of Garveyites but not officially connected to the UNIA, the new church was at first simply called the Independent Episcopal Church. McGuire contacted Vilatte. Though the PEC had officially rejected Vilatte's "Jacobite" consecration, in McGuire's view the eastern lineage was attractive. It transcended the time and space of racist America and linked more closely to the African continent. Others, too, cared little about the "Jacobite" stigma and saw only Orthodoxy, attractive for having a lineage as ancient as Rome's without being Roman. In 1909 New York Russian Orthodox priest Ingram Irvine published a widely read defense of Vilatte in the *Winnipeg Press*, stating that Orthodoxy considered Vilatte's orders authentic and lambasting both Roman and Anglican authorities as "vaingloriously vile" and "un-Christian persecutors" of a fellow "Archbishop of Christ's Church."[94]

Vilatte seems to have regarded McGuire and others of African descent like any other Americans insufficiently served by Rome and Canterbury, but happily afforded Catholic self-determination in a free and democratic nation. Already a quarter of a century earlier, shortly after returning from Ceylon, Vilatte had ordained to the priesthood Henry Hartley, a West Indian deacon of the British Methodist Episcopal Church. So the consecration of McGuire in 1921 was not the first time Vilatte had ordained a black man. But it was the first time he raised a black man to the episcopate. By some reckoning, it was also the first time anyone had consecrated a black man in apostolic succession in North America. To be sure, James Augustine Healy was consecrated as Roman Catholic bishop of Seattle in 1875. But Healy was of mixed Irish and African ancestry and "passed" as white for his entire life. Noteworthy as Healy personally was, his prelacy did not exactly indicate US Roman acceptance of a black bishop, and no other was consecrated in that church until 1965.[95]

Vilatte was willing to consecrate and then leave church administration to the new bishop. McGuire found this a much more attractive offer than those of Orthodox jurisdictions that expected continued oversight. After the consecration, Vilatte and the AOC maintained friendly connections.

When the AOC branched to South Africa, its bishop, Daniel Alexander, communicated with Vilatte, who invited him to join the Order of the Crown of Thorns. When the AOC branched to the West Indies, Henry Hartley—the first black priest ordained by Vilatte—worked for the AOC mission in his native Trinidad.[96]

By far the most innovative of AOC congregations is the St. John Coltrane church of San Francisco, California, which joined the jurisdiction in 1982. More than pushing the racial boundaries of American Catholicism, this community pushes the theological boundaries of world Christianity.

FIGURE 2.5 St. John Will-I-AM Coltrane, by iconographer Mark Dukes, c. 1991. Copyright © Mark Dukes.

Founded by musician Franzo King in 1967, the community was initially a temple of "Coltrane Consciousness," which revered the famous jazz saxophonist as an avatar whose music can lead to divine union. For a time it was attended by Alice Coltrane herself—Coltrane's widow, fellow seeker, and jazz harpist. When the AOC reached out, Franzo King saw a natural evolution of Coltrane Consciousness toward Catholicism. "Music is a universal language, a cosmic language that is beyond this particular galaxy," King told me. "So I understand 'Catholic' in that sense."[97]

In the process of joining the AOC, Coltrane was "demoted," King mischievously said, from divine incarnation to human saint. But St. John Coltrane's centrality remains. So does an aural sacramentalism of "sound baptism"—which is how King describes his experience of getting washed with Coltrane's "sheets of sound" in a live gig in 1966. In the early twenty-first century, the church still celebrates the sonic sacrament, each mass a liturgical jam session riffing on "A Love Supreme." It is often packed with visitors and guest instrumentalists from around the world. "If you play an instrument," recommends the St. John Coltrane website, "bring it." The website proudly proclaims origins in Coltrane, but also in the AOC and Syrian Orthodoxy. Its founders, it says, are not only George McGuire and Franzo King, but also Mar Julius and Archbishop Vilatte.[98]

◆　◆　◆

South of San Francisco, a few years before Franzo King received his "sound baptism," another Californian inherited another portion of Vilatte's legacy. This was Herman Adrian Spruit, founder of the Church of Antioch. When Vilatte's successor Lloyd died, one branch of the American Catholic Church was led by Lowell Wadle in Laguna Beach. In 1957, Wadle and two other bishops consecrated Spruit. Founding a church several years later, Spruit chose the name "Antioch" to recognize Vilatte's lineage. He wished to evoke a primal eastern faith that was also expansively modern. In Antioch, Spruit shared his forebear's hope to shape a full and free American Catholicism, "Neither Protestant nor Roman."

The line from Dominique-Marie Varlet to Herman Spruit shows that contemporary US independent Catholicism dates to times before Vatican II and also before Vatican I. It has roots in counterconducts sparking across three centuries of modern Catholicism, a period in which it is too often assumed that Roman ultramontanism handily established a Catholic monopoly and snuffed out reform possibilities. Instead, independents roamed in Rome, Constantinople, and Canterbury, disordering Catholic boundaries and reinventing its traditions. They said mass in the vernacular by 1750, held a church council with lay input in 1763, revived clerical marriage in 1875, consecrated a female bishop in 1892, and witnessed black ecclesial self-governance in 1921. Big-body Catholicism would replicate these moves only much later or never.

Liberal independents are not some heaven on earth of progressive Catholicism. They suffer from religious sidelining, workaday penury, and the constant balkanization of their institutions, among much else. Stories of Varlet's idealism and Vilatte's initiative can sound heroic or quixotic, depending on your perspective. You may be intrigued; you may be repulsed. For almost everyone, however, the history sketches an irrevocably altered "big picture." Modern Catholicism turns out to be far more multiple and complex than we usually think, partly because independents are right there all along. Independents keep succession, sacraments, and saints. But since 1724, modernity has never seen a Catholicism lacking independents' challenges to big-body ways, including changes in the parameters of Catholicism itself.

3

LOVE AND META-CATHOLICISM

FOUNDING THE CHURCH OF ANTIOCH

IN 1959, WHEN Herman Adrian Spruit founded a body called the Church Universal-Christian Catholic, he started a new phase of a long spiritual quest. Though the name of the church changed several times—it was the Church of Antioch by the late 1960s—Herman Spruit had arrived at a vision of Catholicism that would drive the rest of his life. For the next forty years, he pastored, mentored, and ordained people in independent churches. He also studied and wrote, restlessly seeking union with God for himself and the whole world. For Spruit, Catholicism was a capacious vehicle for this ultimate search. Distinctively sacramental, it still accommodated the myriad and metaphysical goods of the whole California spiritual marketplace.

At the time of founding the church, however, Spruit did not really know where he was going. US independent Catholicism was a frontier, like California itself, and Spruit was pioneering. He ended up in a vanguard of independent leaders that ordained Catholic women as priests and bishops. And then he went further than almost anyone in elevating his partner Mary— later known as Meri—to the level of coleader and successor. A letter from 1981 gives a glimpse of what Herman and Meri called "the conjugal episcopate." "Dearest Meri, Sweetheart and Archbishop," Spruit wrote. "This is a unique relationship we have, probably the first of its kind in Christendom." Patriarch and matriarch, they would lead the church together. They would embody the male-female complementarity that they believed characterized a "meta-catholic" future.

But it took Herman and Meri a long time to see things that way. It took them a long time just to find each other. The future "conjugal episcopate" would depend on tutelage in European independent Catholicism, American metaphysicalism, and globe-trotting Theosophy. It would involve sanctuary with Methodists, Masons, and mediums. It would hinge on the life experiences of two twentieth-century Californians who relished the state's vibe of experimentation even as their projects risked failure over and over.

NEW CATHOLICISMS FROM LONDON TO LOS ANGELES

The state of California has always featured greater religious diversity than most parts of the country. By the middle of the nineteenth century, people moving westward from the states, eastward from Asia, and northward from Mexico had transplanted to California everything from Confucianism and Shinto to Mormonism and Orthodoxy. The Gold Rush brought another several hundred thousand people in less than a decade. In the twentieth century, when Los Angeles became a major port of entry, new and old arrivals converted to one another's religions or invented new flavors like Pentecostalism. They founded institutions trained on the transformation of consciousness: Religious Science, the Cultural Integration Fellowship, the Esalen Institute. As decades passed, well-noted new Protestantisms like Robert Schuller's Crystal Cathedral supplemented evangelical Christianity with meditation techniques, interfaith acceptance, and "positive thinking."[1]

Less noted, however, are the new Catholicisms of California. As we have seen, shoots of the Mexican Catholic Apostolic Church sprouted and died north of the border. A hardier new Catholicism also took root in the City of Angels: the London-based Liberal Catholic Church. Arriving on American shores in 1917, the Liberal Catholic Church originated in a short-lived Old Catholic venture in England. That venture was led by Bishop Arnold Harris Mathew, consecrated in Utrecht in 1908. In the Mathew church, most priests were Theosophists, then also a trend among Anglican divines. When the Mathew church folded in 1915, Bishop James Wedgwood—scion of the Wedgwood china company—joined with Australian Theosophist Charles Leadbeater to found the Liberal Catholic Church. Wedgwood and Leadbeater conceived of the new church as "an independent and self-governing body; neither Roman Catholic nor Protestant—but Catholic."[2]

FIGURE 3.1   Charles Leadbeater (*left*) and James Ingall Wedgwood (*right*) at St. Francis of Assisi Liberal Catholic Church, Tekels Park, England, 1930. Photo by M. Bayly. Copyright © Liberal Catholic Church of St. Francis & Richard B. Bayly.

The Liberal Catholic Church made full use of Theosophy to fulfill, as the founders saw it, the promise of Catholicism. Like the esoteric revival in France, the hugely influential Theosophical Society offered rational but reenchanted pathways through modernity and general optimism about human spiritual evolution. All reality registers different levels of consciousness, as described by Theosophy founder Helena Blavatsky in her magnum opus *The Secret Doctrine* (1888). Yet from earthly life to the starry sky, the "Law of Correspondence" reverberates. Features of the human being correspond to patterns of the universe and vice versa, "as above, so below." Humanity can advance to higher planes, then, by aligning with the Law of Correspondence and learning from *mahatmas*, or "masters," who teach the art of alignment. These masters—elevated beings akin to bodhisattvas—are understood to be scattered throughout world religions and to deliver messages to human designates like Blavatsky.

By 1891, the Theosophical Society was led by Annie Besant, who from the organization's base in Adyar, India, could boast a global membership of tens of thousands. It stood up for progressive causes from socialism and feminism to Irish independence and Indian self-rule. It sponsored "Oriental" religious teachers to translate eastern ideas into metaphysical terms, and those teachers took metaphysicalism back home, creating what historian Catherine Albanese calls a dialectical "metaphysical Asia." The Theosophical Society popularized perennialism, the idea that religions share a single timeless core, as well as the idea that that common core is mysticism. It seeded dozens of philosophical and religious movements, among them several new Catholicisms.[3]

As high-ranking members of the Theosophical Society, Liberal Catholic Church founders Wedgwood and Leadbeater shared Theosophy's commitment to the evolution of human consciousness. In their view, the Catholic sacraments are ancient techniques for accelerating that evolution. But as Theosophy distilled archaic wisdom, so Liberal Catholicism would extract a Catholic essence. Separating the theological wheat from chaff, Wedgwood and Leadbeater immediately dispensed with the concept of sin—and with it sacrifice, atonement, and damnation. Like Hodur drawing up Polish National Catholic Church documents a few years earlier, Wedgwood and

Leadbeater saw no place for sin in their high view of human nature. Sacraments do not fix people, they said, but rather enlarge their capacity for the divine. "The Christ"—spoken as a title, not a surname—is a "master" who models the fullness of divinization available to all.[4]

So when the two founders used several historic masses to compose a new Liberal Catholic rite, they removed all "expressions which indicate fear of God, of His wrath and of the prospect of everlasting hell," Wedgwood wrote. The phrase "Lamb of God" was excised, since "zoological characterization of our Lord" inspires only "a sense of the ridiculous." In general, the new rite aimed "at combining the traditional sacramental form of Catholic worship—with its ritual, its deep mysticism, and its abiding witness to the reality of sacramental grace—with the widest measure of intellectual liberty and respect for the individual conscience." It is, Wedgwood wrote, both "historic" and "modernist." Those word choices were not accidental at a time when Roman Catholicism was well known for rejecting critical history and modernist outlooks, most recently condemned by Pope Pius X in *Pascendi dominici gregis* in 1907. Versions of the Wedgwood/Leadbeater Mass, first published in 1919, have been used in Liberal Catholic churches ever since.[5]

Even more influential, Leadbeater's *The Science of the Sacraments* (1920) refused any idea that "science" opposed religion or led to atheism. On the contrary, Leadbeater detailed how Catholic ritual, especially the Eucharist, esoterically orchestrated "unparalleled" cosmic good that was visible and palpable, if you were attuned. Leadbeater did not think you had to be Catholic to participate in the sacraments, and he did not think unattuned priests blocked the benefits overly much. The technology itself produced "floods of spiritual force." Still, Leadbeater gave instructions for maximizing the potential. Six hundred pages of descriptions and diagrams illustrated how to create energetic flows by means of postures and prayers, candles and colors. Leadbeater saw these flows clairvoyantly, but he generously suggested that most people can learn to see them if they practice. *The Science of the Sacraments* became a second bible among Liberal Catholics and other esoterically inclined Christians.[6]

Leadbeater and Wedgwood were friends of Annie Besant. While the Liberal Catholic Church never formalized ties with the Theosophical

Society, the three friends came to think of the church as a major vehicle of preparation for the soon-coming World Teacher. Blavatsky named this World Teacher "Maitreya" after the future-Buddha of Buddhist traditions. Leadbeater wrote to Besant that Maitreya told him in a vision that "He" had divinely orchestrated "this curious result, that a branch of the Catholic Church, having Apostolic Succession in a form that cannot be questioned, should be entirely in the hands of the Theosophists, who are eager and willing to do exactly as He wishes." Besant was already quite taken with the Old Catholic church, from which Liberal Catholicism's orders derived. She called it a "living" church, perhaps echoing "red priests" in Bolshevik Russia who called their attempted new Orthodoxy the "Living Church." Besant now helped with Liberal Catholic evangelism. Rumors that Besant herself was ordained are unlikely to be true: Leadbeater believed that female celebrants' subtle energies unraveled the dynamic work of the sacraments. But he did ask Besant to offer benedictions at mass. He also founded a spiritual order of women priests intended to parallel Liberal Catholicism and prepare for the "World Mother."[7]

In America, many Theosophists officially split from Besant, often over the religious overtones of the World Teacher Project. They also spoke strongly against Liberal Catholicism, calling it another form of "Catholic bondage" wholly incompatible with real spiritual freedom. But American Theosophy still saw much cross-pollination with this sympathetic new Christianity. The US province of the Liberal Catholic Church was founded in Los Angeles shortly after Wedgwood completed a missionary tour of major American cities in 1917. Churches sprang up across the country. One of the most prominent converts was the mystically minded Henry Agard Wallace, who in 1925 helped establish Liberal Catholicism in Des Moines, Iowa. By the time Wallace served as Franklin Delano Roosevelt's vice president, he had jettisoned this alternative religious association as a political liability.[8]

A wrenching problem in the church was a series of accusations of pederasty against founders Wedgwood and Leadbeater, levied by fellow Theosophists. Some thought Leadbeater had harmed the anointed World Teacher himself, the young Jiddu Krishnamurti, identified by Leadbeater as Maitreya incarnate at age thirteen. Investigations and temporary suspensions of both founders disturbed the Liberal Catholic Church, but did not derail it. Neither did the retirement in 1923 of presiding bishop Wedgwood, who was suffering from syphilis. Seamlessly Leadbeater took over.[9]

What did derail the church was when the grown-up Krishnamurti abruptly abandoned the Theosophical Society, the institution that groomed him for greatness for so long. In a dramatic speech in 1929, Krishnamurti disavowed messianic identity and, much more radically, the possibility of anyone's gaining spiritual advancement through external guidance of any sort. "Truth, being limitless, unconditioned, unapproachable by any path whatsoever, cannot be organized; nor should any organization be formed to lead or coerce people along a particular path," he told a huge gathering in the Netherlands. "Truth is a pathless land" became Krishnamurti's refrain for decades of teaching. This disavowal dashed the cosmic hopes of many Theosophists, including many Liberal Catholics. "The Coming has gone wrong," Leadbeater famously said. Both organizations lost members in droves.[10]

Still, Liberal Catholicism continued. Leaders studied eastern religions and adapted their findings, as in Leadbeater's book *The Chakras*, published in 1927, which formulated the concept of the energy-body, or Wedgwood's talk called "The Priest's Craft: Mass as Yoga," delivered in 1928. Though Leadbeater was never well known outside theosophical circles, he "influence[d] . . . popular occultism to a greater extent than could be estimated," writes biographer Gregory Tillett. Through the years, the perceived flaws of Liberal Catholic leaders were well noted even by insiders. Still, their innovation "must be seen in the larger view as a truly remarkable breakthrough," writes independent Catholic scholar-bishop Lewis Keizer. Liberal Catholicism "adopted a church format for what was essentially a highly personal, mystic, and individualistic path, . . . brought the Apostolic ministry into dialogue with world religions," and revived "awareness of the mystic and subtle dimensions of liturgy." Together with French independents, Old Catholics, and esoteric Catholics, Liberal Catholics made up a popular assemblage that harbored Catholic liberalism, modernism, and magicalism in the late nineteenth and early twentieth centuries.[11]

THE CHARLES HAMPTON LEGACY

One of many Theosophists inspired by Wedgwood's stop in Los Angeles was a young American named Charles Hampton. He immediately joined the Liberal Catholic Church and was ordained to the priesthood by Wedgwood himself. In 1935 Hampton became regionary bishop for the American church. From his base at the lovely St. Alban on North Argyle Avenue in Hollywood, Hampton spread the Liberal Catholic gospel. He had already penned a pamphlet explaining occult meanings of the mass in 1918, two years before Leadbeater's *Science of the Sacraments*. As bishop, he followed the new media trail blazed by Hollywood evangelist Aimee Semple McPherson, speaking on associate pastor Edward Matthews's KFAC radio show "The Liberal Catholic Quarter Hour." "The sacramental life is identical with the Path of Holiness whereby man attains human perfection," Hampton said on a show in the summer of 1940, "and all human beings are treading that path blindly or consciously. It is better to tread it with self-conscious intelligence." But, Hampton continued, Liberal Catholicism does not condemn those outside its purview. "It must not be thought that Sacraments are the whole of religion," he said, "or that People who do not use them will be lost forever, as some backward Churches teach." Emphasizing the sacraments' wonder and power, not to redeem sinful humans, but to direct their "Path of Holiness," Hampton evangelized a sunny Catholicism to interwar Los Angeles.[12]

There was much evangelizing to be done, because Hampton became a bishop just two years after Krishnamurti repudiated his World Teacher status. The Liberal Catholic Church had issued a statement that all clergy and laity were free to endorse or reject Theosophy. But after Leadbeater died in 1934, the extent of adherence to Theosophy became an issue. On the one side, some American clergy wished to "cleanse" Liberal Catholicism of tenets like reincarnation and the masters. These included Edward Matthews, the radio show host and Hampton's associate pastor. On the other side, some wanted to make Theosophy a requirement for clergy. The latter included the new presiding bishop in England, Frank Waters Pigott.

For his part, Hampton followed the initial announcement: Theosophy should be optional. This was the way that Wedgwood and Leadbeater had always run the church. It was also a pragmatic middle path that would best hold Liberal Catholic followers and evangelize new ones. But in the early 1940s differences between Hampton, Pigott, and Matthews became a full-scale transatlantic fight, culminating when Pigott deposed Hampton and put another bishop in his place. Hampton lost his status in the Liberal Catholic Church and lost St. Alban to Matthew. He then suffered a debilitating heart attack and barely supported himself as a carpenter.[13]

But Hampton had good friends. Most American bishops rejected Pigott's replacement bishop. They sued in civil courts to restore to church authority those they regarded as duly elected prelates. After a decade, they finally won a decision by the California Supreme Court. Hampton had already died, so he never got to savor the legal vindication. But in one respect Hampton won back more than his reputation: his middle way, over time, prevailed. As most observers note, in the twenty-first century Liberal Catholicism counts Theosophy as only one of a number of possible ways to approach the faith. The average Liberal Catholic in the pews today may not be theosophical at all and may not know or care about church history related to Krishnamurti.[14]

Still, Hampton himself was a Theosophist, and it was Hampton's metaphysically oriented Catholicism that led Herman Spruit to seek him out. Spruit had read Leadbeater's *Science of the Sacraments* and wanted to know more. Sometime in the early 1950s, he visited St. Alban. Matthews was then in charge and told him that Leadbeater's ideas were all "illusions and hallucinations." Spruit hardly agreed. He heard Hampton was in exile in Ojai—then the home base of Krishnamurti, too. He searched for Hampton "with a determination unlike any I had ever known," he said, "search[ing] every backroad of the town of Ojai."[15]

Spruit found Hampton living in a trailer in a run-down part of town. He was using a narrow fireplace mantel for an altar and, in his clerical collar, made eggs on a single-burner electric hotplate. Hampton's humble life impressed Spruit. So did his demanding tutelage, as when he urged Spruit to get current on scholarship by reading Lamsa's new translation of the Bible, and that of Smith and Goodspeed, too. Spruit started visiting Ojai every week. Later he bragged that he could improvise any space for liturgy, since he learned to say Mass on Hampton's mantel. Their mentoring relationship was soon a fast friendship that salved the end of Hampton's life. Not least, Spruit assisted Hampton with legal filings. The friendship deeply marked the course of the future Church of Antioch.[16]

HERMAN ADRIAN SPRUIT

A seeker among seekers in postwar southern California, Herman Spruit connected with Hampton, started a church, inherited several more, and assisted dozens of others. But before Herman found Hampton and his life's work, he was a German-speaking immigrant, a Methodist minister, and a Religious Science teacher. At various times he worked as a painter, a legal aide, and a tour guide. He was a husband and a divorcé three times over. He was a father and a stepfather.[17]

The whole time, Herman wrote and wrote and wrote: letters, homilies, tracts, essays, autobiographies, seminary catalogs, and church plans. He incessantly revised, sometimes repurposing the same words, attentive to style but also to self-stylization. Much of Herman's output survives in folders kept for the Church of Antioch by his last great love, Meri Louise Spruit. In an interview, Meri remembered her years with Herman starting in the mid-1970s. Daily he would take care of their domestic life and then sit down to church business and writing. He typed with two fingers, she said, and she made copies of everything using the mimeograph machine at her job. Never legally married, Herman and Meri regarded their life together as the consummation of their sacred work.[18]

Meri, then named Mary, was one year old and toddling around the Carmel Valley when Herman arrived in Los Angeles at the age of sixteen. His parents were Dutch but had emigrated to Germany. Like Vilatte, Herman had family roots in non-Roman Catholicism—the whole paternal side was Old Catholic. His grandfather played the organ and cantored at the parish church in Dordrecht. But since there was no Old Catholic parish near the Spruits' home outside of Berlin, the family attended a Methodist church. Herman recounted later that Methodism suited them partly for what they experienced as its emphasis on spiritual experience over abstract dogma. When they emigrated to America in 1927, they remained Methodist.[19]

FIGURE 3.2 Patriarch Herman Spruit at home on his typewriter, 1988.
Courtesy of Paul Clemens.

Two years later, the stock market crashed and the Depression over-
whelmed an already difficult immigrant existence. Herman and his brother
Helmut joined their father in the workforce to supplement family income.
On the census from 1930, Herman was listed as a painter. Even so, his inner
life bent toward concerns beyond the next coat of Malibu Peach. Shortly
after arriving in Los Angeles, he said later, he accepted a call to Christian
ministry that had been tugging for years. Flush with the big decision, he
took the matter to the Methodists. But the local bishop knocked him back.
He told Herman that with his strong German accent, he could never minister to an American congregation. "Keep painting houses," the bishop said.[20]
Herman redoubled his efforts to speak English perfectly. He attended
night school, but also watched Americans' lips and read comic books to
match words to actions. The dedication paid off. Within a few years Herman
was accepted for Methodist ministerial training. He kept painting while
he attended the Bible Institute of Los Angeles (later Biola University), Los
Angeles Pacific College (affiliated with the Free Methodists), and Chapman
College (affiliated with the Disciples of Christ). When the Methodists ex-
amined him, he passed with flying colors. According to a story Herman told

several times, that same discouraging bishop apologized for nearly depriving Methodism of a fine minister. The story showed Herman's pride that no American who met him as a polished public speaker would guess he knew little English until he was almost twenty years old.[21]

Herman started pastoring at North Redondo Methodist Church in 1936 and continued at First Methodist Church of South Gate, with apparent success. He held numerous positions in the church and served local civic organizations. In 1948 Herman joined a fifteen-member American Methodist delegation that toured Europe and several Communist countries, ending with attendance at the founding meeting of the World Council of Churches in Amsterdam. Convening the group was Georgia Harkness, eminent theologian at Garrett Biblical Institute and the first American woman ever to teach theology at a seminary level. Herman's home life seemed to proceed nicely as well. He rejoiced as his wife Hulda gave birth to two sons, in 1945 and 1950, after doctors had told the couple that they could not have children. To all appearances, Herman seemed ready to stay this course for the rest of his life.[22]

But restlessness encroached. As successful as his churches seemed, Herman started to feel he could not give members what they truly needed. The traditional interpretations of scripture seemed inadequate; theological explanations fell short. Herman felt like a failure at home, too. His marriage to Hulda was difficult. There must be something more—but what?

Maybe the yearning and failing that Herman felt are the classic agony of the Christian mystic. For mystics, the meaning of Christ is the bliss of divine union, but that union is also harrowing and fleeting. Herman was by his own account "a mystic" and was often called that by others, who added that his mystical bent made him "lonely" and "misunderstood." Herman remembered growing away from conventional Christian categories and reaching for new language. What people really needed to understand within themselves—what Herman needed to find for himself—was "the glorious Radiance that fills all things, . . . the Fountain of Being wherein a soul has its beginnings, . . . the Great Amen," he said. This God pursues humans relentlessly, "until they learn to speak of Him, hear Him, know Him, and become ever more fully One in and with Him."[23]

Or maybe Herman's restlessness was just typical in the years that started in the shiny 1950s and led to the revolutionary 1960s. In postwar Los Angeles, "a bipolar city of bright surfaces sharply bounded by shadows," everyday life often took a "Dionysian spin into play, physical perfection, violence, altered states of consciousness and a thirst for the infinite," writes memoirist D. J. Waldie. "The infinite had been a part of the sales pitch for Los Angeles for a long time: in its light, its deserts, its emptiness and its place at the end of roads leading west. Ecstatic religion, New Age thought and UFO cults had satisfied ordinary folk who wanted transcendence. . . . Dabbling in LSD and Zen satisfied some of those who looked for a personal cosmic doorway."[24]

Even Methodist leaders were searching. Perhaps Herman first encountered metaphysics in conversations with fellow pastors at the Graduate School of Religion at the University of Southern California. He was captivated. "Like so many of my colleagues, I too had imbibed at the fountain of Metaphysics," he wrote later. Reading at a rate of about five books a week his entire life, Herman quickly advanced in knowledge of this Americanized strand of hermeticism. He even credited metaphysical principles with successfully raising a million dollars for work on the church at South Gate.[25]

He also watched Methodist colleagues downplay metaphysics in their work, finding it "wise to soft peddle these concepts." Herman tried the subtle approach, but had difficulty containing his enthusiasm. Metaphysics worked, he believed. It was that missing piece that he desperately wanted to offer his congregation. Yet he could not even discuss it openly. "Gradually it began to dawn on me that the Methodist Church was far from ready to accept that point of view," Herman remembered.[26]

The whole situation provoked a personal crisis. Recently a tradesman scrambling for jobs, Herman now pastored a church that afforded him an income, a home, and a car. His wife and two young sons were comfortable. He traveled the world and enjoyed high standing. But his mystical heart kept weighing a riskier calling. Finally, the choice as he saw it was to continue in hypocrisy or leave. After fifteen years as a Methodist pastor, he resigned. His resignation letter from January 1951 cited "a search for . . . deeper spirituality." But the break was "shattering," Herman told people later. "I left my Church without any clear cut idea of what I was going to do."[27]

RELIGIOUS SCIENCE

Soon after he preached his last Methodist sermon, Herman planned to meet a few friends on Wilshire Boulevard in Los Angeles and bat around ideas. It was January of 1951. As he headed into the city on West Sixth Street, he spotted the big sign of Religious Science headquarters. On a whim, "I thought I would stop by there in hopes of finding a book on Metaphysics to help me plan my next [steps]." Entering the building, Herman ran into a friend from the South Gate church, former music director William Hornaday. The two Methodists were taken aback by the chance meeting in this alternative sanctuary. "We both recognized the other, and both of us blurted out: 'What in the world are you doing in this Building?,'" Herman remembered. Hornaday had taken a position running the Religious Science radio program. Hearing of his former pastor's newly unemployed state, Hornaday said, "Well, let's go see Ernest."[28]

"Ernest": that would be Religious Science founder Ernest Holmes, whose successful New Thought organization combined science, philosophy, and spirituality in techniques for healing and thriving, as Holmes described in *The Science of Mind* (1926). By 1951, this tome had sold millions, mainstreamed New Thought, and sent teachers from Holmes's Institute for Religious Science all over the world. That January day, ushered into a swank office to meet Holmes, Herman landed a job. Religious Science leaders had been praying to fill a vacancy in top administration, and Holmes offered Herman the position. For the next five years, Herman served as secretary for the International Association of Religious Science Churches and assisted branches across the globe. In May 1951, Herman received his license as a Minister of Religious Science. He led healing sessions, taught in the Religious Science seminary, and wrote for the *Science of Mind* journal.[29]

For a while, "Religious Science was my thing," Herman said. He once described this time as "hard years . . . as, with God's [help], new consciousness was dug into the Methodist grooves." But he was happy to explore metaphysics. The fundamental Religious Science proposition that "there is a power for good in the universe greater than you are—and you can use it," as Holmes said every week at the start of the radio show, resonated with Herman. Beholdenness to orthodox Christianity evaporated. Yet he still had a structure and a community, making connections and "fast friends." He came to regard Holmes as a "great leader" and a "true prophet." He was buddies with Maude Lathem, editor and reviser with Holmes of the edition of *The Science of Mind* from 1938, and called her "without doubt, the finest" of Holmes's "remarkable staff."[30]

Yet Herman could not settle in for long. He joined the leadership at a time of tension over direction and governance. From the beginning there had been a question of whether Religious Science branches should style themselves as "churches" or "centers," religious or secular. Herman leaned to the prochurch side. So did his friend Hornaday, who had lobbied to start Sunday services at the Belmont Theater in 1951 and later led Founder's Church at Sixth Street and Berendo. Holmes himself sympathized with the church concept—he had long envisioned Religious Science as the true "Church Universal"—and in 1953, Holmes legally changed its name to the Church of Religious Science. A year later Holmes proposed to reorganize the far-flung branches so that each was affiliated more directly with his Church. But the changes met with resistance. A number of leaders questioned these moves in favor of continuing as the International Association, the body of which Herman was secretary. Ultimately dissenting leaders resigned and Religious Science continued as two separate denominations.[31]

Weathering the conflict, Herman longed for even more church. He increasingly found the culture of Religious Science to be rationalistic and cold. The intellectual freedom was great, but left people arguing about theories with no mooring, Herman wrote later. Sunday gatherings lacked aesthetic richness, comparing unfavorably to his experience of the "stately grandeur of the Methodist services." And he worried about imagining God as an abstraction, as he saw idealized in Religious Science. "The seeker for the Abstract may have gotten a hold of a measure of truth," Herman wrote, "but that truth is like a flower lacking in fragrance."[32]

Someone in Religious Science—probably Maude Lathem—gave Herman that copy of Leadbeater's *The Science of the Sacraments*. Shortly thereafter, "as if by accident there came into his possession" an Old Catholic missal. It was a glimpse of his Dutch heritage, and Herman was startled to discover the presence of Old Catholicism right there in Los Angeles. One of Holmes's many friends was Lowell Wadle, the metaphysically inclined inheritor of Vilatte's American Catholic Church in Laguna Beach. Then Herman went looking for Hampton. Between the Leadbeater book, the Old Catholic missal, meeting Wadle, and finding Hampton, Herman realized what metaphysics was missing: the Christ and the sacraments. "The Christ" was personal, not abstract. The sacraments were sensual channels of the divine. Both were much bigger than orthodox tradition. Herman started to fathom a "vital non-Papal form of catholic and universal Christianity."[33]

If Herman's memories were accurate, Ernest Holmes himself had an interest in nonpapal Catholicism through friends like Wadle (pronounced WAHD-lee). In at least five separate writings, Herman recounted that Holmes requested that he write a mass for Religious Science. "Just prior to his death" in 1960, Holmes "asked me to compose a 'Metaphysical Mass' " with the help of Wadle, Herman wrote. " 'Metaphysics,' [Holmes] said, 'needs the crowning touch that only the Mass can confer.' " Herman said the death of Wadle prevented him from taking up the request, because "I was too young and inexperienced to attempt it by myself."[34]

Meanwhile, Holmes helped "burst my bubble of certitude" about the ultimacy of his organization, Herman wrote. "Religious Science is a passing phenomenon," Herman remembered Holmes saying. "Metaphysics . . . will capture the main stream of standard Christianity. Only the Churches that teach it will survive." So Holmes nudged Herman toward that future. "I don't know where your real place of service will be, but it will not be Religious Science," he reportedly told Herman. Having left Methodism and now leaving Religious Science, Herman worried that he would look like some "ecclesiastical tramp." But when he found independent Catholicism, it turned out to be the true calling Holmes had predicted.[35]

The marriage to Hulda finally came apart around the time he left Religious Science in 1956. By 1960 Herman was newly married to Violet, who had a son to add to his two. There were mouths to feed and alimony to pay. Over the next two decades, Herman took a number of jobs. He served as vice president of a short-lived venture to start a new institution called

Golden State University. For eight years he worked in the Superior Court system of Orange County, doing administrative tasks for divorce and criminal cases. He moved to northern California, then back to Los Angeles, and back and forth. He got certified at Paul Popenoe's groundbreaking American Institute for Family Relations and started doing counseling. He served as a chaplain for ninety "lifers" at Soledad State Prison; I cannot tell if that was a paid position. He tried various sales jobs, including "the toughest sales line of them all, selling cemetery property." For three years he worked as a tour guide at the Hearst Castle in San Simeon, California.[36]

Herman later said that being a workingman made him a better minister. He knew "the burden of sweat and toil [and] experienced the frustrations faced in the daily labor market," wrote one of his profilers. Thus Herman could show people "the way out of the squirrel cage of this impersonal and mechanistic society into the fulfillment of the messianic dream of the abundant life." But in fact the abundant life often eluded Herman. As much as he apotheosized the "worker-priest," few of his jobs after Religious Science paid what he considered enough money. There was no structure within independent Catholicism that offered financial security. Even the largest Liberal Catholic church paid no salaries. For the rest of his life, Herman warded off backsliding into uncertain economic conditions, often unsuccessfully.[37]

CALLED TO INDEPENDENT CATHOLICISM

In addition to making contacts among American independents, Herman wrote to the head of the Pre-Nicene Gnostic Catholic Church, then based in England. This neognostic scholar-bishop was known in the secular world as Ronald Powell and took the religious name of Richard, Duc de Palatine. Palatine responded that Herman might be ordained and eventually head the US branch of the Pre-Nicene church, if he began by organizing a study group. So Herman gathered some folk and got started. He named his fledgling parish St. Michael's and convened it in his home. By 1959, when Palatine visited the United States, he and Herman had already ended their association. But Palatine represented yet another independent Catholic presence in southern California circles, even more so when he moved permanently to Los Angeles in 1971. The inheritor of Palatine's church was Stephan Hoeller, who was equally inspired by James Morgan Pryse's Gnostic Society, originally based in Los Angeles. Hoeller went on to found the well-regarded Ecclesia Gnostica, worked with Herman over the years, and, like Palatine and Pryse, became an authority on gnosticism.[38]

Studying with Hampton, Herman was ordained to the diaconate in Ojai in October 1955. The following spring, Hampton, Wadle, and another bishop ordained Herman to the priesthood. That ceremony took place in Wadle's church, St. Francis-by-the-Sea in Laguna Beach. Herman did not join anyone's jurisdiction. Hampton was still fighting for Liberal Catholic recognition. Wadle required of his bishops both celibacy and vegetarianism, neither of which suited Herman. But Herman did take an oath of fidelity to his consecrators' new umbrella organization, the Federation of Independent Catholic and Orthodox Bishops, or FICOB. A little over a year later, in June 1957, the same triumvirate consecrated Herman to the episcopacy at a borrowed church in Huntington. And two years after that, Bishop Herman Adrian Spruit incorporated his "Church Universal-Christian Catholic" in the state of California.[39]

THE CATHOLIC APOSTOLIC CHURCH OF ANTIOCH–MALABAR RITE

Herman united strands of independent Catholicism in California. He was a committed universalist, in the sense of envisioning a "Church Universal" like Holmes, but also in the sense of avowing universal salvation, like early Polish National and Liberal Catholicism. Toward that end, Herman downplayed theological differences in favor of common human participation in the divine. He embraced the independent Catholic practice of multiple consecrations, which repurposed the tradition of *sub conditione* ordination to promote Christian unity. Sometime in the 1940s, bishops started consecrating one another *sub conditione*, not to correct possibly invalid consecrations but rather to concentrate in each bishop many lineages—Roman, Anglican,

Orthodox, Armenian, and so forth—to unite branches and gain validity for the widest possible range of other Christians. Such was the hope, at least.[40]

As he met various bishops, Herman appeared so personable and capable that he bridged gaps between competing prelates. He worked with the Liberal Catholic Church but also its rival Liberal Catholic Church International. He was friends with Wadle, but also with Robert Raleigh, who led the other branch of Vilatte's American Catholic Church. When Raleigh retired in 1965, Herman was his coadjutor bishop and inherited the church, soon enfolded into his own. Herman also inherited the charter and artifacts of American Melkite church founder Antoine Aneed, whom he met in Los Angeles in the 1960s. A priest and bishop who served many years as a Melkite within the Roman communion, Aneed came to believe that the Melkite church should once again establish independence from Rome. As patriarch of the new venture, he moved from Brooklyn to the West Coast to make it happen. Finally, Herman inherited leadership of FICOB and St. Sophia Seminary, founded by his mentors to educate independent clergy.[41]

All in all, Herman's church enfolded several other jurisdictions and encompassed a dozen or more apostolic lineages. These included the Roman line through Varlet and the Syrian line through Vilatte. According to independent Catholic understanding, Herman in turn bequeathed this unified bundle to others each time he performed a consecration. Herman's abundant ordaining and consecrating led some to consider him too liberal, flimflam, or even simoniacal. And for those who did not share the same understanding of apostolic succession, the entire subconditional project could seem grandiose at best, pathetic at worst. Still, many independents soon came to regard the young prelate—raised to the archepiscopate by Aneed and Wadle in June 1960—as a unifier and torchbearer.[42]

In 1967, Herman legally changed the name of his jurisdiction. "Church Universal" was already in use, particularly by some local psychics. "While we are aware of the validity of much of psychism," he said tactfully, "we did not care to be known as a Church of Psychics particularly since this is far from being our most fundamental conviction." The new name was the "Archdiocese of the Church of Antioch, Inc." If Herman was aware that that moniker, too, was already taken—as of 1927 a New York branch of Arab

Orthodoxy was "the Church of Antioch" in the United States—he did not give any indication.[43]

Mindful of Hampton's court battles, Herman added to the official title: "A Corporation Sole, vested in the Office of the Archbishop of the Church of Antioch." Making the church a "corporation sole"—a legal entity locating a company in one person—copied the arrangements of other American religious leaders such as Roman Catholic diocesan bishops and the president of the Church of Jesus Christ of Latter-day Saints. It compromised, however, a tradition of independent Catholicism that Herman in theory shared, namely, conciliarism or governance by the collective of bishops. But the Hampton situation scared Herman sufficiently that he preferred the drawbacks of the monarchical model—or the chief executive officer model—rather than risk getting kicked out of his own church. It was a compromise that would haunt the Church of Antioch during his lifetime and afterward.[44]

In 1984, Herman again legally changed the name to "Archdiocese of the Catholic Apostolic Church of Antioch–Malabar Rite, a Corporation Sole vested in the Office of the Patriarch of the Church of Antioch." The "Malabar Rite" reflected Herman's mystical identification with east Syrian-linked Malabarese Catholicism—though Vilatte's consecration was in the west Syrian-linked Malankarese lineage, and though Herman's own mass was an English translation of the Tridentine Rite infused with Kabbalah, the medieval Jewish mystical tradition. The new name also indicated that Herman was by then using the title of patriarch—passed on to him, he said, as inheritor of the church of Patriarch Aneed.[45]

Herman sometimes allowed himself grand hopes and dreams. He occasionally predicted in print that the patriarch of the Church of Antioch would someday govern the modern western church like the historic patriarchates governed in the Christian past; that Sophia Divinity School would become a world-class seminary; that his little jurisdiction would ultimately unite all of Catholicism. But if Herman talked that way, so do a lot of independents. For that matter so do a lot of big-body Catholics. Catholicism seems eternally wistful for the "one, holy, catholic, and apostolic" church as a visible body.

But mostly Herman did not talk that way. His role would be more modest. Sometimes he even eschewed the idea of establishing parishes. While he personally always said Sunday mass, usually with small groups in his home, Herman's real aim was to cultivate an order of priests that would live in the world and offer the sacraments to all. "When we were originally ordained," Antioch bishop Paul Clemens remembered of Herman's early days, the archbishop envisioned "a secret society of people already doing priest work in the world." This indifference to parish formation was and is controversial. Not only the big bodies but also Old Catholics and Liberal Catholics emphasize parish formation. Those within Antioch, however, appreciate Herman's philosophy—and the freedom to create their own ministries.[46]

They also feel free to leave. In Herman's day and afterward, the church variously grew, shrank, and splintered. In 1967, a church newsletter reported that Antioch had "nine priests, two deacons, . . . a number of men in minor orders, and six congregations, as well as an orphanage." In 1980 Herman wrote proudly that the number of clergy almost tripled in a year, from under thirty to over eighty, likely when a group of Rosicrucians in Washington State adopted him as their bishop. But he also reported frustration and disappointment. "My problem is this Church of Antioch," he said in a sermon in 1981, "and what a thorny problem it is!" He wished for more loyal clergy and laity. His home group included only a few who really contributed, he said—"the rest are content with half-way measures and window-dressing." Still, when the Internal Revenue Service granted Antioch federal income tax exemption on the basis of an application that truthfully described his parish of just five families, Herman was suddenly animated again. He said he felt like a modern-day Gideon, triumphing over massive opposing forces with a tiny, handpicked army.[47]

Clerical departures and jurisdiction-hopping happen throughout independent Catholicism. For that matter splitting and switching are rife in all of modern Christianity—always more so when leaders are unpaid. I found no evidence that independent Catholics jump around more or less than other religious groups with volunteer staffing. In Herman's time, however, the Church of Antioch did contend with the specific tension of a founder dedicated to episcopal collegiality in principle while registered as a corporation sole under US law. The ambivalence meant that Herman's fellow bishops sat on an episcopal council but chafed at his lack of consultation. Repeatedly Herman decided on divinity school policies, tithing standards, and ordination requests without collegial input. Fed up, bishops left. Hurt and angry, Herman lashed back. Numerous letters, sermons, and documents written in the wake of these departures rationalized his moves and tried to shore up the remaining bunch.[48]

LOVE, AND DO WHAT THOU WILT

The Second Vatican Council of 1962–65 riveted the attention of Americans of the Roman church, but there is little mention of its goings-on in independent histories or Herman's papers. This does not mean Herman was not interested. But in general independent Catholics saw themselves as staying ahead of the Roman curve. Sometimes Herman expressed thankfulness to Rome. "We are grateful to them for, in spite of the superficial treatment they give the Sacraments, they have kept them alive through the centuries." Other times he felt free to dismiss the church with little tact: "Most Romanism," he wrote, is "relatively worthless." But Herman said the same of huge swaths of Christianity. Even independent Catholicism overly fetishizes the Christian past, Herman thought, namely, the first seven ecumenical councils, which he called "museum pieces, and not really interesting ones at that." Those documents "might be viable," Herman said, "if, like the US Constitution, they were subject to a process of amendments." From the time of his Old Catholic schooling at his father's knee, he had been exposed to the "amazingly wondrous world" of "real Catholicism," he wrote. His life mission was to pass on the treasure without the baggage.[49]

In the 1960s in the United States, Herman saw signs of the times not in Vatican II, but in the emerging counterculture. By the Summer of Love, Herman was fifty-six years old, so the era belonged more to his sons' generation than his own. Still, he opened his arms wide, telling an interviewer in 1967 that he had recently visited San Francisco to do a "study of Hippie-dom." He considered "Hippie-dom" another sign of the coming new age. But like thousands immersed in California alternative religion, Herman had never waited for an Age of Aquarius. Inwardly, it had already arrived. His interior life teemed with revelations, visions, and experiences of the divine.[50]

Sometimes his writings recounted these moments of extraordinary involution. From the age of fifteen, he wrote, he was repeatedly visited by "members of the Congregations of the Gods." Like Theosophy's Masters, these were visitors from other realms "come to sojourn with us." Sometimes they came in brilliant splendor, and other times just "stopped in for a short visit in the course of the Mass." But always they brought wisdom and "overwhelming, gripping joy." Herman did not think these visits indicated that he was special. The Masters were always around and available to "all humble, dedicated mystics." And if you did not believe in the possibility of such encounters at all, Herman asked, "Don't you wish you could?"[51]

Around 1950, even before he left the Methodists, Herman had a vision of Jesus who gathered a "throng of people" before him, yet "all of them as if incorporated into my being." The multitude heard Jesus call them to "build into one dynamic whole the divergent aspects of my Gospel that now clutter your world." Jesus looked directly at Herman with "brilliant eyes" and asked him to follow him. Herman said yes; then Jesus was gone. "As my eyes cast about in search of Him, with a sudden burst of Joy," he recalled, "I found that His Spirit had made its abode within my heart and soul." Herman experienced mystical agony as well as bliss, however. He once recounted a "dark night experience," echoing the famous phrase "dark night of the soul" as coined by sixteenth-century Spanish mystic John of the Cross. Herman possibly refers to the same "dark night" when he recalls revelations on "the day I died":[52]

1. Help your wife

2. — — boys

3. A teaching and a church

Sometime after 1980, he said, Jesus followed up and "showed me how to put the finishing touches" on a concept for uniting the various Christianities. Called "Integral Christianity" or the "Fourth Way," it blended the best of three paths—Christianity, metaphysics, and esotericism—into a new "meta-catholic" path. It was Catholic because it involved the Christ and the sacraments. It was "meta-" or metaphysical because it assumed resonance between microcosm and macrocosm, the core unity of all religions, and the ultimate oneness of the universe. But like his predecessors, Herman rejected an "ecclesiastical imperialism" that would trumpet the superiority of this way or any other way. "At best," he said, independent Catholicism "has only a few answers," just as "each religious group has a basic purpose and is 'right' for some people."[53]

The meta-Catholic way could be distilled even further: "LOVE." The love Herman felt when he woke up from the Jesus vision. The love of God and neighbor that Jesus hailed as the two greatest commandments. The love of friends, children, spouses, and enemies. "You who are going out to tell the story of Christ and who, with Him, seek to build a new humanity and a glorious order of life, load up on LOVE," Herman wrote in his *Rule for Antioch*. "Act as though it were the only action of worth. The Christ Message begins, continues, and ends in the middle of the stream of love." Herman was not unique in defining "LOVE" as the core of Christianity. But in the mid-century United States, he was unusual among Catholic bishops for reducing almost all ethics and ecclesiology to love. Personally he seemed to emanate love, too, according to those who knew him. "I remember the first time I saw him in person," wrote Archbishop Frank Bugge, head of the autocephalous Church of Antioch in Australia. "I had the incredible urge to hug him and not let go, such was his beautiful energy surrounding him."[54]

"Love" is part of how Herman connected his thought to that of Augustine, leading Herman and others to claim the label "Augustinian." Twentieth-century American independents cite the fourth-century Bishop of Hippo almost as often as eighteenth-century Jansenist forebears. Their respective uses of Augustine, however, have little in common. Early modern Catholic reformers invoked the saint to encourage rigorous self-examination and continual penitence. Herman preferred to recall Augustine's seemingly most permissive words: "Love, and do what thou wilt." Just as Aleister Crowley riffed on Augustine in the Law of Thelema, just as Holmes wrote, "All is love yet all is Law," so Herman wrote, "Love is the law, love under will."[55]

The other Augustine quotation especially cherished in meta-Catholic circles is one in which the saint suggested that Christianity started before Christ. Like others of his time, Augustine believed that Christianity perennially existed in the divine action and human wisdom of the ages. "For what is now called the Christian religion existed even among the ancients and was not lacking from the beginning of the human race until 'Christ came in the flesh,'" Augustine wrote in his first book of *Retractions*. "From that time, true religion, which already existed, began to be called Christian. . . . For this reason, I said: 'In our times, this is the Christian religion,' not because it did not exist in former times, but because it had received this name in later times." Several times Herman approvingly referenced this idea. One of those times, he also said Christians should be divided into two types: not Catholic and Protestant, but rather those who believed Christianity started with Jesus and those who thought it newly "received this name" from Jesus's time. "Look at this second group," he wrote. "It is the Church of Tomorrow."[56]

Apart from references to this sort of Augustinianism, Herman deemphasized theology enough to give some the impression of anti-intellectualism. I think it would be hard to square that characterization with the voracious autodidact who read, wrote, and taught his whole life. But Herman did rank experience over doctrine, reduced all ethics to love, and regarded conventional theology as morose and egg-headed. "We pray God to forgive us our theologizing as we forgive those who have theologized against us," he improvised on the Lord's Prayer. He built up Sophia Divinity School precisely to offer a seminary curriculum that valued metaphysical outlooks and experience-based epistemologies. Maybe this qualifies as anti-intellectual. Maybe it is just a mystic's preference.[57]

"HEALING HANDS"

Herman used a sprawl of resources to reimagine Catholicism. He read everything from *The Book of Mormon* to *A Course in Miracles*, Episcopal bishop John Shelby Spong to self-help author Louise Hay. He was a 32nd-degree Mason and a Rosicrucian. He made friends with several local mediums, mostly women, including Mother Jennie Maiereder, whom he later consecrated among the first female bishops in the United States. He was into astrology, numerology, and personology. He did light work and astral projection, studied Kabbalah and the *Bhagavad Gita*, investigated the Psychosynthesis Institute and Creative Touch Technique. He knew Unity people and Holy Graal (sic) folks. He made contact with California Sufis, Camaldolese monks at Big Sur, and followers of Swami Prabhavananda at the Vedanta Society of Southern California. Most contacts were local, but in time the church attracted attention from afar: a New York professor of comparative religion wrote expressing interest in "neo-Catholicism," as did a gnostic leader in Barbados and some churchmen from Nigeria. Traveling to Australia to collaborate with Frank and Chearle Bugge, Herman was initiated into Druidry. He was, in short, eclectic and then some. He seemed to maintain perspective and humor about it all. Lewis Keizer reported that most of Herman's friends and acquaintances knew him as just "The Bish." And in Herman's files I found paper signage in his handwriting, designed as if for a party or gag:[58]

Spook

Spruit

AsTroloGY — ETC .. 1.ºº

Among all his collected outlooks, it seems that the ones "The Bish" cherished the most had to do with healing. His pastor's heart was broken for Methodists he could not help; he treasured healing techniques acquired as a Religious Science practitioner; he viewed the sacraments as God-given balms. What Roman Catholics called "Extreme Unction" should not be a deathbed anointing but a sacrament of healing for anytime use. Confession does not so much erase sin as heal the heart. All the sacraments loosen karmic knots, advancing recipients through lifetimes of learning. In fact, the power to heal through the sacraments is how a Catholic bishop really proves his calling, Herman believed. Just like the original twelve, if "they are not proficient healers," he wrote, "they are not Apostles of the Galilean Master." One profiler wrote from observation of Herman that "spiritual healing" was "the Number One priority in his ministry." It was so from the start. At Herman's priestly ordination, Hampton whispered special words: "I am [anointing] these hands to be healing hands."[59]

Christian and New Thought healing merged in Herman's practice. In a piece called "Psycho-Pneumatology," Herman traced the modern history of spiritual healing from the woman he considered its inventor, Emma Curtis Hopkins, to Hopkins's last student, Ernest Holmes. Later Herman was especially influenced by D. J. Bussell, founder of the Chirothesian Church of Faith, a neo-Essene group. After Bussell cured Herman of kidney stones, Herman said, he put himself under the older man's tutelage. What Herman learned from Bussell: "Love is the absolute requirement" for healing.[60]

Like a number of New Thought healers since the turn of the twentieth century, Herman listed material prosperity as one result of spiritual health. For him this prosperity was not a phenomenon of "mind over matter," as if one imagines wealth and it materializes. Rather, riffing on mystical notions of inner divinity as well as Albert Einstein's equivalence of matter and energy, Herman understood body and mind as "expressions of the same life Force," "one and interchangeable," he wrote. If God pours forth riches, human beings must manifest the largess both spiritually and materially. "The desire for increase, success, and supply is nothing but your innate divinity seeking to express more good in and through your life," Herman wrote. He used the sacraments to heal in the area of finance, but also verbal affirmations and meditations. "God so loved everybody," he wrote, that tangible "benefits to be derived were just as natural as that the sun would shine everyday."[61]

Well, Herman very much *wished* that material benefits were as natural as sunshine. Being an independent Catholic bishop drained his finances. That is common. Despite the frequent charge that independent clerics are motivated by money, no one seems to get rich. Herman in fact "went broke a couple times with the church," profiler Terry Bell wrote. One of those times happened ten years into his independent Catholic career, when a fire destroyed his home chapel along with the whole house. So at "age 54 he started all over again," Bell wrote. Around that same time, Herman looked into getting stained glass windows—or, rather, "Decra-Led Christian Symbol Windows," advertised as a do-it-yourself stained glass window kit. It was all he could afford to make a planned new chapel look more churchy. Later, Herman again faced a financial crisis. "In 1977, Herman wrote to his associates, sharing that he wasn't sure if he could hang on," according to a history of Sophia Divinity School by priest Linda Rounds-Nichols. "He had just spent his last $10.00, most for church business, and no longer had any resources." In 1985, after Herman suffered a stroke, he wrote to church members asking them to chip in for his medical expenses.[62]

A number of those who knew Herman reported his chronic lack of funds. Some recalled that he embarrassed them by pressing priests or congregations for donations. A few hinted that the reason Herman ordained and consecrated so many people was just to make money. If he did, the amounts were paltry—and customary. Independent clergy, like many other priests and ministers, often "recommend a donation" when they perform weddings or ordinations, as Archbishop Richard always puts it. But accounts of Herman's pecuniary troubles are probably reliable, since Herman said as much himself. He never went hungry or homeless. But he had the immigrant's dream of American abundance, a dream that somehow keeps floating out of reach—and the prosperity preacher's conviction that attainment merely requires strong faith.

Even at age seventy Herman wrote out a list of material goals, likely verbal affirmations for manifesting new realities. "Sufficient and adequate financial resources to function efficiently and productively and comfortably; to be able to fulfill my life mission in prosperity and well being." Specifically, "prosperity to purchase attractive and stylish wardrobe on a Grodin's (sic) or Hastings level," he wrote, naming two nice local department stores. He also declared hopes for "dining in the finest restaurants," "means to purchase books," "a luxury, fuel efficient car, late model," "residence in an attractive neighborhood," church office space "in a prestigious setting," and "labor saving devices such as efficient photo copy machine, lateral filing [cabinets]," "competent secretarial assistance," and "attractive office furniture." Five years later, in 1986, the affirmations had still not materialized. Herman described the humiliating situation of getting free haircuts from a neighbor, since he had no money to visit a barber. But "if we really believed," he still insisted, "then Deliverance would at last come. Listen, it is waiting to deliver you from every limitation . . . and give you the full life right now."[63]

Herman did not find persuasive fellow Christians who might criticize conspicuous consumption at nice department stores, much less follow paths such as voluntary poverty. On the contrary, in the last decade of his life, Herman singled out these confused folk, almost bitterly. "I look with suspicion on all that misplaced effort of looking after the poor. God does not know the poor. He never does," he wrote. If Herman didn't have enough money, it was his own fault, because "we have preached poverty for so long." The monastic traditions of Catholicism were partly to blame. "Many of us have been monks and nuns" in previous lifetimes, he said. "And the recitation of those dreadful poverty vows still stick to our innards."[64]

In this, "The Bish" synched with the New Thought bent that makes change start with the individual and move out to society at large, rather than envisioning a just society that nurtures all individual lives. It is a position far from the social justice traditions of Christianity, if not hostile to them. "All this steam about the world betterment, of social activism, is not a legitimate concern of religion," he wrote in 1966. "A by-product yes, but not a fundamental." Herman was not above being actually "embarrassed" by his priests who were engaged in issues of labor, poverty, homelessness, and, by the 1980s, early HIV/AIDS activism. Though Herman himself did not have adequate resources for health care or even haircuts, still he insisted that individual "activation" was the best response to material lack in human life.[65]

ORDAINING WOMEN

If Herman's belief in wealth manifestation and indifference to social justice seem to place him in the neoliberal Hollywood world of Governor Ronald Reagan's California, there was another side. "The Bish" took radical Catholic stances on divorce, remarriage, and women's ordination, pioneering what I am calling sacramental justice. If social justice aims for the equal thriving of all human beings in society, sacramental justice seeks everyone's full access to the sacraments. In particular, ordaining women earned Herman a lasting reputation as a "renegade," "a seminal figure," one of the "giants on earth," and "a saint," as various observers call him.[66]

Already as a Methodist, Herman had tapped into progressive ideas about women's place in the world. At least since Religious Science, he believed it was only logical to conclude that the whole universe rested on a fundamental complementarity of male and female principles. Some meta-physicals pair cosmic gender complementarity with conservative "separate spheres" tropes, matching the feminine principle with normative descriptions of female humans as nurturing, intuitive, earthy, domestic, and receptive. But Herman did not match gender with bodies or characteristics. For one thing, both men and women have male and female aspects. Herman mischievously supported this human "bi-polarity" with Genesis 5:2, "Male and Female made He them"—an interpretation with precedent all the way back to Jewish *midrashim* stating that God initially created Adam as a hermaphrodite. For another thing, the cosmic female principle is seen best in the free and indeterminate Divine Feminine, according to Herman. For a third thing, he loved the free and indeterminate real-world women who were his teachers, mentors, friends, and spouses. He mentioned traveling with Georgia Harkness, a strong advocate of Methodist women's full ordination. He praised Emma Curtis Hopkins as well as Myrtle Fillmore and Mary Baker Eddy as key religious innovators. He singled out Maude Lathem as the most wonderful of his Religious Science colleagues. He made friends with top women psychics. He married three times, each time deeply attached and, in divorce, deeply sorrowful.[67]

Herman's second marriage to Violet was the shortest. They were split by 1965, the year Herman married his third wife, Helen. Helen had four children from a previous marriage, so combined with his two sons with Hulda, their Santa Ana home "often resembles Grand Central Station," wrote profiler Terry Bell. At this time Herman was working at the Orange County Divorce Court. Helen was a highly driven woman—entrepreneur, counselor, astrologer, and musician—and truly seemed a simpatico partner. Herman was devastated when they, too, landed in Divorce Court—just like so many ruined marriages he witnessed on bureaucratic parade, just as had happened with Hulda and Violet.[68]

But Herman took his own experience as a married and divorced cleric to cue an accommodating approach to the Catholic sacrament of marriage. The Roman Catholic position views as unbreakable any valid sacramental bond between husband and wife, so while they both live, remarriage amounts to adultery. Though a marriage can be nullified through an annulment, that process takes a long time, in many people's experience doing as much damage as healing along the way. For Herman, the cultural combination of the sexual revolution, couples' therapy, and rising divorce rates counted as a revelation for the Catholic institution of marriage. "Legalistic attitudes will not shore up this sagging institution," he wrote.[69]

Divorce, remarriage, and clerical marriage could all become holy and wholly Catholic. Married priests can teach by example that matrimony is a high calling with potential for bliss. "As husbands and wives [clergy] are privy to a whole spectrum of joys," Herman wrote, "of which if there are any greater, God must have kept them to Himself." But if a marriage was failing, clergy should help "work out an amiable separation or divorce," he said, and not "create guilt feelings of any kind." Divorce is sad, but so is the "incurable misery" of some marriages. "Sometimes divorce is a matter of karmic necessity," Herman wrote. Marriage remained a sacrament but, in his view, did not necessarily seal a lifelong bond. Herman even saved a newspaper article titled "A Church Divorce Ceremony." Perhaps he thought it was time for a Catholic ritual to bless the marital parting of ways.[70]

Even more transgressive, of course, was Herman's move to ordain and consecrate women. It is not totally clear when Herman decided to go in that direction, or if it ever took deciding at all, since he never mentioned some big change of heart. Maybe he was moved when a woman close to him was called to the priesthood, for example, his wife Helen, who after their divorce became a priest and a bishop. Herman's first ordination of a woman as priest happened when former Palatine comrade Stephan Hoeller proposed to ordain Rosamonde Miller. Leader of the Ecclesia Gnostica Mysteriorum in Los Angeles, Rosamonde Miller had already been secretly ordained, according to her account.

In independent Catholic circles, Rosamonde Miller's story is well known. In 1962, she was a Cuban-American diplomat's daughter passing through France when she was contacted by hierophants or bishops of the ancient underground Mary Magdalene Order, she said. Soon she was ordained and consecrated into this order, as well as given its highest leadership position of Marashin, according to her account. This order understands itself as dating to Mary Magdalene herself. Historically it ordains only women—"not doctrine, but necessity," Miller wrote, for the sake of survival. When Miller moved to California in 1973, she joined the independent Catholic scene there. That was when fellow gnostic Hoeller proposed to ordain her a priest *sub conditione*. She accepted, she said, partly because the Magdalene order had instructed her not to reveal its existence until she joined public apostolic lineages. Hoeller called three other bishops, with Herman responding that he "was more than ready" to take part. The ceremony took place on January 19, 1974. After that, Herman went ahead of Hoeller to consecrate a woman to the rank of bishop, namely, Jennie Maiereder in the spring of 1974.[71]

CATHOLIC WOMEN'S ORDINATION BEFORE SPRUIT

Even before these Hoeller and Spruit ordinations, though, it is likely that the very first ordinations of women as Catholic priests and bishops on US soil took place thirteen years earlier in San Francisco. There, another independent Catholic bishop, Mikhail Itkin, ordained Mary Evelyn Frances Baird as a priest and then bishop in 1961, according to Itkin's episcopal register. The ordination of Baird—and eight other women listed in his register as deacons, priests, and bishops up to 1974—would have been part of Itkin's theology of gay liberation that included denouncing sexism.[72]

Itkin—a small-statured man who became an outsized presence in California's radical and religious circles—appears again in this story. Here, I pause to caution that though the handwritten entries in Itkin's register are detailed and indexed, there is still a chance of unreliability. As noted by James Ishmael Ford, who wrote a thesis on Itkin in 1990 and owns the register, the bishop was "a great exaggerator" who also listed, for example, that he consecrated "Alan Watts." Is there "at least a passing possibility" that not just *an* Alan Watts but *the* Alan Watts—famous philosopher and popularizer of Buddhism—"was an Independent Catholic bishop"? Yes, Ford says. Itkin ran in those circles and Watts was already an Episcopal priest. But if Watts had been consecrated by Itkin, neither Watts nor any biographer of Watts says so. Worse, Itkin's entry for Watts is squeezed between two other lines on an otherwise regular list—"not a good sign," Ford notes. Still, Itkin's entries for the first ordained women are plausible, since he is widely reported to have ordained women as of the late 1960s, losing churches and properties as a result. Even if Itkin's ordinations of women only started in the late 1960s, that is still earlier than Hoeller and Spruit.[73]

After the Second Vatican Council (1962–65) and alongside the feminist movement, the question of women's ordination began rising in all of western Catholicism. In Europe, the grassroots St. Joan Alliance and liberal Roman theologians like Karl Rahner and Haye van der Meer advocated for the cause. In 1965, outspoken Episcopal bishop of San Francisco James Pike ignored General Convention protocols and invested Phyllis Edwards as a deacon. Then the "Philadelphia Eleven" were ordained as Episcopal priests in July 1974 in an unsanctioned rite later regularized by that church. In December 1974, lay Roman Catholic Mary Bernadette Lynch tested the waters for a public call for women's ordination by asking those on her Christmas card list if they thought it was time. Her initiative led to the first Women's Ordination Conference in 1975 and continuous Roman activism on the issue.[74]

Both the "Philadelphia Eleven" ceremony and the founding of the Women's Ordination Conference took place after the first ordinations of women within US independent Catholicism. But even before that, Catholics had been proposing or performing the ordination of women for a long time. Though ordination meant different things at different times, scholars argue for the existence of women deacons, presbyters, and bishops from ancient to medieval times. Some Orthodox churches saw the women's diaconate decline, but never prohibited it. The Armenian Apostolic Church, dating to the third century, maintains an unbroken tradition of women deacons within convents, and as of 2008 these deacons serve the wider public as well.[75]

In modern times, as we saw above, Doinel's Église gnostique consecrated female sophias on mystical authority starting in 1892, and Hodur of the Polish National Catholic Church prophesied women's ordination in 1930. Rudolf Steiner's Christian Community realized a mystical priesthood open to women as of 1922. The next year, the African Orthodox Church in the United States ordained to the diaconate at least one woman, "Sister Phoebe," as noted in *The Negro Churchman*, and continuously maintained an order of deaconesses. During World War I, the Mariavites of Poland ordained women as priests, and starting in 1929, they also consecrated women bishops, the first being Izabela Wiłucka. The first ordination of a woman in the Anglican communion preceded the US "Philadelphia Eleven" by thirty years, when in 1944 Florence Li Tim-Oi was ordained a priest by the bishop of Victoria, Hong Kong, because of the crisis in Chinese Anglicanism when the Japanese invaded. At her bishop's request after the war, Li Tim-Oi gave up her license, though not her valid ordination. In 1947 the previously mentioned Czechoslovak Hussite Church started ordaining women. By 1955, independent bishop Hugh de Willmott Newman in England was consecrating women as deacons.[76]

Even within the modern Roman church, ordinations of women took place in at least one extraordinary circumstance. During Communist rule of Czechoslovakia from 1948 to 1989, an underground Roman church operated parallel to the public institution. The Vatican had ordered its existence for the survival of the faith. But after 1968, when the Vatican worked out an accommodating relationship with the Communist government, underground leaders became very isolated and were especially targeted by the secret police. One of the underground bishops was Felix Davídek, who ordained and consecrated married men with secular jobs, all the better to hide from authorities. In 1970, Davídek called a synod of the underground church to ponder the situation of women prisoners, including many nuns, who had no one to give them the Eucharist. The synod voted to ordain women as priests, and Ludmila Javorová was ordained late that same year. She served as a priest for two decades and vicar-general to Davídek until his death in 1988. At least five other women were ordained as well.

After the fall of Communism in 1989, when the Roman church in the Czech Republic resumed normal operations, Javorová remained active in the community, though, like Li Tim-Oi, she complied with her new bishop's request not to exercise her priestly facilities. But in the 1990s she went public with her story, after the *New York Times* reported it and Cardinal Miloslav Vlk of Prague confirmed that what he called invalid ordinations of women and others had occurred. Male priests ordained in the Czech underground church were regularized into Roman clerical ranks. Javorová and the other female priests were not.[77]

THE "RENEGADE"

Back in California, when Herman contemplated ordaining women and the likely resistance they would face, he decided to start "preparing the ground." Around 1970 Herman began initiating women into "a broadly based spiritual and philosophical association" he called the Hermetic Fellowship. Even at this stage, he recalled, "bishops would come and watch the ministrations of these dedicated women and ridicule our attempts." When actual ordinations started a few years later, Herman did them regularly and openly. It was "a great risk," wrote independent bishop-scholar Lewis Keizer. "He carefully sought the advice and support of fellow Bishops, . . . but really had to go the battle alone. In the process he temporarily lost face among his equals and became the center of controversy."[78]

For years Herman had regarded women's ordination as only logical, but by the end of the 1970s he cited new biblical, historical, and feminist scholarship supporting the practice. Like most independents, he also tapped into traditional Catholic veneration of Mary, the mother of Jesus. Independent Catholic Marianism was quite different from Roman Catholic Marianism at that time. On the Roman side, devotion to Mary encoded ultramontanism, focusing on dogmas of the Immaculate Conception and apparitions in which Mary supported Roman teaching and warned of apocalypse. Highly venerated, Mary officially rose no higher than human status as Mother of God. Even naming her "Co-Redemptrix"—partner with Jesus in redemption by being the necessary human mother—was controversial. On the independent side, however, both liberals and traditionalists did different things with Mary. Liberals tended to follow the Utrecht Old Catholics in rationalizing Mary. She was a model for human life and a feminist icon, but they rejected the Immaculate Conception and concerned themselves little with her virginity, perfection, or obedience. Meanwhile traditionalists birthed sedevacantism, which harbored a rare but pinnacle-high Mariology, mostly originating with French priest-cum-pope Michel Collin, also known as Pope Clement XV. The Collin branch of sedevacantism went far beyond Mary as Co-Redemptrix and actually honored her as a second Real Presence in the Eucharist, an incarnation of the Holy Spirit or even God the Mother.

That is why in the early 1970s—possibly before Herman Spruit and Stephan Hoeller though not before Mikhail Itkin—the sedevacantist Apostles of Infinite Love of Montreal, Quebec, started ordaining women as priests.[79]

Herman's Mary was the Divine Feminine. In a way he combined liberal indifference to Mary's ultramontane virtues with sedevacantist avowal of her divinity. But really his thought had more in common with scholars of comparative religion who categorized Mary with other goddesses, earth-mothers, sea-queens, avatars, incarnations, or cosmic principles. So Herman assumed that Mary was divine *and* the Co-Redemptrix, a feminine force complementing the male force in God's unfolding plan. Herman then added an interesting Christological spin. More than Jesus's co-redeemer, Mary was actually part of "the Christ." "Jesus plus Mary equals Christ," Herman wrote. "A deed so great and a task so vast could not be accomplished by the single male polarity." The one cosmic Christ was male and female, he said, represented physically by both Jesus and Mary. Christian leadership, therefore, should feature men and women together, like poles completing circuits of energy. Until then, "the Church lives in violation of Sovereign Divine Law" and "brown-outs and power outages will damn and curse the progress of the Christian movement."[80]

Here Herman challenged not just big-body Catholic takes on women but also the Leadbeater metaphysics of gender, which hinged on the yogic concept of kundalini, an energy of the subtle body that lies coiled at the base of the spine. Leadbeater thought that "women's kundalini runs counterclockwise while the male kundalini runs clockwise and this is the reason that a man can do the Mass and the woman can't," as an interviewer summarized it in 1981. Herman's partner Mary recalled to the interviewer Herman's reaction "when I related to him my experience of some kind of [spiritual] resistance" in celebrating Mass. Herman reportedly exclaimed, "That's just a bunch of old men on the inner planes that say, 'Woman, you can't do that!'" Mary said she soon got past the resistance with a little otherworldly help. "We women" too, she remarked, "are up and down the planes."[81]

Reviewing scholarship, riffing on Mariology, and revising Leadbeater, in the final analysis Herman supplanted all intellectual arguments for women's ordination with spiritual mandate. "How I came to this decision is easily answered: It is God's will," he told another interviewer. "Once that will was perceived, we moved forward without delay." Other independent bishops could do as they wished. Roman and Orthodox bans stayed in place. Within the Anglican communion, controversy endured. Yet Herman made women's ordination in the Church of Antioch a selling point. "Holy orders are open to all members of the Church, regardless of sex or marital status," he wrote in one brochure. If you too believed in open sacraments, "it could be that you are spiritually a member of the Church of Antioch and do not realize it."[82]

Helen Seymour met Herman and realized she was "spiritually a member." Later, so did Mary Reynolds. In the early 1970s, Herman and Helen had been officially divorced for a few years, but still lived together. One day, Mary knocked on the door.[83]

MARY LOUISE FLEMING REYNOLDS

Mary Louise Fleming was born in 1926 and grew up in the Carmel Valley in central California. Her father was a civil engineer and her mother worked for the Carmel water company. But since the family owned about six hundred acres of farmland, Mary always considered herself a "farm girl." In 1945, at nineteen years of age, she married Judd Bradley, a soldier who shortly shipped out to Okinawa. After Judd got back from Japan, he took a job with Lockheed in Los Angeles. Living in North Hollywood, Mary and Judd enjoyed the comfortable life of a postwar middle-class couple. They had three children: Carol, Charles, and Richard. Gleaning from Mary's stories, however, both she and Judd felt increasingly stifled. After eleven years, Judd was cheating and Mary kicked him out. Later she marveled that she could have normalized the straitened life of being a housewife at that time. "Everything was dictated to me: 'This is the way it's done' and 'We're not going to do that.'" But, she said, "I was used to it."[84]

Mary decamped to Carmel, took various jobs, parented three kids during the week, and took them to her parents' farm on weekends. Soon she met her second husband, John Reynolds, and they married in 1964. John was a charismatic real estate broker who earned a good income, so she could be at home with her little boy, Richard. After a few years, she and John had a child together, Mary's last, named Rosemary. When she and John broke up in 1972, Mary made another fresh start, moving to San Jose and taking a job with the Mountain View Board of Realtors. One day she spied an ad for a continuing education class that looked interesting. "I thought I'd like to go see this course and . . . see if it could help me in my life," Mary remembered. She enrolled and attended the Saturday sessions. The teacher was Helen Spruit.[85]

Both of Mary's divorces left her on rocky emotional terrain. She was a Methodist and to her that meant "staying together as a family." Divorcing twice brought a heavy burden of guilt. So did the economic necessity of being a working mom with less energy for her children. Enrolling in Helen's Saturday class was a way to meet people and have fun. She saw right away that her teacher was "talented," caring, and "very psychic," Mary said. Herman showed up to serve tea at one session. Mary remembered that as students took the cups, Herman joked, "Nothing in the tea!" Someone remarked that this was Helen's husband—not knowing Helen and Herman were split—and that he was the bishop of a church. Mary recalled that he seemed "very bishopy-like."[86]

Meanwhile, Helen had told the class that she was available for private counseling. Mary felt low and decided to take her up on the offer. One Friday afternoon she visited the Spruits' house to see Helen. But it was Herman who answered the door. When Mary said she hoped to see Helen for a counseling session, Herman said Helen was away for the weekend. Mary started to cry. Herman said, "Perhaps I would do." He pulled chairs up to the fireplace and offered her one of the martinis he was making for himself. "Oh, yes," Mary replied, "that would be really nice."[87]

Mary and Herman talked and enjoyed a happy hour. As she got ready to leave, Herman said, "Why don't we say a prayer." He took her hands, she remembered, "and he started talking about the very things that were upsetting to me, and I settled down." After they hugged and she left, "I was very high, and happy," she said. "I don't think I got any energy like that from . . . many people." Mary decided to start going to mass at the Church of Antioch.[88]

Soon Mary was a stalwart member of the little community. For Sunday mass, Helen played the piano and organ. Herman had taught Helen's son Craig and his son Dennis to serve at the altar. After mass, Herman might invite everyone to stay for a meal. "He was very, very social and he cooked different things for different occasions," Mary said, for example, special dishes for a Jewish holiday. Or a bunch of them would pop in the car and go see Jennie Maiereder. Mary knew Mother Jennie as "a little old lady who . . . would tell the future," though to Herman and others she was one of the more spiritually accomplished personages in the area. "That was my entertainment," Mary said. "I loved it." Soon the Methodist version of Christianity—and a lot of Mary's other past views—grew distant as if in a rearview mirror. Her Christianity started to merge with other interests, such as her family's long-time Masonic activity. By this time Mary was very involved in the Order of the Eastern Star, and Herman's teaching sometimes sounded like Christian Freemasonry. "It was just like I was pulled into the thing, or just enticed in, trying to understand . . . what he was teaching us," Mary said. "It was a whole new world, and I was interested."[89]

The tumult in Herman and Helen's relationship continued. At that time they were "going through the toughest part before everything just tumbled," Mary said. It was disruptive for the church community when Herman moved out of the house where they held their services. Yet as Herman and Helen parted ways for good and Herman and Mary started dating, the three remained amicable. Helen stayed in the church, was ordained a priest, and in 1976 became Antioch's first woman bishop. Mary started studying for minor orders—a medieval Catholic series of initiations as doorkeeper, acolyte, lector, and so forth that big-body Catholicism had abandoned and many independent churches had resuscitated. Helen helped her study and was "very, very good to me," Mary said. Perhaps Helen saw that Mary was the next right person for someone they both loved. Perhaps Helen intuited that despite the younger woman's awe of her, it was Mary who could be Herman's partner in church work.[90]

In any case, Mary realized that Herman needed a "boost" to restart ministry after his third divorce. Part of the boost came to her in a vision, she said, at the chapel at Stanford University in Palo Alto, where she and

Herman sometimes attended services. It was a "magnificent" and "beautiful" vision of Jesus with sheep, Mary said, that echoed Herman's vision from years ago and encouraged him to start church work again. Around that time, Herman moved in with her in Mountain View. In the living room of their little apartment, Herman set up his altar. "And [he] started teaching me the different things about the vestments" and such, Mary said. Eventually they purchased an organ and invited people from the apartment complex to attend mass.[91]

MERI SPRUIT

By the time I talked to Meri Spruit about all of this, she was matriarch emerita of the Church of Antioch, eighty-one years old and living once more on the central California coast. For secular matters she still used her last married name, Mary Reynolds. But in the church, she was Meri Spruit. Even the different spelling of her first name—meant to be numerologically a more energetic set of letters—signified a different personage. The day before our interview she had attended the events of Antioch's Convocation in Salinas in 2007, including concelebrating the consecration of two new bishops. It was an emotional day, possibly the last time she would attend Convocation. She was "hung over," she said, from all the spiritual highs. She was also still recovering from a recent operation and radiation therapy. Meri spoke slowly and could not always remember the words she wanted to use. Salinas was sunny and arid, but here on the coast, it was cloudy, raw, and wild. As we talked in her two-bedroom apartment, the fog rolled in. Chilly breezes tinkled the wind chimes on her balcony and made us both reach for sweaters. Frequently we took breaks in the interview to talk to Liz, Meri's beloved Border Collie and companion of days.[92]

Meri still said mass. She used the stately "Wadle Mass" composed by Herman's co-consecrator Lowell Wadle. She showed me the Chapel of Miracles. It was a tiny ornate altar that shared space with her office in one of the bedrooms. Some Antioch priests still made the trek to receive ordinations at the hands of the matriarch in the Chapel of Miracles. I could see why. Her halting, self-deprecating speech did not diminish her attunement, charm, and kindness. And when I saw the matriarch process down the aisle of the Episcopal church where the consecration took place, her regal presence took my breath away. A little over five feet in height, she looked much taller in red vestments and a gold-embroidered miter, carrying Patriarch Aneed's golden crozier. She wore dangly amber earrings, a big amber ring, and her bishop's ring. On the altar, she rested a lot, but still seemed the most vibrant force up there.[93]

When Meri and Herman decided to make a go of Antioch together, she was forty-eight and he was sixty-three. For a decade they plunged themselves into church work and made decisions about family and money accordingly. Meri's parents and children found Herman overbearing and possessive, and Meri knew it. Her youngest daughter moved out when Herman moved in. Yet she would not give up him or the church. Instead, she kept the day job and progressed in sacred studies, while Herman was the housekeeper and "The Bish." "Herman knew so many people," Meri remembered, and he would call them on the phone "and talk to them during the day while I was working." Perhaps he would arrange a visit for the weekend, maybe including an ordination. Then he "would figure out what we were going to have for dinner and do that." On Friday evening, they might hit the road. Meri loved the road trips. "Sometimes we would be driving after work, on a Friday; we would be going somewhere because we were going to have a function on Saturday," Meri said. "And he would have little sandwiches made and feed them to me on the way. . . . And then maybe we'd stay at somebody's house." She laughed. "It was kind of a funny setup," she said. "Like some comedy on television."[94]

By 1986 Meri still worked as executive secretary of the Mountain View Board of Realtors, and for church records she was very glad the office had a good copy machine. Many an Antioch document she copied there after hours. Herman "always, always wrote," she said. "Every time I would come home after work, . . . he'd be [writing]." Meri perceived that he was reaching new spiritual levels as time went on. She got to share it all. "We did healings and . . . a lot of special things that were really very interesting." For his part, Herman seemed to have settled into their arrangement as the best way to do church. As always, he wished they had more money. Sometimes he wished he could be the breadwinner for Meri. The hours she spent at work meant time not spent in other ways. On his personal wish list in 1985, Herman wrote that he desired "prosperity to permit Mary to devote the time to home and church."[95]

But Meri already did a lot of church, and progressively more. In 1979 she was ordained a priest in a Sophia Divinity School class of seven. Helen was one of the ordaining bishops. Other independents warmed to women's ordination; Liberal Catholic bishop Edmund Sheehan still did not accept the practice, but he loaned Antioch his Ojai church for the ordination of Meri and her classmates. Before the ceremony, Meri remembered "haunting and plaguing questions" to the effect of "am *I* worthy?" But then she realized that everyone, man or woman, has those questions. "Is any one human being ever worthy enough? . . . How can we refuse our Lord?" After ordination she was a changed woman, Meri said. "Worship of the Mass has changed my life—and my personality!" she recounted in a sermon in 1981. "The experience of Divine Grace—the Absolution of my faults/sins—Mass is a natural catharsis!—Divine Catharsis! A release of pent-up emotions and guilt feelings!"[96]

THE "CONJUGAL EPISCOPATE"

Meri became a bishop and archbishop. She was coming into her own as a woman and a cleric. And she and Herman were becoming more beloved to each other, relaxing into a relationship that lasted. As Herman continued to write, his references to Meri became more frequent and adoring. "Who can measure the thrill of encouragement and inspiration" from "my incomparable wife?" he asked in the acknowledgments of his long work *The Sacramentarion*.[97]

References also got more intimate. This opening sentence, for example, is probably not the first line that most people would expect to see in an essay by a Catholic archbishop: "The other night while we were lying in bed," Herman wrote, "Bishop Meri asked me . . ." If Herman was not already convinced that sex is holy, with Meri he said out loud that he was convinced. "In those most tender moments of affection," he said, "there are times when the sacramental grace of the full sacramental life is communicated to a mate through all the chakras from head to toe," leading to "raptures compounded in heaven itself." Great sex, he believed, is yet another argument for making women priests, because "no one could intelligently deny" that lovemaking itself conveys a "sacramental grace of ordination." Women take part in lovemaking as much as men, so "whom, then, are we kidding when we rail, fume, and object to the ordination of women!"[98]

That same year—1981—Herman wrote the "Sweetheart and Archbishop" letter. Each of the seven Antioch archbishops got a separate missive. But the one to Meri was particular and remarkable. "Dearest Meri, Sweetheart and Archbishop," Herman wrote. "This is a unique relationship we have," which "calls for the writing of a unique kind of letter, and I am hoping I am up to it. Anyway, I will try." He talked about trying to create more democratic procedures that would still allow room for singular spiritual insight. He talked about church conflict and how to deal with it. "Regardless of what organizational priorities or commitments we may establish in the world beyond our hearth," he concluded, "the two of us will always be the ultimate Executive Committee. There can be no closer intimate and advisor than the precious pal who is the one and only bed-fellow." He closed as "Your very own Archbishop-Patriarch!" and signed it "Herman."[99]

Partnering in business and in bed, Herman and Meri took the ordination of women to a whole new level. If Antioch was serious about the cosmic complementarity of male and female, that "Jesus plus Mary equals Christ," then ordaining pairs of men and women fulfills the promise of Christ with particular splendor. Coupled leaders need not be husband and wife; Herman and Meri were not officially married, even if they often called their union a marriage. But being an ordained tandem worked for them. Herman had already said that his "greatest joy so far is my partnership with Mary in life and the episcopate." Now he called that partnership a "conjugal episcopate." A "conjugal episcopate," he said, is "the ultimate boon and benison God could bestow upon the holy and beautiful bond of marriage, as well as on the Holy Order of Bishops."[100]

In the years that followed, Herman and Meri consecrated a number of couples in the "conjugal episcopate." The most famous was Vivian Godfrey and Leon Barcynski, better known by their pen names, Melita Denning and Osborne Phillips, the husband-and-wife team that authored best sellers such as the multivolume *The Magical Philosophy*. Other bishop-couples included fellow Californians Arnold and Shirley Eyre, William and Patricia Cordogan, and Warren and Ellen Watters, as well as John and Miriam Rankin in Texas, and Frank and Chearle Bugge in Australia. The Bugges are big fans of Meri. In 2006 Archbishop Frank was moved to post on the listserv to inform newcomers about the matriarch emerita. "Let us describe Mother Meri," he wrote. "Angelic, font of love, inspiritional (sic), compassionate, down to earth, good sense of humor . . . and these are her worst points." He concluded that "her good points I leave you to work out for yourself, for they are simply wonderfully indescribable."[101]

In 1981, three women bishops of Antioch—Meri Spruit, Shirley Eyre, and Miriam Rankin—sat down for an interview, which was later published in

FIGURE 3.3 Matriarch Meri Spruit and Patriarch Herman Spruit, who called their union a "conjugal episcopate," c. 1986. Courtesy of Richard Gundrey.

the Washington Rosicrucians' journal *AROHN*. They all spoke of wishing to balance the traditional male leadership of Catholicism with a female component. "We have had a male dominated upper echelon as far as ministry is concerned . . . for quite some time," Bishop Shirley said, "and now the balance is taking place." Male and female bishops married to each other put a fine point on it. "I have an ideal in this age . . . that man and woman would learn to relate and cooperate and reverence one another in a new way," said Bishop Miriam, a former Roman Catholic. "Joining together in ritual work . . . helps us come into total communion with one another and that is perhaps the greatest work."[102]

With the interview weighted toward the experience of ordained couples, Meri added that a single woman—or a married woman whose husband wasn't into it—could also pursue ordination. "I would not discourage any person from entering holy orders because the spouse is not interested," she said. A conjugal ordination is "important, but it is not the only way that one can fly." Indeed, Herman and Meri continued to ordain and consecrate women in their own right. Ordinations of women to the priesthood numbered in the dozens, while solo women bishops consecrated or co-consecrated by Herman, Meri, or both included not only Jennie Maiereder and Helen Seymour, but also Janice McLouth-Frederick, Connie Poggiani, Anastasia Voyatjides, Gladys Plummer de Witow, and Lucia Grosch. The latter two successively led the Holy Orthodox Catholic Church, closely linked to the Societas Rosicruciana of America, which had broken away from its parent body in 1916 over the issue of women's membership.[103]

Eventually Herman titled Meri "matriarch." If there was a patriarch, there should be a matriarch. It was a conscious attempt to model a Catholicism that included masculine and feminine aspects from pews to popes. Antioch shows the world "the partnership of a man and woman together at the Head of this Catholic Church," Meri wrote, "equal in authority, and responsibility." There was a very practical side to the new matriarchate, however. Herman's health was failing. In 1983, when Herman was about seventy-two years old, he collapsed while celebrating mass in Mountain View. It was "believed to be a slight stroke" that somewhat affected his memory and speech, he told the church in a letter. Some of Herman's associates suspected that he had been having mild strokes for years already, possibly altering his personality into one they found more difficult to deal with. In any case, the event in 1983 was followed by a fall in the bathroom in 1985. After that, Herman renewed his interest in healing and endured a long physical decline.[104]

On January 26, 1986, Meri was enthroned as matriarch in an elaborate ceremony aboard the *Queen Mary*, a cruise ship docked in Long Beach, California. One of Antioch's priests was the captain of the ship and arranged its use. Though the grand affair coincided with Herman's seventy-fifth birthday, Long Beach was a fifteen-hour drive south and the patriarch was too sick to attend. Instead, he wrote Meri's Protocol of Election. "May we be reminded that such an event as this has never occurred in the whole of the history of the Church," he wrote. "The heavy foot of male domination has been taken from the necks of womanhood to function freely as God has created them, for such throttling of female genius has always been contrary to the will of God." From 1986 to 1990, Herman and Meri handled church oversight together. But in April 1990, Herman officially named the matriarch as leader, no more coleader. "She will hold the position of preeminence," Herman wrote. "I will hold the position of Patriarch, which will have second place to her."[105]

THE MATRIARCH

Meri led with passion for women's issues and compassion for clergy. Antiochians repeatedly recounted her graciousness, encouragement, and professionalism as they progressed from training to ordination. An accomplished seamstress and designer, she would sometimes gift ordinands with handmade embroidered vestments. A lover of travel, she gladly went to India by herself to fulfill her and Herman's plan to reconnect with church heritage in Indian Christianity via Vilatte.[106]

Meri gave homilies on the importance of women in clerical ranks. In 1981 she reminded listeners that "God Himself/HERSELF" said in Isaiah 55:8 that "My thoughts are not your thoughts, My ways are not your ways." So if God had in mind for Catholic women to be ordained, all human ratio-

LOVE AND META-CATHOLICISM | 171

nale against it must fall away. In 1985 she noted the publication of the new Inclusive Language Lectionary with the dry comment, "This is not new to us in the Church of Antioch." More, if first-century "Palestine had been a matriarchy instead of a patriarchy," she said, "surely God would have sent Her Daughter." Still, Meri never envisioned the female priesthood as an end in itself. The task called for both women and men. At her welcome address to the Antioch Convocation in 2000, she exhorted her church to "raise a bountiful crop of Catholic priests, . . . single or married, women and men," she exhorted. "Let us continue to keep the garden gates open wide, . . . for *everyone* is admitted to the Church of Antioch."[107]

Matriarch Meri led in ways that Antioch Catholics said signified the difference of a woman at the helm. She still did the most humble of ecclesial tasks, like serving at the altar. She was known for rehearsing "an entire housefull of Priests" who might not even know she was the matriarch. No one ever made that mistake with Herman. And while Herman was a stickler for proper liturgical form, Meri appreciated improvisation. Bishop Mark Newman described attending a mass celebrated by Meri in her home chapel when suddenly the matriarch discalced herself. "In the middle of the Eucharist, . . . she stopped and she says, 'I think it's time for a shoe break 'cause my feet are killing me,'" Bishop Mark remembered. "Took her shoes off and then continued with the Eucharist."[108]

At the same time, Meri did not have Herman's confidence in leadership or intellect. Herman told her she could do anything. But she never shook self-consciousness about only having an associate's degree and being so nervous about public speaking. "My earthy simile for preaching," she said in a sermon in 1981, "is that it's like being in a nudist camp! There you are—out in the open—in front of God [and] everybody!" She tried to improve, for example, enrolling in a "Painless Public Speaking Workshop."[109]

But Meri's leadership also suffered from sexist attitudes toward her. In the same church that precociously ordained women, Meri found that fellow bishops repeatedly dismissed or ignored her. So women bishops "must be prepared to serve without appreciation," she wrote. When Herman was at her side, she had a champion. Herman would confront a hostile cleric and make Meri's concelebration a condition of his own participation. But when Herman languished, Meri was more vulnerable. "They absolutely left me out," she recalled. "I had things done to me that were very unkind." Antioch bishops ordained people in her absence, erased her name on consecration certificates, and in general acted as if it were an embarrassment rather than a triumph to have her in charge, she recalled. Herman caught wind of it. "I request and encourage you to include her whenever at all possible in any of your functions and events," he wrote. "It is of utmost importance to the future well being of the Church of Antioch to include the feminine counterpart." His intervention did not help. Within the year, all three clerics addressed in his letter had resigned.[110]

In fact, both Meri and Herman dealt with unpopularity in their own church in the last years of his life. Meri tried to handle bishops' strong personalities and could be fierce in her own defense, but she veered between collegiality and imperiousness. For their part, fellow bishops might have reacted against Meri partly as a form of premourning Herman. Many joined the church under Herman and wanted him back. But he was not the same person. Herman's letter on Meri's behalf sounded an authoritarian tone from the sickbed, repealing steps toward conciliarism and insisting that the Antioch hierarchy started and ended with the matriarch. Even the Spruits' favorite bishop, Richard Gundrey, balked. Richard's handwriting on the typed letter said, "Herman, you must have forgotten what you said—or you have changed your mind. It's time to let go."[111]

It is not clear if Herman ever saw Richard's note. He was no longer fully present for earthly life. In 1981 he had written to Arnold and Shirley Eyre that he fantasized about ending life without dying, of being bodily assumed like Mary, of being "translated like Enoch, Moses, and Elijah." But, he said with chagrin, "I commenced the purification of my soul far too late." Still, toward the end of his life, Herman "was onto something," as Mother Linda Rounds-Nichols judged from reviewing his papers. Close friends also believe something transformative happened to him near death. The patriarch who seemed to be wasting away may have concluded his purification after all. If so, however, it was too late to restore his earthly reputation. When Herman finally died on August 5, 1994, Meri sent the announcement of his funeral Mass far and wide. Almost no one attended. Richard Gundrey, who made the trip from Santa Fe to California, called it a "scandal" and a "shame."[112]

After Herman died, Meri started the tradition of yearly Convocations. She fortified the Federation of Independent Catholic and Orthodox Bishops, or FICOB, which by 1996 listed twenty-four prelates of various independent Catholic jurisdictions, many of whom became movement notables. She published the newsletter *FICOB and Friends*, oversaw the work of Sophia Divinity School, and mentored everyone from seminarians to bishops. There were departures and even attempted coups. But those who remained in Antioch became very loyal. Often they traveled to see her, even when she moved to Creswell, Oregon. The reality of belonging to a Catholic church headed by a woman increasingly inspired Antiochians and identified them among independents.[113]

Meri grew especially close to Richard Gundrey, who had been ordained by Herman in their Mountain View home chapel in 1985. When Richard was elected bishop, Meri happily traveled to New Mexico to perform the consecration. After the festivities, she got support from an unexpected visitor. Father Jay Nelson remembered helping the matriarch carry her vestments back and forth to Loretto, and on the way out, "she was stopped by an actual Sister of Loretto, who was in town on business and had dropped in to see the old place," Father Jay wrote on the listserv. This Roman Catholic sister had "walked in during the ritual [and] was amazed and obviously delighted that a woman could be an Archbishop." As for Meri, she "took it completely and graciously in stride, and I'm sure left the nun's head spinning with new possibilities," Jay wrote. "Meri's done that for a lot of people, myself included."[114]

The decade of Meri's solo leadership was deeply marred, however, by a traumatic relationship. In Oregon, in late 1994 or 1995, Meri met a man who wanted to join the church and ease her workload. In short order, though they were not romantically involved, the man moved in with Meri. Church members met him when he accompanied her on trips. He started classes toward ordination, established FICOB's first webpage, and handled Meri's new email account. She ordained him a deacon and, in 1996, a priest. And, somewhere along the way, he started abusing her. Meri's church and family watched the unfolding scene with great alarm. They were horrified to find out, only deep into Meri's entanglement, that the man had done stints in prison for incest and arson. Part of his problem was certainly alcoholism. With a little help from her friends, Meri finally kicked the man out of her house. He proceeded to stalk her and threaten her life. So, at the beginning of 1998, Meri moved away from "dangerous, and utterly impossible circumstances," as she wrote later. Again she settled in central California. But the entire episode "permanently damaged her psyche," Archbishop Richard said. Meri asked Richard unofficially to take over day-to-day operations of the church. She became nervous and secretive. She wanted no one to know where she lived. She moved four times in seven years—to "downsize," she said, but also likely because she was frightened. Usually she did not attend Convocation.[115]

In September 2004, given continued reclusiveness and advancing years, Meri realized it was "time to officially pass the baton," she wrote to the whole church, "to my chosen successor, Archbishop Richard A. Gundrey." When she fled Oregon in 1998, Meri had already shipped to New Mexico the boxes of church records and archives, plus much of Herman's personal library. Richard put the books on his shelves and stashed the boxes in his garage. Now he officially sent out Meri's resignation and added a cover letter. He thanked Herman and Meri profusely. "I pledge to uphold the standards set by our founder, Most Reverend Herman Adrian Spruit, and his successor, the Most Reverend Meri Louise Spruit," he wrote. "I cannot thank Mother Meri enough for her support of me and all that she taught me."[116]

But Richard also sounded a note of change. Though he would be enthroned as patriarch of the Church of Antioch sometime the following year, a title "called for in our legal documents" as a corporation sole, he wished not to be known as a patriarch. "I have chosen to use the title of Presiding Bishop," Richard wrote, "which I think is more appropriate for our times."

◆　◆　◆

Meri was relieved to step back from active duty and even more relieved that Richard, pastoring the church in Santa Fe and leading the Diocese of the Southwest, had already proved dedicated and able. "If some of you don't already know him," she concluded her letter, "you will be favorably impressed. He is a fine fellow!" Soon Meri made for Richard an exquisite pallium, a traditional vestment given and worn by popes, patriarchs, and archbishops. "Popes and Archbishops are buried with their full vestments and their Pallium," Richard wrote in a public note of thanks. "I will be buried with mine."[117]

So Richard took over as patriarch of one of the flagship US independent Catholic churches. Through the work of Herman and Meri, its influence ranged far beyond Antioch itself. By the start of Richard's tenure, many left-leaning independent Catholic churches ordained women. Even so, most independent women bishops worldwide were still found within the Church of Antioch or had been ordained by Antioch bishops. Meri remained among the very few women ever to lead a Catholic church.[118]

As for Herman, he ordained women and men by the dozens—indiscriminately, some said. Yet even critics acknowledged that Herman's ways buoyed US independent Catholicism in the latter half of the twentieth century as so many original American jurisdictions splintered and sank. While Antioch cannot "be placed in a particular tradition of thought," wrote independent bishop-scholar Lewis Keizer, its founder's "ecumenism" was itself "at the forefront of innovative theology." Herman "caught a vision of free Catholicism . . . and kept it alive through difficult years," wrote priest-scholar Thomas Hickey. Herman "both embodies and sacramentalizes all the choicest possibilities of Neo-Catholicism," added scholar-bishop Robert Burns. None of those men were part of Antioch when they wrote these words, but they all saw something in Herman that made them testify despite time and conflict.[119]

A final legacy of the Spruits came from the sale of their Mountain View home. Proceeds created a small endowment for the Church of Antioch, $45,000 as of 2005. Occasionally the endowment provides waivers for Convocation fees or scholarships for Sophia students. But mostly it sits accruing interest and waiting for some future capital project—a permanent building for the church and its archives, for example. If Herman and Meri felt they never had enough money, still they managed to give the Church of Antioch a small bequest.[120]

PART III
SACRAMENTS AND SAINTS

◆ ◆ ◆

4

DANCE AND BALANCE

◆ ◆ ◆

LEADING AMERICAN INDEPENDENTS

WHEN I HUNG out with Archbishop Richard, mostly what I did was attend weddings. On the same Friday in May 2008 that we went to Pojoaque Pueblo where the guest muttered, "Antioch?!," the archbishop did two more ceremonies. One of the couples had booked Loretto. Bookings went through hotelier owners of the chapel, but Archbishop Richard was on a short list of officiants they called. He also celebrated more affordable weddings in his home chapel on Cordova Road. There a spacious room with a vaulted ceiling comfortably held thirty people. That's where Manuel and Pilar met Richard for his last wedding of the day. They were Roman Catholic. It was their second marriage—to each other. They had divorced but, with four kids, wanted to try again. The bride wore red. The groom wore khakis. Accoutrements consisted of two drugstore rings and one disposable camera. The kids crawled under the chairs, fought, and cried.

Richard was unflappable. "Love comes in all different forms," he said to me later. The United States was hit by a major economic recession in 2008, and Richard worried about Santa Fe residents who found the city too expensive, who could not afford the high gas prices, who were eating more often at McDonald's. The groom worked on and off in construction and Archbishop Richard hoped the family could stay together this time. Concluding the matrimonial rite, he turned to bless the children. They became rapt as he anointed each sweaty forehead with oil. The big girl kept her hands on her hips, but looked at the archbishop with wide eyes.[1]

In 2008, marriage between opposite-sex couples was the only type recognized by the state of New Mexico, but Archbishop Richard married all kinds. Gay and straight. Second weddings—and third and fourth and fifth weddings. Romans and ex-Romans. Protestants, any religion, no religion. Interfaith duos who sought a Catholic mass at which all guests could receive communion. Couples with kids and couples who were pregnant—in which case Richard anointed the mother's tummy. He did weddings for Roman priests who had left their dioceses to marry. He did a "friendship blessing" for a Roman Catholic nun and her best friend, a divorced mom of two. "Talk about an education," Richard marveled.[2]

He was criticized, of course, for taking all comers. "People say, 'Well, how many of your weddings *stick*, Richard?'" He said it is not for him to judge the circumstances. The partners are responsible for making the marriage stick, not he. Yet for all the seeming permissiveness, Richard did not fulfill all requests. He did not do "secular" weddings in which God or the sacred was not mentioned. He did not do weddings without his collar and stole signifying that he was a Catholic priest. And he did not do weddings where he saw no love. Once I heard him on the phone, taking down a couple's information. The groom was a fifty-five-year-old white American. The bride was a twenty-something from Taiwan. Richard questioned him. "I hope you're in love with this woman? This is not an immigration thing, right?" Every couple scheduled two in-person sessions with Richard apart from the wedding—a planning meeting and a rehearsal. If they missed either, Richard canceled.[3]

The planning meeting at Richard's house involved filling out paperwork and choosing readings, but also light counseling. I saw this one day in a meeting with Annie and Jake. When Richard positioned them as if on the altar, Annie was overcome with emotion and started to weep. "Don't cry," Jake said. Annie sniffled at the floor, "He keeps saying, 'Don't cry.'" Richard stepped in. "Let's talk gently about 'Don't cry,'" he said. "I'm totally against saying 'Don't cry.' People who keep it all stuffed in don't get it, don't get what they're doing." He pointed at them. "When she cries, when he cries, it means"—Richard hit his heart—"you get the significance of what you're doing." Later, Annie broke out in tears again. "I'm getting it out now, Jake!" she apologized. "Oh, honey, you cry anytime you want," Jake said. "I was just teasing you." When the meeting wrapped up, it was Richard himself who was welling up with tears. He was well known in his church for getting "SOUPY," as he put it. Of course the archbishop would tell people it is OK to cry.[4]

Taking all comers, yet setting boundaries and dispensing advice, Archbishop Richard did likewise in his leadership of the Church of Antioch from 2005 to 2010. He inherited a wide-open meta-Catholic jurisdiction from the Spruits and carefully cultivated the same expansiveness. But he also moved to institute policies and procedures that gave the thing some kind of container. Critics said the church was still too wide open. Others said he made it too rule-bound. From Richard's perspective, however, it was all a matter of "balance." Repeatedly invoking the concept of balance in the face of church conflicts, Richard took steps toward realizing what might sound like an oxymoron: a church with no dogma, a Catholicism that included everyone. It was not easy. But, like Varlet, Vilatte, and the Spruits before him, Richard had found his calling in independent Catholicism. "I would never have made it twenty years if I was not completely happy and spirit-filled with my ministry," he wrote in 2009.[5]

Still, sometimes it just made him cry.

ON THE PLAZA

Richard Alston Gundrey was born in 1934 in Flushing, Queens—"Archie Bunker's neighborhood," he said. Back then, a great day was taking a three-cent trolley to see swimming star Esther Williams perform at the Queens Aquacade. Richard got very involved in the "high" Episcopal church attended by his family, becoming an acolyte, joining the youth group, and singing in the boy soprano choir. Episcopal sacramentalism captured his heart. He didn't really "get behind" the traditional theology, he said, but the "love and understanding of ritual" lasted. Later in life he would explain his involvement in Antioch by saying, "I'm just an old Episcopalian who loves to do church."[6]

In young adulthood, practicalities set in. Richard attended the State University of New York at Farmingdale on Long Island, graduated with a degree in Animal Husbandry, and promptly got drafted. It was 1954 and he expected to ship out to Korea. Instead, he did sixteen weeks of security training and went to Albuquerque, New Mexico, to guard atomic weapons. "Two thousand guys in an airplane hangar," he said. But he got outdoors enough to fall in love with the western half of the country, never to return east. After the two-year Army stint, Richard spied a notice that the Arthur Murray Dance Center was looking for instructors. "They agreed to train a dance teacher for $40 a week, guaranteed for six weeks," Richard remembered. So he decided to try out San Francisco as a professional ballroom instructor.[7]

A few years earlier Richard had met Georgia Maryol, the daughter of a Sante Fe Greek Orthodox family in the restaurant business. She too had moved to San Francisco, so now Richard looked her up at her family's coffee shop on Market Street. The two rekindled things and soon married. Then they went back to New Mexico and together bought a restaurant on the famous Santa Fe Plaza, the Mayflower Cafe. Managing the Mayflower for seven years, Richard and Georgia celebrated the birth of two sons, George and James. When the marriage broke up in 1972, Richard was heartbroken. They sold the Mayflower, split the proceeds, and went their separate ways. At least for a while. Within five years Richard got a call from Georgia. She had moved her new restaurant, Tomasita's, to a bigger location on South Guadalupe Street. Would Richard help her manage it? "So I went to work for my ex-wife for seventeen years," he said.[8]

Notwithstanding the renewed business relationship with Georgia, Richard was "looking for more answers in my life," he said. Around 1973 he took a course in Transcendental Meditation, the method popularized by the Maharishi Mahesh Yogi. "That was a very meaningful change for me," Richard recalled. "It quieted me down." Soon he stumbled upon a local unit of the United Church of Religious Science, Ernest Holmes's organization. He liked the emphasis on human goodness, "getting away from dogmatic teachings," and grasping "the power of our consciousness." Richard became a licensed

Religious Science practitioner in 1978. Soon he considered ordination as a minister, too. But he was not willing to leave Santa Fe to attend the organization's Los Angeles seminary. Instead, he got ordained in a New Orleans independent Religious Science church in 1982. Still in good standing in Holmes's organization, he served on his district's board of directors for four years. When I first visited the Church of Antioch in Santa Fe, Holmes's simple "Universal Prayer for World Peace" was printed on the inside back of the Antioch Order of Mass.[9]

But, like Herman in Religious Science before him, Richard started missing the sacraments. One Sunday he and Ursula, his girlfriend at the time, attended mass at the Roman Catholic Cathedral of St. Francis of Assisi in downtown Santa Fe. As the priest was celebrating the Eucharist, "his aura popped up," Richard said. "It was beautiful." Metaphysically attuned people often say they see auras—colored light emanating from people's bodies. Seeing this Franciscan priest's aura during the elevation of the host reminded Richard that there was more to mass "than a human being standing behind a table," he said. It drew him back to longing for "a sense of spell." Soon after that, Richard ran into an old friend on the Santa Fe Plaza who said he'd been ordained in a "metaphysical Catholic church." "Those were the buzz words"—metaphysical *and* Catholic—that "sounded like a perfect home and combination for me," Richard said. The friend was an Antioch priest who connected him with the Spruits in California.[10]

In 1985 Richard started studying for the priesthood with Herman and progressed through minor orders. When he traveled to California on business, he would pass through Mountain View to see the Spruits and do the next step. On October 31, 1987, he was ordained a priest in the Spruits' home chapel. Meri later remembered something telling about that ordination, which took place on Halloween. A trick-or-treater "knocked on the door, peeked in, turned to his friends outside and said, 'Oh, there's some kind of wedding going on in there.'" Indeed, while Richard never married a woman again, he surely did "marry" his church that night.[11]

Late the next summer, in space rented from the Santa Fe Woman's Club, Richard celebrated the first mass of the newly established Church of Antioch at Santa Fe. Forty people came—"all my friends," he said. The next

Sunday, only twelve. But he kept celebrating Mass and handfuls of people kept coming. In 1993, the Woman's Club gave Richard notice to find another space—it would lease to another group for more money. Richard's eyes turned toward the gorgeous Loretto Chapel, then solely a tourist site. He had business connections to the owner, developer Jim Kirkpatrick. Through Kirkpatrick's manager, Richard asked if they could rent the chapel. "Jim says absolutely no," the manager reported back, as Richard recalled it. "He wants to keep it secular." But two months later, Richard saw Kirkpatrick himself walking toward him on the Plaza, all alone. "Something inside of me just said, 'Hit him hard.'" He approached and asked again. Kirkpatrick "stopped, looked at me, and said yes," Richard said. "I about fell over." So, the Church of Antioch started celebrating mass in Loretto—the first and only group to hold religious services there since the Roman Catholic archdiocese sold it in 1971.[12]

Kirkpatrick never wrote up a lease, so they could be kicked out at any time. And the rent was high—$1000 a month in 2006, just for a few hours each Sunday morning. "It takes prayer," Richard said. There were other drawbacks. Incense was too much of a fire hazard, their landlord decided. And there was no space to offer childcare, which limited the ability to attract families with small children. Still, Richard judged that Loretto was worth it. The tiny Gothic Revival church burst with white marble, stained glass, and ornate carvings, seeming to deepen and heighten everything that took place there. Richard was "in heaven" every Sunday, he said.[13]

CHURCH AND COMMUNITY IN SANTA FE

So the Church of Antioch at Santa Fe kept celebrating mass, putting its own sign in front of the formerly Roman Catholic chapel every Sunday. Starting each mass, Richard promised that everyone attending would "have a spiritual experience." It seems that many do, both regulars and visitors. Cradle Roman Catholic Melissa joined Antioch, she said, because "everything I was looking for was here." Bennie, eight years with the church, said Richard had given him "a whole new concept of God." Baruch was "not really a church-goer," he said, but a Jew from New Jersey who ran a bike shop in Los Alamos. Still, playing the organ and receiving communion at the Antioch Mass were just part of his thing. A Methodist couple visiting Santa Fe said the experience "was mind-blowing."[14]

Church member Cassandra frequently saw Richard's aura, just as Richard had seen the aura of the Franciscan at the cathedral. After mass at Loretto Cassandra would give him pictures of what she'd seen. Richard kept the drawings in an envelope in his library, which is where I saw them. "Real woo-woo stuff," Richard said. I laughed and said that the whole church seemed pretty "woo-woo" to me. But to Richard, "woo-woo" was relative. Several of Cassandra's drawings show a golden fleur-de-lis over Richard's head. "I get that all the time," he said. "People see the fleur-de-lis over me."[15]

Richard's family supported him and sometimes came to church. His sister's husband, Dick Lemieux, was an enthusiastic regular. Originally from Boston, Dick had been a dedicated Roman Catholic, but when he married a divorced woman—Richard's sister—he was officially barred from communion unless they got her previous marriage annulled. "Go back and say her husband was bad?"—Dick couldn't square the logic of annulment, he said, especially when compared with the situation of Roman bishops who were not penalized for protecting priests who sexually abused kids. "Wait, I'm a sinner because my wife was divorced, and they take (Bernard Cardinal) Law and give him a cushy job in Rome!?" Dick lost his faith. But Richard, he said, restored it. In the Church of Antioch, "I find out I'm not a sinner, I'm a good person, I can take communion," he said. He was "happy about" how "they really include women." Dick served as Church of Antioch greeter every Sunday and cleaned the church afterward. Recently diagnosed with Parkinson's disease, he knew he might not be able to serve forever. The weekly Masses "help me handle what's coming my way," he said.[16]

Ex-wife Georgia was still family, too, while both she and Richard dated new people. When Georgia's longtime boyfriend died, Richard officiated at the funeral. On Richard's side, his "lady friend" was Ilene, and "we've been on and off for ten years," he said. His workaholism got in the way. "I don't have a relationship in my life because I'm not willing to put the time in," he said. But he and Ilene stayed in touch. When Georgia's family had their big holiday gatherings, both Richard and Ilene were always invited, whether they were together or not. The sons and their wives and the grandchildren were all there. Son George continued the family restaurant dynasty, heading the Santa Fe Farmers' Market and then taking over Tomasita's in 2011.[17]

Retiring from restaurant management for good in 1996, Richard was thrilled to focus on church work full-time. He concentrated on publicity, since most people don't even know that independent Catholicism exists. Tourists always come to Loretto just because it is Loretto. But Richard wanted to build a real parish in Santa Fe. "A lot of stuff is local," he said. He ran ads for Easter and Christmas masses in the weekly *Santa Fe Reporter* and the daily *New Mexican*, though they cost $500 each. He lobbied journalists to feature the Church of Antioch in any special religion section. He did radio interviews. He participated in the national Clergy Letter Project as part of the annual "Evolution Sunday." He made a promotional video with the help of Ilene, a professional photographer. He sent a handwritten "thank you" note to every mass attendee from the local area. His public relations philosophy, said Santa Fe seminarian Lian Reed, was "to be out there in the community."[18]

Richard reached out to other independent Catholics when possible. Like most urban areas in the early twenty-first century, Santa Fe and Albuquerque are thick with independents. Traditionalist groups keep their distance, such as the Society of St. Pius X chapel and Bishop Oscar Trujillo's Holy Spirit Cathedral in Albuquerque. But others, such as Albuquerque's Christ the King Independent Catholic Church and Rio Rancho's Our Lady Queen of Angels Liberal Catholic Church, make friends and sometimes collaborate. "A great guy. Give him my love," Richard said when I told him I would visit the Rio Rancho pastor. Richard also had good relations with Holy Trinity Orthodox Church, situated just east of his house on Cordova Road and affiliated with the large Self-Ruled Antiochian Orthodox Christian Archdiocese of North America. Holy Trinity's packs of friendly young monks are often seen around downtown Santa Fe. In addition Richard worked with Bishop Sharon Hart of the Contemporary Catholic Church in Las Cruces and Bishop Chet Stachewicz of the Orthodox-Catholic Church of America in Albuquerque.[19]

As for relations with the city's Roman Catholics, Richard is "good friends" with a Loretto sister still in town and the three local Roman priests who "give me weddings," Richard said. Several times a year he attends events at the cathedral, the seat of the archbishop of Santa Fe, who until 2015 was Michael Sheehan. Richard had a reasonable if occasionally tense relationship with Sheehan. Sometimes Richard is specifically invited to Roman church events along with other local clergy.[20] When he participates in the annual interfaith peace walk sponsored by the Archdiocese of Santa Fe, he takes turns with other religious leaders to say the blessing over bread shared at Chimayó.

Building a church is difficult, including financially. But Richard "married" for richer or poorer. He funded the ministry out of his own pocket by donating all of his wedding honoraria to church accounts. Averaging between seventy and eighty-five ceremonies a year, Richard kept the small church afloat. Father Daniel Dangaran at the Santa Fe parish joked that Richard was "Marryin' Sam," the "Li'l Abner" comic strip preacher who specializes in two-dollar weddings. Richard's honorarium was more than two dollars, but at $150 in 2008, it was still well below market rate. Most Antioch priests do weddings, including Father Daniel and Mother Carol Calvert, the third Santa Fe parish priest. Matrimony is the second-most frequently performed sacrament among independents, after the Eucharist. But in Antioch Richard was by far the "wedding king," as Matriarch Meri once teased him.[21]

By 2004, a critical mass of parishioners gave enough money in the weekly collection basket to cover the Loretto rent. That helped a ton, though Richard still donated his wedding honoraria to the church. A few more dollars came from sales of Antioch books, pamphlets, crosses, and jackets. The Sunday bulletin had a standard back page titled "A Word About Financial Support." But Richard did not want to make money a focus—he had heard too many Catholics complain about fundraising homilies. He worked more hours at church than he had at the restaurant, but he loved it, and did not mind backing it up financially. "I feel very comfortable and at peace with myself when I function as a priest," he said. But "no one," he said, "does it for money."[22]

Highlights of parish life at Santa Fe came when Richard was raised to the episcopate in 1990 and enthroned as patriarch in 2004. Both were glorious

Loretto affairs headed by Meri Spruit, who processed with other Antioch bishops and an assortment of visiting bishops, abbots, and priests. But Richard far preferred another kind of highlight, namely, just lots of people coming to Mass. In December 2006, Richard's new duties as patriarch had doubled his workload. At home he checked email three times a day and constantly worked two telephone lines, one for parish work and one for "Church Central." So when he could report in the newsletter that Christmas Eve and Christmas Day masses on Sunday and Monday had been attended by 150 people, somehow it all seemed worth it.[23]

To ALL,

. . . The Sunday service led by Fr. Daniel with the Baptism was just outstanding. The official count was 61 people in attendance. The Baptism alone drew at least 12 family members. Fr. Daniel had Baptized their first child two years earlier. The special music was great and all who attended that service appeared to be spiritually inspired. My two sons, their wives, and all four of my grandchildren attended that Sunday service. My Granddaughter Lily Kalila Gundrey TEN MONTHS OLD gave her first sermon in a church during that service. She really was very pleasingly loud in expressing what ever she was feeling at that time. All present were very happy about her squealing, feelings, etc.

The Monday AM service was PACKED. It was 13 degrees at 8 AM . . . here in Santa Fe. IT WAS COLD. And in spite of that the official count was 89 people in attendance. We drew some of our regular community (many were out of town to celebrate Christmas with family at other locations) but the rest were tourists from the downtown hotels and of course some of our regular people had friends and relatives in town and they brought them to our service.

Words are so inadequate to describe the spiritual experience . . . but the Holy Spirit really was flowing throughout that service. . . . There were also MANY tears shed as the people approached the altar to light a candle on the high altar at Loretto as they passed by our clergy and received a special Christmas blessing. Many hearts and minds

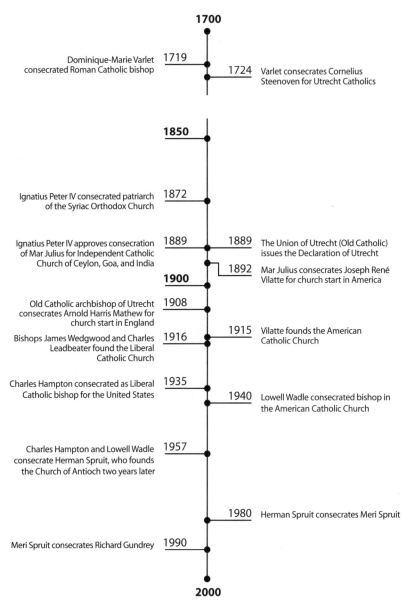

1700

Dominique-Marie Varlet consecrated Roman Catholic bishop — **1719**

1724 — Varlet consecrates Cornelius Steenoven for Utrecht Catholics

1850

Ignatius Peter IV consecrated patriarch of the Syriac Orthodox Church — **1872**

Ignatius Peter IV approves consecration of Mar Julius for Independent Catholic Church of Ceylon, Goa, and India — **1889**

1889 — The Union of Utrecht (Old Catholic) issues the Declaration of Utrecht

1892 — Mar Julius consecrates Joseph René Vilatte for church start in America

1900

Old Catholic archbishop of Utrecht consecrates Arnold Harris Mathew for church start in England — **1908**

Bishops James Wedgwood and Charles Leadbeater found the Liberal Catholic Church — **1916**

1915 — Vilatte founds the American Catholic Church

Charles Hampton consecrated as Liberal Catholic bishop for the United States — **1935**

1940 — Lowell Wadle consecrated bishop in the American Catholic Church

Charles Hampton and Lowell Wadle consecrate Herman Spruit, who founds the Church of Antioch two years later — **1957**

1980 — Herman Spruit consecrates Meri Spruit

Meri Spruit consecrates Richard Gundrey — **1990**

2000

FIGURE 4.1 A sketch of episcopal lineage from Varlet to Vilatte to Spruit to Gundrey. By the author.

were opened that morning. There were many people who had great spiritual experiences that they claimed (on the way out) that they had NEVER had such an experience in any church they had been to before.

My words cannot explain MY experiences that day as well as what happen[ed] to all present. It was truly an experience of the Christ being born in us all AGAIN and AGAIN.

Peace. +++Richard

A year and a half later, Richard marveled to celebrate the twentieth anniversary of his first mass in the Santa Fe Woman's Club. A twenty-year-old parish in independent Catholicism is indeed a feat of labor, steadiness, and—according to Richard and his parishioners—the Holy Spirit. "I just can't believe it," he wrote in the Antioch newsletter. "We never missed a Sunday."[24]

THE SACRAMENTS AT SANTA FE

Saying Mass rotated between Archbishop Richard, Father Daniel, and Mother Carol as celebrants. After mass parishioners convened for what they called a "second communion" at a local bakery, drinking coffee and sharing fresh bread. On Wednesday nights, the group gathered for a healing service and social hour at Richard's house. Other times—true to Herman's vision of a mobile corps of priests—Richard, Daniel, and Carol met people for other sacraments.

Like Herman, Richard is not big on sin. He does not baptize, confess, or heal people to handle sin, he said. Rather, he baptizes to awaken the Christ that already lives within. With a theological anthropology espousing innate human divinity, there is really nothing to prevent Antioch's "altars and orders" from being open to everyone, as Richard often put it. Deacon Douglas Walker in Santa Fe said he once told Richard that his dream was to draw the church circle big enough to include everyone. Richard replied, "Why not just not draw a circle?" "What I got from that conversation," Deacon Doug said, was that "everyone is already in, always was in and can't be otherwise."[25]

None of this is absent from big-body Catholicism. The mystics of the Christian tradition repeatedly glimpse humanity as ever of and within God. Some in the Christian tradition eschew original sin, from the late ancient Greek theologian Origen and much of Orthodoxy, to the twentieth-century former Dominican priest Matthew Fox, whose talk of "original blessing" led to his excommunication from Rome but jibes with many progressive Catholics. Still, it is unusual for a whole Catholic church to reject the concept of any kind of sin and infuse the sacraments with that orientation. Why have the sacraments at all? Because "we're here to learn stuff," Richard explained. There's "no way you and I are going to wind up perfect walking around the streets, not in these bodies." The sacraments "teach" union with God, esoterically, incrementally, and beyond words. They allow everyone gradually to become a mystic, not just a few spiritual adepts.[26]

Not being "perfect" is not the same thing as being sinful. "I just have different semantics," Richard said. "The way I, as a kid, got to know sin was that when you're a sinner, [it] means you're no good. It means you're screwing up, doing bad things." Richard was explaining this to me shortly after I met him in May 2005. "I don't believe in that kind of thinking at all," Richard continued. "[People] make human mistakes, like a woman getting pregnant at sixteen or something. . . . Some people will say that's bad. No. That's who she is. . . . It was a mistake, maybe, but there's nothing bad about that." For that reason, he said, "we stay away from the word 'sin,' not trying to paint a rose-colored picture for people, but just trying to emphasize the positive." He had faith in the process of humans becoming more Christ-like, even if it took eons. "I really believe that there can be peace in the world," he said. "It's up to all of us humans, which are part of this power of God to think in a certain direction and they can bring peace." Offering this outlook with the aid of the sacraments was the foundation of Richard's life in Antioch.[27]

I pressed him on certain points. Was he the kind of metaphysician who thinks "these bodies," as he put it, are a problem? Does he pretty much toss out the Catholic doctrine of the Incarnation, the full humanity of Christ, the insistence that "this world matters," as another Antiochian put it? Doesn't that put Antioch at risk of minimizing Christian concern for material injustices against the poor and powerless? Doesn't "no sin" amount to a completely relativistic ethics?[28]

Like all metaphysically inclined Catholics, Richard had heard these questions before, and he had good answers. But, like Herman, he suspected theology of head games and instead tried to lead with the heart. "See," he said to me, "my simple answer would be [that such questions came from] a belief system. You learned that someplace, you read it in a book someplace, a teacher told you. . . . I'm not saying [it's] wrong. . . . I just say, 'I don't believe that.'" He continued: "If they are throwing some theological point at me that was hashed over for four hundred years by the council [of bishops], I just don't believe it," Richard said. "Even what I'm telling you is a belief system, but that belief system [has] integrity in the development of [my] consciousness." For him, he said, the "biggest thing [is] coming from a place of love."[29]

It was my first time really talking to Archbishop Richard, and I didn't know quite what to make of the tall, lean man in his clerical collar, purple shirt, and black Reeboks. But as I followed him around in the coming days and years, I understood more. A belief system "gets you through the night," Richard said, but is ultimately fungible. A sacrament, on the other hand, is real. It's a human ritual attended by family, strangers, holy objects, and, Catholics believe, presences and powers beyond human ken. It may be rote or raggedy, but it always nudges everyone closer to divinity, as Antiochians understand it. It's a channel of energy you don't need to believe, because you can feel it. Richard felt it, almost too much sometimes. In the middle of a ritual his voice would catch, a tear would fall. Others felt it watching Richard celebrate the sacraments. I felt it, too. He seems to impart visible swirls to empty space. I noticed the substance of air as I breathed in and out.[30]

These performances were Richard's best argument that he does not devalue the physical realm at all. He vests in beautiful garments, a pueblo-woven stole or one of the antique "fiddleback" chasubles that he collects. He arranges for good music, always paying church musicians. Apart from Loretto he uses incense abundantly. He speaks like a Shakespearean actor. He moves lightly, hands flowing. He seems to dance, bringing Arthur Murray ballroom steps onto the altar. "Nobody performs a sacrament like Richard Gundrey," said Deacon Liza Molina, a Santa Fe seminarian. "Nobody. Every baptism that I have witnessed, every wedding that I have witnessed, just sends me into a different plane. Well, why is that? Richard is all heart. All heart."[31]

Which is not to say that Richard entrances everyone all the time. "He tells some of the worst jokes in the world," said Santa Fe seminarian Lian Reed. "And I'm like, 'Oh man. He didn't really say that. On Sunday morning in front of everybody' . . . if . . . they don't understand why an archbishop is saying that, you know, they may not come back." But Lian said she had seen initial "mistrust" turn into attachment. "After a couple of times of being with him, . . . they're like, 'hmmm,' " she said. "And when that shift happens, they're sold, 'This is my church.' "[32]

Lian is right—I heard a few clunkers in Richard's company. But mostly Richard seems a man of easy humor, often about himself. Once over lunch he made fun of himself for not listening to his kids to get a mobile phone— until he got stranded and had to sleep on a cot in an airport. That night "I had an epiphany about cell phones," he said. Another time at his home chapel, Richard was showing me his special things, including a paper packet of dust from Sai Baba, an Indian saint known for materializing ash out of empty bowls. The dust was huffing out of the paper and I told Richard he should put it in a plastic baggie. He looked at me and deadpanned, "How long have we been married?" The next day at lunch, he joked that leading Antioch was the same as managing a restaurant, except while employees could take orders, volunteers required persuasion. " 'I would *highly* suggest that you con*sider* . . .' " he said theatrically. "See?" he laughed. Then he took me along to drop off church mail and pay Loretto rent.[33]

Richard led clergy by persuasion, but also developed practical guidelines. There are instructions for how to get and maintain nonprofit status. The Church of Antioch is a 501(c)(3) organization per US tax codes, so any chartered ministry that keeps up its dues ($153 annually in 2005) can share in those benefits. Richard told heads of chartered ministries to get church insurance. Richard needed his insurance once, when someone fell off the stage during mass at the Woman's Club. Practicalities, protocols, plans— these would be some of Richard's major contributions to Antioch. Herman was often in the clouds and Meri in later life could not keep up with church business. Richard got Antioch's house in order.[34]

Richard gave practical advice on the sacraments, too. For baptisms he strongly recommended using the traditional Trinitarian wording: "I baptize you in the name of the Father, and of the Son, and of the Holy Spirit." That wording is theologically recognized for valid baptism by almost all other Christians, and as much as Antiochians love to experiment, they should also want their baptisms to count. Keep meticulous records, Richard said. He had file cabinets full and could produce certificates years later. These certificates have civil as well as spiritual uses. Undocumented immigrants in the United States can sometimes use baptism certificates like birth certificates. Once Richard baptized six children of a Roma family in his home chapel, he said, partly to provide them with means of semiofficial identification.[35]

For the Eucharist he issued guidelines, too. Antioch masses range widely —priests celebrate contemplative masses, online masses, and *puja* masses. In the past, the church approved liturgies with titles such as "Omnipresence Mass," "Ritual of the Immaculate Conception," and "Lone Star Mass." Richard himself includes in his Eucharistic liturgy an *OM* chant and a "Hail Mary." For independents, the movement's openness to new liturgies is at least as attractive as alternative theology. But two aspects of the Antioch Eucharist are constant church-wide: masses centered on Christ and communion open to all.[36]

The first dates from a decision of the late 1990s, when some priests wished to say mass centered on the goddess Diana. Meri and Richard were both into goddesses in their own ways, but together they decided no. "There's nothing wrong with Diana," Richard said, "but you got to be centered on the Christ. When you leave the Christ, you leave our church. But go ahead and do all these other masses you want to. There's nothing wrong with that, except that's not what our organization is about."[37]

The second of the two commonalities is open communion, a foregone conclusion with Herman as founder. His Methodists practiced an "open table" and he had no reason to do otherwise. But it is a controversial practice among big-body and independent Catholics alike, since many official positions state that only members in good standing or those officially "in communion" can receive the sacrament in any particular jurisdiction. Such "closed communion" policies aim to revere Eucharistic theology and strengthen church bonds. But Antioch Catholics—to paraphrase Richard—just don't believe that. They believe in access above all. In this they join other open-communion Catholics: independents like themselves, all churches of the Anglican communion, Roman Catholic parishes where closed communion is not enforced, and underground big-body communities that actively reject it.

Richard offers communion to all couples he marries and all their guests. The weekly Order of Mass booklet states, "Our communion is open to all who choose to partake." Richard happily remembered the time he "had ten Buddhist monks come up one morning—served them all." Serving everyone, Antioch clergy also let recipients decide for themselves what the Eucharist means. Mother Linda Rounds-Nichols embraces varied interpretations at the drug rehab center mass. "For some of you this is the body and blood of Christ," she says before communion. "For others it is nice grape juice and bread. For others it is a snack you enjoy. However you understand it, you are welcome." One Palm Sunday, she told me, a young man took communion, accepted a palm, and then folded it into the shape of a pentagram, giving it to Mother Linda as a gift. "I kept it until it fell apart," she said.[38]

Antiochians often tell stories about Roman Catholics taking communion for the first time in years, after "they've missed and yearned for" that. When seminarian Lian Reed's sister Susan visited Santa Fe for the first time, Lian told her she could take communion at Loretto. "Well, I know you say that," Susan replied, "but I'm not able to participate in the sacraments." Susan in spiritual terms "saw herself as very sinful, not clean," Lian said, because she had married in a civil ceremony. Lian tried to persuade her. "That has nothing to do with God," Lian said. "God isn't going to strike you dead!" Susan's two daughters chimed in that they wanted to receive the sacrament with their mother. But Susan said, "I don't know about that."[39]

When it was time for communion at Mass the next morning, Lian stood up and held out her hand. Susan stood up too, and then sat back down. Lian said to her, "Didn't you hear Richard? He just said, 'All are welcome.'" Susan stood up again. "So she went and took communion for the first time" since her marriage, Lian said. "And she was crying through the whole thing. The little girls were crying. Richard took one look at her, had no idea why she was crying. He started crying." But later, the daughters were jubilant. "We have a new church! It's the Church of Antioch in Santa Fe!" "And even when they went back home and . . . they would meet new kids or people would say, 'Where do you go to church?' 'We go to the Church of Antioch in Santa Fe!'" Lian said Susan and the girls actually still attend the same Roman Catholic parish back home. But now Susan feels all right taking communion there. "She was sure that the priest just looked at her and paused," Lian said. "She put her hand out [to receive the host], and he gave it to her, and she's been going ever since."[40]

THE DIVINE FEMININE

While an open-communion rite centered on Christ is common to all Antioch masses, there is no requirement to mention Mary. But many Antioch masses do mention her, and Santa Fe leads the way. Merged with the Divine Feminine and the Trinity, Mary is all over Richard's mass. He starts, "In the name of the Father-Mother, Son, and Holy Spirit." He names the Trinity as "God the Father, God the Mother, God the Son, and God the Holy Spirit" and repeatedly references God as "Father-Mother God" or "the Father and Mother of us all."[41]

Most prominently, the congregation says the "Hail Mary" right before the consecration of the Eucharist. Preparing the Loretto sanctuary early each Sunday morning, Richard always lights a candle in front of the white marble statue of Mary on the left-hand side of the sanctuary. When people arrive and take a mass booklet, they can read that the "Hail Mary" is "Dedicated to the Divine Feminine," just as the Lord's Prayer is "Dedicated to the Divine Masculine." When it comes time for the "Hail Mary," everyone turns and prays in the direction of the Mary statue.[42]

Richard changed the traditional wording of the prayer in three ways: not naming Jesus as the fruit of Mary's womb, omitting supplicants' self-reference as "sinners," and calling Mary "Mother God" instead of "Mother of God."

FIGURE 4.2 Archbishop Richard Gundrey lighting the candle in front of Mary, part of his early morning preparation for Sunday mass at Loretto. Courtesy of Ilene Dunn.

Hail Mary, full of grace, the Lord is with You.

Blessed are You among women and blessed is the fruit of your womb.

Holy Mary, Mother God, pray for us, now and at the hour of our death.

The changes reflect his understandings of things, Richard said, for example, "emphasiz[ing] the universal womb of all humanity not just 'Jesus' in that one particular womb." The boldest change, though, is naming Mary "Mother God." If Herman put Mary in the Christ, Richard puts Mary in the God. Both are widely accepted in Antioch. Many Antiochians long ago decided that Mary is basically the Catholic version of the Divine Feminine.[43]

Not everyone who attends Loretto says the revised "Hail Mary." Those with Roman associations may just say the prayer as they remember it, not noticing the changes. If they do notice, they may be surprised. Presumably some are displeased and do not return. But others appreciate hearing about a feminine God in a Catholic church, including numerous clerics who said they joined the church for that very reason. Mother Linda said her best memory of Antioch was "the first time I walked into church" at Santa Fe "and heard 'Father-Mother God.'" Lian agreed. "The core for me here is that they completely embrace, embody, believe in the Divine Feminine," Lian said. "She is alive and well."[44]

Bishop Jorge Eagar, too, said the Divine Feminine was the distinction that drew him to ordination in Antioch. From long experience in Roman Catholic seminaries and Siddha Yoga practice, Jorge already associated Mary with the divine when, in 1998, he first attended Loretto for the Feast of the Assumption, a Marian holy day. Richard gave a homily in which he asked people about Mary in their lives and invited them to come to the altar and light candles. "It's like the floodgates opened and I realized . . . that I wanted to celebrate what he was celebrating," Jorge said. He became a priest and opened the Shrine of Holy Wisdom in Tempe, Arizona, which evolved into one of Antioch's most active communities. It is a "calling card" of the Shrine and Antioch "that we really honor and emphasize the Divine Feminine," Bishop Jorge said, who named the shrine for Wisdom, or Sophia, another traditional invocation of the Divine Feminine in Catholicism. "Whether people see it as the exaltation of Mother Mary, or it goes beyond that to see her as an incarnation of Holy Wisdom, or Sophia itself as an entity that progresses and emanates from the Trinity . . . whether you see [her] as Durga, Kali, or Mother Earth, Mother Nature, you know, there is that reverencing of the female and all that imagery engenders, that brings a sense of balance into our lives that we need desperately, in western societies especially."[45]

Across the ages, reverence for female deities rarely translates into leadership for actual women. In Antioch, however, honoring the Divine Feminine includes ordaining real live females. Many Antiochians are gratified to find the "sense of balance" of which Bishop Jorge spoke. In Santa Fe, Carol Calvert was ordained for parish work in 2006 and soon served alongside Richard and Daniel. When she tells people about Antioch, Mother Carol said, she first affirms that if "you're Catholic, it's going to look Catholic to you, it's going to look pretty normal." Then she adds, however, that if she were celebrating mass, one glance at the woman priest and "you'd know instantly it wasn't Roman Catholic!"[46]

Mother Carol works weekdays in an art gallery. She is also an accomplished singer and harpist who recorded an album of Celtic chants. Carol discovered the Church of Antioch on a winding path from childhood Congregationalism to Transcendental Meditation, Kriya Yoga, the I AM Fellowship, Religious Science, and Spiritual Science. But she remembered having a bit of "Catholic envy" since she was a child. When Carol started studying for the priesthood at Sophia, she was already ordained in the Eternal Life Church, a "church without walls" founded by Santa Fe healer Jay Victor Scherer. She was also initiated into the Order of Bards, Ovates, and Druids, a neo-Druidic group based in London. But, she said, "Had I known [the Church of Antioch] existed, I would probably not have gone to any of these other places." Sacraments plus metaphysics were precisely what she wanted. In Antioch she had what she considered "the whole package."[47]

Like everyone studying at Sophia, Carol started as an acolyte. "I was petrified," she said. "I used to lie awake worrying about ringing the bell on the altar . . . just that I would get this good sound. Cause if you miss, it's a bad thud. And Richard will shoot you a nasty look." Then one Sunday she spilled burning incense in Loretto and set off the fire alarm, which is why their landlord banned incense ever after. The resulting "shame" and "impostor syndrome" made her feel crazy, she said. Even after ordination, Carol said it was difficult not to compare herself to someone like Father Daniel, who before Antioch was a Roman priest in the Jesuit order for over a decade.[48]

One weekend Mother Carol had her "baptism by fire," she said, doing mass on her own when both Richard and Daniel were out of town. "And I loved it," she said. When I interviewed Carol in 2007, she was "still a baby priest" with "a lot to learn," she said. But she was finding her groove, with support from staff and parishioners. She described her manner on the altar as kind of "goofy," the "fool for Christ." But when I watched her say mass, she was as ceremonious as Richard and Daniel. She just smiled a lot more. When Richard's friend Ilene made the church promotional video, Mother Carol was the star, face aglow as her hands blessed the bread and wine. She could also be very solemn. At Good Friday mass at Loretto in May 2007, the reading of the gospel Passion story was traditionally split up into speaking parts. Carol was Jesus.[49]

THE CATHEDRAL BASILICA AROUND THE CORNER

With women priests and open communion in a Catholic sanctuary only a block away, personnel of the Roman Catholic Archdiocese of Santa Fe, centered at the Cathedral Basilica of St. Francis of Assisi, sometimes feel compelled to say something. First, according to Richard, he got an angry call from the leader of the cathedral's parish council, telling him not to take communion at the cathedral, since he is well known in the community for being not Roman. Richard tried to explain that he heartily believed in the Catholic doctrine of transubstantiation but, he said, the caller hung up. Of course Richard realizes that his belief in transubstantiation is not the issue. By Roman rules Richard is barred from communion in Roman churches.[50]

Then, in October 1994, the Franciscan priest who pastored the cathedral parish put a notice in the Sunday bulletin that Roman Catholics "may not attend" "Masses at Loretto Chapel" because they were not celebrated "ac-

cording to our Roman Catholic rite." Richard took action, writing Archbishop Michael Sheehan, the Franciscan provincial, and the archdiocesan
ecumenical officer that the wording "may not attend" is not worthy of the
post–Vatican II church. The ecumenical officer, whom Richard knew from
past positive interactions, wrote back, admitting that the bulletin language
"left something to be desired," but what the Franciscan pastor intended to
say was that Sunday mass at Antioch did not satisfy the holy day of obligation for Roman Catholics. Archbishop Sheehan himself wrote back a few
days later, saying much the same thing. Richard responded that if that had
been the wording, he would not have had any complaint.[51]

A conservative prelate, Sheehan was known for his ecumenical spirit and
good community relations. In a *National Catholic Reporter* article in 2009,
Sheehan called fellow conservative bishops "combative" and "hysterical" in
episodes such as their protest of the University of Notre Dame's speaking
invitation to President Barack Obama because the president was prochoice.
Instead, "I believe in collaboration," Sheehan said. "Consultation, collaboration, building bridges not burning them." This outreach extends to Richard, too, who meets "him a lot around town at various things," Richard said.
"We're always shaking [hands] and talking," and don't "get into debating
theology." Richard attends ecumenical events at the cathedral and Sheehan
always specially welcomed him. When Richard attended the elevation of the
cathedral to the status of basilica in October 2005, he and Sheehan chat-
ted outside afterward. Father Daniel Dangaran snapped a shot of the two
archbishops, both in black cassocks, purple sashes, and zuchettos, standing
under a big duck-shaped umbrella.[52]

But the friendliness is "on the surface," Richard said. Other actions by
Sheehan carry a less accepting message. In June 1997, Sheehan published an
article in *People of God*, the archdiocesan newspaper distributed monthly to
all ninety-two parishes, titled "What Is an Independent Catholic Church?"
Sheehan answered that "there is really no such thing as an Independent
Catholic Church." Real Catholicism was the Roman version alone. "There
may be incense and statues, collections and socials, but those are not the essential elements of the Catholic Church. If a church is not connected to the
Holy Father and the bishop appointed by him, then it is simply not Catholic

FIGURE 4.3 Church of Antioch archbishop Richard Gundrey (*left*) and Roman Catholic archbishop Michael Sheehan (*right*), Santa Fe, N.M., October 4, 2005. Courtesy of Daniel Dangaran.

at all." The article does not forbid Roman Catholics from attending independent Catholic churches, but instead says that it is not "proper" for "a good Catholic to attend" and that "Catholics are not to participate in the services of such churches any more than in any other non-Catholic church." Therefore "I urge our Catholics," Sheehan concluded, "to stay away from those groups and to stay with the Church that goes back to the Apostles and to Christ himself."[53]

Again Richard wrote to Sheehan, copying his ecumenical officer and others. Richard suggested that in the future Sheehan add "Roman" to each use of the word "Catholic" to clarify that there are multiple Catholic churches, only some of them in communion with Rome. He asked that Sheehan inform his people about the difference between sacramental legality versus sacramental validity, rather than imply that Rome views all non-Roman sacraments as invalid. Of course Loretto masses do not satisfy a Roman Catholic's Sunday mass obligation, Richard wrote, and the non-Roman status of Antioch is clearly advertised. But "to tell your people" that they should not attend or participate "is absurd." Do not attend "the Methodist Church, the Presbyterian Church, the Baptist Church"? Richard was incredulous. "Archbishop, you have blown away completely any thoughts of your church being ecumenical in any way," he concluded.[54]

Richard described the follow-up. Sheehan replied that adding "Roman" would confuse people even more, since the archdiocese included Eastern Catholics in communion with Rome. Richard said to me that he "didn't buy that argument at all." But he wrote to Sheehan that the situation called for education of the Roman faithful, not others ceasing to use the name "Catholic." Sheehan penned back that they would have to agree to disagree on the issue.

Subsequently Sheehan issued at least two other communications repeating the wording to which Richard had objected. In 2004 he issued a notice that was printed in all archdiocese Sunday bulletins. "In order to be Catholic, a church must be in union with the Holy Father, Successor of St. Peter and the local Bishop he sends," the notice reads. "The following churches are therefore not Catholic and Catholics should not attend them." Then listed are about eleven "not Catholic" churches, including the Church of Antioch and the local Society of St. Pius X chapel. Building on this list, the archdiocese later added to its website a document titled "Churches: Who's Who?" In several sections, it lists thirteen Eastern churches in communion with Rome and fourteen Protestant churches in formal ecumenical dialogue. But by far the longest section is a list of "churches that call themselves 'Catholic' but not in union with Rome." Over eighty groups across North America are included. Both the "Who's Who" list and a slightly edited version of Sheehan's bulletin message, now labeled "Schismatic Churches: Albuquerque," are available with one click from the main page of the archdiocesan website.[55]

Then, in 2006, Sheehan wrote what Richard considered another highly offensive editorial in *People of God*. Headlined "Don't Be Fooled!," the article warned that some local churches "perhaps have the 'bells, smells and pretty vestments' but are certainly not Catholic." Catholic "means universal," which Sheehan glossed as "throughout the world." But "churches such as the ones that I have mentioned are not universal at all," he continued. "They have a presence here and there and are very small in number indicating they are not universal and that the Holy Spirit is not with them." In truth, those "who protest the teachings of the Church [should] have the honesty to call themselves Protestant," Sheehan wrote. Finally, readers should not "be surprised by the churches to the left and to the right of the true Catholic Church as the scriptures promised that there would be divisions among Christ's followers," he said. "Be concerned, however, for your own eternal salvation. . . . Only the Catholic Church has the fullness of the means of salvation."[56]

These are not the formulations of Sheehan alone, of course. The "fullness of the means of salvation" is a quotation from the Vatican II document *Unitatis redintegratio*, which is repeated in the Roman catechism (1997) and in the Congregation for the Doctrine of the Faith's *Dominus Iesus* (2000), which adds that those outside Rome are "in a gravely deficient situation in comparison with those who, in the church, have the fullness of the means of salvation." Richard was not angry about that—he knows Roman ecclesiology and does not begrudge Sheehan teaching it. But he considers Sheehan's characterization of the scope of Catholicism to be disinformation, even by Rome's standards. "I am very confused by why he keeps information like this going out to the public," Richard wrote on the Antioch listserv. Richard also wondered online if he himself was being "hypocritical," participating in "cordial . . . conversation" at public events that might signify a level of camaraderie "that does not exist." "Pray for me and my judgments," Richard wrote. Fellow Antiochians wrote back, encouraging Richard to continue with public and private cordiality regardless of Sheehan's actions.[57]

Truly it would be out of character for Richard to do anything else. Sheehan's editorial and "Who's Who" list personally "dishearten" him. So do "TOO MANY" instances in which other Antioch clergy find themselves similarly enmeshed in conflict with local Roman authorities, sometimes very publicly. They are not the only US independents in that position. In 2014, Bishop Trujillo just down the road in Albuquerque had a similar exchange of letters with Sheehan and published them on his website. Still, US independents have it pretty good, never dealing with the serious Roman or government persecution faced by independents in other times and places—

the Philippines, Poland, Brazil. So Richard always exhorts leaders to take the high road. "Stay away from the ego attitude of clericalism," he said. If independent Catholic clerics would all check "egos at the door," others "will see who and what we are eventually." They should not "badmouth" anyone, "especially the Roman Catholic church," Richard said. "I get too much business from them!"[58]

It is a joke with an element of truth. As much as any independent cleric, Richard appreciates the rare moments when their little movement seems to get an edge on the powerful Roman church, like David besting Goliath. Once he told me with suppressed glee that he would soon do a wedding in a Roman Catholic sanctuary, usually not allowed for anyone but priests in communion with Rome. But this particular sanctuary is St. Francis on Nambé Pueblo, whose building is owned by the tribal government, not the Archdiocese of Santa Fe. A Native couple requested Richard for the ceremony and the reservation majordomo got approval from tribal leaders. The majordomo also duly informed Archbishop Sheehan, whose office did not approve. But "they couldn't do anything about it," Richard said.[59]

A "POWERFUL HEALING"

After the Eucharist and marriage, the sacrament most frequently performed by Richard and other Antioch clergy is Anointing of the Sick. For them, the sacrament encompasses dozens of modes of healing. The "Wednesday Night Prayer and Healing Service" at Richard's home was advertised weekly in the Sunday bulletin. "Everyone is welcome to attend." Church members brought food, so afterward there was a shared meal and social hour in Richard's living room. Someone might give a presentation, like when Deacon Doug Walker showed his esoteric paintings of goddesses or when local Jewish Renewal rabbi Andy Gold shared his interpretations of some *midrashim*.[60]

Before the healing service, Richard would arrange twenty chairs in the chapel, two rows facing each other. Around six o'clock, people started to take their seats. At half past the hour, Richard, Dan, and Carol processed in. The service moved through censing, intercessory prayer, and laying on of hands. The threesome of Richard, Dan, and Carol moved up and down the two rows. At each chair, they invoked the healing power of "God the Father, God the Mother, God the Son, and God the Holy Spirit," laid six hands on the person's body, and anointed her forehead with oil. After the service everyone adjourned to the living room for the potluck. By this point sometimes Richard fell asleep. The last cars pulled out of the little parking lot at around half past nine.[61]

The healing services were a lot of work for Richard. Every Wednesday morning he cleaned his whole "bachelor pad," as he called it, and fielded calls from people who wanted to drop off their potluck dishes early. He set up the chapel, arranged tables in the kitchen, and put out tea and coffee supplies. There is no sugar in the house—Richard is borderline diabetic, so all he has for sweetener is stevia. Taking meals mostly at Furr's Family Dining or Bagelmania, he actually doesn't keep much in the kitchen at all. One day he showed me his essentials: sprouted-barley bread for toast, fresh fruits and nuts for snacks. His beverage is lemonade that he makes from lemons, stevia, and water. He used this lemonade instead of milk, he said, on his high-fiber cereal. Then Richard did some dance moves around the kitchen, grinned, and struck a flexing pose like a body-builder. I laughed. He was indeed in great shape. But the church required so much time. Richard also ironed all his own altar linens on Saturdays and set up for Sunday Mass at Loretto starting at six in the morning. Once I asked him how he avoided depletion, especially in healing. He said he let "the Christ Consciousness energy" move through him, rather than expending personal effort. But Richard did admit that he was "addicted" to work. In the next few years, he would undergo a hernia operation and a heart operation, and in general become exhausted.[62]

Still, he continually did healings, first as a Religious Science minister and now as a Catholic archbishop. Occasionally Richard anointed during Sunday mass, after communion. At these times he would pause and announce, "I move to do a spiritual healing," and then leave the altar and walk to the person or group who he discerned could use some holy oil. Lian, her sister, and her nieces found themselves the recipients of anointing on that day the sister took communion at Loretto. Another time Richard walked to lay hands on Deacon Liza Molina and Archbishop Dexter Woods, both sitting at the back of a Convocation mass in wheelchairs.[63]

I heard of two people who attributed to Richard miracles of physical healing. One was a complete stranger. In November 2003, the Loretto business office received a letter from Barbara Jean B. of Indiana, who had attended Antioch's mass while on vacation. "I have felt compel[l]ed to write for some time to share with you a Miracle which I had when my husband and I were there March 2002," she wrote. She knew the Loretto story from the television movie about its mysterious staircase, which she watched "repeatedly," she wrote. "An Arch Bish[o]p was there that day. . . . We were so impressed." During the service, the archbishop greeted everyone. "After shaking my hand, he came back to me again"—and here Barbara Jean started to write in all capital letters—"and said, 'I'm real glad that you are here today.' 'Me too,' I said. . . . He blessed me, placed a kiss on each cheek and placed his hand on my forehead and said, 'Whatever is troubling you, just let it out!'" Barbara Jean then gave some background. "He had no idea I had been told I had several places with cancer and I wanted to go [to Loretto] before I had surgery." Her doctor told her surgery was the only option, but go "have a good time." When she got home, she "got up and looked in the mirror and the cancer was gone and has not returned," Barbara Jean wrote. "I even went to another specialist and it is gone!! Praise God!" She concluded that "there is a strong powerful healing there" and enclosed a check made out to Loretto. The business manager sent Barbara Jean's letter along to Richard, with a note and all funds from the check. "We felt the money should come on to the Church of Antioch," he wrote. I found out about this event when looking through Richard's binders of important documents, where he kept the letter.[64]

The other testimony came from Antioch church member Belinda Wong, employed as a scientist at US government research labs at Los Alamos. Belinda said her cancer of the eye disappeared a week after she was baptized by Richard. Richard himself informed me that Belinda was going around saying the baptism healed her, but he was more interested in her ongoing conversion to Catholicism, for example, her making the annual Good

Friday pilgrimage to the shrine at Chimayó. To Richard and to many Antioch clergy, it is just a matter of course that sacraments occasionally result in physical cures. Healing of some sort is a sure thing whenever hands meet bodies and holy oil touches skin with intentions to attune, salve, and cure. Clerics use versions of the Catholic rite of the Anointing of the Sick, but also other methods—simple chrismation, massage therapy, Reiki, chiropracty, crystal work, angel intercession, and flower essence healing. Father Joshua of Sedona, Arizona, does something called Philippine psychic surgery, a folk method with historical links to US spiritualism as well as Filipino shamanism and Catholicism.[65]

Antioch clerics' healing practices also extend to visiting hospitals, nursing homes, and prisons. Bishop Diana Phipps works as an operating room nurse and said her job was the better part of her ministry. "I listen to people," Bishop Diana said. "I'm being a person and I'm just sharing with them. That's a sacrament." Dozens of others have full-time jobs as nurses, social workers, home health aides, hospital chaplains, hospice workers, or counselors for "conscious dying." Many contexts of Antioch clerics' healing work are Roman Catholic institutions. Several Antioch clergy work in spiritual care divisions of Roman Catholic health care systems.[66]

Finally, several independent Catholic clergy, including in Antioch, were at the forefront of the "survivors movement," as early groups of clergy sexual abuse survivors called it. A decade before the *Boston Globe* investigations brought Roman Catholic clerical sex abuse and episcopal cover-up to national attention, Father Tom Economus of the Independent Catholic Church founded Survivors of Clergy Abuse Linkup, for a while the leading advocacy group on the issue. Father Jay Nelson of the Church of Antioch joined Father Tom and edited Linkup's newsletter for years; both worked with Roman Catholics, including priests, as part of Linkup. Focused on healing, communication, and activism, Linkup tried to raise awareness and "really made a difference to victims and survivors," said Father Jay. And because Richard supported Jay's healing ministry, Richard ran a seminar in Santa Fe on pedophilia "at a time when the Romans were still denying there was any such thing amid their ranks," Jay recalled.[67]

A THEOLOGY OF BALANCE

The far-flung and diverse church required Richard's constant attention. Sometimes he clarified guidelines, as when he and Meri decided goddess masses were a no-go. Other times he gave free rein for experiments. Father Jack Sweeley was already approved for celebrating mass online when he asked Richard if he could mail consecrated communion hosts to his congregants. Richard "almost fell out of his chair, I think," Father Jack recalled. But "he said, 'Well, write it up.' Which is his response." So Father Jack wrote up a theological justification and Richard took it to the bishops. Some liked the idea. Others worried that hosts would be desecrated. Richard's "bottom line was, 'Try it for six months and see if it works. And I'll support you.'" "So I did," Jack said. "And I got no takers." But Jack appreciated being able to "call him on the phone, anytime I want, day or night, including Sundays because he's always working, and say, 'Richard, hey, let me run this by you.' He'll say, 'Okay, Jack, go ahead.'"[68]

Richard did not always give final permission, but clerics said he at least listened. All religious leaders make choices on a continuum between stasis and change. But in independent Catholicism, there is "great freedom to create new structures [or] a new synthesis of inherited elements," as bishop-scholar John Plummer put it. Not interested in systematic theology, Richard nevertheless operated with what I would call a practical theology of balance. "I always try to go for BALANCE," he wrote on the church listserv in 2008. "We are a Christian Catholic Church centered on the teachings of Jesus the Christ but not limited to those teachings. That is our center but we are not STUCK there. We WANT to stretch and grow and change as the consciousness of our church grows." At the same time, a river's strength comes partly from its banks, and he aimed not to "get so loose that the water runs all over the mountain with no strength or power," he wrote. In conclusion, Richard wrote, "We simply must find the balance that works NOW. That balance may change in the future."[69]

Deciding when to brave the rapids and when to bank the boat risked capsizing at every turn. Sometimes Richard expressed himself strongly. He had firm opinions about ordination liturgies and wanted them done quite traditionally. This was partly so his priests might be accepted as widely as possible, but also partly because Richard loved high-church ceremony. Deacon Jeff Genung remembered calling Richard from his Austin home for a preordination conversation and broaching the subject of a simpler ritual. Richard was not having it. He "was . . . going down the list of the things we need, you know," Deacon Jeff said. "'Do you have a chasuble?' And I said, 'No, I don't.' And I said to him, 'Do we really need that?' And he scolded me. He says, 'Hey, man!' He says, 'We are Catholics! We are not a Protestant church here!'" Other seminarians knew they were doing things Richard "really would have a fit" about, for example, consecrating the Eucharist before they were ordained. So they just didn't tell him.[70]

Though a stickler on some things, Richard mostly developed soft standards that let people figure out on their own if Antioch was right for them. For example, Richard preferred to understand Jesus more as a cosmic principle than a historical person from Nazareth. When he talked about "seeing the Christ in everyone," as he often said, it was not "Jesus-the-bearded-man in everyone, but the consciousness that is God, the Holy Spirit." When Jesus at the Last Supper "opened himself to becoming Christ," as Richard put it in his Eucharistic prayer, the "Holy Cosmic Christ [was] spiraling through him. Get that concept? Not Jesus standing there." But, Richard continued, that was just his own take. Other Antiochians had different Christologies. "Some people look at Jesus as God. Some people don't," he said. "I don't debate with people on those issues. Jesus the Christ is to you who Jesus the Christ is to you."[71]

This sort of statement is par for the course in a church that champions "freedom" and requires "no dogma." But there are ironies. For one thing, Antioch inherits from historic Catholicism a gigantic patrimony, so taken for granted that it rarely enters the realm of assent or refusal. In particular, as I suggest, succession, sacraments, saints including Mary, and the word "Catholic" itself make up a core of continuity between big-body and independent Catholicism. Much is predecided in that foursome, including the authority of Richard and the other bishops.

And of course all principles, even the principle of freedom, imply constraint. The Santa Fe church "Statement of Principles," given in the Order of Service, affirms "the freedom of each person in matters of belief." The church-wide "Our Spiritual Principles," written by Herman and posted on the website for years, affirms "an individual's right to complete freedom of thought, interpretation, conscience, and inquiry in all matters of our faith and belief." Both limit, then, the "freedom" of the person who would dare call for more boundaries and standards. Indeed, when Father Jay Nelson wished aloud for a standardized Antioch theology of the Trinity, Richard wrote him on the listserv that the principle of freedom constrained the setting of standards. "With our general mind set of freedom of choice and interpretation I can tell you that many of our people if required to [subscribe to a particular theology] would be gone in a New York Minute because of a feeling of LACK of freedom." Later, Richard weighed in on a discussion in which some participants were advocating adopting a Roman norm. "Our church would blow up in the middle of the night if we were to impose that type of stuff on our people."[72]

Still, "freedom" and "no dogma" are accurate characterizations, if they mean that Antioch leaders consider no doctrine beyond question, require none for good standing, and encourage spiritual investigation beyond traditional Catholicism. For those who find themselves "aligned with" Antioch, as Richard often puts it, this spiritual freedom is consistently cited as the best thing about the church. There is "freedom to search for your own spiritual guidance and direction," said Mother Sara Yonce in Montgomery, Texas, "whether it's a medicine wheel in Native American spirituality or the eastern teachings." Deacon Roberto Foss in Los Angeles said the church is "not perfect, because it's a church," but "what it stands for is freedom. And that's what all of us wanted . . . freedom to continue our journey, but still stay in the sacramental world."[73]

Almost as often as Antiochians say freedom is the best church characteristic, however, they also say it is the worst. "Many times the greatest strength can be the greatest weakness," Deacon Jeff Genung said. "Whether we want to embrace it or not," seminarian Lian Reed said, "there is strength in dogma." Seeker-types like "no dogma," she continued, but others could rightly ask, "What's right and wrong? You guys don't even agree as to what is right and wrong."[74]

And how does one describe such a free Catholicism to outsiders? In her hospital chaplaincy, Mother Linda Rounds-Nichols finds it challenging "to explain to people . . . what you stand for if you don't have any dogma." One night she met a family at the hospital in the midst of a tragic situation and "the first question was, 'What denomination are you?'" she recalled. "Well, I mean, OK. . . . This is not the place for an in-depth discussion explaining independent Catholicism." Mother Linda said she responded, "I'm here to serve everyone. The more important question is, 'What denomination are you?'" That worked, she said. "But if it hadn't worked, it would have been like, your loved one is in there dying and I'm going to explain independent Catholicism? This is not OK."[75]

Others fear losing touch with historic Catholicism, despite continuities. "No dogma" is "the perfect position for a postmodern church to take," said Deacon Roberto, but "I get a little afraid for the future" when people are overly revisionist. "And so there's people who want to leave the sacraments behind and move on to the dolphins and space aliens," he said. "And I'm not sure I see myself in that church." Still, initiated as a Mayan priest and studying for Catholic ordination, Roberto saw the potential hypocrisy of his concern. He would not appreciate anyone "put[ting] the brakes on my Mayan fusion," he said. "So if I'm going to say that I want that space, I [have to] give other people that space."[76]

Roberto and others were also concerned that sacramental power might be lost in messing with liturgies. Several priests, feminists though they were, hewed to the traditional masculine language of the mass to give the Holy Spirit time to change it for the whole of Catholicism, rather than take it upon themselves. "I was sticking with 'Blessed is He,'" Father Ted Feldmann said of lines in his mass. "I do not think it should say 'Blessed are we.' It's a very ancient text. . . . It's not up to every stinking priest to rewrite everything." Bishop Mark Newman too said he is cautious about "playing fast and loose" with liturgy, since it might well "undercut the energy, . . . undermine the efficacy." In which case "freedom," he said, just amounts to "shooting ourselves in the foot."[77]

Finally, Antiochians worried that "no dogma" could camouflage unacknowledged dogma. Seminarian Becky Taylor said she realized this when she was reading about Mormonism for Sophia studies and reacted with skepticism to Latter-day Saints' self-description as Christians. She checked herself. Did she, an open-minded, freedom-loving independent Catholic, harbor the same type of prejudice for which she criticized others? "I had never thought of it," Becky said. "I never thought [that] the 'no dogma' principle [would be] words that we would ever have to eat."[78]

A number of Antiochians are less reflective than Becky. Here and there and without heed they spout prejudices against megachurches, fundamentalists, prosperity preachers, the Roman hierarchy, or anything conservative. A few mutter bigotries about Islam and Pentecostalism, as well as fellow independent Catholics they consider "zooey." They talk about people whose faiths involve "killing chickens" or "sacrificing goats" as if they are clearly crazy. Very "other" themselves, Antiochians are still capable of otherizing other religions. Then Deacon Roberto the Mayan priest or Bishop Jorge the former Siddha Yoga devotee jumps in to caution about condemning possession or *pujas*. How exactly, they challenge their colleagues, is the mysticism of the sacraments or the sacrifice of the mass so different?[79]

Amid lively and sometimes tense discussions, Antiochians seem to appreciate that church harmony requires everyone to tolerate an unusually broad definition of Catholicism. They also appreciate Richard's hard work to keep the balance. He was "in the huge position of having to oversee this entire church, and remain . . . neutral," Mother Carol Calvert said. "I don't know how he does it." Making hard decisions as patriarch, Richard said he relied on conscience. He prayed, consulted various sources, and talked to fellow bishops, but then acted on conscience. Usually he called his decisions "opinions." Sometimes he even described them as "hang-ups." This Catholic patriarch, then, claims nothing like infallibility. Still, Richard holds "opinion" in high regard. He "walks that talk," said seminarian Jack Pischner of Santa Cruz, California. "He says, 'This is my opinion. Your opinion's equally valid.'" Yet, having decided something, he is "not wishy-washy," seminarian Lian said. "He never wavers."[80]

"WATER SEEKS ITS OWN LEVEL"

Archbishop Richard faced some of his toughest decisions in his role as head of Sophia Divinity School. But there, too, "water seeks its own level," he said.

The doors of the virtual seminary are wide open. Young, old, female, male, straight, and LGBTQ seminarians of Antioch are enrolled in this, the oldest continuously operating independent Catholic school in the United States. Seminarians of other jurisdictions can study there, too, with the permission of their bishops. Sophia is not accredited, since accreditation requires satisfying criteria of faculty, infrastructure, and curriculum that Antioch cannot afford. Most enrollees arrive with an accredited bachelor of arts degree, though it is not required. They appreciate Sophia's flexible and economical programs.[81]

Rare exclusions on the part of Richard and Sophia advisors have to do with qualifications of character more than education. Vetting character is part of the application process, as much as a tiny nonprofit distance-learning school can manage. All inquirers—between seventy-five and a hundred annually—receive by mail the Sophia information packet. Then a "great SELF SELECTING process eliminate(s) MANY from applying," Richard said. If inquirers go forward, Antioch asks for disclosure of mental health history and sixty dollars for a criminal background check.[82]

Like many religious groups, Antioch found out the hard way that the criminal background check is necessary. But if anything turned up, Richard said, he still used his judgment. Domestic violence, sex abuse? No way. Bad checks, speeding tickets? It depends. Even felony imprisonment is not absolutely an impediment. One Antioch deacon was O. C. Fero, who is serving a life sentence for murder at a prison outside Santa Fe. He was referred to Sophia by beloved Antioch priest Dennis Bryan, now deceased, who was Fero's prison chaplain. After careful vetting, Fero seemed to Richard just another person whose genuine vocation could not find acceptance in mainstream Catholicism. Richard ordained Fero despite media scrutiny and public criticism. "This is not a [w]hite bread world," he wrote about it later.[83]

Mostly, however, Richard's broad acceptance pertained to people's educational histories. On the one side were folks with degrees from Ivy League universities, Roman Catholic seminaries, or prominent divinity schools. On the other side were those whose formal education ended with a high school diploma or GED. "My attitude as the guy who sets the policy when I'm in the chair," Richard said, "is that no one should be denied the opportunity to study based upon education, age, anything." Aptitude became clear over time. "What really happens is that if they don't have the educational thing to read the books and [write] the reports, they wash themselves out," Richard said. "I would never say, 'Oh, you don't have a bachelor's degree, you can't start.' You see? . . . I feel like it's all about the Holy Spirit, not about your PhD," Richard said. "It's about the essence and the energy of who you are." Richard was happy about all the highly educated people increasingly attracted to Antioch. But he was also proud that "people with very little education . . . are doing wonderful work in our church."[84]

"DAILY WORKING FOR A LIVING"

Archbishop Richard's theology of balance fit well with the worker-priests of Antioch, since factually he had limited leverage with priests he did not pay. The worker-priest structure is also known as the "tentmaker" model, so called after the apostle Paul, who made and sold tents to avoid encumbering new congregations with supporting him. According to scholar J. Gordon Melton, the independent Catholic adoption of this model starts with English bishop Arnold Harris Mathew in 1908, who faced "demands of building a church in a relatively short time, and lack[ed] the resources to pay full-time clergy." After that, Melton writes, independent bishops repeatedly "elevated Mathew's expedient program into a norm."[85]

But even before Mathew, Vilatte and other independents procured support apart from church stipends. And while independent tentmaking is surely expedient, it is also continuous with Catholic reform concerns. The famous Irish Jesuit reformer George Tyrrell (a friend of Arnold Harris Mathew), for example, advocated decoupling the priesthood from financial security as a way to combat clericalism and spur change. "Cut off the pecuniary advantage, and you cut off the rest of sacerdotalism," Tyrrell writes, "and all the doctrinal and other corruption it entails." In 1941, the famous French worker-priest movement began as part of the Catholic Revival, but fell out of favor with the Vatican as it experimented with socialism and clerical marriage. In the twenty-first century, Antioch leaders and other independents hope to grow the worker-priest tradition as it lies fallow in the big bodies.[86]

Richard did not require worker-priests to live their priesthood in any particular way. He did not mandate that they recite the hours, say Mass, or celebrate the other sacraments—requirements for some big-body priests—much less start a parish. But he did encourage regular sacramental service. "Get in the habit of saying Mass . . . if you want to help the planet," Richard told the assembly at Convocation in 2006. "You're adding to the consciousness of the world." Many Antioch priests did keep mass schedules with congregations large and small. At the populous end were Richard in Santa Fe and Jorge in Phoenix. At the quiet end were Mother Sara Yonce in Montgomery, Texas, and others who did solo masses—forbidden in some Catholic contexts but completely accepted in Antioch. Those who say masses alone usually add that they are never really alone, since angels and saints accompany them. "I've always believed there's invisible guests there, . . . so I never felt bad [if] I didn't have actual people," said Mother Sara. "The energy, oh, is just beautiful." Solo masses "bring energy down," she said, and "out into the world."[87]

Most Antioch clerics like the worker-priest model not only for its reform of the economic structure of Catholicism, but also for its freedom. Even if they don't like it, they know it comes with the territory of independent churches—according to my survey, only 2 percent of independent priests work full-time in ministry. Still, getting paid little or nothing for the work they consider most important is not always their ideal. Some fret about doing so much uncompensated labor. Others lament that nine-to-five jobs keep them from doing ministry as often as desired. They are police officers, social workers, massage therapists, music teachers, office managers, electrical engineers, attorneys, artists, and nurses. Yes, sometimes those jobs *are* their ministries, but some want to do more explicit ministry, too. Some train to become full-time chaplains as a way to merge ministry and income. Others, like Richard, retire to spend time on priestly work.[88]

Outside Antioch, a few independent churches attempt to pay priests as full-time pastors of congregations, for instance, the Ecumenical Catholic Communion. That means that priests are required to have accredited seminary degrees and work in parishes big enough to support a full-time salaried employee. With salaries, you have clergy with recognized credentials and compensated labor, including health insurance and retirement plans. Such clergy have more time to devote to ministry. On the other hand, it is extremely difficult to pay salaries outside a big connectional church system. And with salaries comes beholdenness to bishops and parish boards.

In contrast, operating with unpaid priests, independent Catholics can survive and do exactly as they wish on very little money. The whole setup of "gypsy churches" with "stealth" priests even has environmental benefits, some said. "We discourage building churches," Bishop Diana Dale told a reporter, explaining that her Apostolic Catholic Orthodox Church always rents existing churches. "We do not want to waste money paving new parking lots." Independent polity can also function to purify intention. With no ties to property or livelihood, no incentive of 401(k)s, worker-priests decide if it is enough payment to "get back spiritually tenfold in returned love and appreciation," as Richard put it. Antioch laity did seem to appreciate their worker-priest leaders. To them it means priests "do this because they love it," said Santa Fe parishioner Dick Lemieux. He identified with them more, too. "Being in the workforce brings them closer to us people."[89]

But worker-priests function with what many outsiders consider alarming levels of unaccountability. They cannot do as much ministry. And for what they can do, they are not only not paid, but often shell out their own money. Richard praised the worker-priests of Antioch as often as he could. "I am amazed," he wrote on the listserv, "at how many of our clergy are daily working for a living AND trying to run a ministry. It ain't easy."[90]

SIMON'S SHADOW

Trying to run a ministry without a salary isn't easy. It also makes independent Catholic priests a target for charges of simony, a serious sin in Catholic tradition. Named for the Book of Acts figure Simon Magus, who is reprimanded for trying to buy spiritual power, simony refers to selling a sacrament for money. Simony occurs, as Richard put it in a note to the church, "when a Cardinal or Bishop says, 'For $1,000 I will ordain you to be a priest or Bishop' without any training or authorization from a church or seminary or governing body . . . 'and if you do not pay me I will not do it.'"[91]

Richard added that the practice is "very prevalent in the past history of the church." It is of course especially prevalent whenever the servants of God deal with financial insecurity. Herman Spruit himself is occasionally named among simoniacs in US independent Catholicism. It is hard to assess these accusations without evidence other than hearsay. But as we have seen, Herman suffered financial vulnerabilities, both material and emotional. He might very well have told potential ordinands that he and Meri could not travel to do a ceremony unless their costs were covered. Though that was true, it surely would come close to making a sacrament conditional upon payment. In any case, many independent bishops feel an especial burden to steer a clear financial course. "We must get away from renegade bishops making priests or bishops of their friends, for a fee or even for nothing," he wrote to fellow bishops. "We must each have our own integrity to dispense Holy Orders to really qualified people and get rid of simony." Richard handled Church Central's finances with sparkling transparency and encouraged Antioch clerics to do likewise.[92]

The western church as a whole is widely regarded to have fixed its simony problem with the Gregorian reforms of the eleventh century. But the line between simony and support remains blurry, since customary offerings for baptisms, weddings, and memorial masses remain permissible, described as supporting the priest rather than paying for a sacrament. And payment is required of Catholics in other ways. In the United States, Roman sacraments cost the time and money associated with obligatory preparation classes. It is another reason that millions of Roman Catholics receive sacraments at the hands of independents. Independents are cheaper.

This situation simmers between Roman dioceses and independent churches and sometimes boils over. As reported by the *Los Angeles Times*, in 2009 popular Roman Catholic pastor Raymundo Figueroa of Baja, Mexico, was accused of simony by Roman bishops in southern California. Father Figueroa had been crossing the border and contracting with independent priests to perform sacraments in people's homes, collecting cash "donations" that were then used, Robin Hood–style, for parish revitalization and social work in Baja. Roman prelates in southern California charged that Figueroa targeted poor Latino-Americans who could ill afford to help

Bajans. Figueroa responded that his US clients would rather donate to him than take time off from work to transport kids to two years' worth of First Communion classes. Figueroa was later suspended by the Vatican, but continued to serve his Rosarito Beach parish anyway.[93]

It is a story once again about surprising collaboration—in this case a Roman priest hiring independent priests to do sacraments for Roman Catholics and eventually going independent himself. It is also a story about the fuzzy lines that define simony. As Richard told his church, there were "so many DIFFERENT factors involved in money given to churches and priests . . . that it is hard to lay out rules on this matter." But in the final analysis, "what the Roman Catholic Church does . . . is none of our business." As for Antioch, Richard's opinion is that it is "OK to mention a donation or honorarium for sacramental services performed," especially weddings and baptisms, "as long as you do not refuse to do the service if they do not pay you something. These sacraments ARE freely given as Jesus the Christ said." In the case of funerals, Richard said he personally never mentions money at all. And if any promised donation does not come through, so be it. "Believe me, I have done many weddings without any honorarium as well as several bad checks," he wrote. "I NEVER go after them. I let it be." I also met Antioch clergy who do not ask for donations at all. Some even return donations when they show up—this on the example of the Orthodox saints known as the "Holy Unmercenaries," who healed sick people and always refused payment.[94]

ELECTED BISHOPS AND THE FUTURE OF ANTIOCH

While Richard often followed in Herman's footsteps, Richard's ideas about future structure departed from the founder's path. He thought the church should become more democratic. Herman had set up a corporation sole and tapped Meri as successor, and Richard respected the rationale, namely, wanting to avoid ending up in Hampton's situation. "Our Herman Spruit did not want to have any possibility of that happening to our Church of Antioch," Richard explained on the listserv. But, he added, "legally we can change anything through due process." For the time being, that meant he as sole could change anything. Richard voluntarily consulted with "people on ALL levels of our church," he wrote, "before I drop the AX." But he wanted consultation baked into the cake, so to speak.[95]

So Richard and consultants developed a new leadership protocol. When Richard retired, they decided, he would appoint one bishop to lead for an interim period, during which she or he would convene the council of bishops to vote for a new presiding bishop, whose term would be limited to five years. The election and the term limit were new. What did not change— though it was discussed—was church structure as a corporation sole. During each five-year stint, according to the plan, whoever was presiding bishop would also serve as legal sole. Richard had the papers drawn up accordingly. "We needed Herman to do what he did for that time period, just like with anything," he said. "But things have moved along since then."[96]

Richard thought about Antioch's future a lot. He had a brain for business, so this included Antioch's material future. First and foremost, the church archives should move out of his garage. When Mother Linda, Father Spencer, and Father Jack organized the archives and I used them for research, the activities only underlined how important climate-controlled storage and lack of mice would become in the future. For years Richard tried to buy the property of his next-door neighbor on Cordova Road. But the guy would not sell. Richard then posted an open letter on the church website, asking for the donation of a house to use as permanent archives. No offers. Finally Richard simply used $125,000 of his own money to pay a contractor to build a home addition. He would put the archives there, at least for the time being.[97]

With that decided, Richard turned his thoughts to hopes of accumulating some land and buildings. Should he donate his Cordova Road property to his children and grandchildren, or to the Santa Fe parish? The parish might have more use. Richard's ultimate dream, of course, was somehow to buy Loretto Chapel itself. Then Antioch would permanently dwell in one of the most beautiful little cathedrals in the world, right in the heart of the City of Faith.[98]

"ALWAYS A RUCKUS"

Richard tilted for balance. But with such diverse membership, geographic spread, and loose structure, imbalance constantly threatened. Richard shed tears during baptisms and weddings because the sacraments moved him. But he also wept because the Church of Antioch had its share of issues and personalities. It made administration a headache.

Serious conflicts happened mostly behind the scenes. But in muted form Antiochians' arguments showed up on the listserv and illumined persistent church tensions. They argued about if or how to grow, to what extent Catholic tradition was Roman tradition, whether priests should be required to say mass, how much priests could remix Catholicism, how much woo-woo was too woo-woo, whether the Divine Feminine was an orthodox concept, whether women in Antioch were treated equally, whether Christianity mandated voting Democrat, the existence of evil, the line between creating "safe space" and honoring free speech, how "formational" it is to read things you disagree with, and how difficult it is to use the delete key. As with all email communication, people often wrote less tactfully than they would speak in person. Sometimes a post went ad hominem or an entire thread turned poisonous. As list moderator, Richard wished he had been patriarch before the age of electronic media. "The email list has given me a fit," he told me. There is "always a ruckus."[99]

Sometimes Richard used humor to deflect tension. Once Father Jack posted a strongly worded statement against prayer at public events, only to recall that Richard prayed before legislative sessions of the New Mexico state government. Jack posted again to say that was all right with him. Richard wrote back, "Thanks, Jack. I thought for a moment you did not love me anymore." When there was a tense discussion of the Trinity, Richard posted that the "three in one concept was thunk up by a bunch of men in a back room smoking cigars." He added, "joke of course." In 2006, when an argument about the Divine Feminine went on for two months, Richard finally posted, "You folks are REALLY making me work." At the Convocation in 2007, he gently suggested that the assembled could try a little harder to work out problems among themselves, rather than call and email Church Central "all day, every day," he said. "I'm here and dedicated and I haven't gotten a raise in a long time."[100]

The listserv was crucial for communication, given a far-flung church. "Sharing individual ideas and stories about ourselves and our families" strengthened church bonds. Indeed, these sharings, plus prayer requests and church announcements, made up the vast majority of posts. But given the "ruckus," there had to be guidelines. Richard made a rule that people could not post overtly political items—"the Democrats VS the Republicans, this candidate is better than that candidate," he wrote. The rule prompted an outcry that the social gospel was inherently political. Richard made another rule not to post material that was ostensibly "sex-positive" but potentially offensive. Listserv members cried censorship. Finally Richard reminded people they could be taken off the list if they wanted. "I can tell you that every time there is a major brewhaaww type of upsetting discussion on this list PEOPLE ASK TO BE REMOVED." Richard's words calmed troubled waters—at least until the next "major brewhaaww." "Richard is so adamant that nothing can be on the list that sort of ruffles anybody's feathers," said Father Jack Sweeley, who was definitely a prime "ruffler." "Intuitively he knows that it would be very easy for people to get going at each other."[101]

In the spring of 2007, a fracas started over conflicting views on gun control. After it settled down, Richard wrote that for the first time, no one asked to be taken off the list. "I guess we are getting used to each other," he wrote. But the cautious optimism did not last. Later that year, discord over the Divine Feminine burst forth again. One side argued it was not a Christian concept and should not be invoked within Antioch. The other side called that sexist and yet another sign that Antioch had not rid itself of society's diffuse misogyny. Mediators pled to keep perspective: it was not required to believe in the Divine Feminine, but in a church where half the bishops were women, at least one could point to progress. But the posts got ugly. Then they got so bad that Richard intervened. "PEACE, PEACE." Richard apologized to everyone for his leadership, which had not prevented the circumstances and feelings that led to such a row.[102]

Still, Richard could only do so much. The conflict was so painful. The argument about the Divine Feminine and several others permanently alienated handfuls of Antiochians. Two bishops who had already voiced other criticisms departed Antioch and formed a new jurisdiction. Richard said it was ultimately "for the best." He did not fetishize institutional unity. But he much preferred Antioch to come together rather than fly apart. "Peace," he signed off every letter and post.[103]

The peace balanced so carefully by Richard was a fragile one, as Father Jack had said. Others echoed that. Deacon Roberto had "a slight sense of foreboding," he said, "about, 'can this thing really hold together?'" There are so many diverse perspectives. "If we don't have a metanarrative, how are we going to stay together in one group?" Seminarian Jack Pischner predicted that the future of Antioch would involve "a lot of suffering . . . as part of the growth process." In an interview in 2007, Father Jack again put it even more strongly. "There's going to be a schism," he said. "I don't see any way out of that . . . if one side feels threatened by the other side and their perceptions trying to take over the church or something, there's going to be a real problem."[104]

Father Jack named the "two very diverse groups in this church" as "Catholic traditionalists" and "the New Age, eastern, esoteric folks." Jack himself is a traditionalist, which in Antioch means, funnily, someone who avows the historic creeds as part of a modern and postmodern liberal-to-radical Catholicism. "Coming from my perspective of a Catholic background," Jack said, some Antioch colleagues are certainly "not Catholic, even with a small c, and may not even be Christian." Still, Jack backed the "New Age, eastern, esoteric" side because he wants a church as open and free as possible.[105]

◆ ◆ ◆

In truth, the "two" sides Father Jack described were about fifteen sides, since Herman was a mixer of faiths and so are many Antioch leaders. In 1947, in the foreword to Henry Brandreth's book on the *episcopi vagantes*, Anglican canon J. A. Douglas considers mixing a very bad thing. Independents in America, he writes, arise from a "macédoine of religio-nationalities" and "have equipped with a valid ministry what in effect were derelict secessions from the historic communions of Europe, or strange and fortuitous congeries which had come together from racial and other causes."[106]

Antiochians tend to consider Douglas's insults a great compliment. Mixing makes the best kind of Catholicism, they say, since additions only enhance universalism. "We're something new," Bishop Jorge Eagar said. "It's a new hybrid." Even "traditionalists" like Father Jack relish identification as Brandreth's "macédoine [of] strange and fortuitous congeries." Jack just didn't think it could last. "Five years, ten years, fifteen, I don't know how long, but . . ."[107]

5

MIX AND MYSTICISM

EXPERIMENTING WITH US CATHOLICISM

IT WAS A Friday afternoon in November 2007, and Roberto Foss was putting on another hat. At his law practice in a downtown Los Angeles high rise, he was literally putting on another hat. He had arrived an hour earlier in a fedora and casual clothes. Litigating mostly immigration and asylum cases, Roberto finds that few clients feel comfortable talking to a suit. Now on a break between appointments, the fedora hung on a hat rack and Roberto tied a white handkerchief over the top of his head. Paula, a colleague from law school, had asked him to consult the *abuelos* for her.

Paula's father had died before she got the chance to confront him about whether he abused her when she was small. Her father was abusive in other ways and symptoms of sexual victimization plagued her life. But she could not remember anything and "there's so much doubt," she said. Now Paula was tormented by dreams in which her father asked her for something but she could not hear what. Part of Roberto's work as a priest in a modern Mayan tradition—specifically an initiated Day-Keeper (*ajq'ij*) in the Maya-K'iche' lineage—was contacting the *abuelos*, or ancestors, on behalf of their children on earth. Roberto told Paula that this was not a simple matter and he was not sure the *abuelos* could help. But he would ask.[1]

In a small, sunlit conference room, Roberto closed the door and sat across the table from Paula. He used a stone to make the Sign of the Cross.

He said, "I need a question." She said, "Just, what he wants." Over about fifteen minutes Roberto opened a woolen bag and murmured prayers while arranging piles of beans and stones on a colorful square of Guatemalan cloth. He orchestrated the actions of his right hand and left hand precisely. He counted days of the Mayan calendar to sort the stones. He stirred the beans. He looked at the assemblage on the cloth for several minutes and penciled notes on a pink Post-it pad to one side.

Then he said, "Yes, when you were young," and "not only you," and "the ancestors know it." "He went to his death with this," Roberto said. "He's stuck in front of the ancestors and they are very angry with him." Paula started to weep. "The communication is cut off, not just with you," Roberto continued, because "the ancestors shunned him. But it's OK, he's out of purgatory. The dreams are a final goodbye." Roberto looked up. "Now the story comes back to you," he said. "The seeds tell the story of his punishment and your rehabilitation. You can keep the anger and stay in prison. Or you can release it to the village. Mother Earth is powerful in her embrace of you at this moment." Paula still wept but listened and nodded. Roberto said several more things and concluded, "That is what the *abuelos* are saying about that." Then he took her hand and prayed. He gave her a stone to make the Sign of the Cross. He carefully gathered arrayed items and put them back in the woolen bag. He kissed the bag. Paula blew her nose.

Roberto was a deacon in the Church of Antioch, soon to be a priest. His job is part of his ministry, applying for US asylum for clients fleeing terrors in Mexico and Central America. Another part of his ministry is Day-Keeping—a tradition separate from Catholicism but also the same, the conquistadors' Christianity mixed with the Guatemalan highlands. Roberto is the epitome of Canon Douglas's diagnosis of "strange and fortuitous congeries" in American independent Catholicism. Indeed, the range of practices among Antioch Catholics can be startling at first. But I soon got used to members who are eclectic and experienced, spiritually speaking.

If anything holds together all the mixing, it is a shared orientation toward the mystical, metaphysical, and esoteric. Herman and Meri gave Antioch this accent. It attracted like-minded people. It established much stronger bonds than the founding couple's occasional attempts at authoritarianism.

Richard knew this. Essentially he allowed the mystical to function as the highest authority in the church—higher than other Catholic traditions, higher than the bishops, higher than himself as patriarch.

But exactly how a common mysticism holds it all together is less than clear. The irony of mystical experience functioning as the highest authority is, of course, that it is the most indeterminate authority of all. How can unseen ultimate oneness or personal apprehension of the divine help decide anything? To take just one issue, if church leaders by normal means do not authorize the ordination of women, it is not as if everyone accepts that a private revelation to Herman Spruit settles the matter.

Then again, some do. A churchful of mystics does. Deacon Roberto does.

DEACON ROBERTO FOSS

At one level of narration, Roberto is a middle-class white Catholic kid from Washington State who grew up to be an immigration lawyer, with influences along the way from the Catholic charismatic movement, Latin American base communities, Roman seminary, and Mayan shamanism. At another level, Roberto is a mystic. He has always experienced invisible realities. As an adult, he made choices partly to give those realities room. One misty day in his house in the Highland Park neighborhood of Los Angeles, he told me all about it. He showed me his chapel, painted blue with gold stars to recall the mantle of the Virgin of Guadalupe. There was a kneeler facing the altar with consecrated hosts and a *reredos*, surrounded by saint images, or *santos*, and an eagle's wing of fantastic provenance. Back in the kitchen, Roberto served chai tea, memorably home-brewed with a few threads of saffron.[2]

He is widely known as Roberto, having lived and worked with Spanish-speaking people for much of his life. But he was born Robert Foss in 1959, the son of East Coast Roman Catholic parents of mixed ethnic roots. When he was growing up, family practice was more "tribal" than devout, he said, except for his pious grandmother, to whom he was very close. The Fosses moved to Washington State when he was little. Starting at three years old, Roberto had unusual experiences he still remembers. Among them: a dream of "the inner aspect of time unfolding"; feeling a hand on his forehead "that I took to be an angel"; a Quinault Indian elder seeing him and stopping to tell his grandmother that "your grandson has spiritual gifts." At his first communion, he had "a tremendous experience of knowing Jesus," Roberto recalled. There was "luscious yellow light . . . all around me," and feelings of "joy," "intimacy," and "belonging." When he was about eleven years old, his mother became deeply involved in the Catholic charismatic movement. Roberto went along and "got saved, too," he said. This also he places "in the stream" of mysticism. Later, he would do Jungian psychotherapy and in his first session spot the Virgin of Guadalupe over his therapist's shoulder. "So therapy began with a manifestation of the Divine Feminine," he said.[3]

The call to be a Catholic priest started early, too. When he was in kindergarten, Roberto announced this vocation to a Presbyterian minister. The man "didn't miss a beat" and gifted the little boy with a Latin missal. Roberto studied the missal, and then read the whole Bible. He first caught wind of social justice activism in middle school, hearing Martin Luther King, Jr., speak on the radio. "I thought Martin King sounded like the Bible," he said. He fell in love with Bobby Kennedy, César Chávez, and George McGovern. But at the same time Roberto was a charismatic Catholic, starting his legal career by investigating how he could convene a prayer group in his public school. As an evangelical Roman activist child-mystic in liberal Seattle, he said, "the only person weirder than me was the Mormon kid."

A ragingly smart youngster, Roberto was attracted to the priesthood partly because he thought studying for ordination might give him the intellectual challenges and travel opportunities he craved. But there was a family fight over his vocation. His rosary-praying grandmother predicted he'd be a priest. His charismatic mother supported that calling but wanted him close. His father derailed plans for him to attend the local minor seminary. So Roberto finished public high school and enrolled at a nearby community college. Finally, he heard about the College of Steubenville, the Franciscan institution in Ohio headed by Father Michael Scanlon and full of charismatics. He'd be safe, his family believed, so he could go.

When Roberto arrived at Steubenville in 1978, the Catholic charismatic movement had not yet taken its conservative political turn. Participating students mostly joined covenant communities on the model of the Word of God movement originating in Ann Arbor, Michigan. That first wave was about "inner healing," Roberto said. "We weren't right-wing." Living in a covenant community, he dove into the writings of King, as well as Dorothy Day and Óscar Romero. He was antinukes and moving toward pacifism, he said, when the climate of exploration abruptly ended. Suddenly, to be charismatic meant "denouncing secularism, Islam, and communism as the three enemies . . . of Christ," he said. "The Contras are good, Reagan is good, and women [are] being booted out of leadership." Plus, Roberto knew he was gay and that was hardly welcome. He started to feel that the covenant community was too isolated and disciplinary, kind of like the People's Temple in Jonestown, Guyana, which had made headlines for a mass suicide a few years earlier. "So I 'deprogrammed' myself," he said. But leaving the community was extremely disorienting. "I believed with all my heart that this is the place where God is acting," Roberto said. "How do you . . . deliberately move away from where God is acting?"[4]

To take more advanced Spanish classes—and to get some breathing room—Roberto moved four hours away to the State University of New York at Buffalo. There, a professor told him about Catholics and Mennonites doing justice work together in Bogotá, Colombia. "I saved up my money and I decided, I'm gonna do this. I'm gonna finally do this." In one heady summer month, he got a "crash course in Colombian reality," he said, from US neocolonialism and covert operations to liberation theology and base communities. "Radical East Coast nuns" were his running buddies. He quickly sensed a Latin American Catholicism that was about history, justice, and "the magical, mystical world" all at the same time. It was new but somehow already familiar, "a kind of homecoming," he said.

Over the next decade, in and out of parish work and seminary studies in the United States, Roberto went back to Latin America numerous times—Colombia, Nicaragua, El Salvador, Guatemala. He worked in overlapping circles of Roman Catholics, peace church people, social justice activists, and Marxist revolutionaries. He did retreats with liberation theologians such as Gustavo Gutiérrez and José Comblin. He met Mother Teresa when she stayed with activist Mary J. McCormick in Bogotá. He served as translator for one of Mother Teresa's brothers who set up a new Missionaries of Charity house in Guatemala. He watched *National Catholic Reporter* correspondent Penny Lernoux piece together what would become the book *In Banks We Trust* (1984) on her big kitchen table.

Roberto thought he would get ordained in a religious order and work in Latin America forever. But after painful conflicts with superiors during his novitiate, he went to an El Salvador fishing village and life took another direction. The community there said he should go work with marginalized people in the United States. "I was sort of using the base community as an oracle," he said. So he headed for Los Angeles and took a job working on amnesty cases for Catholic Charities, the social services wing of the Roman Catholic church. That led him to get a law degree at Loyola, one block away from the Catholic Charities building. Later he switched jobs to work for El Rescate, an organization that did free legal work for Central Americans. Then he opened his own practice.

It was an El Rescate colleague named David who introduced Roberto to Mayan shamanism in the mid-1990s. A K'iche' Guatemalan married to a Mayan priest, David was convinced that he survived torture at the hands of the military regime because his wife had been "burning"—performing fire ceremonies—on his behalf. So, after the Guatemalan Civil War, David joined efforts to reconstitute Maya-K'iche' religious ranks decimated by the death squads. In the Guatemala highlands, Roberto had witnessed ceremonies mixing indigenous Catholicism, Mayan traditions, and underground resistance in a way that seemed immediately familiar, just like base communities that layered justice work with feasts for the *santos*. David was looking for a place to do "burns." Roberto offered the backyard of his house. After a few years, Roberto became part of the local K'iche' community, including interpreting dreams and doing divinations. He started to "recognize" the Mayan priesthood in himself, he said. Among several reconstituted lineages in Guatemala, one was willing to initiate a foreigner in Los Angeles. So Roberto became a Day-Keeper in 2003.

But he remained devotedly Catholic and "want[ed] to do both." In a city rife with independents, Roberto started to run across non-Roman priests and churches. At Catholic Charities, a coworker was the lover of a priest in a Free Catholic church—possibly one of several "Free Catholic" churches that

FIGURE 5.1 Deacon Roberto Foss giving a Convocation presentation on Mayan divination, August 25, 2012. Courtesy of Alan Kemp.

stemmed from Antioch in the 1990s. Roberto was "skeptical" if not "disgusted" by this other Catholicism, he said. He liked the coworker "and was very challenged by his thoughts, but I wasn't ready" to think about leaving Rome. Another time he helped his friend Gene Boutilier, cofounder of El Rescate and a United Church of Christ minister, by doing the Spanish portions of a bilingual wedding. Gene complimented his assistance. "You should find some independent Catholic bishop to ordain you," Gene told him. "There's a lot of them running around." Again Roberto was rather horrified. But then he realized he had known of independents way back in Washington State—the Polish National Catholic parish then in Pe Ell, as well as the Mount St. Michael traditionalists in Spokane. "So Gene planted that seed," he said. "I started feeling that independent Catholicism really did have the juice."

He remembered wishing he could just find "a theosophical Catholicism open to ordaining women." Shortly he discovered the Ecclesia Gnostica right there in Los Angeles, headed by Stephan Hoeller, Herman Spruit's associate from back in the day. Roberto had also found the Church of Antioch online. "I picked up the phone and I called Richard Gundrey," he said. "I was very impressed by Richard Gundrey." He received Richard's Sophia information packet in the mail and it sat on his desk for two years. But finally he filled out the application and joined the Church of Antioch. To Roberto, it seemed doctrinally diverse, sacramentally open, and interpersonally friendly. In addition, Sophia Divinity School gave him a loose structure for unfettered intellectual exploration. As an "average immigration lawyer," if it were not for Sophia, he said, "where would I be doing this?"

As part of Sophia studies, Roberto was putting together a Mozarabic Rite–inspired "Flamenco Mass," layering liturgies that traveled the same lands and oceans as the flamenco and its influences, from Africa, India, and Spain to the Americas and back again. He celebrated feast days with the people in his neighborhood, did burns on request, and spoke to community groups about immigration-related scams. He consulted the *abuelos*, mostly for young women in romantic distress. In a few years, when he was ordained a priest, he would say his first mass at the Los Angeles chapter of Dignity, the noncanonical organization founded for LGBTQ Roman Catholics and allies.[5]

When Roberto was at Catholic Theological Union in Chicago as part of his Roman novitiate, one of his favorite teachers was Ukrainian Catholic priest and patristics scholar Andriy Chirovsky. "People do not fight over doctrine," Roberto said he learned from Chirovsky. "They fight for their spiritual experiences." Over the course of his life, Roberto's experience has included mysticism, enthusiasm, devotionalism, queerness, magical realism, social justice, Mayan ministry, Roman training, and postcolonial liturgy. He reads critical theory for fun, so he constantly deconstructs experience, especially his own. He is not keen on the individualism of the liberal subject and thinks church disciplines helpfully check rampant self-authorization. Still, "experience is key." From his Steubenville days, "around the question of 'does God exist?,'" he said, "I didn't even find the questioning interesting. I knew God existed." He heard out all his friends' counterarguments. He more or less agreed with them. But "I'm not sure I cared . . . because whatever this God is that I'm talking about isn't what you're deconstructing," he said. "And I still can't really get down with intellectual accounts that don't have a convincing account of experience."

Roberto is still pinching himself to have discovered a church that could handle all the mixing, all the mysticism, all the experience. He would fight hard for that kind of church. In Antioch he found good company.

MILD MIXING

Like Roberto, Richard is a "strange and fortuitous congeries." He came from the Episcopal Church, spent years in Religious Science, kept Sai Baba holy dirt, and said the *OM* at mass. As archbishop, however, Richard "mixed" mostly in the mild form of ecumenical and interfaith work. He joined Santa Fe's Interfaith Alliance and served a term as president. He rotated with other religious leaders to say opening prayers for the state legislature. He invited others into his pulpit, such as when local Sikh leader Yogi Bhajan gave a homily at Loretto. In 2008–9 Richard supported Antioch seminarians Doug and Jenni Walker as they organized an official preparatory event for the World Parliament of Religions to be held in Melbourne, Australia. The weeklong event showcased the Antioch interfaith sensibility, bringing together Santa Fe's numerous congregations of Catholics, Protestants, Jews, Buddhists, Native Americans, Buddhists, Wiccans, metaphysicians, and more.[6]

While Richard did this irenic work, some independent Catholic bishops pursued a more ambitious ecumenical goal—to reunite with the big bodies. In the past many individuals and a few groups had seceded, for example, the Carfora churches and former Campus Crusaders that joined Orthodox bodies. In May 2006, a group of American independents made an overture toward joining the Union of Utrecht. Episcopalians convened the meeting, since the Episcopal Church represents Utrecht in the United States. At the Bethsaida Spirituality Center, a Roman retreat house in Queens Village,

New York, Bishops Peter Hickman, Peter Brennan, Charles Leigh, and Robert Fuentes, all with Old Catholic lineage, met four representatives of the Utrecht-Episcopal alliance, including Old Catholic priests Björn Marcussen and Gunter Esser. Marcussen served as rector in an Episcopal parish in southern California, and Esser was an envoy of Utrecht's International Bishops Conference.[7]

There is one historical precedent for Utrecht communing with US churches apart from Episcopal jurisdiction. From 1907 to 2003, the Polish National Catholic Church was a member of the Utrecht Union even though the PNCC overlapped with Episcopal dioceses. Utrecht leaders had no formal ties with Episcopalians until 1931, so the PNCC was grandfathered in. At Bethsaida in 2006, the Utrecht representatives offered little hope for a new exception. Björn Marcussen's summary of the proceedings emphasized that Utrecht considers US Old Catholicism illicit and often invalid. Even if valid, to join Utrecht, independents would have to give up jurisdictional claims and mesh with the diocesan structure of the Episcopal Church. Certainly such terms would amount to dismantling the four US independent bishops' churches as such.[8]

In light of that discouraging prognosis, three of the bishops—Hickman, Brennan, and Leigh—left the meeting and continued as before. Only Fuentes set a new course. He led a merger of three jurisdictions to form the Old Catholic Church, Province of the United States (TOCCUSA), and—though it seemed a long shot—trained it on eventual union with Utrecht. In 2013, bishops of TOCCUSA happily announced that Utrecht Old Catholic archbishop Joris Vercammen had appointed Gunther Esser from the Bethsaida meeting to act as official liaison between their two churches. Suddenly and surprisingly, future union seemed to have a prayer.[9]

Richard knows Hickman personally and thinks well of Brennan, Leigh, and Fuentes. But he doesn't dream of one big happy Catholic church. Like many independents, he does not see the point. All jurisdictions are already part of the Catholic church, from his perspective. All Christians and "all humanity" are mystically unified. Some independents go much further than Richard to repudiate visible union. Desiring one institution, they say, amounts to desiring ultramontanism and among independents is basically internalized self-hatred. By this logic, even intercommunion agreements are actually divisive, since they implicitly distinguish between those with whom a church will and will not forge such pacts. That is true for Antioch, in the sense that Richard did not sign agreements with churches that exclude anyone from the sacraments. In turn, some will not sign with Antioch, due to the "strange and fortuitous congeries."[10]

MIXING WITH ROMAN CATHOLICS

Like most independents, Antiochians mix with Roman Catholics. About 64 percent of Antioch members were raised in the Roman communion. A proportion, like Roberto, had been Roman seminarians, deacons, priests, nuns, or monks. Others remain part of Roman Catholic families, best friends with Roman Catholic clergy, subscribers to the *National Catholic Reporter*, members of Roman progressive groups like Dignity or Call to Action, or parishioners at Roman Catholic churches. Father Jack Sweeley's wife and two sons are Roman Catholic and he attends mass with them; Richard had told Jack from the start that he didn't have to leave Rome to join Antioch. Seminarians Bob and Darleen Mitchell often attend Roman churches, too, and Sophia student Marian Bellus said she always looks for a Roman parish when she travels for work. "Roman Catholicism and Mc-Donald's," she said. If any small town has "the Golden Arches and the Catholic church . . . you'll be all set."[11]

Antiochians not only worship with Roman Catholics but also work with them in voluntary capacities. They invite to their Convocations and pulpits "open" Roman Catholic speakers such as Sister Helen Prejean and a renowned monk who wishes to remain unnamed. Sometimes they are in turn invited into Roman contexts. In 2008 Antioch archbishop Richard Gundrey and now-bishop Daniel Dangaran served on a spiritual advisory group for the local St. Vincent Hospital during its transition back to Roman Catholic affiliation. St. Vincent had origins in a hospital founded by the Roman Catholic Sisters of Charity in 1865 and became a nonaffiliated community hospital in 1977. In 2008 it merged with Christus Health, a "Catholic-related" "faith-based" system headquartered in Texas. Santa Fe community concern that new Catholic policies might exclude people was such that Susan Rush, head of hospital spiritual care, convened the multifaith advisory panel, including Richard and Daniel. "Susan is a Roman Catholic and a teacher of [contemplative prayer]," Richard wrote in the Antioch newsletter. "She is very open."[12]

Antiochians who serve in hospitals always work on teams with Roman lay chaplains, priests, or nuns. Several Antioch clergy serve as celebrants for their local chapters of Dignity, Rome-identified while not canonically Roman. Many get referrals for work from Roman Catholics, just as Richard does, sometimes even substituting for Roman priests. Father Jim St. George recounted a visit to his father's nursing home where he concelebrated mass with a Roman priest who then asked him to fill in the next Sunday. This and similar accounts suggest that some overworked Roman priests know that independent priests are not officially permitted to substitute for them, but take the break when they can get it. Or Roman pastors bend the rules to allow an independent priest to perform a wedding in a Roman sanctuary. One Antioch priest whose wife works at the chancery of the local Roman archbishop said her whole office refers inquirers to independents whenever they know a sacrament cannot be performed according to Roman regulations.[13]

Other Antiochians work for Roman Catholic institutions directly—not only Roberto, who was a lawyer at Catholic Charities, and many who work at Catholic hospitals, but also Father Ted Feldmann, a professional organist for a Roman parish in Baltimore; Father Jack, who taught a course on independent Catholicism in the Renaissance Institute of Notre Dame of Maryland University (School Sisters of Notre Dame), also in Baltimore; Father Jim St. George, who taught theology as an adjunct faculty member at Chestnut Hill College in Philadelphia (Sisters of St. Joseph); and Bishop Cliff Kroski, who teaches religion and philosophy as an adjunct faculty member at Avila University (Sisters of St. Joseph of Carondelet) in Kansas City, Missouri. In other instances, Antiochians are not "out" as independents at Rome-affiliated jobs for fear of getting fired—not an idle fear, since that has happened to independents in other jurisdictions. But the "out" ones said they experience mostly support from Roman Catholic superiors and coworkers. Roman nun colleagues in particular seem "just so jazzed about the Church of Antioch," as one Antioch bishop reported from the job.[14]

The overflow of "business" from Roman Catholicism is nice, but quite apart from that Antioch Catholics said they admire and respect the Roman church. There is static, of course. Antiochians who are former Romans can be blistering in their critiques, sounding much like other aggrieved progressives inside and outside the Roman communion. But many still speak of love for the Roman church. One of the first responses I got when I formally presented the idea for this book to the Antioch community came from Bishop Michael Adams of Fairfield, Iowa, who requested that I not resort to stereotypes about independent antagonism toward Rome. "I love Rome," he said. Father Tom David Siebert in Richmond, Virginia, sounded the same theme. A former Roman seminarian turned Byzantine Rite priest who was formally excommunicated for performing a same-sex wedding, Father Tom David said he still loves the Roman church. "I love it to this very moment," he told a local reporter. One of the most moving endorsements of Rome I read came from Roberto, who one day posted that he admired Vatican-censured Roman theologians who accepted and obeyed orders of silence. Though he would not or could not do it himself, Roberto said, submission could be a powerful witness—especially submission to (and for) Rome.[15]

Though Antiochians complain about Roman church tendencies, they follow Roman events closely. The publication of Mother Teresa's memoirs, the death of Edward Schillebeeckx, the beatification of Óscar Romero, which Roberto attended in El Salvador—all generated lively listserv conversations. As much as Antioch Catholics decry official Roman exclusions, they celebrate the inclusion of "open" Roman clergy and laity. As much as they gainsaid the leadership of Pope Benedict XVI, they rave about the tenure of Pope Francis. As much as they are happy to have found Antioch, they pray frequently for Rome, "our sister church."[16]

MIXING WITH EVERYONE

Antiochians mix with other religious communities in a variety of ways. Mix is built into their heritage, as they understand it: Jewish, Orthodox, Roman

Catholic, Anglican, Protestant, and metaphysical pasts combine in a church that is at once ancient and modern, eastern and western, Christian and universal.

They mix with other independents, as we saw in Richard's case. Richard let languish FICOB, Herman and Meri's umbrella group of bishops, since leadership of multijurisdictional entities is notoriously like herding cats. But he more than made up for it with collaborations with nearby independents and intercommunion agreements far and wide. In Arizona, Bishop Mark Newman joined with thirty-eight other Phoenix-area clerics of a dozen jurisdictions to form the Arizona Association of Independent Catholic Clergy. This large association stands out among regional independent Catholic collaborations in the country. In addition, many Antiochians have ties to other jurisdictions, like Roberto hanging out with the Ecclesia Gnostica before joining Antioch. Sometimes seminarians also straddle jurisdictions to work simultaneously with Antioch and other independent churches, training with Bishop Tim Cravens in Philadelphia or Bishop John Plummer in Nashville if they are geographically close, for example. A British seminarian of the Liberal Catholic Apostolic Church in England did altar training with Bishop Jorge Eagar when he was in Tempe, Arizona.[17]

Outside the independent movement, Antioch collaborates with Christians and non-Christians. Most often cooperation takes the form of renting worship space. For Convocation in 2006 Richard leased the Ghost Ranch conference center in Santa Fe, owned by the Presbyterian Church (USA). For Convocation in 2008 he reserved four hours in an Episcopal church in Salinas, California. Sometimes Antiochians become regular tenants in other houses of worship, like when Father Ted Feldmann rented Lutheran church space in Baltimore or Father Jim St. George leased a Reconstructionist Jewish synagogue outside Philadelphia.

Leases can lead to invitations, such as when Father Ted agreed to preach at the Baltimore Lutheran church. Monsignor Weldon Bowling—a former Roman Catholic deacon who led an Antioch congregation in Harker Heights, Texas—gave sermons at the Disciples of Christ church attended by his wife. In turn clergy of other groups participate in independent Catholic events, as when on two occasions Episcopal priests gave the homily at Antioch bishops'

consecrations. Sometimes connections develop into extensive co-congrega-
tional relationships: the parishes of Father Ted and Monsignor Weldon organized joint Holy Week services with their Lutheran and Disciples partners.
Sometimes Antioch priests even serve as substitute or interim pastors in other
denominations: Mother Linda Rounds-Nichols at a Presbyterian church in
New Mexico; Mother Deirdre Brousseau at a United Church of Christ in New
Hampshire; Father Gary Knapp at Lutheran and Unity churches in Illinois
and South Carolina; Mother Sara Yonce at a Unitarian church in Oklahoma;
and another priest at an Episcopal church in Washington State.[18]

Antioch Catholics also "mix" with Roman Catholics and Protestants
in the "new monastic" movement, a revival and reformation of Christian
contemplative traditions seen in various forms across the contemporary
United States. One priest of Antioch lives by vows as an "urban hermit"
and another professed as a sarabite, a homebound form of monasticism.
Seminarian Dick Gray formed an ecumenical Franciscan household in Arizona, echoing the nondenominational Community of a New Monastic Way
founded by feminist contemplative theologian Beverly Lanzetta, who gave
the keynote address at Antioch's Convocation in 2008. Another Antiochian
who is particularly committed to the new monasticism as it flows across
religious boundaries is Deacon Jeff Genung, who learned and taught at the
Church of Conscious Harmony in Austin, Texas, and later founded several
organizations to popularize monastic traditions. Practicing what he calls
"householder monasticism," Deacon Jeff combines Christian contemplative
practice with householder traditions of India and adapts both for a suburban family of two working parents, two teenagers, and one dog. Jeff also
teams up with other "monks in the world" to promote the work of his friend
Brother Wayne Teasdale and Centering Prayer guru Father Thomas Keating. Writing his own mass as part of Sophia studies, Deacon Jeff developed a
"contemplative Eucharist." "Fewer words, more silence," he said.[19]

Yet more mixing takes place in the ministries of Antiochians who practice more than one tradition. Roberto is a Day-Keeper and a priest. Jim
Willems is a lay leader in Antioch, but also an Episcopal priest and initiated teacher of Vipassana. Bishop Daniel Dangaran has training in the ka-
huna tradition of Hawaii. Bishop Paul Clemens integrates Catholicism and

Tibetan Buddhism, celebrating mass in a chapel with a Jesus image at one end and a Buddha image at the other. Bishop Alan expanded his *puja* mass into a whole ashram project, inspired by Bede Griffiths's Catholic ashram in India. Bishop Jorge Eagar left Siddha Yoga, but not before seeing its leader Gurumayi Chidvilasananda as a manifestation of the Virgin of Guadalupe. Jorge is a master liturgist, and his bilingual masses incarnate what I would describe as Guadalupean Tantric Catholicism.[20]

A handful of Antiochians mix themselves far afield of any Catholicism of succession, sacraments, and saints, yet they belong to the Church of Antioch. Though Reverend Bill Buehler was ordained by Herman Spruit in 1983, he demurs on the title of priest and calls his esoteric ministry "nonsacramental." He trained with three Antioch priests in Hawaii in sacred geometry—the esoteric study of "earth grids" and other portals of "high

FIGURE 5.2 Bishop Jorge Eagar leading a Palm Sunday procession around the Shrine of Holy Wisdom in Tempe, Ariz., March 16, 2008. Courtesy of Jorge Rodríguez Eagar.

spiritual energies"—and since then has worked with a global network of adepts to contact and aid otherworldly forces for good. He initially joined the church because it could grant nonprofit status to his Sanctuary of Machenim Groves. But he was grateful to Herman and came to count Antioch as part of his community. Antioch loves him back, including a few who remain part of the sacred geometry network. It is sometimes challenging to understand Reverend Bill. When he talks about the cosmic grids, his language gets so arcane that few but his associates can comprehend. Still, fellow Antiochians said absorbing the unfathomable can itself be a sacrament. "Listening to Bill Buehler in person is a holy event," said Bishop Diana Phipps. "I can't make sense of his stuff, . . . but when he's talking about it, he goes into another realm and he becomes what he's talking about. It's awesome."[21]

To be sure, big-body Catholicism mixes too, at both official and vernacular levels. Multiple origins, everyday improvisation, missionary inculturation, spiritual borrowing, and interfaith efforts over two thousand years make the whole of Catholicism constitutively heterogeneous. Even the idea of "mixing" wrongly banks on some original purity of component faiths and gets in the way of understanding, as PJ Johnston argues in her study of a Catholic shrine in Tamil Nadu, India. In the same way, criticism of Catholics who mix or "pick and choose"—and sully purported purity or wholeness— likewise misses the extent to which all religionists pick and choose among elements inside and outside their own tradition. In a sense, looking at independents makes one all the more aware of the extent to which big-body Catholicism too is a "strange and fortuitous congeries."[22]

Still, left-leaning American independents bound ahead in the frequency, volume, and creativity of the medleys. They mix consciously rather than inadvertently and centrally rather than marginally. Especially notable among independent Catholics are combinations with traditions of south and east Asia. Some attempt to create full-fledged Buddhist Catholicisms in the west, such as the Contemplative Monks of the Eightfold Path (Lancaster, Pennsylvania), the previously mentioned White-Robed Monks of St. Benedict (San Francisco, California), and, most recently, the short-lived Society of Saints Baarlam and Josaphat (Iowa City, Iowa). Named for legendary Catholic missionaries to Asia, the Baarlam and Josaphat group practiced "Pure Land

Christianity," according to its website. It was "a Christian (or if you prefer, Buddhist) school of thought holding that Amitabha Buddha and Kuan Yin manifested themselves in the first century as Jesus and Mary."[23]

Mixing with traditions of the Indian subcontinent, Abbot George Burke of Light of the Spirit Monastery in Cedar Crest, New Mexico, is a US pioneer. Born around 1950 into a family of mystics and healers in the Church of God (Anderson, Indiana), Burke spent years of his youth in the Shankaracharya monastic order, Paramahansa Yogananda's Self-Realization Fellowship, and Holy Transfiguration Orthodox monastery in Boston. Founding an Orthodox-Hindu monastery outside Oklahoma City, Burke met Bishop Jay Davis Kirby, a Herman Spruit consecratee who in turn consecrated Burke in 1975. The monastery included a dozen men and women who combined yoga and the sacraments. As featured on national prime-time programs in the 1980s like *PM/Evening Magazine* and *Real People*, members also staffed the local volunteer fire department, raised ostriches, and cooked a lot of vegan food. In 1997 Burke authored a vegan cookbook called *Simply Heavenly,* his best seller among published writings that included an autobiography and a work of theology, *Faith Speaks*. Religion scholar J. Gordon Melton calls *Faith Speaks* "the most complete theological text produced by any American" independent Catholic. In the early twenty-first century, Light of the Spirit monastery—also known as Atma Jyoti Ashram—relocated to New Mexico, where Burke continues to write engrossing essays and publish them on the monastery website.[24]

In short, Antioch and other like-minded independents go further and faster in experiments with ecumenism, interfaith, and admixture. They not only acknowledge non-Catholic religious truth, but also welcome it to reconfigure Catholicism. To them, the tradition is already a bricolage as layered and patchwork as Roberto's Flamenco Mass. A few express concern—and sometimes embarrassment—about fellow independents they consider "fringe" or "way out there." But even the worriers are proud that the Church of Antioch somehow keeps it all together. Someone may be "off in what you consider kind of woo-woo land," said Bishop Kera. "But we always manage to say without rancor, . . . 'That doesn't really work for me. But obviously it works for you. So tell me some more about it.'" Seminarian Jack Pischner too marveled at the "diversity of people" and "the fact that they all can come together around a piece of common ground," he said. "Which is just miraculous as far as I'm concerned."[25]

MYSTICAL MIXOLOGY

Holding it all together is a common mystical orientation. Most basically, there is a shared Catholic "everyday mysticism" of the sacraments. Not only the seven sacraments but a huge range of sacramentals and rituals—from patron saints to home altars, *quinceañeras* to pet blessings, pocket rosaries to lectionary apps—offer occasions for contact with the divine. All practicing Catholics also engage the everyday esotericism of prayers and devotions, from saying grace before meals to fasting on Lenten Fridays to giving money to the church. Some seek deeper communion with the divine through contemplative practices, from Thérèse of Lisieux's "Little Way" to John Main's "Christian Meditation" to Thomas Keating's "Centering Prayer." Antioch as a church emphasizes the ordinary mysticism and esotericism of Catholicism more than your average Catholic parish.

A high percentage of Antioch Catholics, however, also experience mysticism beyond the everyday variety. Many report instances of the other kind—the sudden, unusual, uncontrollable experiences that may involve vast emotions, dramatic visions, or otherworldly travels. Antioch is full of such experiencers, not just Roberto with his dream of time and Richard with his auras. There is also Deacon Jeff Genung, who from the age of ten witnessed "incredible occurrences," including traveling out of his body, speaking with animals, and seeing the oneness of all being. There is Bishop Paul Clemens, who watched his grandmother's burial at age four and "woke up." There is Nancy Clemens, married to Bishop Paul, who was a teenager when Francis of Assisi appeared and told her to seek out a Tibetan lama. Bishop Patsy, who from an early age conversed with angels. Bishop Michael Adams, who in youth "had [an] experience of the Divine Mother" at a South Dakota rosary shrine. Deacon Doug Walker, who was painting one day when he was transported to the eye of God. Mother Virginia Essene, who for decades was visited by an "elder brother" to channel dispatches for humanity. Jim Willems was not even a Christian when Jesus appeared in person and asked him to be a priest. (Jim asked Jesus if he could have a day to think about it and Jesus said no.) Another priest was visited by a twinned pair, Mary the mother of Jesus and an Apache woman-spirit. Many others see auras, hear voices, channel messages, or remember past lives. Almost all Antioch Catholics believe that such experiences occur regularly, even if they themselves do not have them.[26]

The two types of mysticism, ordinary and extraordinary, sometimes overlap. Humdrum sacraments or prayers can explode with colors and manifestations, like Roberto feeling the "luscious yellow light" at his First Communion. Others spoke of sacramentally seeing grace like a "white zone," "leak[ing] tears" like Margery Kempe, levitating while doing prostrations, or sighting a totem animal. Claire Vincent said she used to see the transformation of Eucharistic elements in her local Roman church. It surprised her, since she was a Taoist at the time. "I would see this light," she said. "I mean, not in my eyeballs, but you know what I mean . . . I would feel the transubstantiation happen."[27]

The dramatic type of mysticism can be found in big-body Catholicism, but in a lower percentage of believers with higher contestation from leaders. In the Roman church, mystics may be lionized or even canonized after death—Hildegard of Bingen, Meister Eckhart, Joan of Arc, John of the Cross—but while alive they trouble the church, seeming to have unmediated access to God that challenges the bounds of orthodoxy and authority. A loose group like Antioch may handle mystical lawlessness more easily because it has porous boundaries and unenforceable authority to start with. Do porous churches beget dramatic experiencers, or do dramatic experiencers find porous churches? It is a "chicken and egg" question. But Antioch stands in a long line of independents who assert that western Catholicism represses its mystical heritage, who join churches that not only tolerate mysticism but privilege it. Several Antioch leaders expressed a hope to make America's Christians aware that if they like meditation and mindfulness, these emphases can be found not just in Zen centers and yoga retreats, but also in independent Catholicism.[28]

Mysticism unified Antiochians, but Antiochians still mixed. They had to. Mary the mother of Jesus was friends with the Apache woman-spirit and St. Francis of Assisi said to go find a Tibetan lama. Claire Vincent saw the esoteric Eucharist as a Taoist and Bishop Jorge understood Guadalupe by way of Gurumayi. So while they say novenas, they also practice yoga. While they minister in sacraments and sacramentals, they also do Tarot readings and even "ghostbusting," as Mother Millicent Mountjoy saucily called her exorcism specialty. They read Julian of Norwich and Ignatius of Loyola, but also Swami Prabhupada and Osho, Alice Bailey and George Gurdjieff, *God is a Verb* and *Blackfoot Physics*. It is not that Antiochians think Alice Bailey and the Blackfoot cosmogony are "really" Catholic. Rather, nothing falls outside the circle of Catholicism because no circle has been drawn. At the Convocation in 2009, Jim Willems and eleven other leaders gathered the resources of Antioch personnel into a new Guild for Mystical Praxis. Guild leaders were adepts in various Catholic and non-Catholic traditions who could teach and initiate seminarians and clergy in those paths.[29]

Hoping to revive lost mystical heritage, Antiochians study history. Though mystical types have a reputation for ahistoricism, these Catholics ever collect and recuperate esoteric communities, condemned "heresies," and abandoned liturgies. Some reclaim heretics like Arius and Pelagius, Jacob Baradaeus and Johann Hus. Others read accounts of Atlantis, the Akashic records, Jesus traveling to Asia, and Thomas traveling to India. Or they investigate desert monasticism or Celtic Christianity as "useable pasts" for contemporary Catholicism. Or, reading academic histories of early Christianity by Elaine Pagels or Bart Ehrmann, they recognize themselves in accounts of heterogeneous communities with multiple gospels and contested theologies. Or, like Roman Catholic progressives, they use historical-critical scholarship by John Boswell, Francis Oakley, or Gary Macy to show Catholic precedent for same-sex unions, conciliar governance, and women's ordination. Observers of independent Catholicism often say that the movement is characterized by concern for history over theology. I might say that independents' original contribution to Catholic theology *is* a new vernacular Catholic history—a narrative of ancient and continuous heterogeneity. Even casually informed Antiochians characterize church history in ways that depart drastically from big-body narratives of orthodoxy and unity. Maybe it's a veritable requirement of survival in independent Catholicism to get wise fast about power and positionality from the perspective of critical history.[30]

If Antiochians look to history to support their version of Catholicism, they also value experience and science. Looking to empirical evidence to buttress faith claims, Antiochians take part in a vast discourse of religious modernism dating to the early twentieth century that historian Ann Taves calls "the experiential turn." For thinkers of the "experiential turn" such as Friedrich Schleiermacher and William James, Taves writes, the "self-authenticating experience of the individual seemed like a promising source of religious renewal" at a time when so much of traditional religion was dissolving in the "acids" of historical-critical scholarship. Religious experience could seem empirically grounded and even quantifiable; scientific discoveries seemed to echo religious truths. Antiochians tend to agree. In the introductory textbook for Sophia Divinity School, author and former Antioch priest Thomas Hickey teaches that while experience always eludes capture in words and equations, sacramental effects can nevertheless be seen, felt, and measured. And not only the sacraments of Catholicism. All faiths harbor all truths, including scientific ones. World religions not only synch with science; they prophesy and fulfill it. Quantum physics confirms the Vedas, neurology reveals what Buddhist monks have known for ages, and magic is just an old way of saying science.[31]

The mystical orientation of Antioch, with accents of history and empiricism, knits members together despite their varied Catholicisms. Since Richard let this orientation do its work—both unifying and authorizing—it did not disrupt his own authority. Sometimes Richard personally balked at the mystically discerned decisions of others, like when seminarian Lian Reed told him she was called to ordination in another church. "His heart was very reserved," Lian recalled. "He did not want me to go down this path." But it was unquestionable to Richard and everyone else that new directions are divined in ordinary or extraordinary moments that require no external authentication. Ultimately he attended Lian's ordination in the Eternal Life Church. He even accepted the presider's invitation to do a "special blessing," laying his hands on Lian's head and praying a prayer that made everyone weep. In the workaday world, Richard begrudges the disruption of order and boundaries. But mystically, he too lets things flow.[32]

RACE, ETHNICITY, "THE BOOK," AND THE LAW OF ATTRACTION

The church does not mix all that much across racial and ethnic lines. Like most US liberal organizations, including Roman progressive groups and other independent churches, Antioch is full of well-intentioned white Americans who are bedeviled as to how to diversify their institutions.

There are exceptions. Richard has many Hispanic and Indian clients who find him by word of mouth. Roberto is a white guy completely enmeshed in US Latino cultures and concerns. Bishop Jorge's Guadalupean Tantrism and Archbishop Anastasia Voyatjides's church in Argentina attract mixed populations. And things are shifting overall as the demographics of US Catholicism change from white to brown. More seminarians are of non-white heritage. More priests are bilingual and working with Latino people. Around 2008 a Hispanic Ministries Advisory Committee was formed and started translations of Sophia Divinity School materials. Jorge was appointed Vicar of Hispanic Ministries and dean of a new Spanish-language side of Sophia. The Church of Antioch pledged $10,000 to the new venture and Bishop Jorge started getting requests for information from overseas: Mexico, Spain, the Philippines.[33]

The independent movement as a whole is by no means all white or all unaware. Several early US bishops including Vilatte and his successor, Frederick Ebenezer Lloyd, precociously consecrated black men, and a number of the most important churches are majority black or Hispanic: the majority-Hispanic jurisdiction led by Bishop Oscar Trujillo in Albuquerque; the historic St. John Coltrane led by Bishop Franzo King in San Francisco; the majority-black Nashville congregation of Bishop Jewell Granberry, consecrated in the International Old Catholic Church; and the majority-black Imani Temple, led by Patriarch George Stallings in Washington, D.C. The Imani

Temple in particular is a church of manifold experimentation informed by what scholars call critical race studies. Often pigeon-holed as an Afrocentric breakaway from Rome, really the Imani Temple practices an open-door Catholicism based on the idea that you could start from a norm of blackness rather than a norm of whiteness. From its founding in 1989 the Imani Temple also instituted broadly progressive and eclectic reforms, including ordaining women and noncelibates, both gay and straight.[34]

Still, independent Catholicism remains mostly white and unevenly integrated. In Antioch some bemoan what they consider a shamefully low level of church awareness of issues of race and ethnicity. "It's a little culturally bound," said Jim Willems. "It's white." At the Convocation in 2007 in Salinas, two priests of color were consecrated as bishops. Though Antioch historically had numerous Latino or African American priests, these bishops

FIGURE 5.3 Patriarch George Stallings of the Imani Temple, aka the African-American Catholic Congregation, Washington, D.C., October 2012. Courtesy of Hamil Harris.

were a first. But during the whole Convocation weekend, no one officially pointed out the historic moment, except one of the consecratees herself. The church "really doesn't understand" that significance, said Jim. "It's a sign of how naive the church is."[35]

There is handwringing. The church should be more diverse. It should do better than the big bodies. It should reach out to Latinos. Yet Antiochians have difficulty moving fast on this issue. One reason is the usual all-thumbs whiteness. Another reason is that in a church of worker-priests, few have time, money, or expertise to do advertising beyond a basic website, much less target outreach to people of color. Even if they could advertise, they aren't sure it would work, for Latinos or for anyone. Antiochians talked a lot about a Pew survey from 2008 showing that one in ten Americans is a former Roman Catholic—a "Roaming Catholic," they liked to say—yet ex-Romans are hardly streaming into independent Catholic churches. Still, at others' urging, Richard looked into advertising in the *National Catholic Reporter*. He noticed that two independent churches already ran notices in its pages. He called the bishops of those churches. "They BOTH said they were stopping their ads," Richard reported on the listserv, "because of no results and they were running on a very regular basis and they felt it was not worth their money."[36]

Maybe the Church of Antioch would have more luck with Father Spencer Wood's idea. At Convocation in 2005 and 2006—when Dan Brown's best-selling novel *The Da Vinci Code* captivated readers with the idea that Jesus and Mary Magdalene were married—Father Spencer Wood of Tucson, Arizona, announced that it would be very helpful if someone in the church could have a really big vision, "preferably of St. Mary Magdalene," he said, who would proclaim in the vision that the Church of Antioch was really cool. Father Spencer was joking. Sort of. A fantastic vision of Magdalene, along the lines of the spinning sun of Fatima, certainly might attract devotees quicker than any national marketing campaign.[37]

There was another reason that Antiochians were half-hearted about the idea of an outreach campaign. It was a theological reason and it started at the top. Richard subscribes to the Law of Attraction, or "like attracts like." It is a common metaphysical principle stating that positive energy attracts more positive energy or, from a karmic angle, people who need each other find each other. Locally Richard advertised the church and lost no opportunity to inform the public about independent Catholicism. But he opposed the kind of proselytization that would try to persuade anyone to join, much less target any particular group of people. He considered it a lack of flow, even a sort of violence. "Attraction, Not Promotion," he wrote. "We invite; we do not proselytize." If black or brown people come to church, that is wonderful. If anyone comes, that is wonderful. If not, that is all right, too. At some level everyone always finds whom they need.[38]

"The book" is an example of the Law of Attraction at work, according to some in Antioch. Namely, my book—this book you are reading. To those who pushed for advertising, Richard pointed out that with no planning at all, "Julie's book" would eventually be published, and it would be "the best FREE publicity on a national basis we could get." Antiochians started attributing this kind of importance to "the book" from the time I first met the group in 2005. "When you first stood before us in Richmond to explain what it is you wanted to do, suddenly we were looking at each other like, 'Oh my God,'" recalled Bishop Kera Hamilton. "Because your starting [the book] said, 'This is a thing. This is happening. This is a cultural phenomenon.' And so we were kind of running up behind it going, 'Oh, yeah, I guess it is . . .' And so you've been quite a catalyst." As I worked among Antioch Catholics, the "ethnographic uncertainty principle" revealed itself—the principle by which the observer becomes part of the situation that she is observing. A book lent the church "gravitas," as Bishop Kera said, which meant that the church suddenly congealed more urgency about its future. "Now go home and polish your collars, guys," they told one another, "because, you know, you're going to be more visible."[39]

In this perception, the book promises positive evangelistic outcomes. As I attended Convocations and gave updates over the years, I told Antiochians that the book would have some effect, but I did not know precisely what kind. They, however, are pretty sure it will mean growth. "When Julie Byrne has her book published out there we BETTER be ready," Richard wrote on the listserv. But the possibility of growth is scary as well as thrilling. What will work best for a future in which people are reading the book? they ask one another. Should they reorient and try to set up a lot of parishes? Should they rein in the woo-woo and just be Catholics with open sacraments? Or are the mobility, mix, and mysticism crucial to Antioch's identity—and potential appeal?[40]

Maybe the book will not do much, others said. Maybe Antioch will always be tiny. They wonder aloud about the entire independent Catholic proposition. What are they doing, really? Too mixed for many Catholics, too Catholic for many metaphysicals, too churchy as Americans abandon organized religion in droves, maybe they are doomed to irrelevance. But most Antioch leaders have faced the existential questions so often that it is almost funny. Once when I was talking to Richard, he did a mock freakout—"What am I doing? . . . Why am I here? . . . I need to quit this tomorrow!"—and laughed. The priests of Antioch ruminate, but with a sense of humor. They keep going. They wake up "tomorrow" and clock in at their day jobs. Then they go say mass again. They go marry and baptize more people who say they need them.[41]

"THE NEXT LEVEL"

In 2008, Richard announced his impending retirement from leadership of the Church of Antioch. He was seventy-four years old and "slowing down," though free of major health problems. "No issues with our church have me making this decision," he wrote in his resignation letter on November 17. But the "spiritual reasons are several." "This church has grown and prospered spiritually WAY beyond my ability to lead it effectively," he continued. "The Holy Spirit has blown a great breath of spiritual wind into the sails of our ship. She is moving at a much greater speed and I cannot hang on any longer." Richard trusted, he said, that the "great group of leadership people" and "even greater new seminarians" would carry Antioch to future flourishing.[42]

In terms of countable numbers, the church had grown only slightly under Richard's leadership. Throughout his tenure from 2005 to 2009, there remained about thirty church charters, sixty clergy, and forty-five seminarians, with between ten to fifteen new Sophia enrollees every year. But in other ways, growth was tangible. The bishops consulted as a body and met yearly in Illinois, in addition to Convocation. More people attended Convocation and visited one another during the year. New seminarians were better educated. The website was upgraded, the listserv was active, and a newsletter went out regularly. The church archives were indexed and funds accumulated. The Spanish-language initiatives bore fruit. And in the independent world, Antioch had become even more respected. Father Ted Feldmann said he joined Antioch partly because "it's so stable." "When I move in independent Catholic circles, . . . they know what the Church of Antioch is," he said. "It's got a solid structure, it's organized, . . . it's got transparency, you know, there's a budget."[43]

All of this growth happened in large part because of Richard's work ethic, management acumen, and big heart. Maybe the big heart was most important, not just for pastoralism but for policy. Transgender seminarians were first accepted into Sophia Divinity School with apparently no discussion at all, only on Richard's lead and example. He sat down with Richmond church member Becky Taylor the first time he visited the city and enrolled her in Sophia in one conversation. "He got all sorts of things out of me that other people never would even think to ask," Becky said. "And I was more than willing to share because that's the sort of relationship that's always led to my spiritual growth." By the time Richard left Richmond, "I was absolutely taken" with him, Becky said. "If [Sophia] was a reflection of his mentality," she decided, it must be a good thing.[44]

Richard calls it just being a Virgo, a zodiac sign associated with intuition and order. Others do not chalk it up to the stars. Richard has "an essential goodness . . . about him," seminarian Jack Pischner said. "He's a very remarkable guy." Father Jack Sweeley in Baltimore added that he had "never heard him say . . . an unkind thing about anyone," even "when he was really driven crazy." It was an accomplishment just to "remain sane," said Richard's associate pastor Mother Carol Calvert, much less always "show fairness toward all." Deacon Doug Walker in Santa Fe compared Richard to other spiritual leaders of deep "love" and "holistic awareness," like the Dalai Lama and Thich Nhat Hanh. Bishop Alan Kemp in Washington State, whom Richard appointed as interim after he retired, asked, "Who among us would be able to do what Richard does?" "As far as I'm concerned," Bishop Alan said, "he is a saint."[45]

Richard was much more likely to recount his shortcomings. He worked too much; he could not handle the "ruckus"; he did not take responsibility for his frustrations. It was also unnerving to him that he lost a hundred thousand dollars of his own money in the bid to build a house addition for the church archives. The contractor took the money and did no work. In a lawsuit Richard recuperated about a fifth of the funds. But permanent storage for the archives was derailed. Richard told me that he was glad he had not used the church endowment. But the loss still stung. At the Convocation in 2009, the first night featured a reception for Richard's retirement. Wine was poured, people toasted, and praise ran thick. After just a few minutes, though, Richard gently halted the speechifying. "All ego stories," he said. He had only tried to lead to the best of his abilities, he told the assembly. When he tried to say more, he choked up.[46]

Still, Richard did feel good about the progress under his leadership. He was proud of stabilizing the church inherited from Herman and Meri. He expected numerical growth in the future and the shored-up infrastructure would make that possible. He loved life among fellow clerics, interesting parishioners, betrothed couples, and baby baptisands. Antioch was celebrating its fiftieth anniversary, a milestone by any measure, but especially in the independent Catholic world. Any one of fourteen diverse and wonderful bishops might succeed him. And for the first time the new presiding bishop would be elected, not appointed. "We're always talking about 'the next level,'" Richard said in one Convocation homily. But finally "we're not reaching for it," he said. "We're here."[47]

◆　◆　◆

Richard certainly added his piece to the history of one of the oldest and most venerable US independent Catholic bodies. But he resided in Santa Fe, "the metaphysical headquarters of at least the Western world," as one radio host put it, making his church-building slightly easier than in other parts of the country. Mother Carol once said that living in Santa Fe had warped her perspective on Antioch. "This is a funny little liberal pocket in the universe," she said. "The whole town is a Reiki master," and everyone seemed to be "starting a retreat center." "It's not that people aren't attracted" to Antioch, Mother Carol said. "They're just like, 'Oh yeah, of course.'" Likewise in Los Angeles or San Francisco, independent Catholics are not that much of a surprise.[48]

In contrast, in the US midwest, south, and northeast, churches like Antioch meet less recognition. They stand in considerable tension with much of Protestantism and Roman Catholicism. In some places, Antioch priests find allies in Unity adherents, Episcopal pastors, or, yes, Reiki masters. But they long to preach to those not already in the choir, to offer the sacraments widely, to witness an independent take on "Catholic means universal." So Richard's "like attracts like" approach to evangelism does not always work for them. Might not "Roaming Catholics" like to know Antioch exists? Might some "others" like Catholicism if they knew about an "other Catholicism"? What would it take to grow churches in "the Bible Belt, the North-East and places like Montana, Utah," as Herman once envisioned? To have Richard's success in Santa Fe, clerics in other parts of the country have to work even harder.[49]

The Church of Antioch's Diocese of the Northeast stretches along the Atlantic coast from New Hampshire to Virginia, encompassing some of the most thoroughly Roman and ex-Roman areas of the country. Antioch bishops and priests in places like Philadelphia and Richmond want to reach those ex-Romans. They balance the far-out with the familiar. They practice seven sacraments but also advocate sacramental justice. Geographically their challenge is the greatest, but so is the potential, they believe, to reinvent a tradition and change lives.

6

SACRAMENTS AND SAINTS

HEARING A NEW CALL

IT WAS 1994 before the Church of Antioch had an enduring presence on the East Coast. That year, Kera Hamilton of Philadelphia enrolled in Sophia as a seminarian. She remained the lone Antiochian east of the Mississippi for another seven years. But as the millennium turned, things started popping. JoEllen Werthman, also near Philadelphia, came on board in 2000. A whole church called Gentle Shepherd, led by Deacon Tom Gallub and located in Richmond, Virginia, affiliated in 2004. Then three more priests joined from Maryland and New Hampshire. Though spread over four states, this new bunch counted as a critical mass. One night in 2004 Richard called Kera to ask her to serve as bishop of a new Diocese of the East. "He's from the *Field of Dreams*," Kera said. She was referring to the famous line in that movie: "If you build it, they will come." Richard wanted a diocesan structure in place so that future Antiochians could easily plug in.[1]

So that is how Kera came to be one of three women bishops consecrated at the Convocation in 2005 in Richmond. It had been a long and winding road. Raised Baptist, Kera converted to Episcopalianism and then Roman Catholicism in college. But after a failed marriage and deep malaise, she stopped going to mass. It was a group of Wicca women that nurtured her back to feeling whole and capable. And through the Wicca liturgy she fathomed anew the depth of the Catholic mass.

She also realized that she was called to say mass herself. Kera left a message on an answering machine in Oregon. The callback came from Matriarch Meri Spruit herself. "And I'm like, 'Oh God, I'm talking to the pope here.'" But the Antioch "pope" put her at ease, Kera said. "She just had a way when she spoke to you." Kera took one Sophia course. Then she took another. Matriarch Meri was "dogged," calling regularly to check in with her only easterly seminarian. "I would say to her, 'I have no idea why I'm doing this,'" Kera said. "And . . . I could hear the smile and she would say, 'Oh, you'd be surprised how many people say that. But this is a good thing.'" The matriarch set up an intercommunion agreement with the Friends Catholic Communion of Bishop Catherine Adams—related by consecrations to the Spruits and located in New York—just so Kera could take minor orders in a timely fashion. After minor orders, all sorts of Antioch people called to congratulate her, though she had never met them. "I was this one little point out there" in the east, and they did all that for her. "They were so great," she said.

Kera is temperamentally not a pastor. Shy and introverted, maybe she is better suited to be an anchoress. "Wall me off somewhere," she joked. Yet by the fall of 2001 Kera was saying Mass for a brand-new Antioch church. That is because JoEllen Werthman got hold of her. Described by her friends as the "ultimate extrovert" and a "spiritual diva," JoEllen had recently enrolled in Sophia and materialized a small congregation even before she was ordained. She and Kera met for coffee in the Philadelphia suburbs. Would Kera come to her Fairless Hills home and say mass? Kera agreed. After the first mass, JoEllen asked if she would come again the next month. With that, a new Church of Antioch parish was off and running.[2]

After Kera was consecrated, the Atlantic coast boasted a bishop, a diocese, two parishes, and three additional chartered ministries. Clergy of this new diocese share the strong Roman imprint of the eastern United States, as well as patterns of leaving Rome: one-third of the country's thirty million ex–Roman Catholics live in the eastern seaboard states—about ten million. Kera, JoEllen, and other leaders suspect that a few of those ten million may go back to a more open Catholic church. They know personally "many broken and hurting Roman Catholics who want church, who want sacraments," as JoEllen put it. They understand. They themselves had been broken and hurting Roman Catholics. Maybe independent Catholicism would not "take" in heavily Roman Philadelphia. But Kera and JoEllen were about to find out.[3]

MOTHER JOELLEN WERTHMAN

JoEllen said her vocation to the priesthood started with a "little static" that loudened to spiritual honking horns impossible to ignore. But, like many Roman Catholic girls of her generation, she started out wanting to be a nun. Born in 1946 in the Brownsville section of Brooklyn, New York, JoEllen Caulfield lived among Catholic neighbors in a predominantly Jewish community. In Catholic school, she fell in love with her third-grade teacher, a Capuchin nun named Sister Apollonia. "She loved us children and told us God loved us and I am sixty-one and I am telling you that I remember her," Mother JoEllen said when we talked in 2007. Because óf Sister Apollonia's "emanance of acceptance and love and beauty," JoEllen decided to head for the convent. Even when her family moved to Oceanside on Long Island in the late 1950s, she played nun. Making a wimple out of cardboard, JoEllen hopped on her bicycle and gathered other girls to "play Catholic school." Neighbors complained about her riding a bike in nun gear. "I certainly wasn't being disrespectful," she said. "I just thought, you're going to play nun, you're . . . going to look real." Still, JoEllen was clearly riffing on the genre. She was "Sister Mary Holy Brilliance" and the school was "Our Lady of Perpetual Emotion" and the priest was "Father Absoluto Nonpermissione."[4]

Her membership in the lay Roman organization called the Legion of Mary was no-nonsense, however. The local chapter was "run by this woman who was very pious," JoEllen said. "I would say [she] probably had scrupulosity." As a Legion of Mary member, JoEllen kept a journal of every good deed—ironing, cleaning, visiting nursing homes, saying the Rosary—to offer to the Blessed Virgin Mary as a sacrifice. It gave her more occasion to contemplate Mary, who seemed like the beautiful lady Rose who, when JoEllen was small, used to appear to her in the ceiling at home. It was a "feminine connection, that definite feminine drawing," said JoEllen. Between

Rose, Sister Apollonia, and the Legion of Mary, JoEllen said she always doubted the "meek and mild" characterization of Mary. "That Mary just said, 'Well, whatever,'" she said. "That tweaked me." The "tweak" might have been the start of her non-nun vocation. "There just started to be some . . . some, something. Very nebulous. [A] little static on the radio channel . . . wait a minute, is there another song there? Ah, no, it's gone."

With girlfriends JoEllen was still planning which religious order to join, though now it was largely about fashion priorities. They pored over a vocations guidebook that had "every flavor of nun" in all their habits. "Would I look good in that head gear?" "Does it cinch at the waist or is it an empire [waist] or . . . ?" At the same time she totally assumed she would marry and have babies. "I couldn't quite follow," JoEllen said, "that I would have to make a choice." But then she got a boyfriend, and it was "the hormone explosion of the world," she said. "Handsome. You just see him coming down the block and you could just pass out." Finally, JoEllen said, she started to think, "Hmmm, don't know if I could do the nun thing."

A few years later, married to another handsome man, Rob Werthman, JoEllen moved to Levittown, Pennsylvania, to set up a home while Rob commuted to the New York financial district. It was hard to fit in with Philadelphia-area Roman Catholicism, since most locals "did not want to be with these New Yorkers." More intimately, it was hard to practice the Rhythm Method. Like the method of Natural Family Planning endorsed by the Roman church today, the Rhythm Method involved counting days in the woman's cycle and abstaining from sex on possible fertile days. It was also notoriously difficult and unreliable. "That was a major, . . . horrible suffering for Rob and [me]," JoEllen said, as they tried not to get pregnant in their first years of marriage. "Trying to do it right and . . . [do what] God said," she recalled. "My period was crazy, . . . so forget the Rhythm. And crying, crying. We would hold each other and we would cry because we couldn't figure out how to do this." Eventually JoEllen and Rob had two sons, as planned. After that, they "came to some other understanding," as JoEllen put it. The family planning struggle was another moment of "static"—"a little bit of the parting of the ways" with the Roman church. Still, she and Rob were deeply enmeshed. At St. Frances Cabrini in Fairless Hills, they were active parishioners for twenty years, serving as Eucharistic ministers, members of the hospital ministry, and Pre-Cana leaders, charged to help prepare engaged couples for marriage. JoEllen joined the women's sodality and the choir, too.

In 1994, JoEllen "really started getting strong feelings" about a vocation, she said. She decided to contact her pastor, who was also the priest on her Pre-Cana team, giving him a heads-up that she felt called to the priesthood. When they met in his office, he closed the door. "And he said, 'Look,' he said, 'We are forbidden to talk about this. This is a non-issue. The pope has said that this is a non-issue. And we cannot discuss it,'" as JoEllen remembered it. "Now I could not comprehend that because he was our friend. He was a family friend." She suggested meeting off church property, even at her home, so "that nobody knows." "And it was absolute and complete 'no.'"[5]

JoEllen tried to accommodate the answer. "OK," she said to herself. "I guess that's it." She did other things: a secretarial degree, a physical education degree, a dream job at the YMCA. She was ordained as a metaphysical minister and did distance learning courses to get licensed as a counselor. She took women's studies courses and "met the Goddess." "It was thrilling," she said. At Chestnut Hill, a Roman Catholic college in Philadelphia, she got a master's degree and certification as a spiritual director.

Despite all the activities, "now the priesthood [idea] comes back," JoEllen said. But "I can't do that. I'm a Roman Catholic woman." And "any orthodox person I would talk to, there was a lot [of opinion] that it was about my ego. That I really needed to self-reflect . . . because if God really wanted women [to be priests], blah blah blah." Several generations before JoEllen's birth, there had been a family rupture over a vocation. Her grandfather's father, Patrick, was a so-called spoiled priest. A seminarian in New York, he had fallen in love and left his studies to marry and have children. "Which was like such a come-down from, 'He could have been a priest,' you know?" JoEllen said. For the Irish Caulfields, the priesthood was a "justification of their worthiness, their integration into the good life in America." The woman he married was a Lutheran, so it was a "double whammy." Patrick experienced total "ostracization, cutting off," JoEllen said, a "very heavy-duty thing."

Great-grandfather Patrick Caulfield showed up in JoEllen's psychic landscape. She went to a friend who did guided imagery, "a hypnosis kind of thing." JoEllen closes her eyes and sees a blacksmith in a barn. Patrick was a blacksmith. After being cut off from the family, he moved to upstate New York and took up smithing. JoEllen realizes that while Patrick was cut off because he decided to get married, "I would be cut off because I'm going toward the priesthood." Suddenly she finds herself apologizing to Patrick for everything their relatives put him through. "I had to say to him, as the last of the Caulfields, that I'm sorry," JoEllen said. "Somehow I needed to be the one to make a difference, generationally." Patrick says nothing, but indicates that he has heard and accepted. "That was a piece, that my ordination is not just mine," JoEllen said. It was for Patrick and all of those who were cut off from community in any way. Imaginal interaction with Patrick, she said, overcame real-world voices that blamed her desire for ordination on ego.

The final "piece" of coming to terms with her vocation was a dramatic dream. JoEllen dies and goes to heaven. Her Brownsville youth returns: God is an Orthodox Jewish man—full beard, black hat, Yiddish accent. "'So how vas the priesthood?'" God asked, as JoEllen recounted it. "And I said, 'What do you mean, priesthood? I'm a Roman Catholic woman.'" God responded, "Ai, ai, you made such a mistake! I vas calling you and calling you; why didn't you answer me?!" JoEllen woke up and got online. "That dream pushed me over," she said. She had seen the phrase "independent Catholic" in ads in the *National Catholic Reporter*, so she used that as a search term, plus "women's Catholic ordination." In Antioch, she found a sacramental and metaphysical church. A church that would ordain her. "Wordless," she said. JoEllen started courses at Sophia in 2000 and was ordained in 2006. Alongside Rose, Sister Apollonia, and the Blessed Mother, she added another feminine spirit to her pantheon, choosing St. Mary Magdalene as patron of her new Catholic parish.[6]

ST. MARY MAGDALENE

When I visited Fairless Hills one Sunday in July 2007, the little parish of St. Mary Magdalene was just shy of six years old and in full swing. JoEllen's husband Rob served as sacristan, setting up their big sunroom for mass and cuing meditative music. About twenty people arrived in cars, put covered dishes on the dining room table, and settled into the home chapel. The Werthman family dog lay in a sunny spot near the altar.[7]

Bishop Kera and Mother JoEllen concelebrated mass. Sharing the peace came first, so the liturgy started with about ten minutes of hugging and kissing all around. JoEllen spoke boldly, energetically. Kera talked calmly, deliberately. They used the Liberal Catholic Church *Confiteor*, which talked about "imperfections" and "shortcomings" rather than sins. There was no standing at the gospel, no kneeling at communion. The homily included a casual back-and-forth between the congregation and Kera. They said the Hail Mary after the Our Father. They used pomegranate juice instead of wine in case anyone was in recovery from alcoholism. They used rice-based hosts rather than wheat in case anyone was allergic to gluten. The food of communion was not insignificant—Roman churches are required to use real wine and wheat hosts as the only proper Eucharistic "matter."[8]

After mass there was a potluck, including a big spread of hoagies from the minimarket chain Wawa. I talked to about ten church members as people lingered over the meal. Only Evelyn was not from a Roman background. She and her partner came to St. Mary Magdalene from a nondenominational Christian church where their status as a same-sex couple eventually became a problem. "This church accepts," she said. Cindy was JoEllen's goddaughter, who attended with her husband, a toddler, and a baby who would soon be baptized at St. Mary Magdalene. They had recently moved from Arizona. In Cindy's southwest experience, Roman Catholic parishes were diverse and inclusive, so homilies in the sunroom that made negative comparisons with Rome left her cold, she said. But she loved coming to the monthly masses, and attended a Roman church on the three other Sundays.[9]

Marian Bellus had two teenaged children in attendance. She grew up in Philadelphia's Roman Catholic parishes. When divorce turned her life upside down, fellow Roman parishioners were there for her. "People were good to me," she said. Still, independent Catholicism was "a good fit" now, she said. "Lots of people, they love their ritual, their sacraments, the Mass, but they don't fit into the Roman church." She was also disillusioned with the Roman clergy. "They're not from *The Bells of St. Mary's*, if that was ever close to the truth," she said.

Loretta said she was "dyed-in-the-wool" Roman Catholic, but over the years, the church "devastated me as much as helped me." She recalled confessing her sins to a priest who would not give her absolution while she was still using artificial birth control, which meant that officially she could not receive communion. Then media revelations of Roman clerical sex abuse and cover-up were "the last straw," Loretta said. Even then, it was "very difficult" to decide to come to St. Mary Magdalene. But she loved that it was so "open" and "everyone is welcome to take the Eucharist."

Antoinette also struggled mightily to decide to attend, even though Jo-Ellen was her best friend. "When she said she wanted to be a priest, [I said,] 'Holy shit, how are you gonna do that?'" recalled Antoinette, who back then attended the same parish as JoEllen and Rob. "She was able to share with me her wonderful dreams; it was a girlfriend-secret thing." Still, when JoEllen's

FIGURE 6.1 Antiochians having breakfast before Convocation activities, Richmond, Va., October 15, 2005. *Left to right*: Kera Hamilton, Antoinette Cendali, Rob Werthman, and JoEllen Caulfield-Werthman. Courtesy of Daniel Dangaran.

dream came true, Antoinette felt "unworthiness" after her own divorce and remarriage. She worried she would not get into heaven if she left Rome. But at her first St. Mary Magdalene mass, she sobbed when Kera said her standard words before communion: "The body and blood of Christ is not a prize for being good. It is a food, it is a medicine, it is a tonic, and no one on the face of the earth has the right to refuse it to anyone for any reason." Antoinette received communion for the first time since her divorce and has been coming to St. Mary Magdalene ever since. It was still hard to tell her kids she was attending an independent Catholic parish. Hard for her—not for her kids. "They were like, 'It's about time!'" After a few years of worship at St. Mary Magdalene, Antoinette said, she cannot imagine going back to a church in which anyone is barred from the sacraments.[10]

"I CAN BECOME A PRIEST!"

Like parishioners Loretta and Antoinette, Bishop Kera and Mother JoEllen joined Antioch partly because of the availability of sacraments: in their case, ordination. They felt called to the Catholic priesthood and needed a church in which women could answer that call. The same is true of men with vocations who want sexual relationships as part of their lives, such as Richard and Roberto. Antioch has had "open orders" since Herman's time and still keeps ordaining. "Our holy orders are open to all humanity," Richard often said. Roberto marveled at the strong stance for sacramental justice. "That open Holy Orders thing is taken pretty seriously," he said. "More seriously than almost any other place."[11]

All of the big Catholic bodies put restrictions on the gender, marital status, and sexual practice of clergy. In 2016 the Episcopal Church in the United States is different from other big Catholic bodies in ordaining men and women, married or single, gay or straight; it even acknowledges that some clergy in couples have lifetime loving relationships other than marriage. But until 1997 Episcopal bishops were still authorized to enact tighter restrictions in their own dioceses, and three dioceses continued to limit ordination to straight men who had sex only within marriage. This led to considerable variation—not to mention conflict, breaches, and lawsuits—from place to place and time to time. Though some Antioch clergy had previously been members of the Episcopal Church and pursued ordination there, liberal bishops were not necessarily available when and where they faced pressing vocational decisions. So while Episcopalianism has the most open ordination policies of big-body Catholicism, in the recent past it was not always the solution.[12]

Numbers of women priests said they were elated to find Antioch. Seminarian Lian Reed in Santa Fe recalled knowing she was called to the priesthood at eight years old, when she whispered to her mother at Mass that she "could do what Father Dominic is doing." Her mother replied, "That's very sweet, but you can't; you're a girl." Lian said she remembered "sitting there with my hands on my hips" and saying, "Yes I can and when I want to, I will!" When I asked Lian what was the best thing about Antioch, she simply said, "I can become a priest!"[13]

Seminarian Claire Vincent was also wowed to discover she could be ordained in the Church of Antioch. For years she felt discouraged, feeling called to the priesthood but blocked. "You got the wrong plumbing, sister!" she would remind herself. Living in Nashville, Tennessee, she struck up a conversation with her ex-Roman neighbor, a Vanderbilt Divinity School student who encouraged her to start a Masters of Divinity degree. "And you say you want to be a priest? Women are priests," the neighbor said to her, according to Claire. "I said, 'What are you talking about, women are priests.' He said, 'Women are Episcopal priests and Lutheran priests and there's even independent Catholic churches.'" So Claire "spent the entire summer on the Internet" researching independent Catholicism, she said. "So . . . that's how I got to Antioch."[14]

The men of Antioch share enthusiasm for women's full inclusion. Bishop Michael Adams studied for the priesthood in the Episcopal Church in the 1970s, but there was fractiousness over women's ordination, as well as not enough attention to Mary or the Divine Feminine, in his view. "It didn't seem quite Catholic enough for me in that way," said Bishop Michael, one of a handful who found Antioch after struggling in conservative Episcopal dioceses.[15]

Other men, straight and gay, gravitate to Antioch because they can have relationships while answering a priestly calling. While a few priests in the Roman communion are married, they represent exceptional circumstances, and it remains that once you are ordained you cannot marry. Deacon Jeff, raised Roman Catholic in upstate New York, grew up with that assumption. He recalled a youthful, "very dark" time wrestling with simultaneous calls to priesthood and marriage. "It almost tore me apart psychologically, because I felt like I was turning my back on God," he said. "Finally I had to recognize, 'Well, I'm not called to [the priesthood]' and it must somehow . . . be revealed in time. Because I will not, cannot, take vows that I cannot keep." Shortly after that, Jeff left the Roman church and got married. Two decades later, a friend mentioned Sophia Divinity School. "Here's . . . a Catholic seminary where I can actually be a priest and I don't have to be celibate," he said. "I thought, 'Eureka,' you know, 'thank you thank you thank you Lord.' . . . So, [Antioch] was literally a gift from God." Gay men also said it was a relief to find a church where same-sex partnering, including same-sex marriage, is welcome. In Antioch, "I'm not hiding anything," Father Ted Feldmann said. "The women's issue is over. The gay issue is over. It's fabulous. . . . You can go on to other things."[16]

In fact, the issues are not totally over. Conflict endures, as we have seen, and sometimes opens painful breaches. Women clergy of Antioch in particular are rarely convinced that Antioch has resolved ancient prejudices in one generation. I too noticed differences in how men and women talk about ordination in Antioch. Women clergy, for example, tend to report authorization for their vocations based on unusual communications, like JoEllen receiving dreamy warrant from ancestor Patrick and the Brownsville God. Readying for ordination, women hear in visions or dreams things like "You've done this before" or "You are a continuation." Mother Deirdre Brousseau, a priest in New Hampshire who knew Herman and Meri, remembered Herman telling her that being male or female hardly matters, since everyone spent past lives as the other sex. Perhaps these extraordinary authorizations relate to the fact that women priests have a harder time being taken seriously in the ordinary world.[17]

Which they do. Mother Linda recounted the multiple times she wore her collar around town in Gallup, New Mexico, and was taken for being in costume. She laughed about it. But Bishop Diana put it more starkly. Men in clerical collars "are automatically accepted as a priest," she said. "Women, no." Women do the priestly work, then, but also still fight to do it. In many cases, there is outright hostility. Even within the independent movement, women priests are barred from many altars. Even from supporters, there is subtle sexism. One married woman priest turned to me after her husband interrupted our scheduled interview. "Real-life priesthood," she noted wryly. "A wife would not do that."[18]

Yet precisely because a woman in Catholic clerical garb is unusual, Antioch women priests have an impact on those around them, even just visually. JoEllen always carries pamphlets for St. Mary Magdalene in her purse, because at the grocery store "cashiers will say, . . . 'Are you a minister or just . . . ?' 'Well, actually I'm a priest.' 'You're a priest?! Tell me more about your church.'" Kera could hardly believe it when she was approached twice in O'Hare International Airport in Chicago with inquiries about her outfit. First a woman approached to ask if she was a priest, and Kera said yes. "She says, 'Bless your heart . . . you are just beautiful!'" Kera recalled. "And I thought, wow, that's not going to happen very often." But about fifteen minutes later, "a young lady came over and . . . she said, 'My girlfriend and I were just over there talking,' she said. 'Are you a priest?' I said yeah. She says, 'Tell me about your church.'"

All Antioch women priests have stories like this.[19]

GOING PUBLIC

In the sunroom home chapel, St. Mary Magdalene's first parishioners were JoEllen's former clients in counseling and spiritual direction, as well as family and friends. As I hung out with church leaders after mass that Sunday, the phone rang and Rob picked up. It was a long-ago acquaintance wondering if JoEllen still did spiritual direction. "This is how it happens," Rob said.[20]

Though St. Mary Magdalene might continue successfully, JoEllen and Rob knew its appeal was limited as long as it operated out of their home. The general public did not necessarily feel comfortable coming to a stranger's house for church. So JoEllen, a great believer in the metaphysical idea of manifesting thoughts in reality, bought a little toy church on which to focus prayer and symbolize the search for a public space. Just before I visited, Jo-Ellen was driving home as usual when she noticed a sign outside St. Paul's, a Levittown Episcopal church, announcing a Reiki healing service. Reiki? St. Paul's was a small and diminishing parish. It was already sharing re-sources with All Saints in Fallsington as part of steady US Episcopal down-sizing. Yet the sign seemed to indicate something was happening.[21]

JoEllen called to talk to the new rector. Father Michael Ruk was indeed bent on innovative ideas of any sort, including ecumenical work. After Jo-Ellen and Father Mike met in person, they shortly settled on an agreement that St. Mary Magdalene could rent St. Paul's for weekly Sunday masses. It would be expensive, but, as Kera put it, the St. Mary Magdalene crowd in-cludes "some very generous people." I attended the advertised Reiki service, met Father Mike Ruk, and toured St. Paul's. JoEllen could not get over its beauties, such as the antique baptismal font and the pipe organ. Kera was beaming.[22]

A short time after that, other collaborations were afoot. Father Mike in-vited JoEllen to substitute for him at a St. Paul's mass on Labor Day weekend 2007. Then they planned joint Holy Week and Easter services for the follow-ing spring. Soon St. Mary Magdalene joined St. Paul's and two other Epis-copal churches for a monthly "Food with Friends" ministry, a free sit-down meal for "everyone who would like to get out of the house and spend some time with others," as a local newspaper announced it. Then the group added Zion Lutheran Church, whose pastor was a friend of Father Mike.[23]

As an Episcopal priest, Father Mike knew about the Old Catholics of Europe, since they are in full communion with all of Anglicanism. He also knew about US independent Catholics before he met JoEllen, because he was already friends with local independent bishop Tim Cravens. Because of the formal Episcopal relationship with European Old Catholicism, an

Episcopal rector is not supposed to share altars with Old Catholics outside the Episcopal framework. But JoEllen and Tim Cravens are not Old Catholics, so Father Mike treated them like fellow Catholics in full communion. Not all Episcopalians felt the same. Another local pastor and vestry declined to participate in the joint services because they did not want Bishop Kera and Mother JoEllen on the altar—not because they were women, but because they doubted the validity of Antioch orders. That was "interesting" and "surprising," JoEllen said. But Father Mike's ecumenical enthusiasm was still "affirming to us as independents."[24]

St. Mary Magdalene continued to welcome new parishioners. The Roman Catholic church sex abuse crisis and bishops' cover-up hit Philadelphia particularly hard, with horrific details disclosed in grand jury reports in 2005 and 2011. Like parishioners Marian and Loretta, newcomers sometimes mentioned those reports. "We have a bunch of Romans who come here for two, three, four months because they need someplace to be but they don't know where they're going," Bishop Kera said. "And if they leave afterward, we have served the purpose of being a safe spot for them until they could figure out what to do."[25]

The Archdiocese of Philadelphia also has a history of episcopal conservatism that affects the tenor of parish life, so with ex–Roman Catholics JoEllen introduced change slowly and invited feedback often. For example, only after much discussion the church decided it would offer the option to receive the Eucharist by intinction, that is, by the communicant herself dipping the host in the chalice and eating it. Intinction is favored by a number of progressive Catholics who say it gives a more active and intimate role to the communicant. But intinction is also officially forbidden in the Roman rite, so Philadelphia Catholics are not used to it. Even after collective approval, JoEllen prepared a careful handout for the information table that invites additional feedback.[26]

Having a predominantly Roman or ex-Roman constituency makes the work of St. Mary Magdalene harder. Sometimes people report such painful experiences in the Roman church that it seems "awfully easy" to convert them to an alternative Catholicism, Kera said. But really it is not easy at all. Hurt or not, most Roman Catholic Philadelphians stay with their home church. Even if statistically about a third of those born Roman leave, largely they do not switch to independent Catholicism. Even if some attend St. Mary Magdalene, it may be temporary. And St. Mary Magdalene is not the only independent Catholic option in town.[27]

Still, from the perspective of JoEllen and Kera, it is amazing that St. Mary Magdalene exists at all. Only a dozen years earlier, neither of them had any idea they could become priests. Only in 2007 did they gain public worship space at St. Paul's. Ecumenical relationships now add more bodies to special services. Growth is slow but steady. They are optimistic that more big things can happen in the future.

A NEW CATHOLICISM IN THE NEW SOUTH

Two hundred and fifty miles south of St. Mary Magdalene, another outpost of the Church of Antioch was taking shape in the New South. In Richmond, Virginia, a group of friends was trying to figure out how to do a new Catholicism. Virginia was only half as Catholic as Pennsylvania, with 14 percent of the state claiming the faith. It was also politically more conservative, with large contingents of right-leaning Protestants. Even urban Richmond had not yet shifted from red to blue. The leaders of the group of friends were inclined to Catholicism, but they imagined a church that would welcome all the city's Christians. They imagined a church that welcomed out gay guys like themselves.[28]

Churches with open participation for out gay people and other sexual minorities have existed for years. Unitarian and Universalist congregations hosted same-sex marriages in the United States as early as 1957. The Metropolitan Community Church (MCC) was founded in Los Angeles in 1968 specifically for the inclusion of people of any gender or sexual orientation; it soon spread to urban centers all over the country. In 1969, also in Los Angeles, Dignity took shape as a harbor for LGBTQ Roman Catholics. It too had chapters everywhere within a few years. In the new millennium, the Episcopal Church and a number of of Protestant denominations bar no one from ordination or marriage on the basis of sexual orientation, or at least allow localities to decide to be "Welcoming" and "Open and Affirming" toward LGBTQ people.[29]

Back in the 1990s, however, it was a stretch for the Richmond men to imagine a Catholic church like that. Official Episcopal theology still held that gay members should remain celibate. Same for the Orthodox churches. Same for the Roman church, with a new accent from 1986 that same-sex acts were an "intrinsic moral evil" and that even celibate same-sex-oriented people had an "objective disorder," as formulated by Joseph Cardinal Ratzinger, then head of the Congregation for the Doctrine of the Faith and later Pope Benedict XVI. Taking Ratzinger's cues, one by one US bishops forbade Dignity from meeting on Roman church property and forbade Roman priests from celebrating mass for the group. The harsh phrases and the routing of Dignity dismayed millions of Roman Catholics who wished for a church more hospitable to gender and sexual minorities.[30]

Independent Catholicism ran miles ahead of the big bodies in terms of full sacramental inclusion of LGBTQ people. The Liberal Catholic Church had been the first modern Christianity to hint at a change in views of same-sex love. At first, it could only hint. In England the conviction in 1895 of Oscar Wilde for "gross indecency" silenced public avowal of homosexuality for sixty years. Yet the British left included Anglican groups of self-described "Uranians," who linked same-sex attraction with radical political and spiritual aims. Timothy d'Arch Smith's study from 1970 of these circles named Liberal Catholic Church founder Leadbeater among the Uranians, along with Vilatte's friend Ignatius of Llanthony and Annie Besant's friend Edward Carpenter. Carpenter was quietly influential—a self-described "mystic socialist" who wrote *The Intermediate Sex* (1912) and *Intermediate Types Among Primitive Folk* (1914). Both books celebrate "third sex" examples "in the Service of Religion" from ancient Greece to shamanic tribes, recuperating homosexuals as a high spiritual caste. While Carpenter never joined the Theosophical Society, Besant supported his work with money and publicity. And while Liberal Catholicism never endorsed Carpenter's notions of the nobility of same-sex love, Leadbeater certainly credited the sacraments with freedom from bondage, including repressive sexual conditioning. Merely the fact that the Liberal Catholic Church did not condemn homosexuality—in fact, it demoted the concept of sin altogether—made it a novel Catholic moment.[31]

A few generations later, Carpenter's writings had a huge impact on early homophile churches in the United States. Pioneer activist Harry Hay, founder of the Mattachine Society (1950) and the Radical Faeries (1979), said that reading *The Intermediate Sex* at age eleven changed his life. And independent bishop Mikhail Itkin—as mentioned above, likely the first US Catholic bishop to ordain women—dedicated to Carpenter his book *The Radical Jesus and Gay Consciousness: Notes for a Theology of Gay Liberation* (1972).[32]

Itkin published his book of gay liberation theology a year ahead of the English-language edition of Gustavo Gutiérrez's hugely influential *A Theology of Liberation*, which introduced US readers to Latin American liberation theology. Itkin likely knew of Gutiérrez. But his immediate influence was James Cone, who published *A Black Theology of Liberation* in 1970. Itkin also mentioned reading radical feminist Shulamith Firestone, Beat poet Gary Snyder, and Christian existentialist Nicolai Berdyaev. Ravenous for the best ideas, he reportedly attended conferences to buttonhole feminist theologians Mary Daly, Rosemary Radford Reuther, and the "Sisters of W.I.T.C.H." (Women's Inspirational Theological Conspiracy from Harvard), as well as "death of God" theologians Thomas Alizer and William Hamilton.

Jewish by birth, Mikhail Itkin was raised in Brooklyn as Michael Itinsky. Perhaps in Brooklyn he ran across the African Orthodox Church, then very active in that borough. Itkin repeated an anecdote told by its founder, George McGuire: Was Jesus black? Yes, McGuire had answered, because once an elderly parishioner had told him that "no white man would have died for me." So, Itkin wrote, "when we ask the question, Was Jesus Gay?, we are speaking to a like problem for our Gay brothers and sisters, for ourselves." If Jesus is black in the sense that he died for black lives, so Jesus is gay for the same reason. Itkin established his first San Francisco church in the late 1950s, preceding the founding of Dignity and the MCC by at least a decade. Both he and fellow Carpenter fan Harry Hay inspired more homophile churches, including independent Catholic ones.[33]

But gay-positive American independents went back even further than Itkin. Before his time in California, Itkin had linked with the very first Catholic church to explicitly welcome out gay and lesbian persons, a remarkable venture from 1946 headed by George Hyde in Atlanta, Georgia. In the early 1940s, Hyde was studying for the Roman priesthood at St. Mary's Seminary in Perryville, Missouri. A fellow student accused him of "immoral activity" and, as Hyde told the story, he not only denied it, but also publicly denounced seminary-wide hypocrisy about homosexuality. He was promptly expelled. Moving home, Hyde heard that a gay young man had been refused communion at Atlanta's downtown Sacred Heart church. He contacted the young man and, the next Sunday, knelt with him at the communion rail. The priest "passed by both of us," Hyde recalled. So the two of them just kept kneeling until the end of mass. The next Sunday, they did it again, and a few more people joined them. After five weeks, the solidarity group had grown to eight. They started meeting outside Sacred Heart and soon rented a house together. After Hyde was ordained to the priesthood by former Greek Orthodox bishop John Kazantks, they called themselves the Eucharist Catholic Church and started celebrating mass.[34]

The new church had about eighteen founding members—gay and straight, men and women, black and white, Catholic and Protestant. None of those was supposed to mix in Georgia in 1946. "And we paid for a lot of broken windows as a result," Hyde said. But the Eucharist Catholic Church was never supposed to be only for gay people. "That's wrong," Hyde said. "That would be just as wrong as having an exclusively heterosexual church." Still, the new group held that gay identity was "an intrinsic—even divinely created—part of the self," as Heather Rachelle White put it in her study of early homophile religious groups. Hyde was later consecrated as a bishop in the Vilatte line and led the Orthodox-Catholic Church of America, a small but enduring jurisdiction that combines eastern and western Catholicisms. Hyde advertised in the Mattachine Society's magazine ONE: "We do not attempt to judge."[35]

The Mattachine ad is what prompted Itkin to seek out Hyde for ordination. A small man with a larger-than-life personality, Itkin drew people with his brilliance and devotion. He celebrated mass every day of his adult life, served the cause of liberation Catholicism, and touched the lives of hundreds, including fellow indie priest and Lavender Panthers founder Ray Broshears and Ecclesia Gnostica Mysteriorum leader Rosamonde Miller. But Itkin also alienated people with his moods, hyperbole, and imperiousness. In the gay community he was called "the gay pope," and it was not always complimentary. Yet it is perhaps understandable if a certain personal fragmentation befell an independent Catholic bishop with views unpopular even among other independents, who linked gay rights not only with feminism but also with socialism, pacifism, antiracism, and Islamophilia. Toward the end of his life, Itkin joined the wildly syncretic Moorish Orthodox Church, which has honored him as Saint Mikhail of California since his death in 1989. To champion all those controversial causes for thirty years indeed qualifies Itkin as a saint, or crazy, or both.[36]

Another notable priest to affiliate with Hyde was Robert Clement, who started the Church of the Beloved Disciple in Manhattan as an outreach to gay, lesbian, and transgender persons shortly after the Stonewall riots in 1969. Marching as the only openly gay priest in New York's first Pride Parade on June 28, 1970, Clement carried a Beloved Disciple sign that read, "Gay People, This Is Your Church." A week later, eight hundred people showed up for the first mass, celebrated at an Episcopal church in Chelsea. That same summer, Clement started officiating what he called "Holy Union" ceremonies. They were the first public Catholic same-sex marriages.[37]

There was so much gay liberatory Catholicism in New York and California in the 1970s that some outsiders noticed independent Catholicism for the first time—and assumed that the whole phenomenon was "a gay subset." One widely cited article was Lester Kinsolving's *San Francisco Examiner* piece "The Paper Priests," recycling the familiar anti-independent charge of "playing church" and aiming it at the new homophile clerics. And in the slim book *The Gay Church*, Ronald Enroth and Gerald Jamison included independents in the assessment that while gay clerics seemed sincere and did good, their churches were "merely an extension of the gay life-style clothed in religiosity." Fellow independent Catholics were not all happy, either, about new numbers and notoriety in the gay ghettos. Like the issue of women's ordination, positions on the inclusion of LGBTQ Catholics divided independent churches over and over again.[38]

Yet independent Catholicism continues to provide a fruitful space for LGBTQ Catholics to live out faith and sexuality at the same time. As discussed above, my survey shows that gender and sexual minorities are represented in left-leaning independent Catholic churches at a much higher rate than the general population. In addition, respondents indicate involvement in LGBTQ advocacy at more than triple the rate of any other social cause, from the National Gay and Lesbian Task Force to the Trevor Project to Parents, Friends, and Family of Lesbians and Gays. Key LGBTQ theologian-activists are also independent priests and bishops, including Elias Farajaje-Jones, Richard Cleaver, and Elizabeth Stuart. In the new millennium, many independent Catholic churches marry same-sex couples and ordain transsexual and transgender people. There is even one jurisdiction that does Catholic "poly weddings"—marriages between three or more people in polyamorous relationships.[39]

DEACON TOM GALLUB

In Richmond, the men looking for a new way to do Catholicism found out later about independents' precocious gay-friendliness. For the time being, they figured things out on their own. Tom Gallub was the ringleader. Born in Brooklyn in 1944, Tom grew up "Catholic the Italian way," he said. He realized in his teens that he was gay and determined to confess it to a trusted priest. "And his words to me, . . . I'll remember them [forever]," Tom said. " 'Well, Tom,' he said, 'you might as well never come back to church because you're going to fry in hell.' And those words stunned me." Tom stopped going to church and joined the Army. On his own, he became entranced with ancient gnosticism and started learning modern languages to read the research articles. The Army let him do a degree while stationed in Heidelberg, Germany, in the 1970s. There he joined the Utrecht-linked Old Catholic church. Initially it was for "purely pragmatic" reasons, he said—it was easier to get access to archives as a member of the clergy. So he became an Old Catholic deacon. Only much later did Tom mark this diaconate as the start of a vocation to the priesthood.[40]

Back in the States, Tom moved to Richmond to teach languages in a middle school. A neighbor insisted that he meet a local Episcopal priest named Ulysses Gooch. Tom demurred, saying he was not really a church person. "She said, 'I think you'll get along with Uly.'" Several days later, there was a knock on the door. "I open it and it's Uly and his partner Worth," Tom said. "And they walked in and we bonded almost immediately. Not from the standpoint of anything religious but just as people." Because Uly pastored Richmond's Episcopal parish of St. Barnabas, Tom joined. At that time, the Episcopal Church had an unofficial "don't ask, don't tell" policy regarding noncelibate gay men and lesbians in ministry. So the whole church knew that Uly and Worth were a couple, and it didn't matter. Until it did. In 1994, someone officially notified the Episcopal diocese of the pastor's twenty-five-year relationship and Uly's bishop was obliged to press him to retire.[41]

For a while, Uly, Worth, and Tom attended the local Metropolitan Community Church. Like most MCCs, it was very "low-church," offering unadorned services and usually no communion. "I didn't want it; I didn't like it. But, I made Uly happy," Tom said. "Uly was the sort of person that you made happy." But then Uly was called out of retirement to fill in as rector in a tiny country parish, so he did that. Tom met his partner Fred Sherrill, and a little group of seven formed at the MCC. They even persuaded the MCC to add a liturgical service for high-church types. But when the local MCC leadership changed, the group of seven again found themselves spiritually homeless. Briefly they went back to Episcopalianism, but "then Lambeth came out," Tom said. That would be the Lambeth Resolution from 1998, which affirmed Anglican traditional language on homosexuality, including that it was "not compatible with scripture" and gay people were called to celibacy. "So we were not happy with that."

In 1999, they decided to start a church of their own. The group of seven came from diverse religious backgrounds—three Roman Catholic, two Southern Baptist, one American Baptist, and one Seventh-Day Adventist—but they hoped to be liturgically Catholic and radically inclusive. Tom saw an advertisement for an independent Catholic jurisdiction in one of his gnosticism magazines. So they linked up with that independent bishop and proceeded to spend "countless hours sitting there trying to figure out a formula that would mesh" all of their backgrounds, but also fit the guidelines of their new church. It worked for a while. But soon the new bishop seemed too conservative and his jurisdiction too unstable.

"Lo and behold, I get on the Internet," Tom said. He and his three best eighth-grade students found 260 independent US Catholic jurisdictions. Then Tom called every one. "Well, I didn't call every one," he said. "Our Lady of the Mysterious Turnip, no." So he narrowed it down to about one hundred churches. Twenty percent were "no longer in business," Tom estimated, and another twenty percent had split or merged since the website was last updated. Finally, Tom called the Church of Antioch. It was just one of the calls. "I was impressed by Richard's really simpl[e] attitude toward Christianity," Tom said. After that initial conversation, the Richmond group remained in preliminary talks with Richard for two years. But fairly soon Tom said they felt that the Church of Antioch "probably should be our destiny." It was Catholic, open, and "viable." Uly, back from his country stint, started saying mass for the parish they would eventually call Gentle Shepherd. They began to shop for a building.

Buying a building was more of an ordeal than joining Antioch. Leaders found a little church on a residential street put up for sale by an independent Anglican group. But that group was traditionalist and reneged on selling to a church full of out-gay guys. Instead it sold to "notorious Richmond developer, architect, and sometime political activist" Louis Salomonsky, as a local paper described him. That's when things got rather providential. Salomonsky heard that the traditionalist Anglicans had turned down the gay guys and was disgusted. So he decided to sell the church to Tom Gallub and the group himself. Salomonsky priced the building at cost and then donated another $10,000 to his buyers. He even hooked them up with a new bank when the first one backed out of financing a gay church.[42]

Even with Salomonsky's help, however, buying a church was difficult. "People were talking about us," Tom recalled. "They thought we were some sort of estranged cult." It was also a big fiscal step, since members of the group were named on the mortgage and three of them personally guaranteed it. But they believed their new church would be an important resource for gay people and for Richmond Catholicism. "We wanted to open the eyes of the community," Tom said. In independent Catholicism, Tom "could once again be what I was"—Catholic and openly gay—"and not have to face the flames of hell," he said. He hoped Gentle Shepherd could offer the same to others. Slowly but surely, their presence in the community turned the tide of public opinion. They got some sympathetic local press. One day Uly knocked on the door of a man who lived in the Gentle Shepherd neighborhood. Uly had heard that the man was dying and came to pray with him. "Ah, you're that queer church down the street," the man said. "Well, come in."[43]

At first they named the church after Saints Sergius and Bacchus, Roman martyrs of late antiquity whose traditional iconography always pairs them together. "They are, of course, a gay couple," Tom said. Part of reworking Catholicism in communities of sexual liberation involves "outing" the tradition's considerable potential for eroticism, including homoeroticism, such as the story of Sergius and Bacchus or the trope of John as "Beloved Disciple" of Jesus. A number of gay-friendly Catholic churches display the striking icon of Sergius and Bacchus painted by Franciscan monk Robert Lentz, in which the pair stands especially close. But eventually the Richmond group decided that as a church name Saints Sergius and Bacchus was "sort of masculine." "We didn't intend it to be a gay church," Tom said, or a men's church. So they paired the male saints with another Lentz icon of female saints, Perpetua and Felicity, and changed the church name to Gentle Shepherd. "We figured, oh, you know, . . . everybody likes a Gentle Shepherd."[44]

To them, being gentle and shepherd-like was even more important than being gay or Catholic. It was a "relief" to find Antioch, Tom said—an open Catholic church "that had been around for a long time." But "we could have called ourselves, you know, the First Church of Richmond," Tom said. They were already a viable community and primarily wanted to keep the family feeling and welcome more people. "Ninety-five percent of the people in our church are here because it is our church," he said. "They're not here because of independent Catholicism. And I think, you know, with the possible exception . . . of starting to worship Satan, they would continue to come."[45]

They grew bit by bit, gaining members and losing members, like most independent Catholic churches. When I attended mass on a July Sunday in

2007, there were twenty-six people: many gay white men, but also female, black, Asian, bi, trans, straight, and cross-dressing adults, both couples and singles, and a few children as well. Stalwarts made up the excellent music ministry: Tom's partner Fred on the piano, Gene Abbott on the organ, and Becky Taylor on guitar. After mass about fifteen people decamped for brunch, taking over the back room of a comfy neighborhood restaurant. The gathering had the feel of a family, even maybe a "New York–style Italian family," like the one in which Tom grew up. Everyone was talking loudly, talking over one another, ribbing one another, jumping from topic to topic, and gesturing with hands and whole bodies. Richmond's political climate "made it very very difficult for people that are gay to basically exist peacefully with society at large," Tom said, so "we go out of our way to make people feel like [they] can rely on each other outside of the confines of their traditional, biological families." Gentle Shepherd parishioners can "call each

FIGURE 6.2 Antiochians and saints at Convocation, Richmond, Va., October 2005. *Left to right*: Kathy Perry, Tom Gallub, Uly Gooch, and—in prints by iconographer Robert Lentz, OFM—Saints Sergius and Bacchus and Saints Perpetua and Felicity. Courtesy of Daniel Dangaran.

other up and say, 'I'm having a problem' or . . . 'I'm back in drug rehab' . . . or 'I'm really down.'"[46]

Married at Gentle Shepherd in 2004, Tom and Fred often house Richmond's unmoored or rehabbing young gay men at their home for weeks and months at a time. Tom tells them what Uly told him years ago: "There's no reason to deny God because of the thoughts of some people who don't understand Him, or Her." He and Fred bring the young men to church for more support. "You don't have to come every Sunday. We don't look at you strange." Tom paused. "Well, I yell at them if they don't come." But, he laughed, "it's not an abject requirement."[47]

QUEER CATHOLICISM

Richard was thrilled about St. Mary Magdalene and Gentle Shepherd, two East Coast Antioch parishes that materialized in a few short years. A defender of any "creative" ministries his priests might wish to try, Richard was still at heart a pastor who vibed well with the traditional parish work of JoEllen and Tom. It was no stretch for him to welcome a church full of gay men. As far back as Religious Science, he started to see gender and sexuality on a continuum, rather than as dualities of men and women, gay and straight. Richard loved the ladies and was old-fashioned enough to prompt occasional church grumbling about his sexism. But he also embraced his own "feminine side." Like Herman, he never really stereotyped what such a side might look like.

For Herman and Meri Spruit personally, homosexuality was a nonissue. Both ordained and consecrated noncelibate lesbian women and gay men from the start. When Meri was in charge, one future priest recalled telling her that he was gay and asking if he should even start the process. "Oh no, it's not a problem," Meri said, as he recalled. "At all." But she and Herman harbored enough homophobia to decide against using gay-inclusive language in church brochures and advertising. Some of their bishops felt it would "attract" gay people. "They were right," Richard said, because as soon as he added explicitly gay-inclusive language in 2006, the result was that "there are more gay people." Which is "totally OK," he said.[48]

Then Richard kept ahead of the political curve by performing same-sex marriages and advocating for civil recognition of such marriages by the state of New Mexico. He stood up for LGBTQ acceptance when Santa Fe Episcopal rector Richard Murphy "flew the rainbow flag" at St. Bede's, where vandals repeatedly broke windows. At the time seminarian Lian Reed headed the Interfaith Alliance and organized a controversial Interfaith Support Day for St. Bede's. Richard was "one of the first to say, 'I will be there, Dick, no problem,'" Lian told me. A number of ministers showed up with Richard to provide added security and help replace broken windows. After a while, the vandalism stopped.[49]

The big bodies of Catholicism have plenty of room for LGBTQ people, as millions of queer Roman, Orthodox, and Episcopal church members can attest. LGBTQ Antiochians who are former Roman Catholics have by no means experienced uniform condemnation in the Roman church. Deacon Roberto recalled confiding his sexual confusions to a Seattle-area priest in the early 1970s. The priest told him he "was OK," "it was fine," and "God didn't care." "And I didn't believe him," Roberto laughed. Another Roman priest responded supportively, too. They "pretty much sav[ed] my life, I think." In the seminary, however, Roberto witnessed the negotiations of closeted gay life and became very sad. He is thankful his path led elsewhere.[50]

Like Roberto, Father Ted is a former Roman seminarian. He left the seminary—temporarily, he thought—to explore more radical theology at Matthew Fox's Institute for Culture and Creation Spirituality, then a Roman institution housed at Holy Names College in Oakland, California. But between Fox's excommunication by the Vatican in 1992, the deaths of many friends from AIDS, and meeting some independent Catholics, Ted increasingly dreaded going back into the seminary closet. "What really pushed me over the edge with the Roman Catholic church was the gay issue," Ted said. "I have been banging my head against the wall . . . for all these years, and trying to use all this psychology and theology to make it OK. And it's . . . not OK."[51]

Sophia seminarian Claire Vincent, raised Roman Catholic, said she left Christianity for decades after ingesting the official Roman condemnation of homosexuality. "I was so anti-Christian," Claire said. "I was one of those people that, like, had the bumper sticker 'Jesus Save Us from Your

Followers.'" Bishop Mark Newman, also raised Roman Catholic, said he stayed away from church for twenty-five years. "As a gay man it was not a pleasant environment for me to be in and to be aware that the church didn't accept us as valid, as meaningful, as anything potentially sacred, but as inherently sinful," he said. "So there was always that tension of, how do I relate to an organization that I dearly love but at the same time really doesn't love me? Despite what it says."[52]

For each of them, the Church of Antioch turned it around. Ted and Roberto both said the best thing about the church is providing a context where they can fulfill their vocations as Catholic priests "without compromising . . . integrity to do it," as Ted put it. Roberto said he loves telling other progressive ex-Romans that Antioch is "not hung up on doctrines, so all of the issues that you think of that have separated you from Catholicism, principally issues involving 'pelvic Christianity' . . . aren't issues for us." For straight Antiochians too, the full inclusion of gender and sexual minorities is "huge," as Mother JoEllen put it. Seminarian Jack Pischner said he appreciates "that sexual orientation is not an issue, . . . because it exemplifies the fact that we do walk the talk. We truly are an inclusive rather than exclusive organization."[53]

At least they truly try. LGBTQ Antiochians still contend with fellow church members who are discomfited by their presence, theorize their difference, or talk about "them" in the third person, as if "they" weren't present on the same listserv. One priest finally posted to say she found it odd that straight Antiochians discuss "gay and lesbian issues" so frequently. What about straight people "issues"? The straight people have issues. Sometimes LGBTQ Antiochians attempt to educate or explain. Other times, it is too tiring. At the first Convocation with a separate men's meeting, it was too tiring. The women of Antioch had held separate women's meetings at Convocation in the past, so in 2009 the men decided that they would have a separate meeting, too. But none of the gay guys attended. When I asked them why, they said, "Straight men's issues." For their whole lives as gay men they had journeyed to deconstruct stereotypes of masculinity. For survival and sanity, they had to. They didn't feel like circling back around for straight guys who were suddenly discovering the whole topic.[54]

ANOTHER TOM

Gentle Shepherd faced another hurdle. Though finding Antioch was hard and buying their building was even harder, the greatest challenge of the little church came with the unexpected death of one of their own. One day Uly Gooch was his usual captivating, laughing, pain-in-the-ass self. The next day he was seriously ill, with partner Worth at his hospital bedside. It was October 2006, and a core group of Gentle Shepherd was scheduled to go to Convocation in Santa Fe. Worth said to fly without them. Tom, Fred, and everyone else were at the airport when they heard the news that Uly had died. He was seventy-four and, it seemed, way too young. He was their priest.[55]

It was also the Richmond church's finest hour, in a way. They came to Convocation. They were shocked and grieving, but knew Uly wanted them to get on the plane. In the bustle of the gathering, the hushed, reflective pack of men participated but also prayed madly and turned in early. After Convocation, Bishop Michael Adams flew from Iowa to Virginia to help lay Uly to rest. The whole Diocese of the East drove south. The funeral was held at St. Paul's Episcopal church right next to Richmond's state capitol—big enough to handle the crowd, and grand enough for Uly. But Uly asked that donations in his memory go to Gentle Shepherd. The small community was still distressed, but felt the grace and love from Uly and fellow Antiochians.[56]

They felt graced yet more when a new man among them quietly took his vestments out of their dry cleaning bags and started saying mass. This was Tom Siebert. Another Tom. They called him Tom David to distinguish him from Tom Gallub. Their new priest just walked forward from the pews.

Tom David had known Uly for only a few months. So his shock was less about the loss of a friend and more about the strange path that led from his teenaged conversion to Roman Catholicism in Racine, Wisconsin, to saying Sunday mass for an independent parish in Richmond, Virginia. He could hardly believe it. In Richmond he was just minding his own business, making a life with partner Rick Goff and working for Brooks Brothers. He and Rick found Gentle Shepherd and liked it. But the last time he had said mass was years ago. He thought he had left all of that behind. Yet now he was again called to serve as a priest, a pastor. He was just trying to go with the flow.[57]

Flow was not Tom David's strong suit in his school years. When he graduated from college at St. Mary's in Baltimore in the mid-1970s, he had so thoroughly molded himself into the perfect candidate for Roman Catholic ordination that his professors told him to take a year off. Tom David was "dumbstruck and horrified," initially thinking they were "calling my vocation into question." Slowly he comprehended that some faculty thought he really needed to see the world. So Tom David went home to Racine, pondered Lake Michigan for a while, and decided to make the most of the opportunity.

That summer after college launched his transformation from collared-up seminarian to intrepid spiritual explorer. Working in construction in Mobile, Alabama, he and his foreman would have philosophical conversations. The foreman said that "his conception of God was kind of this amorphous cloud of gases," Tom David said. "And I just didn't, I just couldn't even begin to wrap my head around that, . . . [it was so] out of my category." But it opened his mind. So did riding in a coworker's pink Cadillac Eldorado, tricked out with lanterns, pillows, and a killer stereo system. So did falling in love with the daughter of the family with whom he was staying. He had a whole year totally out of his category. Still, something told him "it wasn't the right track for me to be pursuing a relationship with a woman," he said, "just very, very deep down, coming to terms with my sexuality and so on." And something else told him he still wanted to be a priest.

So he went back to Baltimore. But after that summer, it was never a straight line again. He switched to the Byzantine Rite within the Roman communion, was ordained as a Byzantine priest, and tonsured as a monk in the Eparchy of Passaic, New Jersey, in 1981. Then he went fully Orthodox and was received into the Carpatho-Russian diocese in Johnstown, Pennsylvania. In 1989 he and a monk-friend founded the Monastery of the Holy Cross near Catholic University in Washington, D.C. For funds and outreach they ran the Icon and Book Service a few doors away. Ministering at the forefront of ecumenical work in canonical American Orthodoxy, they celebrated a Divine Liturgy open to the whole Catholic University community, mostly Roman Catholics. But by 1995 Tom and his confrere were back in the Roman communion, partly because of Orthodox leaders' resistance to their efforts. They reestablished status as Byzantine priests, now in the Ukrainian diocese of Philadelphia.

Counseling younger seminarians, Tom David started to mind his own status as a gay priest in the Roman communion. He would recite "the party line" that gay or straight, "what the church expects of you" as a priest is celibacy. "I started hearing myself," Tom David said, and "understand[ing] that I didn't really believe everything that I was having to tell them. That I had told myself." He was approaching middle age and "decided to leave no stone unturned." Then he met Rick—or, rather, remet him. They had known each other in seminary at St. Mary's. "And that just kind of took off." So Tom David took a leave of absence from the Byzantine diocese.[58]

Then came a defining moment, though Tom David did not recognize it at the time. A fellow Byzantine cleric who left and wanted to marry his male partner asked Tom David to do a rite of "holy union." Tom David agreed, since the ceremony took place apart from any church jurisdiction. But a year later, he got notification that his diocese had charged him with violating "sacramental norms." And in December 2006, he received documents confirming excommunication. The documents also said church leaders decided not to laicize him, in hopes he "would repent and return." But by then Tom David had moved to Richmond and married Rick. He had also vested for mass when Uly died. "I could never repent in terms of that holy union ceremony," Tom David said. "And I can certainly never repent on anything that I've done with Gentle Shepherd."[59]

When I spoke to him in July 2007, Tom David was still reeling from the whole trip. From his time in Roman Catholicism and Orthodoxy, he knew about "*vagantes* groups, . . . independent groups," he said, because "Rome follows all those things, as do the Orthodox, pretty closely. And here I am, in the pews of one of these churches on a Sunday. You know, with my partner." He laughed. "Oh, I don't understand this. But this is exactly why I'm supposed to be here. Because it's . . . pushing me to grow." Tom David felt "betrayal" from Rome, he said, but "the Roman church would say 'betrayal,' too." In any case, he was seeing fewer lines between varieties of Catholicism.

On the contrary, he was seeing much flow among all conceptions of the divine. "All these years later," that "cloud of gases" the Alabama foreman described as God seemed "not . . . all that far off," he said. It was all "part of the mystical reality of the Body of Christ," Tom David said. "I'm the same person, in some ways, that I have always been. But then again, I'm a radically different person."[60]

◆　　◆　　◆

By 2008, the Diocese of the East had taken shape according to Archbishop Richard's *Field of Dreams* strategy. Tom David was earning a certificate in Clinical Pastoral Education in order to work professionally as a hospital chaplain. Tom Gallub as an Old Catholic deacon had been incardinated into the Church of Antioch, then ordained a priest. Claire Vincent did her Masters of Divinity degree at Vanderbilt and her pastoral internship at Gentle Shepherd. To the south in Goldston, North Carolina, Father Carl Matthews-Naylor had joined. To the north in Baltimore, Ted Feldmann said mass for a small community called Beloved Disciple—named after Robert Clements's vanguard church in New York City, which Ted had visited back in the day. Also in Baltimore, Father Jack Sweeley celebrated his weekly online mass at the St. James Catholic Community website. Further to the north were Jo-Ellen and Kera at St. Mary Magdalene, which had spun off another congregation, St. Miriam's, led by Father Jim St. George. Even further north, Mother Deirdre Brousseau said mass at her New Hampshire home and grew a wedding ministry.

The saints accompany them, as they do all Catholics. Mary the mother of Jesus is invoked in many forms, as are Sergius and Bacchus, Perpetua and Felicity, Mary Magdalene, the "Beloved Disciple," and the apostle James. The Blue Bell church of St. Miriam symbolically canonized Miriam, the biblical older sister of Jewish patriarch Moses, to honor its borrowed worship space in a synagogue. To Antiochians, this new Diocese of the East came about not just because of Herman's vision, Meri's leadership, Richard's hard work, and all their efforts. It was confected by the whole communion of saints, on earth and in heaven. It manifests God as Father, Mother, the Christ, the

Holy Spirit, the "Goddess, Ascended Masters, and a Galactic Being or two," as Bishop Patsy Grubbs put it. Thanks be to God and all the galactic beings, the East Coasters seeded a new kind of Catholicism in geographic strongholds of the US Roman church and conservative Protestantism. The seeds have barely sprouted. There are difficulties and drama. But that is true in any church. Despite tensions, diocesan leaders are awed to be part of what they consider God's work. They are getting the word out that Catholics can be divorced and receive communion, be women and get ordained, be gay and say yes to a vocation. Catholicism really is for everybody.[61]

"Catholic means universal."

CONCLUSION

ALL CATHOLICS

THE CHURCH OF Antioch did not last.

At least, it did not last as one church body. In 2010, the Church of Antioch split. Despite careful planning, the leadership transition from Richard to an elected presiding bishop did not go well. Bishops reported after their meeting in spring 2009 that the election process was wrenching. In September 2010 a series of latent conflicts burbled to the surface. People spoke harsh words and did rash things. And while in theory new governance would enhance episcopal collegiality, in reality, past a certain point, the retained structure of the corporation sole left no room for mediation. There were rulings, resignations, ultimatums, and excommunications. A "holy implosion," as Mother JoEllen later called it, had commenced.[1]

By the time the dust had settled, everything was rearranged. In 2016, the Church of Antioch still exists, but it is a much smaller body, now headed by Bishop Mark Newman and based in Phoenix, Arizona. Initially his term as presiding bishop was to last five years, as Richard had specified. But in 2011 Bishop Mark announced that for the sake of stability, he would serve for ten years. He steadily led the new Church of Antioch away from metaphysics and mixings and toward the Christianity of new progressives like Jeff Procter-Murphy and Fred Plumer. But Antioch still retains the Catholic difference: succession, sacraments, and saints.

Most former Antiochians sojourn with Ascension Alliance, founded by former Antioch bishop Alan Kemp and based in Seattle, Washington. The leadership of Ascension Alliance is shared between Alan acting as permanent president and doing all administration and Roberto Foss serving as presiding bishop, a position of spiritual leadership. Roberto became a bishop in 2009 and succeeded Bishop Patsy Grubbs in 2015. Ascension harbors more of the range of the old Antioch, and adds notes of the Emergent Church and Jewish Renewal as embodied in the organization Aleph, of which Bishop Alan was a member for many years.

Out on the East Coast, St. Mary Magdalene in Fairless Hills joined another jurisdiction, the Independent Catholic Church of the Americas. St. Miriam in Blue Bell joined yet another jurisdiction, the International Old Catholic Churches.

Mother JoEllen could joke about the "holy implosion" later, but for her and every Antioch leader, the division was devastating. They all knew that independent churches split, but hoped theirs would be different. They could not understand how reasonable and kind colleagues had behaved so badly. Sometimes they could not fathom their own words and actions, looking back on hasty assumptions and bombastic declamations, mostly exchanged by email. Conflict sparked about all the usual things, from authority structures and ordination standards to theological parameters and future directions. Why in the world did previously manageable conflict suddenly detonate?

Then again, they knew why.

As they discussed in the months and years afterward, they knew. They always knew that church diversity would be hard to hold together over the long haul. That Richard worked daily miracles of order and balance. That new leadership always occasioned fresh tilts at old quarrels. That change meant vulnerability. That "the book" would soon be published—this book—which seemed to raise the stakes of decisions.

Still, the split rocked Antiochians to their cores. They lost ecclesiastical and spiritual mooring. They lost friends. They were ashamed. A number of them got sick. Their very flesh protested this latest cut within the Mystical Body of Christ.

They worried about me. Some controversial decisions that precipitated the split had attempted to adjust organizational structure partly "based upon the assumption that your book will cause people to flock to the [Church of Antioch]," as Bishop Michael Adams wrote me. In other words, the book was part of the end of the church. And for a while we all wondered if the end of the church would also be the end of the book. But I was certainly OK. I loved these people and felt for them. They loved me and felt for me. Observation changes the observed and the observer. The knowledge is the relationship. I got on the listserv of Ascension as well as Antioch and started going to both Convocations.[2]

Richard himself was absolutely shattered. If he ever wept over the Church of Antioch, he wept now. Freshly retired, he just wished to be a proud patriarch emeritus. Instead, his life's work lay blown to pieces around him. He remained autocephalous for a while. But in 2012, Richard joined Ascension Alliance, too. At Loretto, Dan Dangaran and Carol Calvert took full responsibility for the Santa Fe parish, but Richard wanted to start a new ministry and needed the nonprofit status that Ascension Alliance conferred. He found a small space in downtown Santa Fe and opened it as the Chapel of Inner Peace—not a church, just a space for residents and tourists to get away from the hustle and bustle. It was a slower and more contemplative ministry, which suited Richard just fine.[3]

After a few years, everyone had recovered and gained perspective. In presentations at the dual Convocations, I commented that while the breakup hurt, the two new jurisdictions were actually more representative of independent Catholicism than the one long-lasting Church of Antioch. Fragmentation characterizes the movement. It also continually challenges members—and scholars—to notice their attachment to size, stability, and status. What counts as success? Who is worth studying? Leaders at Antioch and Ascension could hear what I was saying. Some even took comfort from the fact that in view of independent Catholic history, the split they experienced as so horrific was actually a totally normal occurrence.

So, the new Antiochians and new "Ascensionistas," as they nickname themselves, continue to make their way in independent Catholicism. Antioch has the church archives that I cite in this book. Ascension also has a significant historical collection. Both jurisdictions claim to be the authentic continuation of the Spruit church. Both posted yearly listserv notices of Matriarch Meri's August birthday, with the suggestion that everyone send her cards as she continued to live with Alzheimer's disease in the care of her oldest daughter, Carol Lauderdale.

FIGURE 7.1 Meri Spruit with her Himalayan cat, March 2014.
Courtesy of Carol Lauderdale.

And on June 3, 2014, both listservs posted news of Matriarch Meri's death. One of the first and still one of the only women in the world to lead a Catholic church had passed from earthly life. But if Antioch and Ascension had anything to do with it, Meri would not pass from memory.[4]

It was long the wish of the matriarch that Archbishop Richard preside at her funeral. Perhaps more people would attend Meri's final event than made it to Herman's. Perhaps Meri and Richard would be able to gather everyone together, one last time.[5]

REDEFINING CATHOLICISM

As I've told the story of Antioch and Ascension Catholics—or a story, one of many that could be told—I've shown that left-leaning independents maintain and modify modern Catholicism in a number of ways. They keep succession, sacraments, and saints, as well as identification with the word "Catholic." But they practice those traditions in new ways, especially in the direction of mixing, mysticism, and what I call sacramental justice—opening the sacraments to all. Their idea of "one" Catholic church assumes that many institutions are invisibly united. As if church boundaries are indeed so porous, independents flow in and out of big-body Catholicism all the time.

Telling this story, I suggest that independents function as the "other" within the totality of Catholicism by sheltering, reshaping, and showcasing what the big bodies block or expel. Left-leaning independent Catholics showcase conciliarism, liberalism, and modernism. They precociously consecrated black men, ordained women, and married gay people. They dropped sin and universalized salvation. They are worker-priests and liturgical innovators. Sometimes the big bodies move in those directions after years, decades, or centuries—as in the Roman church's Vatican II reforms or the Anglican communion's ordination of women. Yet independent Catholics remain at the cutting edge of exploration and experimentation.

As such, independents represent the once-and-future possibilities of Catholicism. Sometimes they actually influence the big communions. When the Holy See established new US southern dioceses in 1820, when the bishop of Green Bay invited the Norbertines to Wisconsin in 1893, when Hans Küng heralded the example of Old Catholicism after Vatican II, when Pope Benedict XVI announced that women's ordination was a "grave crime" in 2010, these events are evidence that independents change the big communions. In a bigger view, the conciliarist leanings of popes like John XXIII and Francis and the growing interest of Catholics worldwide in participatory church governance could suggest that reform elements inside and outside the Roman communion prophesied the future of Catholicism a long time ago. Meanwhile, at the local level, every time a Roman priest calls an independent colleague to do a sacrament, every time a Roman couple books an independent priest for a wedding, independents change the big communions.

Usually the changes are local and barely perceptible. Big-body and small-church Catholic leaders watch each other and warn each other and work together. They come into contact and collaborate or condemn. Either way, they are having a much wilder and more creative conversation than the one you hear if you only listen to the big bodies. Where is the church? Who is the pope? What is Catholic? And who says? The all-Catholic conversation features appropriation, cooperation, and reunion among the different institutions. It also involves silence, repudiation, and excommunication. All interactions continually morph small bodies and large churches in minute and unpredictable ways. Though most changes are small, clearly the bounds of Catholicism are not identical with any one church. You need to see all the churches to get the big picture.

INCLUDING ALL CATHOLICS

I hope that the story of independents opens new vistas on the US history of religion, women, and LGBTQ communities, as well as small faith groups, fluid institutions, religious mixing, and the lives of leaders. Most of all, however, I hope the story of independents can shift how we see Catholicism. Maybe we can start talking as if Catholicism includes all Catholics. In Roman contexts, of course, Catholicism may still solely or normatively indicate the Roman communion, and that is fine. But outside Roman contexts, equating all Catholicism with Roman Catholicism is just habit.

In the United States, it is a habit with a history. That history is the demographic and political dominance of the Roman church and its role as foil for American identity. In the early twentieth century, Roman Catholic power coalesced with the popular idea of America as a nation where many Protestantisms contended with monolithic Catholicism. This coalescing eclipsed the common awareness of "other Catholics" and the common usage of the word "Catholic" for anyone but members of the Roman communion. Scholars picked up the habit. By the time of the invention of American church history in the 1840s, this interpretive funneling was well underway. By the time of the invention of religious studies in the 1960s, the widespread American equation of all Catholicism with Rome was done and dusted. By the time of the invention of Catholic Studies in the 1990s, the diverse Catholic perspectives it aimed to represent all fell within the bounds of the Roman communion. All of this is to say that in the United States, Catholicism apart from Rome is difficult to conceptualize, even where there is no ideological resistance or theological reason.

It was not always so. To recall, in the early 1890s there were six different Catholic churches in play for Joseph René Vilatte and his missions: Protestant Episcopal, Old Catholic, Roman Catholic, Russian Orthodox, Syrian Orthodox, and Polish Catholic. The US Census Office listed "6 bodies" of "Other Catholics." And the Protestant Episcopal Church was debating changing its name to the "American Catholic Church." But about seventy years later, when the Protestant Episcopal Church became "The Episcopal Church" and dropped the "Protestant" from its name, it was by then completely out of the question to add "Catholic."

In the twenty-first-century United States, the equation of Catholicism and Rome remains in place. Take the huge study "America's Changing Religious Landscape," conducted in 2015 by the Pew Research Center. The survey separately lists and counts over a hundred Protestant denominations. Many of these denominations come in at less than 0.3 percent of the population, meaning fewer than 960,000 people. The line for Catholic, however, is just that: one line, Catholic, 20.8 percent. The Pew report does not detail respondents' exact words in this telephone survey, but identification as "Catholic" is presumed to indicate Roman Catholic. Pew counts separately Orthodoxy and Episcopalianism, the latter listed as Protestant. But not any other Catholics. Pew did not do anything wrong. This is a normal view of the US religious landscape. As Lawrence Cunningham puts it in *An Introduction to Catholicism* (2009), Catholicism is "almost instinctively identified with the papacy."[6]

Yet the lightest exposure to other Catholics quickly reframes that instinct as habit. Perhaps at least we can start noting the habit, which Cunningham does. "We will understand 'Catholic' in the generic way (i.e. as opposed to the Orthodox or Protestant or Anglican Churches)," he writes, "as is commonly used unless otherwise stipulated." So does scholar Mark Jordan. "I will often use 'Catholic' to mean Roman Catholic and 'the church' to mean . . . the network of Roman Catholic institutions," he writes. "I don't mean to suggest by my usage that the sum of Roman Catholic institutions is the true church or that other Christian institutions couldn't make an equal claim to being 'catholic.' I only intend to begin with our ordinary shorthand for talking about these things." Catholicism is "our ordinary shorthand" for Roman Catholicism. Shorthand is fine and often useful. But by definition it stands in for the full transcript.[7]

Maybe US observers of Catholicism can take a cue from global Catholicism, since in places like the Netherlands, Greece, Lebanon, Egypt, England, and Brazil, Catholicism does not refer only to the Roman communion. In some countries there is more popular awareness that though the Roman church claims global unity, Catholicism obviously split many times in the Reformation, and before that in the Great Schism, and before that in rifts with purported heretics, and before that in a long, slow fissure with Judaism. Outside the culturally ultramontane United States, it can be easier to see the truth of so many "separation[s]" and "segregations" or, as the Rastafarians say, "isms and schisms." Irish pop singer and independent Catholic priest Sinéad O'Connor likes to quote her wordsmithing Rastafarian friends. Catholicism? No, they say. Catholi*schism*.[8]

FIGURE 7.2 Sinéad O'Connor, independent Catholic priest, performing at Parkpop in The Hague, the Netherlands, June 30, 2013. Courtesy of Geert Heldens.

SHIFTING CATHOLIC STORY LINES

If Catholicism includes all Catholics, other shifts may follow. Perhaps we can explore what religious studies scholar Manuel Vásquez calls "the production of Catholicity." Maybe Catholicism can be defined less by institutions and creeds and more by discourse about succession, sacraments, saints, and the word "Catholic." Who talks about these things, and when, why, and how? What is the cultural work of the discourse in different times and places? How does it function as capital or counterconduct? When do genealogies of "Catholic" and "catholic" merge and separate?[9]

We may also rethink anti-Catholicism. Maybe historical anti-Catholicism is sometimes more helpfully described as anti-Romanism. I am not saying that anti-Catholicism never existed. But given Orthodox, Anglicans, independent Catholics, and Protestant Catholics, all of whom were critical of Rome and sometimes passionately hated Rome, while claiming Catholicism, the label of anti-Catholicism is not always accurate.[10]

We may also reconsider denominationalism. It is a bulwark of American religious historiography and Catholic exceptionalism that Catholicism was the only American religion not to succumb to the Protestant denominational model. Judaism, Islam, Buddhism—they all showed up in the United States, started splitting, and organized themselves denominationally. As it turns out, Catholicism is not an exception. It too has split over and over, and continues to split. If that is the case, then the exception no longer proves the rule. Maybe splitting is not a Protestant thing at all. Maybe it is just the way of human institutions.[11]

We can rewrite the timeline of US Catholic history, and not only by adding dates for women's ordination and same-sex marriage. US Catholic history features a lot more modernism and liberalism than is usually recognized. In the years leading up to the papal condemnations of 1898 and 1907, modernist Catholicism was not limited to the Americanist bishops and Dunwoodie priests. Hundreds of other reform-minded Catholics were the ones founding and populating ultrajectine churches since the late eighteenth century. And even when the US Roman church repopulated its liberal ranks before and after Vatican II, only a few Roman liberals ever challenged the ultramontane papacy as such. By contrast, left-leaning independents maintained a radical critique of papalism and acted on it, forming new churches with alternative authority structures. In short, if you count independents, Catholics were part of progressive religion in the United States earlier, more radically, and in greater numbers than we generally acknowledge.

Catholics also turn out to be a big part of US metaphysical religion, usually identified primarily with Protestants, Freemasons, transcendentalists, and New Age types. Looking at independents, it seems clear that from European origins to the American twenty-first century, metaphysicalism is often simply a flavor of Catholicism—subversive, underground, or separate from Rome altogether. Metaphysically inclined Catholics share much with other mystics and esotericists. But they are unusually interested in history, hoping to newly narrate a Catholicism of lost essences restored, of heterogeneity rather than unity.

Despite all these shifts, I guess it is still possible to argue that the small size and perpetual chaos of independent Catholics render them ever peripheral and irrelevant, just so many rogue satellites to the Roman center. But after spending a decade among independents, I say the center cannot hold. If independents highlight the shared emphases of Catholics as well as the fault lines between them, if they dart ahead where big bodies follow years later or never, if they harbor people and practices that roil the large communions, if they nudge the history, frame, and name of Catholicism, then it seems to me that independents are more like a vanguard than a margin. Independents know they are considered "fringey." "I don't think of it that way," Bishop Michael Adams said. "I think of us as the cutting edge. The pointy [end] of the spear has a very small surface area. And that's us."[12]

At the very least, independents are provocative for thinking about modern Catholicism. The extent of their difference, continuity, and interaction with the big communions suggests we may not fully understand modern Catholicism without them. If we add independents to the story, "the orderly Catholic/non-Catholic, form/matter world of the neo-Thomist revival no longer exists (if it ever did)," writes scholar and blogger Marian Ronan. "There isn't just an inside and outside anymore."[13]

THE FUTURE OF US INDEPENDENT CATHOLICISM

Those outside of independent Catholicism tend to predict its future in extremes. It will soon disappear from the face of the earth. Or there will be explosive global growth starting tomorrow. In 1947, Canon J. A. Douglas not only disdained independent "congeries" but also "forecast that twenty years hence only traces of [independent Catholics] will remain, and that they will be little more than a souvenir, as of a disease." Canon Douglas turned out to be quite wrong. But more positive observers were also wrong, for example, the hopeful Anglicans who predicted that the formation of the Union of Utrecht portended "a vast movement carrying with it a large minority of the members of the Church of Rome."[14]

Independents themselves are more moderate, tempering hope with realism. In 1985 English independent Catholic bishop Alan Bain drew up a list of bishops that since his first count in 1961 had grown from two hundred to twelve hundred. Nevertheless he only commented mildly that "numbers will continue to increase." Antiochians and Ascensionists too make modest claims about future growth. Though many wish for bumper crops of new members, that desire takes a backseat to history and experience. Survey respondents in other jurisdictions also predict a good but quiet future. When asked if the movement would get bigger or smaller, about 76 percent said it would "stay the same size" or "grow modestly."[15]

In comments, however, respondents allowed themselves to wonder why "ridiculous numbers of disgruntled Romans" do not result in an independent Catholic boom. Many Roman Catholics want what independents are already doing, yet they stay with Rome. Why? Some respondents said Roman Catholics have just not heard of independent Catholicism yet. A few noted that Roman Catholics are sometimes just highly committed to the Roman communion, and commitment is a good thing. Others suspected that fears of disobeying Rome or even not gaining eternal life play a role: the norm "not to 'leave the Church'" is very powerful. Still others said they think people prefer their religions more organized, established, or prestigious than independent Catholicism, so many stick with Rome even when "they disagree with some of that church's doctrine or method." Inertia could also be part of it, they guessed. Some people just don't change. Some people just don't care.[16]

While independents are realists, they also believe in what they are doing, and can handle the reality partly because they see God acting in and through them. English bishop Bain predicted modest growth but added an apocalyptic edge. "Is [independent Catholicism] a sickness?" he rhetorically asked Canon Douglas. "If so, the whole church Catholic is infected with similar symptoms. If . . . not, then we must presume that God is trying to tell us something." But Bain didn't know quite what. "What is God up to?"[17]

Antioch and Ascensionist independents have an answer for that. If big numbers are not part of God's plan, their churches still play a role in a new era in human evolution, a quantum leap of consciousness, the realization of the Beloved Community. "We are coming up to an energy/consciousness event of massive proportions," Jim Willems wrote on the Antioch listserv in 2010. This "event is spoken of in different ways by different lightworkers, mystics, contemplatives, scriptures, etc.," he said. "What is involved is a massive change of vibration that will offer many the opportunity to translate to a higher plane/dimension of Being." While most modern Catholic apocalypticism describes a harrowing end of time and final judgment, as in Marian revelations endorsed by Rome, the apocalypticism of Antioch and Ascension forecasts a glorious global revolution of consciousness.[18]

Their prophecy also involves Mary. No one in Antioch or Ascension ended up having that big vision of Mary Magdalene that Father Spencer Wood encouraged. But the imminent transformation of humanity is, in their view, deeply entwined with the soon coming of Mary as "Mother God" and Divine Feminine. Enter the Spruit churches, whose cosmic role lies in rebalancing masculine and feminine energies of the universe. How can it be otherwise, with Herman and Meri as leaders and now advocates on the other side? "When I came into the church, [Meri] was the matriarch," Deacon Jeff Genung said. "I thought, this is perfect . . . because . . . I fundamentally believe that we're entering into a phase of the Divine Feminine Mother." Archbishop Frank Bugge in Australia connects the apocalypse not only to Mary and Meri, but also to the Second Coming of Christ. He believes that the Church of Antioch is preparing the way for the next avatar of Christ, who will be female, he said. Herman and Meri are beings who "in many past lives contributed much" to the unfolding era and are "still working [vigorously] on the other side for this event," Archbishop Frank said.[19]

It is intriguing, though of course not dogma. Much more low-key than the prophecy of the coming of the female Christ by Archbishop Frank, Bishop Kera sees signs of the new age simply in the fact that popular perception of independent Catholicism has changed. When she used to tell people about Antioch, she said, the first reaction was fear, as if responding to danger. But just a few years into the new millennium, "they're not so skeptical anymore," she noticed. Now people are "more neutral to [it], 'I don't understand that, tell me about it.' "[20]

MAY "A THOUSAND CATHOLICISMS BLOOM"

In 2013, global modern Catholicism witnessed a huge change. Pope Benedict XVI resigned from the Roman Catholic church's highest office and cardinals elected Jorge Bergoglio, archbishop of Buenos Aires, Argentina, as the new pontiff. Taking the name of the humble saint of Assisi, Pope Francis immediately set a "new tone" for the seat of Peter, more pastoral and less dogmatic than immediate predecessors. Social justice and stewardship of the earth, not sexuality issues, should be the church's priorities, he says. Bishops are to understand themselves as servants, not potentates. They should evangelize with "the joy of the gospel." About gay Catholics Pope Francis famously said, "Who am I to judge?" He walks the talk, too, eschewing fancy digs, hanging out with "the least of these" and posing for selfies. All of this is incredibly popular, and not just among Catholics. After years of doctrinal hardball, clerical sex abuse, episcopal cover-up, and financial scandals, commentators credit Pope Francis with rehabilitating Rome's international image in record time. He made the cover of *Rolling Stone* and was named *Time*'s Person of the Year. He toured the United States and won more fans as "the people's pope."[21]

Like 90 percent of Catholics everywhere, Antioch and Ascension Catholics are wild about Francis. They consider each Roman pope "their" pope, even if they are not under his jurisdiction. So they are happy to have a pope they like. "Ascensionistas" in particular inundate the listserv with articles and discussion about Francis's latest wonderful deeds. To them, his tenure is the work of the Holy Spirit, a sign of "Christ Consciousness," a ripening of the age to come. As a bishop in Argentina, he infamously became close friends with the widow of a married former Catholic bishop who used to concelebrate mass with her husband. Now as pope, Francis won more favor with independents when he welcomed to the Vatican a delegation of bishops from the Union of Utrecht and lauded the ongoing work of the International Roman Catholic/Old Catholic Dialogue Commission. Francis also continued his predecessor's outreach to the traditionalist Society of St. Pius X.[22]

Despite the enthusiasm, however, no Antioch or Ascension leaders are considering rejoining the Roman church. Why not? Because Pope Francis will not and possibly cannot change things enough to accord with Catholicism as they are committed to practicing it. Francis may create more leadership roles for women, but he will not ordain them. He may decline to judge LGBTQ brothers and sisters, but he will not marry them. He may evangelize with joy, but as a "son of the Church" who sees Rome alone as having "the fullness of the means of salvation."[23]

Even in the era of Francis, then, Antiochians and Ascensionists are content to understand themselves as already part of the whole Catholic family. They can celebrate an astonishing new pope with no need to incur the costs of joining his jurisdiction. They embrace an "other" role. They have endured since the eighteenth century. They implement change at a rate impossible in the bigger bodies. They fly across jurisdictional boundaries like bees pollinating far-flung orchards. They are "Catholic but not Roman Catholic," and get to reinvent the faith over and over again.

A year into Francis's papacy, the *New York Times* ran an op-ed by journalist and author Peter Manseau titled "What It Means to Be Catholic Now." Manseau reminds readers that while Pope Francis is changing the church, it may be too late. Millions of Catholics already left Catholicism, or left the Roman church, or are otherwise going their own way. Whether the pontiff can gather them back in the pews remains doubtful.[24]

Some Catholics going their own way, Manseau notes, are independent Catholics. He would know. Manseau is the son of William Manseau, a US Roman priest who married a former nun, helped found CORPUS, and later became an independent Catholic bishop. As Manseau tells in his book *Vows: The Story of a Priest, a Nun, and Their Son*, his whole family trod a rocky road of Catholic identity. But like others with contact with independent Catholics, Manseau senses intimately "the opportunity and risk Rome faces in the age of Francis," he writes in the *New York Times* piece. Though Pope Francis "surely did not intend it this way, 'Who am I to judge?' would be a fitting motto for a papacy that saw a thousand Catholicisms bloom."[25]

◆ ◆ ◆

In the ten years I watched, Antioch and Ascension bloomed. So did dozens of other independent Catholic jurisdictions. And just as many faded and disappeared. But if churches come and go, independent Catholic individuals keep going. If nothing else, independents are Catholics who care.

FIGURE 7.3 Archbishop Richard Gundrey, Gig Harbor, Wash., August 16, 2008.
Courtesy of Alan Kemp.

They go to church. They pray. They want change. They make change happen whether the world is ready for it or not. They work against huge odds. They get really tired. But relentlessly they chase a Catholicism more open, more "universal." They see a wounded world and want very much to heal it, especially through the sacraments.

Despite the split, there is no end of Antioch. No end of the book, except the normal one. At the end, I find myself remembering meeting them for the first time at the Convocation in 2005. I drove to Richmond. Tom Gallub and the gang welcomed us from all corners of the country. Uly Gooch was strong like Superman.[26]

On the first night, the gathering lit a candle to signify the presence of Matriarch Meri, who was with them in spirit though she remained in California. West Coasters Roberto and Daniel mingled with East Coasters JoEllen and Ted. Everyone met all the Gentle Shepherd regulars. Ghostbusting Mother Mountjoy was there, as was Argentina church head Anastasia Voyatjides.

On the second night, Patsy, Diana, and Kera were consecrated as bishops.

On the third night, Uly hosted one of his famously fabulous parties. He and Worth had renovated a country manor into a sprawling bed-and-breakfast. The warm autumn evening was easy with food and drink, music and laughter. Late into the night, people got on their feet to dance. Salsa, disco, and oldies played. Shoes came off. Richmond friends and Antioch guests boogied on the hardwood, collapsed in chairs, and accepted refills.

In the middle of it all was Richard. The former dance instructor and patriarch of the Church of Antioch twirled Becky on the hardwood floor, and then Kera. Watching, I caught again that "sense of spell." Richard danced like celebrating a sacrament, like baptizing a baby, like laying hands on soft hair. He seemed to be in heaven.

APPENDIX

INDEPENDENT CATHOLICISM SURVEY

THE INDEPENDENT CATHOLICISM Survey was created on SurveyMonkey .com and culled a convenience sample of 407 people over eleven months in 2011–12. For more on its aims and methods, please see the introduction (p. 21) and chapter 1 (pp. 58–63). Here I add a few notes.

What follows includes the complete text of the survey. But not all respondents saw all the questions. Online, the survey was designed to jump questions not relevant to certain respondents. For example, if a respondent answered "yes" or "other/not applicable" to question 50, or if she skipped it, the survey proceeded to question 51. But if a respondent answered "no," it jumped him to question 58. For this reason, the listed number of respondents who "skipped" each question could be misleading. It seems a high number of respondents skipped question 51. But really the only respondents who saw question 51 at all were the 270 who dealt with question 50, as described above.

What follows also includes tabulation of all responses to quantitative questions, plus a few open-ended questions tabulated by me (questions 7, 15, and 44). For reasons of space and confidentiality, I do not include answers to qualitative questions or various comments.

Breakdowns of percentages of answers to each question do not always add up to 100% since some figures were slightly rounded.

Percentages cited in the main narrative do not always match percentages in these tables since I always analyzed groups of respondents separately where appropriate, such as laity and clergy.

Q1. What is your present religion? You will have a chance to explain more.
Answered: 402
Skipped: 5

ANSWER CHOICES	RESPONSES (%)	RESPONSES
Independent Catholic	71.64	288
Roman Catholic	6.72	27
Eastern Rite Catholic	0.75	3
Orthodox	2.74	11
Protestant	4.98	20
"Just Christian"	2.99	12
Other, non-Christian	0.50	2
No religion	1.99	8
None of the above	7.71	31
Total		402

Q2. Please explain your last answer, if you wish.
Answered: 268
Skipped: 139

Q3. Are you currently a member of an independent Catholic community?
Answered: 389
Skipped: 18

ANSWER CHOICES	RESPONSES (%)	RESPONSES
Yes	78.92	307
No	15.42	60
Other/not applicable	5.66	22
Total		389

Q4. Of which independent Catholic jurisdiction or denomination are you a member, if any? This question is asking about the larger body.

Answered: 306

Skipped: 101

Q5. What is your particular group, parish, or ministry within the larger independent Catholic body, if any?

Answered: 280

Skipped: 127

Q6. Why did you join independent Catholicism?

Answered: 299

Skipped: 108

Q7. How many years have you been involved in independent Catholicism?

Answered: 303

Skipped: 104

ANSWER CHOICES	RESPONSES (%)	RESPONSES
0–5	38	115
6–10	24.8	75
11–15	17.5	53
16–20	9.6	29
21–25	4.3	13
26–30	3.3	10
31–35	1	3
36–40	1.7	5
Total		303

Q8. What is your main role(s) in independent Catholicism?

Answered: 306

Skipped: 101

ANSWER CHOICES	RESPONSES (%)	RESPONSES
Occasional attendee	8.82	27
Lay member	18.95	58
Lay leader	12.09	37
Seminarian	8.82	27
Monastic	6.21	19
Permanent deacon	1.63	5
Priest	33.33	102
Bishop	18.95	58
Other/not applicable	5.88	18
Total		306

Q9. If you are not a current member, what is your association with independent Catholicism?

Answered: 52

Skipped: 355

Q10. If you wish, describe your typical involvement in the church—what you did once or twice, or what you do on a weekly, monthly, or yearly basis.

Answered: 311

Skipped: 96

Q11. Besides your main religion, with what other religious or spiritual traditions do you identify, if any?

Answered: 303

Skipped: 104

Q12. Besides religious and spiritual affiliations, what organizations or social causes are a main part of your life, if any?

Answered: 299

Skipped: 108

Q13. This survey uses the term "independent Catholicism"—is that what you call it? You will have a chance to explain your answer.

Answered: 350

Skipped: 57

ANSWER CHOICES	RESPONSES (%)	RESPONSES
Yes	51.43	180
No	20.86	73
Sometimes	25.71	90
Don't know/not applicable	2.00	7
Total		350

Q14. Please explain your last answer, if you wish. If you do not call it "independent Catholicism," what label do you prefer, if any?
  Answered: 229
  Skipped: 178

Q15. What year did you first hear about independent Catholicism?
  Answered: 342
  Skipped: 65

ANSWER CHOICES	RESPONSES (%)	RESPONSES
1960–65 or earlier	2.6	9
1966–70	0	0
1971–75	2.6	9
1976–80	4.6	16
1981–85	4.6	16
1986–90	7.2	25
1991–95	12.4	43
1996–2000	19.1	58
2001–5	16.2	56
2006–11	23.7	82
No year specified	8.1	28
Total		342

Q16. How did you first hear about independent Catholicism? Choose all that apply.
  Answered: 350
  Skipped: 57

ANSWER CHOICES	RESPONSES (%)	RESPONSES
Person who was an independent Catholic	44.29	155
Person who was not an independent Catholic	10.86	38
Book	12.00	42
Article in a newspaper or magazine	14.29	50
Advertisement in a newspaper or magazine	12.00	42
Internet	29.14	102
Other/don't know	8.29	29
Total		350

Q17. What is the best thing about independent Catholicism?
    Answered: 329
    Skipped: 78

Q18. What is the worst thing about independent Catholicism?
    Answered: 319
    Skipped: 88

Q19. How important is your religion or spirituality to you personally?
    Answered: 344
    Skipped: 63

ANSWER CHOICES	RESPONSES (%)	RESPONSES
The most important part of my life	47.67	164
Among the most important parts of my life	40.41	139
Quite important to me, but so are many other areas of my life	10.17	35
Not terribly important to me	0.87	3
Not very important to me at all	0.87	3
Don't know/not applicable	0	0
Total		344

Q20. Aside from weddings and funerals, about how often do you attend Mass (including if you say Mass)?
   Answered: 344
   Skipped: 63

ANSWER CHOICES	RESPONSES (%)	RESPONSES
At least once a week	68.02	234
Two or three times a month	16.28	56
About once a month	5.23	18
A few times a year	5.81	20
Seldom or never	3.78	13
Don't know/not applicable	0.87	3
Total		344

Q21. How regularly do you pray, apart from Mass?
   Answered: 344
   Skipped: 63

ANSWER CHOICES	RESPONSES (%)	RESPONSES
More than once a day	56.10	193
Daily	30.81	106
Occasionally or sometimes	11.05	38
Seldom or never	1.45	5
Don't know/not applicable	0.58	2
Total		344

Q22. Regarding Catholicism, how important is each of the following to you?

Answered: 341

Skipped: 66

	VERY IMPORTANT	SOMEWHAT IMPORTANT	NOT AT ALL IMPORTANT	DON'T KNOW/NOT APPLICABLE	TOTAL
The sacraments, such as the Eucharist	84.46% (288)	12.32% (42)	2.64% (9)	0.59% (2)	341
Catholicism's traditions about Mary	35.00% (119)	40.00% (136)	22.94% (78)	2.06% (7)	340
Social justice	78.14% (261)	18.86% (63)	1.80% (6)	1.20% (4)	334
Having a regular daily prayer life	73.53% (250)	20.59% (70)	5.00% (17)	0.88% (3)	340
Helping the poor	78.53% (267)	19.12% (65)	1.47% (5)	0.88% (3)	340
Belief in Jesus's resurrection from the dead	59.00% (200)	23.30% (79)	15.34% (52)	2.36% (8)	339
Participation in devotions such as Holy Week or praying the rosary	39.00% (133)	40.76% (139)	17.60% (60)	2.64% (9)	341

Q23. Regarding Catholicism, how important is each of the following to you?

Answered: 339

Skipped: 68

	VERY IMPORTANT	SOMEWHAT IMPORTANT	NOT AT ALL IMPORTANT	DON'T KNOW/NOT APPLICABLE	TOTAL
Apostolic succession	45.40% (153)	30.86% (104)	21.36% (72)	2.37% (8)	337
Having deacons, priests, and bishops	51.93% (175)	38.28% (129)	9.20% (31)	0.59% (2)	337
Mystical aspects of the faith	72.70% (245)	21.07% (71)	5.04% (17)	1.19% (4)	337
Leaders required to have rigorous intellectual training	48.21% (162)	44.64% (150)	6.25% (21)	0.89% (3)	336
"Open table" communion	78.99% (267)	14.20% (48)	3.85% (13)	2.96% (10)	338
Holy Orders open to anyone who has a vocation and completes training	72.19% (244)	21.01% (71)	3.25% (11)	3.55% (12)	338

Q24. For each of the following statements, please mark what best suits your views.

Answered: 341

Skipped: 66

	STRONGLY AGREE	SOMEWHAT AGREE	SOMEWHAT DISAGREE	STRONGLY DISAGREE	DON'T KNOW/NOT APPLICABLE	TOTAL
How a person lives is more important than whether he or she is Catholic	81.76% (278)	14.12% (48)	3.24% (11)	0.59% (2)	0.29% (1)	340
Catholicism contains a greater share of truth than other religions do	13.39% (45)	25.60% (86)	22.92% (77)	29.76% (100)	8.33% (28)	336
Being a Catholic is a very important part of who I am	55.16% (187)	25.37% (86)	10.62% (36)	5.90% (20)	2.95% (10)	339
The sacraments are essential to my relationship with God	58.65% (200)	27.27% (93)	7.62% (26)	5.57% (19)	0.88% (3)	341
It is important to me that younger generations of my family grow up as Catholics	16.22% (55)	33.92% (115)	25.07% (85)	16.52% (56)	8.26% (28)	339
I often feel I cannot explain my faith to others	13.20% (45)	23.17% (79)	24.05% (82)	37.24% (127)	2.35% (8)	341
I cannot imagine being anything but Catholic	29.03% (99)	26.98% (92)	22.87% (78)	18.18% (62)	2.93% (10)	341

Q25. Following are some statements about social and political issues. Please mark what best suits your views. There should be …

Answered: 339
Skipped: 68

	STRONGLY AGREE	SOMEWHAT AGREE	SOMEWHAT DISAGREE	STRONGLY DISAGREE	DON'T KNOW	TOTAL
More government funds to provide health care for children	74.85% (253)	19.23% (65)	3.55% (12)	1.78% (6)	0.59% (2)	338
More government funds for the military	7.37% (25)	13.27% (45)	32.15% (109)	45.72% (155)	1.47% (5)	339
Stiffer enforcement of the death penalty	4.14% (14)	6.21% (21)	13.31% (45)	74.26% (251)	2.07% (7)	338
Reduced spending on nuclear weapons	64.01% (217)	20.65% (70)	7.37% (25)	6.49% (22)	1.47% (5)	339
Further cutbacks in welfare programs	5.33% (18)	10.65% (36)	20.41% (69)	61.83% (209)	1.78% (6)	338

Q26. *What is your best guess about future independent Catholic numerical growth? You will have a chance to explain your answer.*

Answered: 341

Skipped: 66

ANSWER CHOICES	RESPONSES (%)	RESPONSES
It will explode with numbers	11.44	39
It will grow modestly	67.16	229
It will stay the same size	8.80	30
It will be absorbed into another group(s)	4.40	15
It will decrease in size	1.76	6
It will die out	0.59	2
Don't know/not applicable	5.87	20
Total		341

Q27. *Please explain your last answer, if you wish.*

Answered: 221

Skipped: 186

Q28. *If you are currently a member of an independent Catholic community: On a scale of one to seven, with "1" being "I would never leave independent Catholicism" and "7" being "Yes, I might leave independent Catholicism," where would you place yourself on this scale? You will have a chance to explain your answer.*

Answered: 337

Skipped: 70

ANSWER CHOICES	RESPONSES (%)	RESPONSES
1—I would never leave independent Catholicism	27.89	94
2	23.44	79
3	10.09	34
4	10.09	34
5	2.08	7
6	2.37	8
7—Yes, I might leave independent Catholicism	8.31	28
Don't know/not applicable	15.73	53
Total		337

Q29. *Please explain your last answer, if you wish. If you could imagine departing independent Catholicism, what other religious group would you join, if any, and why?*

Answered: 221

Skipped: 186

Q30. *Were you at any point in your life a Roman Catholic (or Eastern Catholic within the Roman communion)?*

Answered: 340

Skipped: 67

ANSWER CHOICES	RESPONSES (%)	RESPONSES
Yes	72.06	245
No	26.47	90
Other/not applicable	1.47	5
Total		340

Q31. If you were once a Roman Catholic (or Eastern Catholic within the Roman communion) and now are not, what is the main reason(s) you are not?

Answered: 223

Skipped: 184

Q32. How did you receive the link for this survey?

Answered: 341

Skipped: 66

ANSWER CHOICES	RESPONSES (%)	RESPONSES
Sent via church or seminary listserv	19.65	67
Clicked on link at church website	3.81	13
Sent in mail or email by clergy member	45.75	156
Sent in mail or email by layperson	7.33	25
Sent in mail or email by author of survey	16.13	55
Other/not applicable	7.33	25
Total		341

Q33. Marital status? You will have the chance to explain more.

Answered: 339

Skipped: 68

ANSWER CHOICES	RESPONSES (%)	RESPONSES
Married	51.03	173
Living as married	14.75	50
Separated	0.88	3
Divorced	11.21	38
Widowed	2.65	9
Never married	16.81	57
None of the above/not applicable	2.65	9
Total		339

Q34. *If you wanted to elaborate on the marital status question, please do so here.*

Answered: 159
Skipped: 248

Q35. *What is the highest level of education you have completed?*

Answered: 339
Skipped: 68

ANSWER CHOICES	RESPONSES (%)	RESPONSES
Less than high school (0–11)	0	0
High school graduate (12)	1.18	4
Some college	10.32	35
Trade/technical/vocational training	2.95	10
College graduate	15.93	54
Postgraduate work/degree (academic or professional)	69.62	236
Other/don't know	0	0
Total		339

Q36. *Were you brought up in any religious tradition(s)?*

Answered: 339
Skipped: 68

ANSWER CHOICES	RESPONSES (%)	RESPONSES
Yes	92.33	313
No	6.78	23
Other/not applicable	0.88	3
Total		339

Q37. What were your parents' religious tradition(s) if any and in what religious tradition(s) were you brought up?

Answered: 307

Skipped: 100

Q38. Did you ever attend a Catholic school or college for any of your education?

Answered: 336

Skipped: 71

ANSWER CHOICES	YES	NO	DON'T KNOW/ NOT APPLICABLE	TOTAL
Attended Catholic elementary school	41.28% (135)	58.72% (192)	0% (0)	327
Attended Catholic high school	27.67% (88)	72.33% (230)	0% (0)	318
Attended Catholic college or university	36.02% (116)	63.04% (203)	0.93% (3)	322

Q39. If you ever attended Catholic schools, how many TOTAL years of education did you receive in Catholic schools?

Answered: 326

Skipped: 81

ANSWER CHOICES	RESPONSES (%)	RESPONSES
0	16.87	55
1–2	5.21	17
3–4	10.74	35
5–6	5.83	19
7–8	4.91	16
9–10	4.60	15
More than 10	24.54	80
Don't know/not applicable	27.30	89
Total		326

Q40. Are you yourself of Hispanic origin or descent, such as Mexican, Puerto Rican, Cuban, Honduran, Dominican, Salvadoran, or other Hispanic or Latino background?

Answered: 335

Skipped: 72

ANSWER CHOICES	RESPONSES (%)	RESPONSES
Yes	4.78	16
No	94.03	315
Other/not applicable	1.19	4
Total		335

Q41. How do you identify yourself racially?

Answered: 307

Skipped: 100

ANSWER CHOICES	RESPONSES (%)	RESPONSES
White, Anglo, or Caucasian non-Hispanic	91.86	282
Hispanic	2.93	9
Black or African American	1.63	5
Asian, Native Hawaiian, or other Pacific Islander	1.30	4
American Indian or Alaskan Native	2.28	7
Total		307

Q42. How do you identify your gender?

Answered: 335

Skipped: 72

ANSWER CHOICES	RESPONSES (%)	RESPONSES
Woman	36.12	121
Man	62.09	208
Genderqueer	0.60	2
Intersex	0	0
MtF Trans	0.90	3
FtM Trans	0.30	1
Total		335

Q43. How do you identify your sexual orientation?
  Answered: 325
  Skipped: 82

ANSWER CHOICES	RESPONSES (%)	RESPONSES
Lesbian	8.31	27
Gay	31.38	102
Straight	50.46	164
Bisexual	8.62	28
Polysexual	0.62	2
Asexual	0.62	2
Total		325

Q44. What year were you born?
  Answered: 336
  Skipped: 71

ANSWERS TRANSLATED INTO AGE AT TIME OF SURVEY	RESPONSES (%)	RESPONSES
18–34	7.1	24
35–49	19	63
50–64	45	151
65+	28.6	96
No age specified	0.6	2
Total		336

Q45. *Do you live in the U.S. now?*
Answered: 337
Skipped: 70

ANSWER CHOICES	RESPONSES (%)	RESPONSES
Yes	97.33	328
No	2.67	9
Other/not applicable	0	0
Total		337

Q46. *If you live in the U.S. now, in what region of the country do you live?*
Answered: 327
Skipped: 80

ANSWER CHOICES	RESPONSES (%)	RESPONSES
East	31.50	103
Midwest	11.62	38
South	22.94	75
West	32.72	107
Other/not applicable	1.22	4
Total		327

Q47. *Where do you live, outside the U.S.?*
Answered: 13
Skipped: 394

Q48. *Generally speaking, in terms of U.S. politics, do you usually think of yourself as a Republican, a Democrat, an Independent, or what?*
Answered: 334
Skipped: 73

ANSWER CHOICES	RESPONSES (%)	RESPONSES
Democrat	58.68	196
Republican	7.19	24
Independent	23.95	80
Some other party	5.09	17
Other/not applicable	5.09	17
Total		334

Q49. *What is your total annual HOUSEHOLD income before taxes?*
    Answered: 334
    Skipped: 73

ANSWER CHOICES	RESPONSES (%)	RESPONSES
Under $25,000	11.68	39
$25,000 to $34,999	6.89	23
$35,000 to $49,999	13.17	44
$50,000 to $74,999	18.26	61
$75,000 to $99,999	15.87	53
$100,000 to $149,999	17.66	59
$150,000 or over	7.49	25
Decline to answer	8.98	30
Total		334

Q50. *Are you a seminarian, clergy, or monastic in independent Catholicism?*
    Answered: 335
    Skipped: 72

ANSWER CHOICES	RESPONSES (%)	RESPONSES
Yes	54.93	184
No	40.90	137
Other/not applicable	4.18	14
Total		335

Q51. As a seminarian, clergy, or monastic, are you . . .

Answered: 200

Skipped: 207

ANSWER CHOICES	RESPONSES (%)	RESPONSES
Active	90.00	180
Nonactive/retired	4.50	9
Other/not applicable	5.50	11
Total		200

Q52. As a seminarian, clergy, or monastic, do you serve people of the church or community in a ministry apart from prayer? (Ministry is anything you consider your ministry.)

Answered: 186

Skipped: 221

ANSWER CHOICES	RESPONSES (%)	RESPONSES
Yes	90.86	169
No	4.84	9
Other/not applicable	4.30	8
Total		186

Q53. If you wish, estimate how many people you serve in your ministry, beyond prayer, in an average week.

Answered: 144

Skipped: 263

Q54. If you wish, estimate the percentage of those you serve (beyond prayer) who are members of independent Catholic churches—yours or others.

Answered: 126

Skipped: 281

Q55. Please mark the one that best describes your financial compensation for ministerial work. This could be work in the church, in the community, or in a job that you consider your ministry. You will have a chance to choose more.

Answered: 181

Skipped: 226

ANSWER CHOICES	RESPONSES (%)	RESPONSES
Paid full-time by independent Catholic entity	1.66	3
Paid part-time, stipend, or donation by independent Catholic entity	5.52	10
Paid full-time by another organization	7.73	14
Paid part-time, stipend, or donation by another organization	2.21	4
Paid honoraria for specific services	13.26	24
Volunteer	14.92	27
I fund my own ministry (worker-priest)	50.83	92
Other/not applicable	3.87	7
Total		181

Q56. Please mark any other options that characterize your financial compensation for ministerial work. Choose all that apply.

Answered: 161

Skipped: 246

ANSWER CHOICES	RESPONSES (%)	RESPONSES
Paid full-time by an independent Catholic entity	1.24	2
Paid part-time, stipend, or donation by an independent Catholic entity	3.73	6
Paid full-time by another organization	4.97	8
Paid part-time, stipend, or donation by another organization	4.97	8
Paid honoraria for specific services	27.95	45
Volunteer	29.81	48
I fund my own ministry (worker-priest)	48.45	78
Other/not applicable	8.07	13
Total		161

Q57. If you have or had what you consider a non-ministerial job or profession, what is/was that line of work?
Answered: 158
Skipped: 249

Q58. Please use this space for other comments or clarifications about yourself and/or independent Catholicism, if you wish.
Answered: 77
Skipped: 330

NOTES

INTRODUCTION: OTHER CATHOLICS

1. Field notes, Church of Antioch Convocation, Richmond, Va., October 14–17, 2005.
2. Field notes, Antioch Convocation, October 16, 2005.
3. Ibid. "Sheep not of this fold" is a paraphrase of the Gospel of John 10:16.
4. Independent Catholics tend to call their bodies "churches" or "jurisdictions" rather than "denominations," since the latter is a historically Protestant term with Protestant ecclesiological assumptions. That said, many independents do not find "denomination" objectionable and use it interchangeably with "church" and "jurisdiction."
5. United States Department of the Interior, Census Office, *Report on Statistics of Churches in the United States, Eleventh Census: 1890* (Washington, D.C.: Government Printing Office, 1894), p. 3 (first listing of "Other Catholics [6 bodies]").

   After I adopted the working title "The Other Catholics" and before I found the phrase in the Census of 1890, I read that Father Jim Callan, a priest associated with the independent Spiritus Christi Church in Rochester, N.Y., called his parish "the other Catholic Church." See Benjamin Zeller, "'We're the Other Catholic Church': Feminism in a Radical Catholic Renewal Community," *Journal of Feminist Studies in Religion* 19, no. 2 (2003): 123–43, at pp. 123, 143. I also read journalist Nicholas Kristof's column "The Other Catholic Church" (*New York Times*, April 17, 2010), which discusses not independent Catholics but rather Roman Catholic religious orders and laypeople committed to social justice and charity work.

6. Scholars of American religion often point out that labels borrowed from US political life such as "right," "left," "liberal," and "conservative" are not satisfying and often inaccurate for religious groups, including Catholicism. But Catholics themselves use

these words all the time, so for the sake of subjects' self-description and fluid communication, I use them as well.

7. See Michael Cuneo, *Smoke of Satan: Conservative and Traditionalist Dissent in Contemporary American Catholicism* (New York: Oxford University Press, 1997), which is the best work on the traditionalist side of non-Roman Catholicism.

8. In 2015 the Pew Research Center published "America's Changing Religious Landscape," a study that calculates religious groups' memberships as percentages of the population, with Catholics (presumptively Roman) coming in at 20.8 percent. The next largest body is the Southern Baptist Convention, which claims 5.3 percent. Pew Research Center, "America's Changing Religious Landscape," full report, May 12, 2015, p. 21.

9. In 2010 the United States Census Bureau estimated the national population at 308,745,531 people. To arrive at numbers for religious groups, I used percentages in the 2015 Pew study, "America's Changing Religious Landscape," p. 21: Orthodox 0.5, Muslim 0.9, Episcopalian 0.9, Mormon 1.6, Jewish 1.9, Pentecostal 3.6, Catholic 20.8. For the estimate of the number of US Quakers, I used the more accurate number of 87,000 (in 2007) cited on the website of the Friends General Conference.

10. In 2011, Roman Catholic Womenpriests split into two groups, the second of which is the Association of Roman Catholic Women Priests. For more on Spiritus Christi, see Jody Caldwell, "From Corpus Christi to Spiritus Christi: The R/Evolution of an Independent Catholic Church," PhD diss., Drew University, September 2010. For more on the *Santa Muerte* church, see R. Andrew Chesnut, *Devoted to Death: Santa Muerte, the Skeleton Saint* (New York: Oxford University Press, 2012).

11. Robert Foss, Church of Antioch deacon, age forty-eight, interview, Los Angeles, Calif., November 24, 2007.

12. *A Catechism of Catholic Doctrine, Prepared and Enjoined by Order of the Third Plenary Council of Baltimore* (Rockford, Ill.: Tan Books, 1977), lesson 11, q. 496. Originally published by Benziger Brothers in New York in 1933.

13. On the Anglican origin of the term "Roman Catholic" and the opinion that it is a "qualification of the name Catholic commonly used in English-speaking countries by those unwilling to recognize the claims of the One True Church," see, for example, Herbert Thurston, "Roman Catholic," in *The Catholic Encyclopedia*, vol. 13 (New York: Robert Appleton, 1912).

14. For examples of these discussions, see Richard P. McBrien, *Catholicism: New Study Edition*, new ed. (New York: HarperOne, 1994), pp. 4–5; Gerald O'Collins, *Catholicism: A Very Short Introduction* (Oxford: Oxford University Press, 2008), p. xi; Lawrence Cunningham, *An Introduction to Catholicism* (Cambridge: Cambridge University Press, 2009), pp. 7–8; and Evyatar Marienberg, *Catholicism Today: An Introduction to the Contemporary Catholic Church* (New York: Routledge, 2014), p. 3. My thanks go to William T. Cavanaugh for consultation on this question: email to author, January 27, 2015.

15. This line paraphrases Eve Kosofsky Sedgwick, *Epistemology of the Closet* (Berkeley: University of California Press, 1991), p. 27. There are some self-identified US Catholics who do not do "sacraments, saints, and succession," such as John Alexander Dowie

and his "Christian Catholic Church," many bishop-headed Catholic or "Cathol-ish" black Spiritualist and Pentecostal groups, and millions of Catholics who do not practice their faith. In these cases, I would still count them as Catholics on the basis of self-identification, with riffs on Hans Baer's argument that the claim to Catholicism still means something about Catholicism, even in these cases, such as positioning for heritage, prestige, or authority in contexts of racism (or antienthusiasm or presumptive religiosity). Baer, *The Black Spiritualist Movement: A Religious Response to Racism*, 2nd ed. (1984; Knoxville: University of Tennessee Press, 2001).

16. There was no formal Church of Antioch Annual Report in 2009, so for these numbers I used the Annual Reports of 2007 and 2008 (distributed at Convocations in Salinas, California, and Santa Fe, New Mexico, respectively). States where the Church of Antioch had official presence in 2009 were Arizona, California, Colorado, Hawaii, Iowa, Maryland, New Hampshire, New Mexico, Pennsylvania, Texas, Virginia, Washington, and Wisconsin. For reasons of national and international law, Antioch's presence in Argentina under Archbishop Anastasia Voyatjides and in Australia under Archbishop Frank Bugge is as legally separate entities that maintain intercommunion agreements with the US body.

17. Richard Gundrey, Church of Antioch presiding archbishop and patriarch, age seventy-one, interview, Santa Fe, N.M., May 28, 2005.

18. Call to Action conferences featured masses celebrated by independent women priests from Spiritus Christi and Roman Catholic Womenpriests starting in 2002. On July 19, 2008, I sat in on the "Alternative Catholic" workshop: field notes, Joint Conference (Federation of Christian Ministries, CORPUS, Women's Ordination Conference, and Roman Catholic Womenpriests), Boston, Massachusetts, July 18–20, 2008.

19. I spoke to two independent Catholic priests who were at that time serving as full-time pastors in Protestant churches: Richard Mapplebeckpalmer, White-Robed Monks of St. Benedict priest, interview; and Ken Babauta, Independent Catholic Churches International (ICCI) priest, telephone call with author, both in San Francisco, California, both on August 9, 2005. Mapplebeckpalmer served Grace North in Berkeley, California, a historically Congregational church. When he left, Grace North called another independent priest as its pastor, John Mabry of the American Catholic Church. Ken Babauta was called to two Disciples of Christ pastorates: St. Victor Catholic Community Church in Vallejo and then Barrett Avenue Christian Church in Richmond. Babauta said that Frederic Jones and Judith Jones, leaders of ICCI (now dispersed), also served as pastors of Congregational and Disciples of Christ churches in Vallejo and Chico. In addition, I heard about an independent priest working full-time on the ministry team of a Presbyterian church via my survey (Independent Catholicism Survey, question 29, respondent 395, April 11, 2012). Instances of the same are uncommon but not unheard of in American independent Catholic history.

On the "third stream," see Catherine Albanese, *A Republic of Mind and Spirit: A Cultural History of American Metaphysical Religion* (New Haven: Yale University Press, 2007), p. 6. In this reading, the other two streams are "mainline-denominational" and "evangelical."

20. Albanese, *A Republic of Mind and Spirit*, p. 515.

21. I am thinking here of broad poststructuralist and decolonial projects (from Jacques Derrida and Michel Foucault to Frantz Fanon and Ashis Nandy, and many more) to describe social systems riven with the interests of capital, surveillance, and subjection but never completely homogenized. As such, even repressive systems signal the heterogeneous other and the potential for change in micropolitical or even macropolitical ways. Interestingly, in this literature a consistent description of the heterogeneous other involves its weirdness and eccentricity—words that are often applied disparagingly to independents but that in this literature count as compliments. As Ashis Nandy quotes a character in E. M. Forster's novel *A Passage to India*, "There are many kinds of failure, some of which succeed." Nandy, *The Intimate Enemy: Loss and Recovery of Self Under Colonialism* (Delhi: Oxford University Press, 1983), p. 107. On religion as flows, see Thomas Tweed, *Crossing and Dwelling: A Theory of Religion* (Cambridge, Mass.: Harvard University Press, 2008).

   I am indebted to others who think about independent Catholics as "other" in similar ways. Scholar-bishop John Plummer writes that maybe the "anarchic confusion" of independent Catholicism actually constitutes "creative ferment" and "valuable ecclesiastical experiments," in Plummer, *The Many Paths of the Independent Sacramental Movement: A Study of Its Liturgy, Doctrine and Leadership in America* (Dallas: Newt Books, 2004), p. 3. Kathleen Kautzer sees what she calls an "underground church" (including some independent Catholics) operating in resistance to imperial models of Catholicism, as described in Kautzer, *The Underground Church: Nonviolent Resistance to Vatican Empire* (London: Brill, 2012). Independent Catholic layperson Claudia Patchen heard my presentation on "other Catholics" and said she was reminded of the Jungian "other," describing unknown or shadow parts of the self (field notes, Ascension Alliance Convocation, Seattle, Wash., August 20, 2011).

22. Michel Foucault, *Security, Territory, Population* (New York: Palgrave Macmillan, 2007), pp. 207–16.

23. Roger Finke and Patricia Wittberg, "Organizational Revival from Within: Explaining Revivalism and Reform in the Roman Catholic Church," *Journal for the Scientific Study of Religion* 39, no. 2 (June 2000): 154–70; H. Richard Niebuhr, *The Social Sources of Denominationalism* (New York: Holt, 1929). Max Weber and Ernst Troeltsch had developed the vocabulary of "church" and "sect" in earlier works.

24. Dena Ross, "Sinéad O'Connor's Act of Love," *Beliefnet*, no date (late June 2007); and Ted Olsen, "Sinéad O'Connor's Theology and 'Theology,'" *Christianity Today*, July 9, 2007. For the New York show, see Ben Ratliff, "Old-Time Religion in Modern Guise," *New York Times*, July 28, 2013.

25. Plummer, *Many Paths*, pp. v, 66–67; Lewis Keizer, *The Wandering Bishops: Apostles of a New Spirituality* (1976; Aromas, Calif.: Home Temple Press, 2001), pp. 21–22. The *episcopi vagantes*, or "wandering bishops," date to the fourth century. These bishops were usually recognized by church authorities as bishops but were not associated with

a particular diocese in regular ways; rather, they roamed and ministered across diocesan boundaries, sometimes causing problems for jurisdictional order.

26. J. Gordon Melton, *Encyclopedia of American Religions*, 8th ed. (Detroit: Gale/Cengage, 2009).

27. Field notes, Church of Antioch Convocation, [midwestern city and state], September 10–14, 2009.

I. WEEPING AND WOO-WOO:
OBSERVING INDEPENDENT CATHOLICISM IN AMERICA

1. Karen Arthur, dir., *The Staircase* (BWE Distribution/Craig Anderson Productions/ TeleVest Entertainment, 1998).

2. Field notes, Santa Fe, N.M., May 23, 2008.

3. On the "proximate other," see Jonathan Z. Smith, "What a Difference a Difference Makes" (1985), republished in *Relating Religion: Essays in the Study of Religion* (Chicago: University of Chicago Press, 2004), pp. 251–302.

4. On my Independent Catholic Survey, 64 percent of Antioch respondents said they were formerly Roman Catholic or Eastern Catholic within the Roman communion (question 30). I talked with Marian and Cindy after mass in Fairless Hills, Pennsylvania: field notes, Philadelphia, Pa., July 29, 2007.

5. Field notes, Santa Fe, N.M., April 7, 2007. As Bryan and his fianceé learned in a Pre-Cana class in a Roman Catholic parish, Roman canon law requires a Petrine Privilege or a Pauline Privilege to go forward with a marriage such as theirs. These Privileges are somewhat similar to annulments, granted to dissolve nonsacramental marriages in favor of marriages in which one of the parties will first be newly baptized a Catholic. See Congregation for the Doctrine of the Faith, *Norms on the Preparation of the Process for the Dissolution of the Marriage Bond in Favour of the Faith*, April 30, 2001.

6. Conservative Roman takes on left-leaning and right-leaning independents can be found in many fora of conservative Catholic opinion. Richard Chonak, for example, used the word "kooks" for sedevacantists. Richard Chonak, "Come Home, Traditionalists," *Catholic Light*, July 10, 2004.

Roman excommunications of independents have been covered in the US media. In the cases of Father Anthony Garduno and Father Ned Reidy, their former Roman Catholic Diocese of San Bernardino held heresy trials in 2003 and 2005, respectively, after they left Rome to found independent Catholic parishes. In 2003, the Archdiocese of Atlanta sued the *Mision Catolica: Capilla de la Fe*, headed by Bishop Julio Cesar Freitas, possibly associated with the Mexican Catholic Apostolic Church, charging that it falsely claimed to be Catholic. The church protested that it was Catholic but not Roman Catholic. The archdiocese won the suit, as reported by the Associated Press, "Judge Sides with Archdiocese in Lawsuit," October 7, 2003. In addition to other coverage, see Michael McGough, " 'Property of Rome'? Does the Vatican Have Exclusive Rights to the Word 'Catholic'?," *Slate*, October 31, 2003.

For the Hotchkin quotation, see Margaret Ramirez, "A Confusion of Churches," *Los Angeles Times*, February 27, 2000. For the Cairo quotation, see Julie Gallego, "Old Catholic Mission an Independent Success," *Press-Telegram* (Long Beach, Calif.), July 9, 1990, in J. Gordon Melton American Religions Collection, University of California at Santa Barbara Archives, Folder: American Catholic Church–Old Catholic (St. Matthew's).

7. Vatican Council II, *Unitatis redintegratio*, November 21, 1964, sections 1, 3, 4, and 13.

8. See the Congregation for the Doctrine of the Faith, "General Decree Regarding the Delict of Attempted Sacred Ordination of a Woman," December 19, 2007, and Vatican Information Service, "Modifications Made in the *Normae de gravioribus delicts*," July 15, 2010. Both documents deal with specific canons in the Code of Canon Law, cc. 1365 and 1378, in *The Code of Canon Law: Latin-English Edition* (Washington, D.C.: Canon Law Society of America, 1983).

9. For the Vilatte quotation, see Serge A. Theriault, *Msgr. René Vilatte: Community Organizer of Religion, 1854–1929* (Berkeley: Apocryphile Press, 2006), p. 171. For the Ramerman quotation, see Angela Bonavoglia, "One Woman Who Refused to Wait: The Ordination of Mary Ramerman," in *Good Catholic Girls: How Women Are Leading the Fight to Change the Church* (New York: ReganBooks, 2005), pp. 237–56, at p. 248.

10. In 2012 the Polish National Catholic Church website claimed twenty-five thousand members in the United States. In his study of traditionalists, Michael Cuneo says the SSPX has thirty to forty thousand members: Cuneo, *The Smoke of Satan: Conservative and Traditionalist Dissent in Contemporary American Catholicism* (New York: Oxford University Press, 1997), p. 92.

11. Reverend Phil, "Thou Shalt Love," television interview of Archbishop Richard Gundrey and Bishop Daniel Dangaran on "Words of the Prophets," Santa Fe Community TV, Comcast Cable Channel 16 (Santa Fe, N.M.), Program #21 (November 2, 2009).

12. Herman Spruit, "Toward a Synthesis of the Metaphysical and Sacramental Schools of Spirituality," Church Archives CD, Document 99, no date, p. 1.

13. Usage of "independent Catholic" by independents themselves became common in the 1990s, likely due to increased use by authors of encyclopedias and compilers of directories. J. Gordon Melton's first edition of the *Encyclopedia of American Religions* was published in 1978 and includes, under "Western Liturgical Family," a section for "Independent and Old Catholic Churches." Alan Bain's *"Bishops Irregular": An International Directory of Independent Bishops* (Bristol, UK: A. M. Bain, 1985) and his directory (compiled with Gary Ward and Bertil Persson) *Independent Bishops: An International Directory* (Detroit: Apogee Books, 1990) mention "independent bishops," not "independent Catholics," but in the latter volume Melton supplies a preface that calls its subjects "independent Catholic bishops" (p. v). Antioch founder Herman Spruit certainly used the term. One work from 1980, for example, mentions the "free and independent Catholic Movement," "Independent Catholics," and (in a draft version) "Independent Catholic Christianity." See *The Conquest of the Rings: A Writing by Patriarch Herman as an Introduction to Sophia Divinity School and a Few Other Brief Articles*, book C, ed. Richard Gundrey (Santa Fe, N.M.: Sophia Divinity School Press,

2008), first item, no pagination, original pagination 1–12. Also available in Church of Antioch Archives/Box: Herman & Meri's files—1/File: Faith. See also Herman Spruit, "The Conquest of the Rings," draft of *The Conquest of the Rings*, Church Archives CD, Document 31, January 1, 1980.

Possibly the earliest usage of "independent Catholic" in the United States, how-ever, dates to 1819, when a Roman Catholic priest was solicited by parish trustees in Charleston, South Carolina, to help start an "Independent Catholick Church of the United States," as I describe more in the next chapter. See Peter Guilday, *The Life and Times of John England, First Bishop of Charleston, 1786–1842*, vol. 1 (New York: America Press, 1927), pp. 271–79. After that, players in various church ruptures as well as historians of these episodes continually used terms such as "independent Catholic church," "Independent American Catholic Church," and "independentism."

14. Thomas Siebert, Church of Antioch priest, age fifty-two, interview, Richmond, Va., July 22, 2007. Michael Adams, email to author, February 10, 2011. Roman Catholic Womenpriests (RCWP) claims its first ordinations took place at the hands of Roman bishops operating outside of Roman protocols, a common independent pattern. But RCWP wishes its ordinations to be seen as prophetic and transformational within and for Roman Catholicism, not for an independent body. It models itself on the "Philadelphia Eleven," unauthorized women priests in the US Episcopal Church who were later accepted by its General Convention. I acknowledge here that my discuss-ing RCWP alongside independents does not accord with many Womenpriests' self-understanding. I stop short of calling them independents, but do believe there is war-rant to include Womenpriests in a discussion of independents.

15. John Plummer, *The Many Paths of the Independent Sacramental Movement* (Dallas: Newt Books, 2004). As Plummer acknowledges, part of the term was first used in the 1980s by the Synod of Independent Sacramental Churches. See J. Gordon Melton, *En-cyclopedia of American Religions*, 8th ed. (Detroit: Gale/Cengage, 2009), pp. 721, 1207. Then Richard Smoley wrote of "independent sacramental" groups in Smoley, *Inner Christianity: A Guide to the Esoteric Tradition* (Boston: Shambhala, 2002), pp. 223–24. But it was definitely Plummer who catalyzed the widespread discussion and common use of it among independents themselves.

On the Independent Catholic Survey, I asked: "This survey uses the term 'inde-pendent Catholicism'—is that what you call it?" Of all respondents, 54 percent said yes, 21 percent said no, and 26 percent said sometimes (Independent Catholicism Survey, question 15). Of those who responded no or sometimes and gave a further ex-planation in the Independent Catholicism Survey, question 16, almost all mentioned "independent sacramental" or Plummer's work specifically.

16. Lewis Keizer, *The Wandering Bishops: Apostles of a New Spirituality* (1976; Aromas, Calif.: Home Temple Press, 2001), p. 41.

17. Cuneo, *Smoke of Satan*, pp. 100–108. See also Plummer, *Many Paths*, pp. 21–25.

18. On the word "tradition" as used in religions and religious studies, as well as the idea that some traditions serve to authorize other traditions, see Ann Taves, "Catholic

Studies and Religious Studies: Reflections on the Concept of Tradition," in *The Catholic Studies Reader*, ed. James Fisher and Margaret McGuinness (New York: Fordham University Press, 2011), pp. 113–28.

19. Cyprian, *De unitate* (251), in St. Cyprian, *The Lapsed/The Unity of the Catholic Church*, trans. Maurice Bévenot, Ancient Christian Writers: Ante-Nicene Era Collection 25 (Mahwah, N.J.: Paulist/Newman Press, 1957), pp. 43–65.

20. Augustine, *Contra epistolam Parmeniani* II: 28 (c. 400 CE). See Augustin, *Contra epistulam Parmeniani*, in *Oeuvres de Saint Augustin*, Bibliothèque Augustinienne, vol. 28, 4e série, *Traités Anti-Donatistes*, vol. 1, trans. G. Finaert (Paris: Desclée de Brower, 1963), pp. 208–481. See also canon 6 of the Council of Chalcedon (451 CE); and Edward Schillebeeckx, *The Church with a Human Face: A New and Expanded Theology of Ministry* (New York: Crossroad, 1985), pp. 154–56, 191–94. The phrase *ex opere operato* was defended in the Council of Trent document *On the Sacraments* (Seventh Session, First Decree, c. VIII) to counter the Protestant idea of *ex opere operantis*, which held that sacramental efficacy was affected by the moral standing of the priest and the recipient. The idea of the "indelible" mark of ordination can be seen in c. IX of the same Trent document, which anathematizes anyone who would deny that "in the three sacraments, Baptism, to wit, Confirmation, and Order, there is not imprinted in the soul a character, that is, a certain spiritual and indelible Sign, on account of which they cannot be repeated." Council of Trent, *On the Sacraments*, March 3, 1547.

21. For an account of eastern Christian churches, see Michael Burgess, *The Eastern Orthodox Churches: Concise Histories with Chronological Checklists of Their Primates* (Jefferson, N.C.: McFarland, 2005).

22. Taves, "Catholic Studies and Religious Studies," p. 118; see also pp. 124–26.

23. Jordan Stratford, quoted in Siobhan Houston, *Priests, Gnostics and Magicians: European Roots of Esoteric Independent Catholicism* (Berkeley: Apocryphile Press, 2009), p. 6.

24. Pope Leo XIII pronounced Anglican orders invalid in *Apostolicae curae*, September 18, 1896.

25. Alan Bain, *"Bishops Irregular,"* p. 12.

26. "Magic hands theology" is a phrase I first heard at the Joint Conference (Federation of Christian Ministries, CORPUS, Women's Ordination Conference, and Roman Catholic Womenpriests) in Boston in 2008 (field notes, July 19, 2008). Various progressive Roman Catholics since Vatican II experimented with or even standardized in their communities such practices as communal consecration of the Eucharist, lay presidership, or priestless masses, usually shielding local bishops from the knowledge of such practices.

27. For the Schüssler-Fiorenza quotation, see Peter Steinfels, "Women Wary About Aiming to Be Priests," *New York Times*, November 14, 1995. Women-Church Convergence describes itself as "Catholic-rooted" on its website homepage. Dutch Province of the Dominicans, "Church and Ministry," January 11, 2007. Garry Wills, *Why Priests? A Failed Tradition* (New York: Penguin, 2013), p. 256. Hans Küng, *Why Priests? A Proposal for a New Church Ministry* (New York: Doubleday, 1972).

28. Marian Ronan, "Living It Out: Ethical Challenges Confronting the Roman Catholic Women's Ordination Movement in the Twenty-First Century," *Journal of Feminist Studies in Religion* 23, no. 2 (2007): 149–69, at p. 162. Field notes, Intentional Eucharistic Communities Conference, Chevy Chase, Md., May 15–17, 2009 (IEC Conference 2009). Michele Dillon, "Lived Spirituality," PowerPoint presentation at IEC Conference 2009, May 16.

29. Archbishop Irene (no last name given), quoted in Karl Pruter and J. Gordon Melton, eds., *The Old Catholic Sourcebook* (New York: Garland, 1983), pp. 86–87. Rosemary Radford Ruether, "Women Priests Offer Different Approaches to Valid Ordination," *National Catholic Reporter*, August 10, 2010.

30. Richard Gundrey, Church of Antioch listserv, March 1, 2008. Diana Phipps, Church of Antioch bishop, age sixty-three, interview, Fredericksburg, Tex., June 16, 2007. Pope Paul VI, *Lumen gentium*, November 21, 1964, sec. 10. Plummer, *Many Paths*, p. 103.

31. On these "inner" lines of apostolic succession, see Plummer, *Many Paths*, pp. 31–36; Houston, *Priests, Gnostics and Magicians*, pp. 37–66; Rob Angus Jones, *Independent Sacramental Bishops: Ordination, Authority, Lineage, and Validity* (Berkeley: Apocryphile Press, 2010), pp. 154–81; and Phillip Charles Lucas, *The Odyssey of a New Religion: The Holy Order of MANS from New Age to Orthodoxy* (Bloomington: Indiana University Press, 1995).

32. John Plummer, Twitter @priestcraft, June 3, 2012.

33. Field notes, Church of Antioch Convocation, Santa Fe, N.M., October 21, 2006.

34. Bain, *"Bishops Irregular,"* p. 14.

35. Bob Ross, radio interview of Archbishop Richard Gundrey, "Live from the Santa Fe Farmers' Market," Santa Fe Public Radio KSFR (March 15, 2008); and Richard Gundrey, "Starting a Real Church and Keeping It Going," presentation at Sursum Corda II Conference, October 5–8, 2003, DVD by Jim Waters/Sanctus Media. Gentle Shepherd Church, brochure, obtained by author in church vestibule, October 2005. "All of the sacraments" was on the website of the Ancient Apostolic Communion. "Vatican-Free Catholics!" was on the website of the National Catholic Church of America.

36. Richard Gundrey, "What Is an Independent Catholic Church?," brochure (Church of Antioch, 2002), obtained by author at the information table before mass at Loretto.

37. Peter Levenda, "A Field Guide to Wandering Bishops," in *Sinister Forces: A Grimoire of American Political Witchcraft*, book 1, *The Nine* (Walterville, Oreg.: Trineday), pp. 333–45, at p. 339.

38. Scholars who have analyzed the roles of Catholicism and Protestantism in American imagination and ideology include Jackson Lears, *No Place of Grace: Antimodernism and the Transformation of American Culture, 1880–1920* (Chicago: University of Chicago Press, 1994); Jenny Franchot, *Roads to Rome: The Antebellum Protestant Encounter with Catholicism* (Berkeley: University of California Press, 1994); Tracy Fessenden, *Culture and Redemption: Religion, the Secular, and American Literature* (Princeton: Princeton University Press, 2007); and John T. McGreevy, *Catholicism and American Freedom: A History* (New York: Norton, 2003).

39. Jeff Diamant, "Some Dissenters Quit the Church but Don't Stop Being Catholic," *Washington Post* (Religion News Service), January 10, 2007. Catherine Albanese, *A Republic of Mind and Spirit: A Cultural History of American Metaphysical Religion* (New Haven: Yale University Press, 2007), pp. 8, 510.

40. Adolph Schalk, "The New-Fashioned Old Catholics," *U.S. Catholic*, May 1974, pp. 35–38, at pp. 35, 38. Richard P. McBrien, *Catholicism: New Study Edition*, new ed. (New York: HarperOne, 1994), pp. 242–46. Garry Wills, *Papal Sin: Structures of Deceit* (New York: Doubleday, 2000). Hans Küng, *The Catholic Church: A Short History* (New York: Random House, 2001), p. 167.

41. David Haldane, "Faithful, Yet Not Traditional Catholics," *Los Angeles Times*, June 24, 2006. Independent Catholic Survey, question 32. Thomas Reese, "The Hidden Exodus: Catholics Becoming Protestants," *National Catholic Reporter*, April 18, 2011. William Byron and Charles Zech, "Why They Left: Exit Interviews Shed Light on Empty Pews," *America*, April 30, 2012. See also Jerry Filteau, "Unusual Study Asks Former Catholics Why They Left Church," *National Catholic Reporter*, March 23, 2012; and the Pew Research Center, "U.S. Catholics Open to Non-Traditional Families," full report, September 2, 2015, pp. 12–17.

42. On the Ecumenical Catholic Diocese of America, see Melton, *Encyclopedia*, p. 115. Call to Action conference programs publicized the celebration of mass by women priests as of 2006, but Mary Ramerman of Spiritus Christi presided at conference altars earlier: field notes, Joint Conference, July 19, 2008.

43. Field notes, Joint Conference, July 19, 2008. For the story of cooperation between CORPUS, the ECC, and the Community of John XXIII, see the link on the Community of John XXIII's website.

44. Kathleen Kautzer, *The Underground Church: Nonviolent Resistance to Vatican Empire* (London: Brill, 2012), pp. 9, 23, 25, 36–37.

45. On trends of Roman Catholic laity, see William D'Antonio, James D. Davidson, Dean R. Hoge, and Mary L. Gautier, *American Catholics Today: New Realities of Their Faith and Their Church* (New York: Rowman and Littlefield, 2007), esp. pp. 173–83; and William D'Antonio, Michele Dillon, and Mary Gautier, *American Catholics in Transition* (Lanham, Md.: Rowman and Littlefield, 2013), esp. pp. 167–79. I found the review of "keelynelson" not on Yelp but on a wedding website forum, projectwedding.com (dated July 29, 2010).

46. Field notes, Santa Fe, N.M., May 23, 2008.

47. Robert Dittler, White-Robed Monks abbot, and Tom Dowling, White-Robed Monks priest, joint interview, San Francisco, Calif., August 10, 2005. Dittler, email to author, August 5, 2012, and "About the Monks" on the White-Robed Monks website. In the same interview, Tom Dowling described Roman priests' referrals as "totally off-the-radar."

48. For "entrepreneurial," see "While We're at It," *First Things*, April 2000, pp. 89–90, which mentions Antioch's Sophia Divinity School by name. Old Catholics of Europe and the United States also criticize US independents for being "entrepreneurs"

running "sacrament mills" who have "objectified the laity as consumers of religion": see Robert Caruso, *The Old Catholic Church* (Berkeley: Apocryphile Press, 2009), pp. 95 and 139, as well as the introduction by Björn Marcussen, p. xi. Plummer, *Many Paths*, p. 92.

49. Tim Townsend, "St. Stanislaus in Discussions to Join Episcopal Diocese of Missouri," *St. Louis Post-Dispatch*, September 3, 2013.

50. Currently the community church movement manifests primarily in the International Council of Community Churches. See Melton, *Encyclopedia*, pp. 262–63; Theriault, *Msgr. René Vilatte*, pp. 32–41; and Ralph J. Shotwell, *Unity Without Uniformity: History of the Community Church Movement*, 2nd ed. (Frankfort, Ill.: Community Church Press, 2000). Peter E. Gillquist, *Becoming Orthodox: A Journey to the Ancient Christian Faith*, rev. ed. (1992; Ben Lomond, Calif.: Conciliar Press, 2001).

51. Field notes, Shabazz African Orthodox Church, The Slave Theater #1, Brooklyn, N.Y., October 16, 2011. I used the population of Goldston as listed in the 2010 US Census for zip code 27252.

52. Thomas Merton, *The Seven Storey Mountain: An Autobiography of Faith*, 50th anniversary ed. (1948; San Diego: Harcourt Brace, 1998), pp. 357–58.

53. Linda Rounds-Nichols, Church of Antioch priest, age fifty-eight, interview, Salinas, Calif., October 7, 2007. Field notes, Gig Harbor, Wash., September 14, 2008.

54. For attendance figures: Richard Gundrey, "Seeing the Christ in All Life," in *A Strange Vocation: Independent Bishops Tell Their Stories*, ed. Alistair Bate (Berkeley: Apocryphile Press, 2009), pp. 72–77, at p. 75; Richard Gundrey, Church of Antioch listserv, April 17, 2006; Gundrey, Church of Antioch listserv, December 26, 2006; field notes, Santa Fe, N.M., April 8. Archbishop Richard defined membership as "Show up and give money" at a Convocation business meeting: field notes, Antioch Convocation, October 21, 2006.

55. On Roman Catholic counting, see Clifford Grammich, Kirk Hadaway, Richard Houseal et al., *2010 U.S. Religious Census: Religious Congregations and Membership Study*, Association for Statisticians of American Religious Bodies (Kansas City, Mo.: Nazarene Publishing House, 2012), pp. 655–56.

56. See the appendix for my Independent Catholicism Survey and detailed results. The questions it replicates are found in D'Antonio, Davidson, Hoge, and Gautier, *American Catholics Today*, pp. 173–83. I compared responses on my survey with results in that volume, and in D'Antonio, Dillon, and Gautier, *American Catholics in Transition*, pp. 167–79.

I also consulted books that focus on Roman Catholic progressives: William D'Antonio and Anthony Pogorelc, *Voices of the Faithful: Loyal Catholics Striving for Change* (New York: Herder and Herder, 2007), pp. 226–35; and Michele Dillon, *Catholic Identity: Balancing Reason, Faith, and Power* (Cambridge: Cambridge University Press, 1999). Dillon's small survey of IEC attendees was a final source of comparison with Roman church members whom she calls "pro-change Catholics": Michele Dillon, "Lived Spirituality," PowerPoint presentation at Intentional Eucharistic Communities Conference, Chevy Chase, Md., May 16, 2009.

Though I copied D'Antonio's questions in *American Catholics Today* wherever possible, my comparisons of independents and Romans are inexact for several reasons. The biggest reason, as I state in the main text, is that the aforementioned surveys of Roman Catholics are large national polls of statistically random samples, and my survey is a convenience sample of only 407 respondents. To compare results from these two poll genres is to compare the proverbial apples and oranges.

Comparison is also problematic because my survey could not ask all the same questions or ask them in the same way. For example, the D'Antonio survey asks a question that assumes "the Catholic Church" teaches against same-sex marriage (D'Antonio, Davidson, Hoge, and Gautier, *American Catholics Today*, pp. 173–74). I could not replicate this question, given the vagueness of "the Catholic Church" to my respondents and their lack of supposition that Catholic teaching opposes same-sex marriage. In this case and other cases, I adapted questions to fit independent respondents. Conversely, my survey asks questions that these surveys of Roman Catholics do not, such as what kind of Catholicism respondents follow and their sexual orientation. But whenever I adjust or add questions, comparability suffers.

A final drawback to the comparison is the difference in the clergy component of respondents. My survey culls a majority of clergy—64 percent—because independent churches are made up primarily of worker-priests who minister outside their own group. Surveys of Roman Catholics poll almost exclusively laypeople. However, for my purpose of a very rough comparison between independent and Roman Catholics, this is a difference I can live with, for three reasons. First, in analyzing my results I always separate lay and clerical responses where that status is relevant. Second, independent worker-priests with day-jobs, the option to marry, and children live lives structurally more similar to Roman Catholic lay leaders than Roman Catholic professional priests. Third, more of the independent Catholic population can receive Holy Orders—not just celibates and not just men. This means that more independents are priests because they can be, and also because "open orders" actively attract those who understand themselves to be called to the priesthood but who are unable to answer the vocation in another communion.

57. For these numbers: Dillon, "Lived Spirituality," slide 8; D'Antonio, Davidson, Hoge, and Gautier, *American Catholics Today*, p. 178; D'Antonio and Pogorelc, *Voices of the Faithful*, p. 226; and Independent Catholicism Survey, questions 35, 19, and 20.

58. Dillon, "Lived Spirituality," slide 8. Independent Catholicism Survey, questions 36, 37.

59. Independent Catholicism Survey, question 43, asked, "How do you identify your sexual orientation?," and question 42 asked about gender identity, listing transgender and four other choices. Figures on the prevalence of gender transitioning in the general population are disputed, but are usually given in the range of one in tens of thousands, for example, at the website of the Center of Excellence for Transgender Health. So no matter what figures you use, the independent Catholic answer—1 in 66—is a much higher prevalence. For my gender totals, I counted transgender persons in the category of the gender to which they transitioned.

60. For a poignant and provocative discussion of Catholicism's non-cis qualities, see Mark Jordan, *The Silence of Sodom: Homosexuality in Modern Catholicism* (Chicago: University of Chicago Press, 2000). On the past innovating functions of religious orders, see Roger Finke and Patricia Wittberg, "Organizational Revival from Within: Explaining Revivalism and Reform in the Roman Catholic Church," *Journal for the Scientific Study of Religion* 39, no. 2 (June 2000): 154–70.

61. Gundrey, interview by Ross, 2008.

62. "Wildcat" is a characterization that shows up successively in William Whalen, *Separated Brethren: A Survey of Protestant, Anglican, Orthodox, Old Catholic, and Other Denominations in the United States*, rev. and enlarged (Huntington, Ind.: Our Sunday Visitor, 1972), p. 228; Schalk, "The New-Fashioned Old Catholics," p. 37; and Richard Newman, "Black Bishops: Some African-American Old Catholics and Their Churches," in *Words Like Freedom: Essays on African-American Culture and History* (West Cornwall, Conn.: Locust Hill Press, 1996), pp. 107–48, at pp. 111–12.

63. Claire Vincent (pseudonymized at interviewee's request), Church of Antioch seminarian, age forty-five, interview, Salinas, Calif., October 7, 2007.

64. I presented work at the American Religious History Workshop at Princeton University on October 22, 2009, and the next day Father Ted Feldmann reported to the group on the listserv. Father Ted's partner John DeLoach as well as Mother JoEllen Werthman and her husband Rob Werthman made the trip.

65. Field notes, Church of Antioch, Santa Fe, N.M., May 2005, April 2007, and May 2008.

66. Herman Spruit, *The Conquest of the Rings*, inner front cover.

67. On the "ethnography uncertainty principle," see Sarah McFarland Taylor, *Green Sisters: A Spiritual Ecology* (Cambridge, Mass.: Harvard University Press, 2007), pp. xviii–xx.

68. Field notes, Church of Antioch Convocation, Richmond, Va., October 16, 2005; Antioch Convocation, October 20 and 22, 2006; Austin, Tex., June 23, 2007; Richmond, Va., July 22, 2007; Church of Antioch Convocation, Salinas, Calif., October 7, 2007; Santa Fe, N.M., May 27, 2008; Gig Harbor, Wash., September 14, 2008; and Arizona (mostly Phoenix area), April 7–9, 2009.

69. Field notes, Ascension Alliance Convocation, Seattle, Wash., August 20, 2011; Ascension Alliance Convocation, Tahlequah, Okla., August 24, 2014; and Church of Antioch Convocation, [midwestern city and state], October 25, 2014.

70. Field notes, Antioch Convocation, October 21, 2006; Antioch Convocation, October 7, 2007; [Arizona city], Ariz., April 8, 2009. Daniel Dangaran, Church of Antioch priest (later bishop), age fifty-three, interview, Santa Fe, N.M., April 5, 2007. In my field notes I count five other times that Antiochians counseled me to answer a call to the priesthood.

71. Field notes, Santa Fe, various; Antioch Convocation, October 21, 2006; Houston, Tex., June 20, 2007; [Arizona city], Ariz., April 8, 2009.

72. Field notes, Antioch Convocation, October 16, 2005; Antioch Convocation, October 21, 2006; Santa Fe, N.M., May 25–26, 2008.

73. Field notes, Antioch Convocation, October 16, 2005.

2. MISSION AND METAMORPHOSIS:
NARRATING MODERN CATHOLIC HISTORY

1. For accounts of Varlet's life, see Basil Guy, ed., *Domestic Correspondence of Dominique-Marie Varlet, Bishop of Babylon, 1678–1742* (Leiden: Brill, 1986); Serge Theriault, *Msgr. Dominique M. Varlet: Originator of the Old Catholic Episcopal Succession, 1678–1742* (Berkeley: Apocryphile Press, 2008); Pierre Hurtubise, "Dominique-Marie Varlet, 1678–1742," in *Dictionary of Canadian Biography*, vol. 3, *1741–1770*, ed. Marc La Terreur et al. (Toronto: University of Toronto Press, 1974), pp. 639–41; J. M. Neale, *A History of the So-Called Jansenist Church of Holland* (1858; New York: AMS Press, 1970), pp. 241–77; and C. B. Moss, *The Old Catholic Movement, Its Origins and History* (London: Society for the Propagation of Christian Knowledge, 1948), pp. 119–23. Throughout this section I use common information in these biographies, and add footnotes for unique or contested information.

2. Charles E. Peterson, *Notes on Old Cahokia* (Cahokia, Ill.: Jarrot Mansion Project, 1999).

3. Guy, *Domestic Correspondence*, pp. 84–85.

4. On the European religious scene from the ancien régime to Revolutionary France, I consulted Jean Delumeau, *Catholicism Between Luther and Voltaire: A New View of the Counter-Reformation* (London: Burns and Oates, 1977); Dale Van Kley, *The Religious Origins of the French Revolution: From Calvin to the Civil Constitution, 1560–1791* (New Haven: Yale University Press, 1996); Jeffrey Burson, "The Catholic Enlightenment in France from the *Fin de Siècle* Crisis of Consciousness to the Revolution, 1650–1789," in *A Companion to the Catholic Enlightenment in Europe*, ed. Ulrich Lehner and Michael Printy (Leiden: Brill, 2010), pp. 63–126; and Derek Beales, *Prosperity and Plunder: European Catholic Monasteries in the Age of Revolution, 1650–1815* (Cambridge: Cambridge University Press, 2003).

5. See Francis Oakley, *The Conciliarist Tradition: Constitutionalism Within the Catholic Church, 1300–1870* (Oxford: Oxford University Press, 2003); and Dale Van Kley, "Catholic Conciliar Reform in an Age of Anti-Catholic Revolution," in *Religious Differences in France: Past and Present*, ed. Kathleen Perry Long (Kirkland, Mo.: Truman State University Press, 2006), pp. 91–140.

6. Following the practice of historians of the era, I have not used the word "Jansenism" for Augustinianism prior to the turn of the eighteenth century, before which the label would be "anachronistic," says historian Charles Parker, "impos[ing] a view that they would not recognize or accept" (email to author, January 22, 2009). On Jansenism here and throughout this section, see Dale Van Kley, *The Jansenists and the Expulsion of the Jesuits from France, 1757–65* (New Haven: Yale University Press, 1975); Brian Strayer, *Suffering Saints: Jansenists and Convulsionnaires in France, 1640–1799* (Brighton, UK: Sussex Academic Press, 2008); and Catherine Maire, "Port Royal: The Jansenist Schism," in *Realms of Memory: Rethinking the French Past*, vol. 1, *Conflicts and Divisions*, ed. Pierre Nora and Lawrence Kritzman (New York: Columbia University Press, 1996), pp. 301–52. For "campaigns," see Strayer, *Suffering Saints*, pp. 10–11.

7. On widespread Catholic experimentation, see Van Kley, *The Religious Origins*. For quotation, see Strayer, *Suffering Saints*, pp. 10-11; see also 280-81.

8. Owen Chadwick, "The Italian Enlightenment," in *The Enlightenment in National Context*, ed. Roy Porter and Mikuláš Teich (Cambridge: Cambridge University Press, 1981), pp. 90-105, at p. 103. Ulrich Lehner, *Enlightened Monks: The German Benedictines, 1740-1803* (Oxford: Oxford University Press, 2011), p. 2. Lehner, "Introduction: The Many Faces of the Catholic Enlightenment," in *A Companion to the Catholic Enlightenment in Europe*, ed. Ulrich Lehner and Michael Printy (Leiden: Brill, 2010), pp. 1-62, at p. 12. On the stateside reputation of Jansenism, see Lawrence McCaffrey, *Textures of Irish America* (Syracuse, N.Y.: Syracuse University Press, 1998), pp. 56, 191-92.

9. Lynn Wood Mollenauer, *Strange Revelations: Magic, Poison, and Sacrilege in Louis XIV's France* (University Park: Penn State University Press, 2007).

10. Guy, *Domestic Correspondence*, pp. 3, 24-25.

11. Ibid., p. 10.

12. Ibid., pp. 3-4.

13. On Mobile, Cahokia, and Kaskaskia, see Jay Higgenbotham, *Old Mobile: Fort Louis de la Louisiane, 1702-1711* (1977; Tuscaloosa: University of Alabama Press, 1990), and Natalie Maree Belting, *Kaskaskia Under the French Regime* (Urbana: University of Illinois Press, 1948). In addition, John Gilmary Shea discusses the "famous Jansenist Varlet" by name in Shea, *History of the Catholic Missions Among the Indian Tribes of the United States, 1529-1854* (New York: Dunigan and Brother, 1855), pp. 12, 424; he tells of the death of Bergier and the celebration of the medicine men (p. 422). See also Shea, *The Catholic Church in Colonial Days, 1521-1763* (New York: John G. Shea, 1886), which features sections on "The Seminary Priests at Tamarois," "Very Rev. Dominic M. Varlet, V.G.," and "Cahokia" (pp. 535-38, 543-44, 554-57).

14. On Cahokia's population, Shea says Cahokia had "forty-seven families" in 1715, the year Varlet arrived. Shea, *Catholic Church in Colonial Days*, p. 554. "White collars" vs. "black robes": Higgenbotham, *Old Mobile*, p. 102.

15. Guy, *Domestic Correspondence*, p. 5. Belting, *Kaskaskia Under the French Regime*, pp. 12, 41. See also Hurtubise, "Dominique-Marie Varlet."

16. Here and following, I use Laurence Lockhart, *The Fall of the Safavid Dynasty and the Afghan Occupation of Persia* (Cambridge: Cambridge University Press, 1958), pp. 9, 31-33, 74-79; Roger Savory, *Iran Under the Safavids* (Cambridge: Cambridge University Press, 1980), pp. 120, 176; and Sebouh David Aslanian, *From the Indian Ocean to the Mediterranean: The Global Trade Networks of Armenian Merchants from New Julfa* (Berkeley: University of California Press, 2011), p. 151.

17. Guy, *Domestic Correspondence*, pp. 5-6, 25-26.

18. Ibid., p. 6. Neale (*History of the So-Called Jansenist Church*, p. 242) and Moss (*The Old Catholic Movement*, p. 120) give different accounts of the route change.

19. Charles H. Parker, *Faith on the Margins: Catholics and Catholicism in the Dutch Golden Age* (Cambridge, Mass.: Harvard University Press, 2008), pp. 1-58.

20. For "never forgotten," see Neale, *History of the So-Called Jansenist Church*, p. 244. For "charity" and the rest, see Guy, *Domestic Correspondence*, p. 7.

21. Guy, *Domestic Correspondence*, p. 8. Moss, *The Old Catholic Movement*, p. 121. Alexander Hamilton, *A New Account of the East Indies*, vol. 1 (London: C. Hitch and A. Millar, 1744). For consular reports of detainment in Shamakhi, see Savory, *Iran Under the Safavids*, pp. 117, 176–77.

22. Guy, *Domestic Correspondence*, pp. 8–9. Neale, *History of the So-Called Jansenist Church*, p. 245.

23. Guy, *Domestic Correspondence*, pp. 9, 26, 31–32.

24. Ibid., pp. 11–12.

25. Neale, *History of the So-Called Jansenist Church*, pp. 249, 253.

26. Ibid., p. 256.

27. Ibid., pp. 256–57, 266–67.

28. Guy, *Domestic Correspondence*, p. 20. Neale, *History of the So-Called Jansenist Church*, p. 277.

29. Guy notes (*Domestic Correspondence*, p. 22) that brothers attending Varlet's room at his death reported the *odeur de sainteté*—the supernaturally floral scent traditionally said to rise from the bodies of expired saints. John E. Holman writes that the Old Catholic Church of America celebrates Varlet's anniversary of death as a feast day: Holman, *The Old Catholic Church of America* (n.p.: Old Catholic Church of America, 1977), p. 72. Raphael J. Adams, "Meet the Ultrajectines: A Brief Introduction to Old Catholic Thought," *New Perspectives* (Louisville, Ky.) 3, no. 1 (2002): 11–14.

30. Van Kley, "Catholic Conciliar Reform," p. 99.

31. Peter Guilday, *The Life and Times of John Carroll: Archbishop of Baltimore, 1735–1815* (New York: Encyclopedia Press, 1922), p. 769. Jay Dolan, *The American Catholic Experience: A History from Colonial Times to the Present* (Notre Dame: University of Notre Dame Press, 1992), pp. 184–85.

32. Guilday, *Life and Times*, pp. 786, 752, 784. James Hennesey, *American Catholics: A History of the Roman Catholic Community in the United States* (Oxford: Oxford University Press, 1981), p. 97.

33. For a portion of the trustees' letter and "Independent Catholick Church," see Peter Guilday, *The Life and Times of John England, First Bishop of Charleston, 1786–1842*, vol. 1 (New York: America Press, 1927), pp. 271–79. John Gilmary Shea, "Jansenists, Old Catholics, and Their Friends in America," *American Catholic Quarterly Review* 14 (January–October 1889): 533–41, at p. 534. For "malcontents," see Peter Guilday, *The Catholic Church in Virginia, 1815–1822* (New York: United States Catholic Historical Society, 1924), p. xiv. For a thoroughly revised history of the people and events of this era, see Michael Pasquier, *Fathers on the Frontier: French Missionaries and the Roman Catholic Priesthood in the United States, 1789–1870* (Oxford: Oxford University Press, 2010).

34. Guilday, *Catholic Church in Virginia*, pp. xii, xiv.

35. United States Catholic Historical Society, *Historical Records*, vol. 2 (New York: United States Catholic Historical Society, 1901), pp. 184–90, 439. The *Gazette* treats the matter

on June 5–6 of 1835, as reported in Thomas Meehan, "Link Between East and West," *Illinois Catholic Historical Review* 2, no. 3 (1920): 339–47, at p. 340.

36. Van Kley, "Catholic Conciliar Reform," p. 93. For "social utility" and "surprise and relief," see Luca Codignola, "Roman Catholic Conservatism in a New North Atlantic World, 1760–1829," *William and Mary Quarterly*, 3rd ser., 64, no. 4 (October 2007): 717–56, at pp. 720–21.

37. John T. McGreevy, *Catholicism and American Freedom: A History* (New York: Norton, 2003), p. 29. For "updated version," see R. Scott Appleby, "The Triumph of Americanism: Common Ground for U.S. Catholics in the Twentieth Century," in *Being Right: Conservative Catholics in America*, ed. Mary Jo Weaver and R. Scott Appleby (Bloomington: Indiana University Press, 1995), pp. 37–62, at p. 39. For "papal internationalism," see Peter D'Agostino, *Rome in America: Transnational Catholic Ideology from the Risorgimento to Fascism* (Chapel Hill: University of North Carolina Press, 2004), p. 7. For "loyalty to . . . the Holy See," see Terence Fay, *A History of Canadian Catholics: Gallicanism, Romanism and Canadianism* (Toronto: McGill University Press, 2002), p. 69.

38. Johannes Ronge, *A German Catholic's Farewell to Rome* (London: Hamilton, Adams, 1845), p. 15.

39. Owen Chadwick, *A History of the Popes, 1830–1914* (Oxford: Clarendon Press, 1998), p. 252. In *Tuas libenter*, Pius IX writes the archbishop of Munich in dismay over a conference Döllinger had convened (on December 21, 1863); this is the letter that serves as the citation for the Syllabus of Errors, proposition 13 (Pius IX, *Syllabus errorum*, December 8, 1864).

English-language sources I consulted on Old Catholicism included J. Bass Mullinger, *The New Reformation: A Narrative of the Old Catholic Movement from 1870 to the Present Time* (London: Longmans, Green, 1875); A. M. E. Scarth, *The Story of the Old Catholic and Kindred Movements, Leading Up to a Union of National Independent Churches* (London: Simpkin, Marshall, 1883); Society for the Propagation of Christian Knowledge, "The History of the Old Catholic Movement," *Church Quarterly Review* 19, no. 37 (October 1884): 130–58; Moss, *The Old Catholic Movement*; and Victor Conzemius, "Catholicism: Old and Roman," *Journal of Ecumenical Studies* (Summer 1967): 426–45.

40. On Utrecht Union numbers: Maja Weyermann, Office of Information of the Old Catholic Bishops' Conference of the Union of Utrecht, email to author, May 20, 2011. Leo XIII, *Iampridem*, January 6, 1886, section 3. Peter-Ben Smit, *Old Catholic and Philippine Independent Ecclesiologies in History: The Catholic Church in Every Place* (Leiden: Brill, 2011). Ludvik Nemec, *The Czechoslovak Heresy and Schism: The Emergence of a National Czechoslovak Church* (Philadelphia: American Philosophical Society, 1975).

41. Franciszek Hodur, "The Eleven Great Principles" (1923), in *The Confession of Faith and the Eleven Great Principles of the Polish National Catholic Church in Polish and English*, ed. Polish National Catholic Church (Scranton, Pa.: Polish National Catholic

Church, n.d.), pp. 25–38, at pp. 33–34. On the future priesthood, see Hodur, *Apocalypse of the Twentieth Century*, trans. Metchie Budka, ed. Albert Tarka, co-ed. Louise Orzech (1930; Scranton, Pa.: Polish National Catholic Church, 1977): "The priesthood of the future will not be a caste of men mercenaries growing rich and fat, but rather it will be a free association of individuals dedicating themselves to higher purposes. It will be a brotherhood of men and women chosen by God, prepared and ordained for this purpose" (p. 219). Within the PNCC, Women's Ordination Now (WON) is working for that cause. For more on Hodur and the PNCC, see Hodur, *Hodur: A Compilation of Selected Translations*, 2nd ed., trans. Theodore L. Zawistowski (Scranton, Pa.: Bishop Hodur Biography Commission of the Central Diocese and the Commission on History and Archives of the PNCC, 1990); Stephen Wlodarski, *The Origin and Growth of the Polish National Catholic Church* (Scranton, Pa.: Polish National Catholic Church, 1975); and Hieronim Kubiak, *The Polish National Catholic Church in the United States of America from 1897 to 1980: Its Social Conditioning and Social Functions* (Zeszyty Naukowe Uniwersytetu Jagiellońskiego: Prace Polonijne, 1982).

42. On the Brazilian Catholic Apostolic Church, see J. Gordon Melton, *Encyclopedia of American Religions*, 8th ed. (Detroit: Gale/Cengage, 2009), pp. 85–86. For numbers, I consulted the website of the Brazilian Institute of Geography and Statistics. For numbers of the Brazilian church's Worldwide Communion of Catholic Apostolic Churches, see Phyllis Zagano, *Women and Catholicism: Gender, Communion, and Authority* (New York: Palgrave Macmillan, 2011), pp. 66, 73. The Brazil-connected church in the United States is the Catholic Apostolic National Church, in 2016 led by Patriarch Robert Gubala. For the Mbewe quotation, see "Splinter Catholic Church Launched," *Times of Zambia*, December 26, 2007, via allafrica.com.

43. Matthew Butler, "*Sotanas Rojinegras*: Catholic Anticlericalism and Mexico's Revolutionary Schism," *Americas* 65, no. 4 (April 2009): 535–58, at pp. 536–37.

44. Ibid. In the United States this church is sometimes called the Mexican National Catholic Church. For example, see Melton, *Encyclopedia of American Religions*, p. 125.

45. Ibid.

46. Kozlowski is quoted in Robert Trisco, "The Holy See and the First 'Independent Catholic Church' in the United States," in *Studies in Catholic History in Honor of John Tracy Ellis*, ed. Nelson Minnich, Robert B. Eno, and Robert Trisco (Wilmington, Del.: Michael Glazier, 1985), pp. 175–238, at pp. 225–26.

47. Hickman is quoted in Scott Fagerstrom, "Old Catholics Retain Roots but Accept Married Clergy," *Orange County Register*, July 11, 1988: J. Gordon Melton American Religions Collection/University of California at Santa Barbara Library, File: American Catholic Church–Old Catholic (St. Matthew).

48. For the backdrop of La Petite Église, see Van Kley, "Catholic Conciliar," pp. 94, 130, 137–39. For Vilatte biographical information and context used throughout this section, see Joseph René Vilatte, *My Relations with the Protestant Episcopal Church*, in *Old Catholic: History, Ministry, Faith and Mission*, by Andre' Queen (New York: iUniverse, 2003), pp. 195–210; Jean Parisot, *Mgr Vilatte, fondateur de l'Église vieille-*

catholique aux États-Unis d'Amérique (Tours: E. Soudée, 1899); A. Parker Curtiss, *History of the Diocese of Fond du Lac and Its Several Congregations* (Fond du Lac, Wis.: P. B. Haber, 1925); Joseph Marx and Benjamin Blied, "Joseph René Vilatte," *Salesianum* (Milwaukee, Wis.: Alumni Association of St. Francis Seminary) 37, no. 1 (January 1942): 1–8; Peter Anson, *Bishops at Large* (1964; Berkeley: Apocryphile Press, 2006); Serge Theriault, *Msgr. René Vilatte: Community Organizer of Religion, 1854–1929* (Berkeley: Apocryphile Press, 2006); Gerard O'Sullivan, "Historical Vignettes: Joseph René Vilatte," *FICOB and Friends* 1, no. 3 (Fall 1996): 3, in the Church of Antioch Archives/Box: Herman & Meri's files—1/File: Fed of Ind. Cath & Orth Bishops. For this section I also consulted extensively with Alexis Tancibok, whose dissertation for the PhD in the Theology and Religion Department at Durham University in England supplements or corrects aspects of Vilatte's biography with a close examination of primary sources: "Early Independent Catholicism in Context: A Re-examination of the Career of Archbishop Joseph René Vilatte (1884–1929)," scheduled for defense in 2016. I cite emails with Tancibok in what follows.

49. Parisot, who likely interviewed Vilatte personally, seems to think that declining numbers in the Petite Église meant that Vilatte was baptized in the Roman church shortly after birth (Parisot, *Mgr Vilatte*, chap. 1, unpaginated, first page).

50. For "rabidly Romanist," see Vilatte, *My Relations*, p. 196. On host-stomping, see Yves Roby, "Charles Chiniquy," *Dictionary of Canadian Biography*, vol. 12, *1891–1900* (Toronto: University of Toronto/Université Laval, 2003). For this section I also use Richard Lougheed, *The Controversial Conversion of Charles Chiniquy* (Toronto: Clements Academic, 2009).

51. Chiniquy's autobiography is *Fifty Years in the Church of Rome: The Life Story of Pastor Chiniquy* (Grand Rapids, Mich.: Baker Book House, 1961). It was a best seller. So was *The Priest, the Woman and the Confessional* (Ontario: Chick Publications, 1979). The latter is so full of boilerplate vitriol that, as you can see, it remains in print per the publishing house of the notoriously anti-Roman American pamphleteer Jack Chick. "Father Chiniquy Establishing a New Church Neither Protestant nor Roman," *Montreal Witness*, September 4, 1858, in Lougheed, *Controversial Conversion*, p. 108, fig. 29.

52. On the Door peninsula, spiritualism, and "Villatte," see Hjalmar Holand, *History of Door County, Wisconsin, the County Beautiful* (Chicago: S. J. Clarke, 1917), pp. 209, 316, 416–18. Vilatte, *My Relations*, pp. 196–97.

53. Thérèse of Lisieux, *Letters of St. Thérèse of Lisieux: General Correspondence*, vol. 2, *1890–1897*, trans. John Clarke (Washington, D.C.: Institute of Carmelite Studies, 1988), pp. 728–30. On Loyson's Gallican Catholic Church (there were several of that name over time), see Henry Lascelles Jenner, ed., *The Gallican Catholic Church: Some Account of Its Progress and of Its Present Condition and Prospects* (London: Church Street Printing, 1888); Moss, *The Old Catholic Movement*, pp. 283–84; and Anthony Cross, "Père Hyacinthe Loyson, The Église Catholique Gallicane (1879–1893) and the Anglican Reform Mission," PhD diss., University of Reading, 2011. James McCartin at Fordham University treats Loyson in a forthcoming book (manuscript in progress, 2016).

The national churches of Old Catholicism gradually accepted clerical marriage: Switzerland in 1875, Germany in 1877, Austria in 1880, and the Netherlands in 1922. Helen Parish, *Clerical Celibacy in the West: C. 1100–1700* (Surrey, UK: Ashgate, 2010), p. 216.

54. Elizabeth Clark, *Founding the Fathers: Early Church History and Protestant Professors in Nineteenth-Century America* (Philadelphia: University of Pennsylvania Press, 2011), p. 85.

55. O'Sullivan, "Historical Vignettes," p. 4. For this section I also consulted William M. Hogue, "The Episcopal Church and Archbishop Vilatte," *Historical Magazine of the Protestant Episcopal Church* 34, no. 1 (March 1965): 35–55; John M. Kinney, " 'The Fond du Lac Circus': The Consecration of Reginald Heber Weller," *Historical Magazine of the Protestant Episcopal Church* 38, no. 1 (March 1969): 3–24; and Glenn D. Johnson, "Joseph René Vilatte: Accidental Catalyst to Ecumenical Dialog," *Anglican and Episcopal History* 71, no. 1 (March 2002): 42–60. The area of the PEC Diocese of Fond-du-Lac, created in 1874, overlapped with the Roman Catholic Diocese of Green Bay, created in 1868.

56. Hogue, "The Episcopal Church," p. 41.

57. Ibid.

58. On Vilatte's thoughts in the interim between Brown and Grafton, see Vilatte, *My Relations*, p. 203. On the Fond-du-Lac diocese, Grafton, Monte Cassino, and the infamous photo of the "Fond-du-Lac Circus," which played a key role in wide PEC acceptance of "Catholic" sensibilities, see Kinney, "The Fond du Lac Circus." On Grafton's involvement with Anglican, Old Catholic, and PNCC monasticism, see René Kollar, "Travels in America: Aelred Carlyle, His American 'Allies,' and Anglican Benedictine Monasticism," Project Canterbury, 2003.

59. Vilatte, *My Relations*, pp. 207–8. On the synod, see Theriault, *Msgr. Vilatte*, p. 94. For the articles of incorporation, see ibid., 238–40. *A Sketch of the Belief of the Old Catholics*, preface by Joseph René Vilatte (Fort Howard, Wis.: James Kerr and Son, 1890), p. 4.

60. Anson, *Bishops at Large*, p. 101.

61. US Department of the Interior, Census Office, *Report on Statistics of Churches in the United States at the Eleventh Census: 1890* (Washington, D.C.: Government Printing Office, 1894), pp. iv, xvi, xviii. For the first use of the column heading "Other Catholics (6 bodies)," see p. 3. For the count of 665, see p. 39.

On the accuracy and utility of the US Census Office's endeavors to count religious adherents between 1850 to 1936, see Roger Finke and Rodney Stark, *The Churching of America, 1776–1990: Winners and Losers in Our Religious Economy* (New Brunswick, N.J.: Rutgers University Press, 1992), pp. 6–13.

62. On the "Reformed Catholics," see US Department of Commerce and Labor, Bureau of the Census, *Religious Bodies: 1906, Part II* (Washington, D.C.: Government Printing Office, 1910), pp. 596–97. The Reformed Catholics are first mentioned on the contents page of the 1890 *Report on the Statistics of Churches*, p. iv. Headquartered on West 21st Street in Manhattan and "incorporated as Christ's Mission," the Reformed Catholic

Church had about a thousand members in a half-dozen parishes in five states, according to the reports from 1890 and 1906. For the tenor of coverage of this church, see the *New York Times*, "Señor Fernando de Ortollak Speaks in Father O'Connor's Church," May 27, 1895.

63. *Religious Bodies: 1906, Part II*, pp. 15–18, 506–8.

64. Matthew Butler, "Ever *Unfaithful*? Independent Catholicism in Modern Mexico," paper presented at American Academy of Religion annual meeting, San Diego, Calif., November 24, 2014. Butler's forthcoming book on this topic will be published by the University of New Mexico Press: *Father Pérez's Revolution: Or, Making Catholicism "Mexican" in Twentieth-Century Mexico.*

65. Alexis Tancibok, emails to author, March 15, 2015.

66. Hogue, "The Episcopal Church," pp. 54–55. On Vilatte's good looks and charming personality, see Anson, *Bishops at Large*, pp. 100–101, and Theriault, *Msgr. Vilatte*, p. 91. For more information on Grafton, including the conflict with Vilatte, see Grafton's own numerous publications, for example, Charles Grafton, *Personal Reminiscences: A Journey Godward of Doulous Iesou Kristou* (Milwaukee: Young Churchman Company, 1910), pp. 155–56, 170–72.

67. On Harding, see Hogue, "The Episcopal Church," p. 48, and Theriault, *Msgr. Vilatte*, pp. 110–12. Mar Ignatius Peter IV is the same person as Mar Ignatius Peter III, depending on the numbering used. On Indian Catholicism, the independent Indian church, and Álvarez, see Amir Harrak, "Trade Routes and the Christianization of the Near East," *Journal of the Canadian Society for Syriac Studies* 2 (2002): 46–61; Susan Bayly, *Saints, Goddesses and Kings: Muslims and Christians in South Indian Society, 1700–1900* (Cambridge: Cambridge University Press, 1989); Abba Seraphim (William Henry Hugo Newman-Norton), *Flesh of Our Brethren: An Historical Examination of Western Episcopal Successions Originating from the Syrian Orthodox Patriarchate of Antioch* (London: British Orthodox Press, 2006), pp. 113–44; and Pratima P. Kamat, "The Goa-Ceylon Religious Connection: A Review of the 'Indian Cry' of Álvares Mar Julius, Archbishop of Ceylon, Goa and India," *Sabaragamuwa University Journal* 12, no. 1 (December 2013): 61–82.

68. Anson, *Bishops at Large*, pp. 106–7. See also George Anton Kiraz, "The Credentials of Mar Julius Álvares, Bishop of Ceylon, Goa and India Excluding Malabar," *Hugoye: Journal of Syriac Studies* 7, no. 2 (July 2004): 157–68, in which Kiraz attempts to reconstruct the original Syriac version of Vilatte's certificate of consecration.

69. For this section, see Hogue, "The Episcopal Church," pp. 49–51, and O'Sullivan, "Historical Vignettes," p. 7. Joseph René Vilatte, "An Encyclical to All Bishops Claiming to Be of the Apostolic Succession," Project Canterbury, 1893.

70. Theriault, *Msgr. Vilatte*, p. 134. In an email, Theriault told me that Vilatte wrote of his participation in the Parliament in his newsletter the *Old Catholic*, likely volume 2 (November/Advent 1893), but the archives of Theriault's church (a member of the International Council of Community Churches, which traces heritage to Vilatte; see Melton, *Encyclopedia of American Religions*, pp. 262–63) no longer have that issue

(email to author, June 24, 2015). See also Anson, *Bishops at Large*, p. 111. On Roman Catholic participation in the Parliament, see John F. Cleary, "Catholic Participation in the World's Parliament of Religions," *Catholic Historical Review* 55, no. 4 (January 1970): 585–609. On Vilatte's relegation to the margins, see Carlos Parra, "Standing with Unfamiliar Company on Uncommon Ground: The Catholic Church and the Chicago Parliaments of Religions," PhD diss., University of Toronto, December 18, 2012, p. 60n40.

71. Parisot, *Mgr Vilatte*, chap. 5, unpaginated, fourth page.

72. Hogue, "The Episcopal Church," pp. 52–53. Theriault, *Msgr. Vilatte*, p. 148n195. On the Order of Corporate Reunion, see Henry R. T. Brandreth, *Episcopi Vagantes and the Anglican Church* (1947; Springfield, Mo.: St. Willibrord Press, 1987), p. 64.

73. Anson, *Bishops at Large*, pp. 126–28. Theriault, *Msgr. Vilatte*, pp. 22, 200–204.

74. For "farmers and fur trappers," see Bayly, *Saints, Goddesses and Kings*, p. 318. Vilatte's anniversaries of consecration (May 29) and death (July 1) are both noted by independents as feast days on listservs to which I subscribed: a Yahoo New York City Independent Catholic/Old Catholic list (July 1, 2007), the Church of Antioch list (May 29, 2002), and the Ascension Alliance list (May 24, 2012). One listserv member wrote a post with a link to a Vilatte relic on eBay (Independent Sacramental Movement listserv, Yahoo, October 1, 2007).

75. Raymond Rudorff, *The Belle Epoque: Paris in the Nineties* (New York: Saturday Review Press, 1972), pp. 193–200. Joanne Pearson, *Wicca and the Christian Heritage: Ritual, Sex and Magic* (London: Routledge, 2007), pp. 43–44.

76. Pius X, *Gravissimo officii munere*, August 10, 1906.

77. On Parisot, see Theriault, *Msgr. Vilatte*, p. 149n196. Jean Parisot, *Mgr Vilatte*. On smoking Cubans with Huysmans, see Anson, *Bishops at Large*, p. 120. Huysmans's novel *L'Oblat* (1903) includes descriptions of his time at Ligugé.

78. On Roman Catholic protests against Vilatte's church in France, see J. F. Boyd, "The French Ecclesiastical Revolution," *American Catholic Quarterly Review* 32 (January–October 1907): 181–83, 269, 653–58. Giraud was consecrated by Jules-Ernest Houssaye, who was consecrated by Paolo Miraglia-Gulotti, who was consecrated by Vilatte.

79. Pearson, *Wicca and the Christian Heritage*, pp. 45–47. Apiryon (Tau Apiryon), "History of the Gnostic Catholic Church," Ordo Templi Orientis, 1995.

80. Pearson, *Wicca and the Christian Heritage*, p. 58.

81. Ibid. Aleister Crowley, *Liber XV—Ecclesiae Gnosticae Catholicae Canon Missae*, Ordo Templi Orientis, 1913.

82. Augustine, *In epistulam Ioannis ad Parthos* (Tractatus VII, 8) (c. 416 CE), in Augustine, *Homilies on the First Epistle of John*, trans. Boniface Ramsey, Works of Saint Augustine series (Hyde Park, N.Y.: New City Press, 2008), pp. 104–14. Pearson, *Wicca and the Christian Heritage*, p. 47.

83. Pearson, *Wicca and the Christian Heritage*, pp. 1–10 and chap. 2, "*Episcopi Vagantes* and Heterodox Christianity." See also Hugh Urban, *Magia Sexualis: Sex, Magic, and*

Liberation in Modern Western Esotericism (Berkeley: University of California Press, 2006).

84. On the number of consecrations, I use Alexis Tancibok's figure: Tancibok, email to author, January 27, 2015.

85. See Trisco, "The Holy See," and Conzemius, "Catholicism," as well as Lawrence Orton, *Polish Detroit and the Kolasinski Affair* (Detroit: Wayne State University Press, 1981), and Leslie Tentler, "Who Is the Church? Conflict in a Polish Immigrant Parish in Late Nineteenth-Century Detroit," *Comparative Studies in Society and History* 25, no. 2 (April 1983): 241–76, at p. 269.

86. Theriault, *Msgr. Vilatte*, pp. 135, 137–39, reproduces press reports of the Cleveland consecration and convention, including in the newspaper of the Jehovah's Witnesses, whose leader, Charles Taze Russell, was a Vilatte correspondent (p. 163).

87. In 1907, when Hodur became the second American Old Catholic bishop and the first PNCC bishop, the Kozlowski group joined the PNCC. The Kaminski group remained separate.

88. Robert Nevin, "The Modern Savonarola," *Churchman* 74, no. 14 (October 3, 1896): 400. Congregation of the Universal Inquisition, "Declaration of Major Excommunication That Was Incurred by the Two Priests Miraglia and Vilatte" (June 13, 1900), *American Ecclesiastical Review* 23 (July–December 1900): 287–88. For more on the North American Old Roman Catholic Church, see Melton, *Encyclopedia of American Religions*, pp. 125–26, and Jonathan Trela, *A History of the North American Old Roman Catholic Church* (Scranton, Pa.: Straz Printery, 1979).

89. Butler mentions the survival of parishes of the Mexican Catholic Apostolic Church in Mexico as of 2009 in *"Sotanas Rojinegras,"* p. 557. Instances of survival in the United States are documented by Paul Schultz, who wrote "The Bishop Who Ran in the 1932 Olympics" about Olympian runner and Mexican church bishop Emile Federico Rodríguez in the *Christian News*, July 30, 1984, p. 5 (J. Gordon Melton American Religions Collection/University of California at Santa Barbara Library, Folder: Mexican National Catholic Church), and Michael Marinacci, "The Mexican National Catholic Church," *Califia's Children* blog, November 19, 2014. Especially notable is St. Augustine's Catholic Church headed by Bishop John Parnell in Fort Worth, Texas.

90. " 'Hippie Priest' Dead at 96," *Daily Freeman* (Kingston, N.Y.), July 23, 1979 (J. Gordon Melton American Religions Collection/University of California at Santa Barbara Library, Folder: Old Catholic Church [Francis]). This article says that Bob Dylan attended Brothers's church and the priest influenced Dylan's "new moral." On the bike shop and photo, see Tusha Yakovleva, "Bicycle Matchmaker: Woodstock's Michael Esposito," *Faster Times* website, October 13, 2009. See also Richard Heppner and Janine Fallon-Mower, "Father Francis," in *Legendary Locals of Woodstock* (Charleston, S.C.: Arcadia, 2013), p. 45; Tobe Carey, dir., *Father Francis, 1974–1975*, Glenford, N.Y.: Willow Mixed Media, no date; and Paul McMahon, "Woodstock's Centennial Anthem," a song written and performed for the town's centennial cel-

ebration in 2002. The song repeats the local legend that Father Francis married Dylan and first wife, Sara Lownds, though I did not find evidence of that in several biographies of Dylan.

91. Theriault, *Msgr. Vilatte*, pp. 138–39. Anson, *Bishops at Large*, pp. 125, 258–59. For "married a Peabody," see J. A. Douglas, "Foreword," in Brandreth, Episcopi Vagantes *and the Anglican Church*, pp. ix–xix, at p. xvii.

92. Richard Newman, "Archbishop Daniel Alexander and the African Orthodox Church," in *The Colonial Epoch in Africa*, vol. 2, ed. Gregory Maddox (New York: Garland, 1993), pp. 65–80, at pp. 65, 75–78. For more on the AOC branches in Africa, see F. B. Welbourn, *East African Rebels: A Study of Some Independent Churches* (London: SCM Press, 1961). On the AOC, I also drew on Melton, *Encyclopedia of American Religions*, pp. 179–80; and Richard Newman, "Black Bishops: Some African-American Old Catholics and Their Churches," in *Words Like Freedom: Essays on African-American Culture and History* (West Cornwall, Conn.: Locust Hill Press, 1996), pp. 107–48. See also the forthcoming book by Tshepo Masango Chéry, as of 2016 a manuscript titled "Kingdoms of the Earth: Daniel Williams Alexander and the Rise of the Black Church in South Africa."

93. William Montgomery Brown, *The Crucial Race Question: Where and How Shall the Color Line Be Drawn*, 2nd ed. (Little Rock, Ark.: Arkansas Churchman's Publishing, 1907), p. 249. For UNIA numbers, see Manning Marable, *Malcolm X: A Life of Reinvention* (New York: Penguin, 2011), p. 20. Newman, "Archbishop Daniel Alexander," p. 69; and Newman, "Black Bishops," pp. 107–12.

94. Newman, "Archbishop Daniel," p. 69; Newman, "Black Bishops," p. 128. On the Irvine essay, see George Augustine Hyde, *Genesis of the Orthodox Catholic Church of America* (Indianapolis: Orthodox Catholic Church of America, 1993), section titled "Ongoing Ecclesiastical Disorientation."

95. Black priests in the big bodies came relatively quickly compared to the long wait for black bishops with standing equal to white bishops. In McGuire's time the PEC allowed black men as "suffragan" bishops without rights of voting or succession to diocesan leadership. This second-class "racial episcopate" was condemned within the PEC in 1957. It changed with the consecration in 1962 of John M. Burgess, who became diocesan bishop of Massachusetts in 1969. On Healy, see James O'Toole, *Passing for White: Race, Religion and the Healy Family, 1820–1920* (Amherst: University of Massachusetts Press, 2003). In 1965, James Lawson Howze was appointed auxiliary bishop of the Roman Catholic Archdiocese of New Orleans.

96. Theriault, *Msgr. Vilatte*, pp. 196, 131.

97. Field notes, St. John Coltrane African Orthodox Church, San Francisco, Calif., August 7, 2005. Franzo King, interview, San Francisco, Calif., August 10, 2005.

98. Field notes, St. John AOC, August 7, 2005. The history that included mention of Syrian Christianity, Mar Julius, and Vilatte was on the church website. See also Newman, "Black Bishops," pp. 115–16; and David Bry, "Ascension," *Vibe* 5, no. 6 (August 1997): 106–9.

3. LOVE AND META-CATHOLICISM:
FOUNDING THE CHURCH OF ANTIOCH

1. On US religion as seen from the West Coast, see Laurie Maffly-Kipp, "Eastward Ho!
   American Religion from the Perspective of the Pacific Rim," in *Retelling American
   Religious History*, ed. Thomas Tweed (Berkeley: University of California Press, 1997),
   pp. 127–48. On the Crystal Cathedral, see Dennis Voskuil, *Mountains Into Goldmines:
   Robert Schuller and the Gospel of Success* (Grand Rapids, Mich.: Eerdmans, 1983).

2. On the British Old Catholic and Liberal Catholic churches throughout this section,
   see James Ingall Wedgwood, *Beginnings of the Liberal Catholic Church, February 13,
   1916* (1937; Lakewood, N.J.: Ubique, 1966); Peter Anson, *Bishops at Large* (1964; Berkeley: Apocryphile Press, 2006), pp. 185–87, 192–98, 323–442; Robert Ellwood and Harry
   B. Partin, *Religious and Spiritual Groups in Modern America*, 2nd ed. (Englewood
   Cliffs, N.J.: Prentice Hall, 1988), pp. 107–9; and Siobhan Houston, *Priests, Gnostics
   and Magicians: European Roots of Esoteric Independent Catholicism* (Berkeley: Apocryphile Press, 2009), pp. 67–120.

   For "neither Roman Catholic nor Protestant," see the Liberal Catholic Church,
   The Liturgy According to the Use of the Liberal Catholic Church, 3rd ed. (San Diego:
   The St. Alban Press, 2002), p. 7; written by Wedgwood for the first edition (see p. 17),
   the formulation repeats throughout Liberal Catholic Church history, in statements of
   principles and on websites.

   Mathew claimed distress at his clergy's involvement in Theosophy. In hindsight,
   it is likely that Mathew was actually more disturbed by the "immorality" of some of
   his priests, namely, same-sex amorous activities, which had upset him in Anglican
   and Roman contexts, too. In particular, Old Catholic bishop Frederick Willoughby
   had been targeted for exposés in the London magazine *John Bull*. In 1915 Mathew dis-
   solved the church. See Anson, *Bishops at Large*, pp. 158–59, 165, 193–94, 198.

3. The number of members in the Theosophical Society at its height is usually given
   as forty-five thousand, for example, in Anne Tyler, *Annie Besant: A Biography* (Oxford: Oxford University Press, 1992), p. 328. Catherine Albanese, *A Republic of Mind
   and Spirit* (New Haven: Yale University Press, 2007), chap. 6, "Metaphysical Asia,"
   pp. 330–93. Besides the Liberal Catholic Church, other esoteric sacramental groups
   started by former Theosophists include Rudolf Steiner's Christian Community, Dion
   Fortune's Guild of the Master Jesus (later called the Church of the Graal), and Richard, Duc de Palatine's Pre-Nicene Gnostic Catholic Church.

   After Blavatsky's death, the Theosophical Society split into a number of organizations. My references to Theosophy refer to the major inheritor, the organization led
   by Besant based in Adyar. As an adjective, I sometimes use "theosophical" to describe
   the general orientation of the assorted organizations.

4. *The Liturgy According to the Use of the Liberal Catholic Church*, pp. 7–8.

5. Ibid., pp. 10–13. For "zoological," I use Anson's quote of an earlier edition, since it
   captures Wedgwood's original colorful language. Anson, *Bishops at Large*, p. 354.

6. Charles Leadbeater, *The Science of the Sacraments* (1920; Adyar, Madras, India: Theosophical Publishing House, 1980), pp. xi–xiv, 3.

7. For "curious result," see Anson, *Bishops at Large*, p. 348, quoting a letter from Leadbeater to Besant. For "Catholic bondage," see Anson, *Bishops at Large*, p. 351, citing a pamphlet published by an American Theosophy group headed by Celestia Root Lang, "Shall the American Section T. S. Be Sold Into Catholic Bondage?," *Divine Life* (1917), published by the Independent Theosophical Society of America in Chicago. Annie Besant, "On the Watch-Tower," *Theosophist* 38, no. 1 (October 1916): 1–8, at p. 5. See also Edward Roslof, *Red Priests: Renovationism, Russian Orthodoxy, and Revolution, 1905–1946* (Bloomington: Indiana University Press, 2002). On Besant's benedictions, see Houston, *Priests, Gnostics and Magicians*, p. 96, and Gregory Tillett, *The Elder Brother: A Biography of Charles Webster Leadbeater* (London: Routledge and Kegan Paul, 1982), pp. 603–4. A photograph understood in independent Catholic oral history to depict Annie Besant vested in the sanctuary of a Liberal Catholic Church is reprinted by Lewis Keizer, *The Wandering Bishops: Apostles of a New Spirituality* (1976; Aromas, Calif.: Home Temple Press, 2001), p. 26, leading him and others to wonder whether Besant was ordained to minor or major Catholic orders. But the provenance of the photograph and its images is not clear. Keizer, emails to author, March, April, and August 2012. On the Order of the World Mother, see Joseph Ross, *Spirit of Womanhood: A Journey with Rukmini Devi* (Ojai, Calif.: Joseph E. Ross/Krotona Archives, 2009); and Leela Samson, *Rukmini Devi: A Life* (Gurgaon: Penguin Books India, 2010).

8. On early growth, see the historical section of the Liberal Catholic Church website. On Henry Agard Wallace and the Liberal Catholic Church, see John Culver and John Hyde, *American Dreamer: A Life of Henry A. Wallace* (New York: Norton, 2001), pp. 76–82, 96.

9. Besant, a lifelong supporter of Krishnamurti, nevertheless stood by Leadbeater against all accusers. She accepted, for example, that Leadbeater gave boys lessons in masturbation techniques, pointing out that all sex education was considered scandalous at the time, and Theosophy should help dispel the miasma of British prudery. Tillett, *The Elder Brother*, pp. 77–86, 104–7, 152, 347–48, 635–36.

10. Jiddu Krishnamurti, *The Dissolution of the Order of the Star: A Statement by J. Krishnamurti* (Eerde, Ommen: Star Publishing Trust, 1929). For "The Coming" quotation, see Tillett, *The Elder Brother*, p. 240.

11. Tillett, *The Elder Brother*, p. ix. Keizer, *Wandering Bishops*, p. 27. On Leadbeater's wider influence, see also Albanese, *A Republic of Mind and Spirit*, pp. 452–65.

12. On Hampton, here and throughout this section, see J. Gordon Melton, *Encyclopedia of American Religions*, 8th ed. (Detroit: Gale/Cengage, 2009), p. 725; Anson, *Bishops at Large*, pp. 350, 363–64; Herman Spruit, *The Sacramentarion: A Record of a Personalized Journey Into the Inner Life of the Least Understood of Christianity's Major Mysteries* (1979; Nevada City, Calif.: Sophia Divinity School, 1999), unpaginated front matter, third page; and Charles Hampton, *The Leadbeater, Hampton, Spruit Story and the Loss of Archbishop Hampton's Church Building* (c. 1955; Nevada, Calif.: Sophia

Divinity School Press/Blue Dolphin Publishing, 2006). For the quotation from the radio show: Charles Hampton, "Sacraments," *Liberal Catholic Quarter Hour*, KFAC (Los Angeles), July 28, 1940 (Church Archives CD, Document 30b), p. 2. (Document 30, titled "Confirmation" on the CD, actually includes two documents that I have informally labeled 30a, "Confirmation," and 30b, "Sacraments.") The former cathedral of St. Alban still stands at 2041 North Argyle Avenue as of 2016. In 1964 it became the home of Protection of the Holy Virgin Russian Orthodox Church.

13. Herman Spruit, "An Interview with Herman Adrian Spruit by *AROHN* a Rosicrucian Publication," in *Herman Adrian Spruit: Articles and Writings About Him and By Him*, book A, ed. Richard Gundrey (Santa Fe, N.M.: Sophia Divinity School Press, 2008), second reprinted article, original date 1981, original pagination pp. 23–29, at p. 26. *AROHN* was edited by Edward Sullivan, at that time the secretary general of the Holy Order of the Rosy Cross and archbishop in the Church of Antioch.

14. John Plummer, *The Many Paths of the Independent Sacramental Movement: A Study of Its Liturgy, Doctrine and Leadership in America* (Dallas: Newt Books, 2004), p. 78. Houston, *Priests, Gnostics and Magicians*, pp. 115–16. Anson, *Bishops at Large*, p. 362.

15. For Spruit's account of his visit to St. Alban, see Hampton, *The Leadbeater, Hampton, Spruit Story*, pp. 28–29. For the other anecdotes, see Spruit, "An Interview," p. 26, as well as Herman Spruit, "Another Interview with Herman Adrian Spruit by *AROHN*," in Gundrey, *Herman Adrian Spruit*, book A, third reprinted article, original date 1981, original pagination pp. 25–30, at pp. 28–29.

16. For a photograph of Hampton making eggs in his trailer, see Hampton, *The Leadbeater, Hampton, Spruit Story*, p. 9. Herman Spruit, "Holistic Meditation of Antiochean Bishops" (Mountain View, Calif.: Church of Antioch Press, 1978), Church Archives CD, Document 47, p. 42. Richard Gundrey, "Historical Background on the Spruit Succession," no date, Church Archives CD, Document 45.

17. After this point in the narrative I mostly call Herman Spruit by his first name, so as not to confuse him with Meri Spruit and to be consistent with my use of other Antiochians' first names after initial citations.

18. Meri Louise Spruit, Church of Antioch matriarch emerita, age eighty-one, interview, Marina, Calif., October 8, 2007.

It is common if not universal knowledge among Church of Antioch leaders that Herman and Meri were not legally married. Consulting public records for Herman, Meri, and family members at Ancestry.com on May 3, 2013, there were incomplete records of the marriage and divorce of Herman and Hulda Zurbuchen (1930s–1950s), Herman and Violet Walp (1960–?), and Herman and Helen Banks aka Helen Seymour (1965 to 1969 or 1970).

Piecing together public records and information from my interviews and field notes, it seems that the children in Herman's life were his two sons with Hulda, Dennis (b. 1945) and Douglas (b. 1950), a stepson with Violet, and four stepchildren with Helen. Meri had four children from two marriages: Carol, Charles, Richard, and Rosemary.

19. Meri Louise Spruit's birthday is August 1, 1926. Herman's birthday is January 26, 1911. On his grandfather, see Spruit, *The Sacramentarion*, p. 131. (Book 5 of *The Sacramentarion* is titled "Search for Truth" and subtitled "An Abbreviated Auto-Biographical Sketch of Herman Adrian Spruit," announced on an unpaginated page and running pp. 118–37.)

    On Herman's emigration, see Edward Sullivan, "Herman Adrian Spruit: A More Detailed History/Archbishop-Patriarch Herman Adrian Spruit," in Gundrey, *Herman Adrian Spruit*, book A, first reprinted article, original date n.a., pp. 40–41. Found at Ancestry.com on May 3, 2013, the "California Passenger and Crew Lists, 1882–1957" show original logs for Helene (age forty-three), Hermann (age sixteen), and Helmut (age nine) sailing from Antwerp and arriving in Los Angeles on December 19, 1927. Hermann the father, listed as of Dutch ethnicity and born in 1886, sailed nine months earlier, arriving in Los Angeles on March 20, 1927.

    I draw on the following sources for Herman's life here and throughout: Spruit, "An Interview" and "Another Interview," as well as Herman Spruit, "How to Demonstrate What You Believe You Have a Right to Expect," in *Herman Adrian Spruit: Various Historical Papers, Pictures and Letters Pertaining to Our Church*, book B, ed. Richard Gundrey (Santa Fe, N.M.: Sophia Divinity School Press, 2008), seventh document, three pages, no original pagination; and, in the same volume, Herman Spruit, "This Piece Is Written by Patriarch Herman About His Life" and "This Piece Is ABOUT Patriarch Herman's Life History," eighth and ninth reprinted documents, one page each; Herman Spruit, *The Conquest of the Rings: A Writing by Patriarch Herman as an Introduction to Sophia Divinity School and a Few Other Brief Articles*, book C, ed. Richard Gundrey (Santa Fe, N.M.: Sophia Divinity School Press, 2008), first item, no pagination, original pagination pp. 1–12, at pp. 7–9) (also available in the Church of Antioch Archives/Box: Herman & Meri's files—1/File: Faith); Terry Bell, "For This Was the Bishop Called," *Contact* (Archdiocese of the Church of Antioch), August 1967, pp. 1+, Church Archives CD, Document 41; Jan Kooistra Van Campenhout, *Apostolic Succession in the Catholic Apostolic Church of Antioch, Malabar Rite*, ed. Richard Gundrey (Santa Fe, N.M.: Sophia Divinity School, 1998), pp. 49–50; Paul Clemens, "Preface," in *The Rule of Antioch*, by Herman Spruit, new ed., ed. Paul Clemens (1979, 2002; Nevada City, Calif.: Blue Dolphin Publishing, 2010), pp. vii–xi; Karl Pruter and J. Gordon Melton, eds., *The Old Catholic Sourcebook* (New York: Garland, 1983), pp. 62–63; Anson, *Bishops at Large*, pp. 364–65; Keizer, *Wandering Bishops*, pp. 62–65; and Houston, *Priests, Gnostics and Magicians*, pp. 119–20.

20. At Ancestry.com on May 3, 2013, the "U.S. City Directories, 1821–1989" for 1930 listed "Herman Spruit Jr" with his parents at 50 Bixel Street in Los Angeles and his profession as "Pntr."

21. Sullivan, "Herman Adrian Spruit," pp. 40–42. Bell, "For This Was the Bishop Called," p. 1. Spruit, "Another Interview," p. 25. Keizer, *Wandering Bishops*, p. 63. Herman Spruit, "Herman Adrian Spruit: The Man," draft of interview (1981; Santa Fe, N.M.: Sophia Divinity School Press, 2007), p. 4. (The first half of the latter interview is re-

produced in "Another Interview," but I cite it separately because it includes more of the interview and other material not included in the published version.)

22. Sullivan, "Herman Adrian Spruit." Spruit, "Herman Adrian Spruit the Man," p. 6. Spruit, "Holistic Meditation," p. 41. For more on Harkness and this trip, see Rebekah Miles, "Georgia Elma Harkness," in *Makers of Christian Theology in America*, ed. Mark Toulouse and James Duke (Nashville: Abingdon Press, 1997), pp. 430–33.

23. Herman repeatedly called himself a mystic and was so named by others, for example, Jim Willems, Church of Antioch member, age sixty-three, interview, Ojai, Calif., November 25, 2007. For "lonely" and "misunderstood," I quote Willems. For the "Radiance" quotation, see Sullivan, "Herman Adrian Spruit," p. 49.

24. D. J. Waldie, "L.A.'s Postwar Art Scene: Hot Rods and Hedonism," *Los Angeles Times*, September 8, 2011.

25. On Herman's rate of reading, see Bell, "For This Was the Bishop Called," unpaginated second page of interview. On "fountain" and building funds, see Spruit, "This Piece Is Written." On Spruit's time at the University of Southern California, see Spruit, "Holistic Meditation," pp. 2–3, 40–41, and Keizer, *Wandering Bishops*, p. 63.

Herman's work at USC fell within the time when Robert J. Taylor was dean of the Graduate School of Religion; Herman mentions Taylor's influence. Herman's classes, however, did not culminate in a degree, which he explained as an effect of concentrating on desired courses rather than degree requirements. Spruit, *The Sacramentarion*, p. 126. Herman's doctorate (or doctorates—he listed both the PhD and DD at various times) may have been granted later by another institution, for example by Sophia Divinity School.

26. For "soft peddle" and "dawn on me," see Spruit, "This Piece Is Written." "Soft peddle" is a common misspelling of the idiom "soft pedal."

27. For the resignation date of January 1951, see Sullivan, "Herman Adrian Spruit," p. 42. For "deeper spirituality," see Clemens, "Preface," p. 7. For "shattering," see Keizer, *Wandering Bishops*, p. 64. For "clear cut," see Spruit, "This Piece Is Written."

28. Spruit, "How to Demonstrate," unpaginated, first page. Herman Spruit, "Letters from the Apostles," no date, Church of Antioch Archives/Box: HA & Meri Spruit's Writings/File: Hermans (sic) Writings loose in box, pp. 2–3.

29. Spruit, "How to Demonstrate," unpaginated, all three pages. *Science of Mind* archivist James Abbott confirms Herman's positions as executive secretary and licentiate minister according to minutes of meetings of the International Association of Religious Science Churches from 1951 (email to author, May 8, 2013). Articles by Herman published in the Institute's *Science of Mind* journal include "I Discovered the Secret of Prayer" (December 1951): 23–24+, and "The Best Is Yet to Come" (March 1954): 4–7. Herman was listed as a Religious Science practitioner in *Science of Mind* through the January 1955 issue (p. 91).

30. For "my thing" and "great leader," see Spruit, "This Piece Is Written." For "Methodist grooves" and "true prophet," see Spruit, "Herman Adrian Spruit, the Man," pp. 6, 11. For "fast friends," see Spruit, *Letters from the Apostles*, p. 3. On Maude Lathem, see Spruit, "Another Interview," p. 28, and Spruit, "Herman Adrian Spruit, the Man," p. 11.

31. On the issues in Religious Science from 1953 to 1954, see Melton, *Encyclopedia of American Religions*, p. 887; John Dart, "Rev. William Hornaday; Religious Science Leader," *Los Angeles Times*, March 20, 1992. On Holmes's idea of the "Church Universal," see Reginald C. Armor and Robin Llast, *That Was Ernest: The Story of Ernest Holmes and the Religious Science Movement*, ed. Arthur Vergara (Camarillo, Calif.: DeVorss, 1999), p. 142.

32. For "stately grandeur," see Spruit, "Letters from the Apostles," p. 3. For Methodists' superior warmth and "flower," see Spruit, *Conquest of the Rings*, pp. 7–8.

33. For Herman's introduction to Leadbeater, his reintroduction to Old Catholicism, and the "vital non-Papal" quotation, see Sullivan, "Herman Adrian Spruit," pp. 43–44. I guess that it is Maude Lathem who gave Herman a copy of Leadbeater because Sullivan says it is a "she." Lathem was among few women employed in the top ranks of Religious Science and Herman mentioned her by name as a friend. Still, I am just guessing.

34. For "prior to his death" and "crowning touch," see Spruit, "Conquest of the Rings," p. 9. For "too young and inexperienced," see "Letters from the Apostles," p. 4. For three other accounts of this Holmes request, see Spruit, "Psycho-Pneumatology," no date, Church Archives CD, Document 68, p. 12; Spruit, "Conquest of the Rings," p. 26; and Spruit, "Another Interview," p. 28.

35. For "passing phenomenon" and other Holmes words as remembered by Herman, see Spruit, "Another Interview," p. 28, and also "Herman Adrian Spruit the Man," p. 11, which is the same document in draft version. For "ecclesiastical tramp," see Spruit, *Conquest of the Rings*, p. 8.

36. On the stint with Golden State University, see Melton, *Encyclopedia of American Religions*, p. 719, and materials in Church of Antioch Archives, Box: Herman & Meri's files—1/File: Golden State. This university had several incarnations, later ones only on paper, and by 2013 it was generally noted as a degree mill, if anything. On the Popenoe certification, see Sullivan, "Herman Adrian Spruit," p. 46. On other employment and activities, see Spruit, "This Piece Is ABOUT"; Herman Spruit, "Upward Still and Onward," no date, c. 1982, Church Archives CD, Document 100, p. 3; Bell, "For This Was the Bishop Called," p. 1; and materials in Church of Antioch Archives/Box: HAS files/ File: Hearst Mansion.

37. Bell, "For This Was the Bishop Called," p. 1 and third page.

38. Melton, *Encyclopedia of American Religions*, p. 721. On Herman and Palatine's relationship, see Sullivan, "Herman Adrian Spruit," pp. 43–45; Sullivan reports that Herman met Hampton at Palatine's "behest." On St. Michael's, see Pruter and Melton, *Old Catholic Sourcebook*, pp. 96–97. For more on Palatine and Stephan Hoeller, see Keizer, *Wandering Bishops*, pp. 48–55, 60–61. For more on Hoeller, see Stephan Hoeller, "Guest Addendum," in *The Sacramentarion*, by Herman Spruit (1979; Nevada City, Calif.: Sophia Divinity School, 1999), pp. 273–75, and A. W. Hill, "Exile in Godville: Profile of a Postmodern Heretic," *LA Weekly*, May 19–25, 2005.

39. St. Francis-by-the-Sea still stands and is pastored by American Catholic Church bishops following Wadle. See Leslie Earnest, "Laguna Beach: Tiny Church Designated a Landmark," *Los Angeles Times*, June 4, 1990.

On Herman's ordinations, see Sullivan, "Herman Adrian Spruit," pp. 45–46, and Spruit, "Another Interview," pp. 28–30. Wadle's requirements are mentioned in the latter. Wadle was married; Melton speculated that his celibacy requirement was aimed at gay men more than straight men, but whatever its goal, Herman seemed put off (J. Gordon Melton, email to author, July 6, 2015). On the start of FICOB, see Gundrey, "Historical Background." For various FICOB documents, see Herman Spruit, "Our Seventeen Lines of Apostolic Succession," undated, Church Archives CD, Document 63; and materials in Church of Antioch Archives/Box: Herman & Meri's files—1/File: Fed of Ind. Cath & Orth Bishops. On various names of Herman's church, see Gundrey, "Our Beginning." For a copy of Herman's certificate of episcopal ordination, see Church Archives CD, Document 35.

The speed with which Herman was ordained and then consecrated would be unusual for the big-body Catholicisms in the twentieth century, but requirements for time (and age and education) before ordination have fluctuated in the history of Catholicism.

40. Melton credits the start of the practice of multiple consecrations to Hugh George de Willmott Newman, who founded the Catholicate of the West in Britain in 1944 (Melton, *Encyclopedia of American Religions*, pp. 84–85). Herman explained in "Our Seventeen Lines" that (in his view) while reconsecrations in the 1940s aimed to shore up validity to a wider Catholic world, within a few decades the "lines" were more a matter of "roots," "historical interest," "identity and pride." More, Melton wrote that "by the 1990s, the several lines of apostolic succession had become well established in the person of a large number of the independent bishops . . . and the practice of multiple consecrations . . . largely disappeared" (Melton, *Encyclopedia of American Religions*, p. 84). For extended discussion of the practice, see Rob Angus Jones, *Independent Sacramental Bishops: Ordination, Authority, Lineage, and Validity* (Berkeley: Apocryphile Press, 2010), pp. 66–92.

41. For more on Herman's accrual of churches, lines, FICOB, Sophia, and episcopal effects, see Spruit, "Another Interview," pp. 29–30; Spruit, "Conquest of the Rings," pp. 24–27; Richard Gundrey, "Our Beginning," Church of Antioch listserv, January 23, 2007; Anson, *Bishops at Large*, pp. 257–61; Pruter and Melton, *Old Catholic Sourcebook*, p. 96; Houston, *Priests, Gnostics and Magicians*, pp. 118–21; Keizer, *Wandering Bishops*, pp. 32–36; and Melton, *Encyclopedia of American Religions*, pp. 1157–61.

42. For the date of his being raised to the status of archbishop, see Spruit, "Another Interview," pp. 29–30.

The apostolic succession of the Church of Antioch is given as an example in John Plummer and John Mabry, *Who Are the Independent Catholics? An Introduction to the Independent and Old Catholic Churches* (Berkeley: Apocryphile Press, 2006), pp. 92–95.

I do not know how many diaconal and priestly ordinations Herman performed, but a church source lists his number of consecrations at forty-one, plus an additional six for which he served as co-consecrator. Of the forty-one, all but eight were consecrations for the Church of Antioch itself. If this record is accurate, Herman consecrated abundantly within his church, but carefully outside of it. Van Campenhout, *Apostolic Succession*, pp. 75–79.

43. For "validity of much psychism," see Spruit, "Another Interview." On western Orthodox independent bishops such as Aneed, Jules Ferrette, Aftimios Ofiesh, and Ulrich Herford, see John Erickson, *Orthodox Christians in America: A Short History* (New York: Oxford University Press, 2007), pp. 58–83; Michael Prokurat, Alexander Golitzin, and Michael D. Peterson, *The A to Z of the Orthodox Church* (Lanham, Md.: Scarecrow Press, 1996); Thomas Fitzgerald, *The Orthodox Church* (Westport, Conn.: Greenwood Press, 1995); Pruter and Melton, *Old Catholic Sourcebook*, pp. 34–37 and 67–76; Melton, *Encyclopedia of American Religions*, pp. 1157–61; and Mariam Namey Ofiesh, *Archbishop Aftimios Ofiesh, 1880–1966: A Biography Revealing His Contribution to Orthodoxy and Christendom* (Sun City West, Ariz.: Abihider, 1999).

44. On Antioch's corporation sole arrangement, see Gundrey, "Historical Background"; and Richard Gundrey, Church of Antioch listserv, June 14, 2006. As Gundrey explained in the latter, the state of California no longer issues corporation soles, but since the Church of Antioch remains continuously the same organization, it remains legally an entity of that status.

45. On the names, see Gundrey, "Our Beginning." In April 2008, church bishops voted to drop the "Malabar Rite" part and make the official name simply "The Catholic Apostolic Church of Antioch." Richard Gundrey, *Church of Antioch Newsletter*, June 5, 2008, unpaginated, first page. Archbishop Leon Hunt, presiding bishop of the Autocephalous Catholic Apostolic Church of Antioch in the United Kingdom, knew Herman personally and described Herman's mass: field notes, Church of Antioch Convocation 2014, [Roman Catholic retreat center, midwestern city and state], October 26. On Herman's title as patriarch, see Spruit, "Another Interview," p. 29.

46. Paul Clemens, email to author, June 3, 2010.

47. On the church newsletter numbers, see Bell, "For This Was the Bishop Called," second page. On the higher numbers from 1980, see Spruit, *Conquest of the Rings*, p. 10. On the "thorny problem," see Spruit, "Our Gideon's Call," June 14, 1981, Church Archives CD, Document 62, pp. 1–2.

From circumstantial evidence, I gather that in 1979, Herman agreed to serve as bishop for the Holy Order of the Rosy Cross (HORC), based in Burlington, Washington, and led by Edward Sullivan, soon a bishop and then archbishop of Antioch. As members of HORC got ordained, too, they accounted for the tripling of clergy numbers by 1980. The HORC-Antioch collaboration remained strong throughout the 1980s, and Meri Spruit mentioned it in a letter to Richard Gundrey. "There were a lot of people involved in the Church work at Washington," she wrote. "They came together for the formulation of the newsletter, writing the articles, mass daily, all the church work, their own jobs for the separate family livelihood, care of children, fixing meals, and meetings ad infinitum." Letter to Richard Gundrey, "At Long Last . . . ," June 20, 2007, in Gundrey, *Herman Adrian Spruit*, book A, first reprinted letter, no pagination.

48. For examples of documents in which Herman wrote of conflict, see Herman Spruit, Letter to Arnold and Shirley (October 1, 1981), Church of Antioch Archives/Box: HA & Meri Spruit's Writings/File: Letters, etc.—HAS; Herman Spruit, "Constitution and Statement of Principles of the Church of Antioch" (Mountain View, Calif.: Church of Antioch Press, 1978), Church Archives CD, Document 77; Spruit, "Our Seventeen Lines"; Herman Spruit, "A Frank Appraisal of My Ministry and a New Year's Message for Myself and Those Who Would Walk with Me," copy of original writing dated 1986, posted to the Church of Antioch listserv by Daniel Dangaran, June 1, 2009.

49. For "worthless," see Spruit, "Psycho-Pneumatology," p. 13. For "museum pieces," see Spruit, "Another Interview," pp. 27–28. For "amazingly wondrous" "real Catholicism," see Spruit, *The Sacramentarion*, pp. 131–32.

50. Bell, "For This Was the Bishop Called," third page.

51. Spruit, *The Sacramentarion*, pp. 10–11, 277. See also Herman's reference to the Masters in "An Interview," pp. 23–24.

52. For the vision of Jesus, see Herman Spruit, "Some Years Ago . . . ," no date (after 1980), Church of Antioch Archives/Box: Herman & Meri's files—4/File: Sophia Divinity School, pp. 4–5. Herman indicated on page 5 that by 1980, thirty years had elapsed since the vision, so it apparently happened around 1950. For the "dark night," see Herman Spruit, "After a Prolonged Period . . ." (a meditation), February 18, 1982, Church Archives CD, Document 14(b). For "Help your wife," see Herman Spruit, "This Is Like a Buffet Supper . . . ," no date, Church of Antioch Archives/Box: Herman & Meri's files—4/File: History & Notes of H.A.S., unpaginated, first page. The latter is a very thick sheaf that looks like notes toward an autobiography.

53. For "finishing touches," the "Fourth Way," and "Integral Christianity," see "Some Years Ago . . . ," pp. 4–7. ("Integral" is generally a hot word in metaphysical circles, but in 1980 the California Institute of Integral Studies was so renamed, that is, around the same time that Herman wrote of "Integral Christianity.") Also for the "Fourth Way," see Spruit, *Conquest of the Rings*, p. 9. For "meta-catholic," see Spruit, "Toward a Synthesis," p. 2. For "ecclesiastical imperialism" and "basic purpose," see Terry Bell, "Liberal Religion," *Cosmos* (June 1973), Church Archives CD, Document 54.

54. Herman Spruit, *The Rule of Antioch*, new ed., edited by Paul Clemens (1979, 2002; Nevada City, Calif.: Church of Antioch by Blue Dolphin Publishing, 2010), p. 2. Frank Bugge, Church of Antioch listserv, June 1, 2009.

55. For characterizations of Herman's theology as Augustinian, see Keizer, *Wandering Bishops*, p. 64; Bell, "For This Was . . . ," second page; Bell, "Liberal Religion"; and Herman Spruit, "Conquest of the Rings" (draft version), p. 25. Augustine's words "Love, and do what thou wilt" are in his seventh homily on the First Epistle of John, section 8. See Philip Schaff, ed., *Nicene and Post-Nicene Fathers*, 1st ser., vol. 7 (Buffalo, N.Y.: Christian Literature Publishing, 1888). For Herman's riff on Augustine's words, see Herman Spruit, "My Philosophical Manifesto," no date, Church of Antioch Archives/Box: Herman & Meri's files—2/File: Philosophy, unpaginated, second page.

56. Augustine, *Retractions* 1.12.3, in *The Retractions*, trans. Mary Inez Bogan, RSM, Fathers of the Church: A New Translation (Patristic Series) 60 (Washington, D.C.: Catholic University of America Press, 1999), p. 52. According to historian Elizabeth Clark, it was a common late ancient Christian trope that Christianity was older than Christ, who completed or fulfilled an older monotheism in which wise pagans partook (email to author, March 14, 2011). For "Church of Tomorrow," see Herman Spruit, "Old Wine for New Skins," 1966, Church Archives CD, Document 59, pp. 3–4.

57. Spruit, *The Rule of Antioch*, p. 4.

58. For Herman's Masonic and Rosicrucian affiliations, see Spruit, "An Interview," p. 29; Spruit, "Holistic Meditation," pp. 7–8; and Herman Spruit, "The Technique: The Development of Spiritual Consciousness, the Jesus Christ Method," no date, Church Archives CD, Document 95, p. 2. Besides Mother Jennie Maiereder, other local intuitives Herman knew personally included Charlotte von Strahl, Edith Gable, and Simon Amador (the latter was an Antioch priest). Additionally he used the work of Louise Hay and Corinne Heline. He might have met the latter—a fellow former Methodist in southern California who was immersed in metaphysics and devoted to "the Madonna," whom Heline saw frequently in visions. For these references, see Spruit, "Holistic Meditation," pp. 10–11, 13–14, 52; Spruit, "Technique," p. 3; and a photocopy of the first pages of Louise Hay's *Heal Your Body* (1984), in the Church of Antioch Archives, Box: Herman & Meri's files—1/File: HAS's notes/musings. Examples of letters of inquiry about the Church of Antioch from far-flung places can be found in the Church of Antioch Archives/Box: Herman & Meri's files—1/File: Independent Churches as well as Church of Antioch Archives/Box: Herman & Meri's files—2/File: Nigeria—this inquiry came to Meri Spruit and near it were notes for her response letter. On the Druid initiation, see "The Ritual of Initiation of Herman and Meri Spruit to the Ancient Order of Druids," author unknown, with a note by Richard Gundrey at the top: "Performed in December 1987 in Australia at the same time Herman and Meri consecrated Frank & Chyrlle (sic) Bugge to the order of bishops," Church Archives CD, Document 92. (Bishop C. Bugge's first name is actually spelled Chearle.) Frank Bugge also posted information about this event to the church listserv in July and August 2003, and it is preserved as "Female Lines of Apostolic Succession," Church Archives CD, Document 38. The website of Bugge's autocephalous Australian Church of Antioch names the consecrator as the archbishop and arch-druid Tim Ryan. References to other techniques, organizations, and persons with whom Herman had contact were rife throughout his writings and papers. For the paper signage, see Church of Antioch Archives/Box: Herman & Meri's files—1/File: Astrology. In all fairness, there is a chance that this sign refers to Helen Spruit, known as a gifted astrologer, but I guess it has to do with Herman poking fun at Herman.

59. For "the Galilean Master," see Spruit, "Holistic Meditation," p. 47. For "Number One," see Bell, "For This Was . . . ," third page. On Hampton's anointing, the sacraments of healing, and "Absolution," see Spruit, "Holistic Meditation," pp. 5–6.

60. Herman Spruit, "Psycho-Pneumatology," pp. 10–14; Herman also talks about Bussell within these pages. For Bussell's cure of his kidney stones and the crucial role of love in healing, see Spruit, "Holistic Meditation," pp. 16–18, 48. See also D. J. Bussell (?), "The Chirothesian Church," no date, Church Archives CD, Document 83.

61. For no "mind over matter," see Spruit, "Holistic Meditation," p. 51. For "innate divinity," see Herman Spruit, "Prosperity Is Up to You," no date, Church Archives CD, Document 67, p. 3. For "sun would shine," see Spruit, "Psycho-Pneumatology," p. 10. For more on the relationship between New Thought and prosperity, see Albanese, *A Republic of Mind and Spirit*, pp. 437–48, and Kate Bowler, *Blessed: A History of the Prosperity Gospel* (New York: Oxford University Press, 2013), pp. 11–40.

62. For "went broke," see William Whalen, *Faiths for the Few: A Study of Minority Religions* (Milwaukee: Bruce Publishing, 1963), p. 74. On the fire and starting over, see Bell, "For This Was . . . ," second page, and Spruit, "Holistic Meditation," p. 20. For the Decra-Led windows ad, see Church of Antioch Archives, Box: Herman & Meri's files—1/File: Architecture. For "last $10.00," see Linda Rounds-Nichols, "Sophia Divinity School: A History," published in four parts, *Antioch Clarion* (January/February 2010–July/August 2010), part 1. For the request for medical funds, see Herman Spruit, "The Full Truth of My Condition," April 15, 1985, Church of Antioch Archives/Box: HA & Meri Spruit's Writings/File: Letters, etc.—HAS, p. 2.

63. For the wish list, see Herman Spruit, "For Myself," August 13, 1981, Church of Antioch Archives, Box: Herman & Meri's files—4/File: Incomplete 1. On the haircuts and "Deliverance," see Herman Spruit, "Escaping the Wheel of Karma and Finding the Full Life," no date, c. spring 1986, Church Archive CD, Document 37, pp. 2–4.

64. Spruit, "Escaping the Wheel," pp. 2–4.

65. For "steam," see Herman Spruit, "Old Wine for New Skins," p. 1. On Spruit being "embarrassed" and repudiating priest Michael Zaharakis, see Keizer, *Wandering Bishops*, p. 76. Melton also mentions that Zaharakis's ministry emphasized social justice issues: Melton, *Encyclopedia of American Religions*, p. 721.

66. For "renegade," see Sullivan, *Encyclopedia of American Religions*, p. 46, quoting a friend of Herman's. For "seminal," see Keizer, *Wandering Bishops*, p. 65. For "giants on earth," a quote of Genesis 6:4, see Robert Burns, *On Being a Bishop* (1980; Santa Fe, N.M.: Sophia Divinity School Press, 2005), unpaginated dedication page. On May 29, 2009, a post on the Yahoo Independent Sacramental Movement listserv named Herman a "saint," as did a post by Archbishop Frank Bugge on the Church of Antioch listserv on June 1, 2009.

67. For "bi-polarity" supported by Genesis, see Herman Spruit, "An Interview," pp. 24, 26. For the midrash tradition of Adam's hermaphroditism, see *Genesis Rabba* 8:1 and *Leviticus Rabba* 14:1. For Herman on Fillmore and Eddy, see "Psycho-Pneumatology," pp. 10–11.

68. Bell, "For This Was . . . ," third page.

69. Spruit, "An Interview," pp. 27–28.

70. Ibid. I found "A Church Divorce Ceremony," an Associated Press article appearing in the *Peninsula Times Tribune* (Palo Alto/Redwood City) (September 16, 1980) on p. A-8, in the Church of Antioch Archives, Box: Herman & Meri's files—2/File: Liturgies 3.

71. For Miller's story, see her own account in Rosamonde Miller, "Wild Gnosis," in *A Strange Vocation: Independent Bishops Tell Their Stories*, ed. Alistair Bate (Berkeley: Apocryphile Press, 2009), pp. 128–43. For "not doctrine," see Miller's shorter account at the website of the Ecclesia Gnostica Mysteriorum. See also Melton, *Encyclopedia of American Religions*, p. 72, and Keizer, *Wandering Bishops*, pp. 55–58. For "more than ready," see Spruit, "An Interview," pp. 25–26. For Spruit's participation, see also Stephan Hoeller, "Independent Catholic Bishop Spruit Dies," *Gnosis* (Winter 1995): 11. In *Wandering Bishops*, Keizer writes in a photograph caption that Jennie Maiereder was consecrated by Spruit as the first female bishop in United States in 1974 (p. 45). In a subsequent book, Keizer says that the ordination date was the spring equinox of 1975. Keizer, *Mother Jennie's Garden: The Life Story of a Great Theosophical Sage, Saint and Psychic* (self-published by Lewis Keizer, 2009), chap. 10. Keizer told me that the former date was correct, that is, 1974 (email to author, March 26, 2012). It also sounds more right because Maiereder died in 1975.

72. Itkin's episcopal register is in the possession of James Ishmael Ford, an author, Zen priest, and Universalist-Unitarian minister who wrote a thesis on Itkin: James Ishmael Ford, "Forever a Priest: *Episcopi Vagantes* and the Myth of Catholic Ministry," MA thesis, Pacific School of Religion, 1990. Ford kindly sent me a copy of the register (emails to author, May 2014).

73. James Ishmael Ford, "Was Alan Watts an Independent Catholic Bishop? An Historical Footnote," *Monkey Mind* blog, May 25, 2009. See also Pruter and Melton, *Old Catholic Sourcebook*, pp. 78–79; Mark Sullivan and Ian Young, eds., *The Radical Bishop and Gay Consciousness: The Passion of Mikhail Itkin* (Brooklyn, N.Y.: Autonomedia, 2014); and "Bishop Michael Francis Augustine Itkin," profile at the Lesbian, Gay, Bisexual and Transgender Religious Archives Network. Several of these sources state without offering specifics that Itkin ordained women as of the late 1960s.

74. On Roman Catholic activism for women's ordination at this time, see Mary Jeremy Daigler, *Incompatible with God's Design: A History of the Women's Ordination Movement in the U.S. Roman Catholic Church* (New York: Scarecrow Press, 2012), pp. 1–52. For Rahner's early advocacy of women's ordination, see Rahner, *The Dynamic Element in the Church* (New York: Herder and Herder, 1964), pp. 42–83. On the diaconal ordination of Edwards by Pike, see Episcopal News Service, "Phyllis Edwards Ordained Priest Declared Deacon in 1964," July 10, 1980. For more on Roman and Episcopal women's ordination, see Fredrica Harris Thompsett, "Women in the American Episcopal Church," in *Encyclopedia of Women and Religion in North America*, ed. Rosemary Keller and Rosemary Radford Ruether (Bloomington: Indiana University Press, 2006), pp. 269–79; and Maureen Fiedler and Dolly Pomerleau, "The Women's Ordination Movement in the Roman Catholic Church," in Keller and Ruether, *Encyclopedia of Women and Religion*, pp. 951–59.

75. See Karen J. Torjesen, *When Women Were Priests: Women's Leadership in the Early Church and the Scandal of Their Subordination in the Rise of Christianity* (1993; San Francisco: HarperSanFrancisco, 1995); Kyriaki Karidoyanes FitzGerald, *Women Deacons in the Orthodox Church* (Brookline, Mass.: Holy Cross Orthodox Press, 1998); Ute Eisen, *Women Officeholders in Early Christianity: Epigraphical and Literary Studies*, trans. Linda Maroney (Collegeville, Minn.: Liturgical Press, 2000); Kevin Madigan and Carolyn Osiek, *Ordained Women in the Early Church: A Documentary History* (Baltimore: Johns Hopkins University Press, 2005); Gary Macy, *The Hidden History of Women's Ordination: Female Clergy in the Medieval West* (Oxford: Oxford University Press, 2008); Phyllis Zagano, *Women and Catholicism: Gender, Communion, and Authority* (New York: Palgrave Macmillan, 2011); and Zagano, "Catholic Women's Ordination: The Ecumenical Implications of Women Deacons in the Armenian Apostolic Church, the Orthodox Church of Greece, and the Union of Utrecht Old Catholic Churches," *Journal of Ecumenical Studies* 43, no. 1 (Winter 2008): 124–37.

76. On the Christian Community priesthood and Czechoslovak Hussite Church, see Plummer, *The Many Paths*, pp. 23, 33. On the African Orthodox Church ordination of Sister Phoebe to the diaconate on June 23, 1923, see an excerpt from *The Negro Churchman* (the African Orthodox Church organ of that time), quoted in Father Furblur, "The McGuire Years," *Trumpet* 2, no. 2 (November 1980): 7 (J. Gordon Melton American Religions Collection/University of California at Santa Barbara Library, Folder: AOC—serials—*The Trumpet*). On the Mariavites, see Jerzy Peterkiewicz, *The Third Adam* (London: Oxford University Press, 1975); Melton, *Encyclopedia of American Religions*, pp. 1151–52; and Anson, *Bishops at Large*, pp. 117–23. On de Willmott Newman's diaconal ordinations, see Keizer, *Wandering Bishops*, pp. 34–35.

77. Miriam Therese Winter, *Out of the Depths: The Story of Ludmila Javorová, Ordained Roman Catholic Priest* (New York: Crossroad, 2001). Fiedler and Pomerlau, "The Women's Ordination Movement," p. 957. "Czech Hierarchy Bars Some Priests," *New York Times*, December 8, 1991.

78. Spruit, "An Interview," p. 25. Keizer, *Wandering Bishops*, p. 41.

79. On the Collin heritage of high Marianism, I consulted bishop-scholar John Plummer (emails to author, January 2015). On the Apostles of Infinite Love, see Michael Cuneo, *Smoke of Satan: Conservative and Traditionalist Dissent in Contemporary American Catholicism* (New York: Oxford University Press, 1997), p. 125. Cuneo gives no definite date for the ordination of women, though a revelation came in the "early seventies" and women of the community were ordained priests "over the next several years."

80. For Herman's words here, see Spruit, "An Interview," pp. 24–25; and Spruit, "Herman Adrian Spruit: The Man," p. 19. These are different versions of the same interview but "Jesus plus Mary equals Christ" appears only in the latter of the two.

     There are Christian (including Catholic) precedents for imagining a complementary female Christ, for example, Shaker theology in the United States and Mariavite theology in Poland. Earl Blighton, or Father Paul, founder of the Holy Order of MANS in the United States, thought of Mary as the female Christ. No one except Herman to my knowledge thought of Mary and Jesus as gendered poles of the same Christ.

81. Jeffrey Isbrandtsen, "An Interview with Three Women Bishops/Women in the Episcopate" (originally published in *AROHN*), in Gundrey, *Herman Adrian Spruit*, book A, fourth reprinted article, original pagination pp. 77–86, at p. 81.

82. Spruit, "An Interview," p. 25. Herman Spruit, "What Is the Church of Antioch?," no date, Church Archives CD, Document 103. There are two slightly different copies of this brochure, one from Creswell, Ore. (no date), and one from Santa Fe, N.M. (revised January 1, 2001, by Richard Gundrey). Here I used the Creswell one.

83. Per public records as noted above, Herman and Helen's divorce was finalized sometime in 1969 or 1970. Mary met them sometime after her split from John Reynolds in 1972, at which time Herman and Helen still lived at the same address.

84. Meri Louise Spruit, Church of Antioch matriarch emerita, age eighty-one, interview, Marina, Calif., October 8, 2007. Carol Lauderdale, "In Memory of Mary Louise Reynolds, August 1, 1929–June 3, 2014," obituary sent via Ascension Alliance listserv by Alan Kemp, July 26, 2014, and published in several newspapers and online sources.

85. Meri Spruit, interview.

86. Ibid.

87. Ibid.

88. Ibid.

89. Ibid. Lauderdale, obituary.

90. Meri Spruit, interview.

91. Ibid.

92. Ibid. Lauderdale, obituary. Field notes, Church of Antioch Convocation, Salinas, California, October 6–8, 2007.

93. Meri Spruit, interview.

94. On the home routine, see Meri Spruit, Letter to Richard Gundrey and Mandate of the Matriarch and Instrument of Succession, September 18 and September 20, 2004, respectively, sent with cover letters by Richard Gundrey to the church on October 15, 2004, and again on July 14, 2009; sent to author on July 14, 2009. On the road trips: Meri Spruit, interview. On Meri's family dynamics: Carol Lauderdale, telephone call with author, July 11, 2015.

95. Meri Spruit, interview. Spruit, "For Myself."

96. One of several southern California Liberal Catholic heads of splinter churches, Edmund Sheehan started the International Liberal Catholic Church. On Meri's ordination class, see "Ordination to the Priesthood, Fall Class of 1979," photograph caption, in Gundrey, *Herman Adrian Spruit*, book B, fourteenth document. The caption notes the seven class members, the five consecrators, the place, and the date. Meri Spruit, "Women in Holy Orders?" (September 12, 1981), Church of Antioch Archives/Box: HA & Meri Spruit's Writings/File: Meri's Writings, p. 2.

97. Spruit, *The Sacramentarion*, unpaginated front matter, third and fourth pages.

98. For "lying in bed," see Spruit, "How to Demonstrate," unpaginated first page. For "are we kidding," see Spruit, "Herman Adrian Spruit: The Man," p. 22.

99. Herman Spruit, Letter to Meri, October 7, 1981, Church of Antioch Archives/Box: HA & Meri Spruit Writings/File: Letters, etc.—HAS.

100. Spruit, "Herman Adrian Spruit: The Man," pp. 8, 21.

101. Most of Herman and Meri's consecrations are listed in Van Campenhout, *Apostolic Succession*, pp. 75–82, but for the consecration of Vivian Godfrey and Leon Barcynski in June 1982, see Melton, *Encyclopedia of American Religions*, pp. 1209–10, and the history at the website of the House of Adocentyn: Ordo Astrum Sophiae. Frank Bugge, Church of Antioch listserv, March 26, 2006.

102. Isbrandtsen, "An Interview with Three Women Bishops," pp. 77–78.

103. Ibid., p. 86. On the consecratees, see Van Campenhout, *Apostolic Succession*, pp. 75–82. On the Holy Orthodox Catholic Church, see Melton, *Encyclopedia of American Religions*, pp. 194, 704–5.

104. Meri Spruit, Letter to Richard Gundrey. Herman Spruit, "The Full Truth."

105. Herman Spruit, Protocol of Election of Meri Louise Spruit to the Office of Matriarch, no date but c. January 1986, Catholic Apostolic Church of Antioch Important Papers, Book #1 (1987–2005). Spruit, "Escaping the Wheel," pp. 2–3. Herman Spruit, Letter (elevating Archbishop Meri Louise Spruit to position of presiding Matriarch), April 6, 1990, Catholic Apostolic Church of Antioch Important Papers, Book #1 (1987–2005).

106. On the India trip: Carol Lauderdale, email to author, July 11, 2015.

107. Meri Spruit, "Women in Holy Orders?," p. 1. Meri Spruit, "Sermon at Phoenix ordination of 14 to Subdeacon and Deacon," November 5, 1985, Church of Antioch Archives/Box: HA & Meri Spruit's Writings/File: Meri's Writings, pp. 1–2. Meri Spruit, "Re-Building the Garden—Re-Building Our Ministries," October 28, 2000, Church of Antioch Archives/Box: HA & Meri Spruit's Writings/File: Meri's Writings, p. 5.

108. For "entire housefull," see Herman Spruit, Protocol of Election of Meri Louise Spruit. Mark Elliot Newman, Church of Antioch bishop, age fifty-nine, interview, Phoenix, Ariz., April 13, 2009.

109. Meri Spruit, "Women in Holy Orders?," p. 4. "Painless Public Speaking Workshop," flyer and other materials, Church of Antioch Archives/Box: Herman & Meri's files—3/"Public Speaking."

110. For "serve without appreciation," see Isbrandtsen, "An Interview with Three Women Bishops," p. 85. Meri Spruit, interview. Herman Spruit, Letter to Most Rev. Michael Daigneault et al., November 3, 1990, Church of Antioch Archives/Box: HA & Meri Spruit's Writings/File: Letters, etc.—HAS. On the resignations, I talked to Richard Gundrey (telephone conversation with author, August 2, 2010).

111. For evidence of conflicts Meri faced, see Meri Spruit, "At My Request That Michael and Timothy Be the Co-Consecrating Bishops of R. Gundrey," no date (c. October 1990), in Gundrey, *Herman Adrian Spruit*, book B, eleventh document, one page. For the letter on which Gundrey handwrote a note, see Spruit, Letter to Daigneault.

112. Spruit, Letter to Arnold and Shirley. For the accounts of Linda Rounds-Nichols and Richard Gundrey: field notes, Church of Antioch, Santa Fe, N.M., May 23–29, 2008.

113. Federation of Independent and Orthodox Bishops, *FICOB and Friends* 1, no. 3 (Fall 1996), Church of Antioch Archives/Box: Herman & Meri's files—1/File: Fed of Ind. Cath & Orth Bishops, p. 9.

114. Father Jay Nelson, Church of Antioch listserv, January 7, 2009.

115. I talked with Bishop Connie Poggiani of Antioch about this episode in Meri's life: field notes, Church of Antioch Convocation, Richmond, Va., October 14–17, 2005 (October 15); others confirmed the information. For "dangerous," see Meri Spruit, Letter to Richard Gundrey. According to information easily available on the Internet, the man remained an independent Catholic priest and then bishop until his death in 2014. He ran street and prison ministries based on the twelve-step program to help people who had simultaneous problems with substance abuse and mental health.

116. Meri Spruit, Letter to Richard Gundrey.

117. Ibid. On the pallium, see Richard Gundrey, Church of Antioch newsletter, February 2006, unpaginated, fourth page.

118. The only other independent Catholic jurisdiction with a sizable number of women bishops was the Mariavite Catholic Church in Poland.

119. Keizer, *Wandering Bishops*, pp. 41, 65. Thomas Hickey, *Free Catholicism and the God Within* (Richland, Iowa: Esoterica Press, 1990), p. 10. Burns, cover page.

120. Field notes, Richmond Convocation, October 15, 2005.

4. DANCE AND BALANCE: LEADING AMERICAN INDEPENDENTS

1. Field notes, Santa Fe, N.M., May 23, 2008. Manuel and Pilar are not the couple's real names.

2. Roman canon law allows for the "non-sacramental" marriage in Roman churches of couples made up of a Roman Catholic and a nonbaptized person, but if such couples want a Catholic marriage at the sacramental level or a wedding mass where both of them can take communion, they may look for an independent Catholic priest. Code of Canon Law, c. 1086, §1, in *The Code of Canon Law: Latin-English Edition* (Washington, D.C.: Canon Law Society of America, 1983).

3. Field notes, Santa Fe, April 2–3, 9, 11, 2007. Richard Gundrey, "Starting a Real Church and Keeping It Going," presentation at Sursum Corda II Conference, October 5–8, 2003, DVD by Jim Waters/Sanctus Media. Field notes, Santa Fe, April 11, 2007.

4. Ibid., April 4, 2007. Annie and Jake are not the couple's real names. For "SOUPY": Richard Gundrey, Church of Antioch listserv, January 30, 2007.

5. Richard Gundrey, "Seeing the Christ in All Life," in *A Strange Vocation: Independent Bishops Tell Their Stories*, ed. Alistair Bate (Berkeley: Apocryphile Press, 2009), pp. 72–77, at p. 74.

6. For life details, see Gundrey, "Seeing the Christ," pp. 72–74. For quotations: Richard Gundrey, interview of Archbishop Richard Gundrey by Bob Ross, Santa Fe Public Radio KSFR, March 15, 2008. On Esther Williams: field notes, Santa Fe, April 4, 2007.

7. On SUNY–Farmingdale, see Meri Spruit, Protocol of Election of the Very Reverend Richard Alston Gundrey (October 27, 1990), Catholic Apostolic Church of Antioch Important Papers, Book #1 (1987–2005). For "airplane hangar": field notes, Santa Fe, April 2, 2007. On falling in love with the west: Richard Gundrey, Church of Antioch archbishop and presiding patriarch, age seventy-one, interview, Santa Fe, N.M., May 28, 2005. On "dance teacher," see Gussie Fauntleroy, "Bishop Juggles Religion, Restaurant Job," New Mexican (Santa Fe, N.M.) (October 17, 1992), p. A-9, also in Church of Antioch Important Papers, Book #1 (1987–2005).

8. Field notes, Santa Fe, April 2 and 4, 2007.

9. For "answers," "dogmatic," and "consciousness," see Gundrey, "Seeing the Christ," p. 73. On TM: Gundrey, interview. On the Religious Science details: Meri Spruit, Gundrey Protocol of Election. Richard Gundrey, Order of Service for Holy Eucharist, Church of Antioch at Santa Fe (May 29, 2005, and October 22, 2006, for example). The Holmes prayer was not printed in mass programs of later years.

10. For "sense of spell," see Fauntleroy, "Bishop Juggles." For "buzz words" and "perfect home," see Gundrey, "Seeing the Christ," p. 74. Otherwise, Gundrey, interview.

11. For dates, see Meri Spruit, Gundrey Protocol of Election. For the anecdote, see Meri Spruit, Letter to Richard Gundrey, Mandate of the Matriarch and Instrument of Succession, September 18 and September 20, 2004, respectively, sent with cover letters by Richard Gundrey to the church on October 15, 2004, and again on July 14, 2009; sent to author on July 14, 2009.

12. On Richard's first space in Santa Fe, see Meri Spruit, Gundrey Protocol. For "all my friends": Gundrey, Sursum Corda. Otherwise, Gundrey, interview.

13. No lease: field notes, Santa Fe, April 2, 2007. "It takes prayer": Gundrey, interview. No incense: Gundrey, Ross interview. For no childcare and "in heaven": Gundrey, Sursum Corda.

14. Field notes, Santa Fe, May 25, 2008; April 8, 2007.

15. Field notes, Santa Fe, April 11, 2007. Cassandra is not the church member's real name.

16. Field notes, Santa Fe, May 23 and 25, 2008.

17. Field notes, Santa Fe, April 2, 2007; May 23, 2008. Richard used "ladyfriend" on the listserv when referring to Ilene.

18. Gundrey, interview. Field notes, Santa Fe, April 2, 2007; May 23, 2008. Ilene Dunn, "The Catholic Apostolic Church of Antioch–Malabar Rite," promotional DVD, October 2006. On the handwritten notes: Gundrey, Sursum Corda. Lian Reed, Church of Antioch seminarian, age fifty-one, interview, Santa Fe, N.M., April 6, 2007.

19. "A great guy": Gundrey, interview. On relations with local independents: Gundrey, telephone conversation with author, February 25, 2015. Seeing Holy Trinity monks: field notes, Santa Fe, April 8, 2007.

20. For "good friends": Richard Gundrey, Church of Antioch newsletter, April 2005, unpaginated, first page. The rest: Gundrey, interview.

21. On Li'l Abner: Daniel Dangaran, Church of Antioch listserv, March 2, 2008. On his rates: Gundrey, Sursum Corda. On the annual number of weddings: field notes, Church of Antioch, Santa Fe, April 2, 2007. Meri Spruit, Letter to Richard Gundrey.

22. For "very comfortable": Gundrey, "Seeing the Christ," p. 75. For "does it for money": Gundrey, Sursum Corda. Otherwise, Gundrey, interview.

23. On the visiting clergy, see Fauntleroy, "Bishop Juggles." Gundrey, Church of Antioch listserv, December 26, 2006.

24. Richard Gundrey, Church of Antioch newsletter, January 18, 2008, unpaginated, third page.

25. Doug Walker, Church of Antioch listserv, February 29, 2008.

26. Gundrey, interview. The vast majority of Antiochians likewise dispute or downplay the idea of sin. It came up in at least four other interviews of clergy.

27. Ibid.

28. For "this world matters": Roberto Foss, Church of Antioch deacon, age forty-eight, interview, Los Angeles, Calif., November 24, 2007.

29. Gundrey, interview.

30. For Richard saying people should stick to their beliefs if it "gets" you "through the night": Church of Antioch listserv, April 19, 2006, and field notes, Santa Fe, April 7, 2007.

31. Liza Molina, Church of Antioch deacon, age forty, interview, Santa Fe, N.M., May 27, 2008.

32. Reed, interview.

33. Field notes, Santa Fe, May 23, 2008; April 3, 2007; May 27, 2008.

34. Gundrey, Sursum Corda. There are additional annual clergy dues that range from $75 for a deacon to $175 for an archbishop. As noted in Richard Gundrey, Church of Antioch newsletter (February 8, 2007), unpaginated, second page, these sums represented a hike in rates for the first time in fifteen years.

35. On using the Trinitarian formula: Gundrey, Church of Antioch listserv, March 1, 2008. On keeping good records: Gundrey, Church of Antioch listserv, April 15, 2007, January 9, 2008, December 8, 2008. On using baptism certificates as identification: field notes, Santa Fe, April 8, 2007.

36. These mass titles can be found among masses collected in the Church of Antioch Archives, Box: Herman & Meri's files—2/Files: Liturgy 1 and Liturgy 2.

37. Richard Gundrey, telephone conversation with author, August 2, 2010.

38. On the Buddhist monks: Gundrey, interview with Ross. On Mother Linda's mass: field notes, Church of Antioch Convocation, Richmond, Va., October 14, 2005. On the pentagram: Linda Rounds-Nichols, email to author, January 13, 2015.

39. Reed, interview.

40. Ibid.

41. Field notes at masses celebrated by Richard Gundrey. Gundrey, Order of Service, p. 6.

42. Gundrey, Order of Service, p. 11.

43. Ibid. For "particular womb": Gundrey, Church of Antioch listserv, April 19, 2006.

44. Linda Rounds-Nichols, Church of Antioch priest, age fifty-eight, interview, Salinas, Calif., October 7, 2007. Reed, interview.

45. Jorge Eagar, Church of Antioch bishop, age sixty-three, interview, Tempe, Ariz., April 13, 2009.

46. Carol Calvert, Church of Antioch priest, age fifty-seven, interview, Santa Fe, N.M., April 5, 2007.

47. Ibid.

48. Ibid.

49. Ibid. Field notes, Santa Fe, April 6, 2007.

50. Field notes, Santa Fe, April 7, 2007.

51. Cathedral of St. Francis of Assisi Sunday bulletin, October 2, 1994. Letters from Bishop Richard Gundrey to Father Gilbert Schneider and Archbishop Michael Sheehan (October 24, 1994); letter from Father Ernest Falardeau to Bishop Richard Gundrey (November 1, 1994); letter from Archbishop Michael Sheehan to Bishop Richard Gundrey (November 4, 1994); all Church of Antioch file copies provided to author by Bishop Mark Newman, March 28, 2015. For Richard's account of the whole story and his response to the ecumenical officer: Gundrey, interview.

52. Tom Roberts, "Bishop Decries 'Combative Tactics' of a Minority of U.S. Bishops," *National Catholic Reporter*, August 26, 2009. On Richard's around-the-town interactions with Sheehan: Gundrey, interview, and Gundrey, Church of Antioch listserv, September 11, 2006.

53. Michael Sheehan, "What Is an Independent Catholic Church?," *People of God*, Archdiocese of Santa Fe, N.M., June 1997.

54. Letter from Bishop Richard Gundrey to Archbishop Michael Sheehan, July 7, 1997, Church of Antioch file copy provided to author by Bishop Mark Newman, March 28, 2015.

55. I do not have copies of the follow-up letters, the gist of which Richard described to me: Gundrey, interview. But a subsequent letter from the ecumenical officer to Richard corroborates that Sheehan argued that "there was confusion in the minds of the laity about which 'Catholic Church' you represent and whether or not they can, in good conscience, accept Sacraments from you": letter from Father Ernest Falardeau to Archbishop Richard Gundrey, February 23, 2000, Church of Antioch file copy provided to author by Bishop Mark Newman, March 28, 2015. "Message from Archbishop Michael J. Sheehan: Attention Roman Catholics," Sunday bulletin notice, May 2004 and continuous, for example, in the "Liturgy" section of the website of Nativity of the Blessed Virgin Mary Catholic Church in Albuquerque, N.M. For one parishioner's analysis and the date of the original notice: Stephanie Block, "The Archbishop's List," *Los Pequeños Pepper* (Albuquerque: Los Pequeños de Cristo) 7, no. 1 (January 2005): 8–10. Archdiocese of Santa Fe website.

56. Michael Sheehan, "Don't Be Fooled!," *People of God*, Archdiocese of Santa Fe, N.M., September 2006, p. 2.

57. Vatican Council II, *Unitatis redintegratio*, November 21, 1964. *Catechism of the Catholic Church*, 2nd ed. (Washington, D.C.: United States Catholic Conference, 2011), section 816. Congregation for the Doctrine of the Faith, *Dominus Iesus*, August 6, 2000, section 22. Gundrey, Church of Antioch listserv, September 11, 2006.

58. For "dishearten": Gundrey, Church of Antioch listserv, September 11, 2006. For "TOO MANY": Gundrey, Church of Antioch listserv, December 15, 2005. Bishop Oscar Trujillo heads the American Catholic Communities based at Holy Spirit Cathedral in Albuquerque; on its website I accessed a link to the exchange with Sheehan on October 12, 2014. For "ego," see Gundrey, "Seeing the Christ," p. 76. For "badmouth": Gundrey, Sursum Corda.

59. Field notes, Santa Fe, May 23, 2008.

60. Deacon Doug's presentation: field notes, Santa Fe, April 11, 2007. Rabbi Gold's presentation: Gundrey, Church of Antioch listserv, April 8, 2008.

61. Field notes, Santa Fe, April 4 and 11, 2007.

62. For "bachelor pad," ironing, and kitchen tour: field notes, Santa Fe, April 3, 2007. On "Christ Consciousness energy," field notes, Santa Fe, April 9, 2007. On being "addicted" to work: field notes, Santa Fe, May 23, 2008.

63. Reed, interview. Field notes, Church of Antioch Convocation, Santa Fe, N.M., October 21, 2006.

64. Church of Antioch Important Documents, Book #1.

65. Field notes, Santa Fe, April 4, 2007.

66. Diana Phipps, Church of Antioch bishop, age sixty-three, interview, Fredericksburg, Tex., June 16, 2007.

67. Jay Nelson, email to author, June 24, 2015. Father Jay created an online tribute with links to national media coverage of Father Tom's death and the history of Linkup: http://archives.weirdload.com/economus/index.html.

68. Jack Sweeley, Church of Antioch priest, age sixty-four, interview, Baltimore, Md., July 24, 2007.

69. John Plummer, *The Many Paths of the Independent Sacramental Movement: A Study of Its Liturgy, Doctrine and Leadership in America* (Dallas: Newt Books, 2004), p. 37. Gundrey, Church of Antioch listserv, March 1, 2008.

70. Jeff Genung, Church of Antioch deacon, age forty-seven, interview, Austin, Tex., June 23, 2007. On "a fit": I keep this interviewee anonymous here.

71. Gundrey, interview.

72. Gundrey, Order of Service, p. 3. Herman Spruit, "Constitution and Statement of Principles of the Church of Antioch" (Mountain View, Calif.: Church of Antioch Press, 1978), Church Archives CD, Document 77. Gundrey, Church of Antioch listserv, April 19, 2006. Gundrey, Church of Antioch listserv, March 7, 2008.

73. On the Independent Catholicism Survey, question 17, and in my interviews, respondents said "no dogma" or "freedom" was the "best thing" about the church more than

any other answer, at least fifty times. Sara Yonce, Church of Antioch priest, age sixty-five, interview, Montgomery, Tex., June 19, 2007. Foss, interview.

74. Genung, interview. Reed, interview.

75. Rounds-Nichols, interview.

76. Foss, interview.

77. Ted Feldmann, Church of Antioch deacon, age fifty-seven, interview, Baltimore, Md., July 23, 2007. Mark Elliot Newman, Church of Antioch bishop, age fifty-nine, interview, Phoenix, Ariz., April 13, 2009.

78. Becky Taylor, Church of Antioch seminarian, age fifty-six, interview, Richmond, Va., July 23, 2007.

79. For "zooey": field notes, Antioch Convocation, October 6, 2007. "Killing chickens," "worshiping Satan," and otherwise accusing "nutsos" came up in several interviews, as well as in a Church of Antioch listserv discussion.

80. Calvert, interview. Jack Pischner, Church of Antioch seminarian, age sixty-two, interview, Salinas, Calif., October 7, 2007. Reed, interview.

81. For "water": Gundrey, Church of Antioch listserv, April 19, 2006.

82. For "great SELF SELECTING": Gundrey, Church of Antioch listserv, December 12, 2007. On other Sophia processes: field notes, Antioch Convocation, October 15, 2005; and Gundrey, Church of Antioch listserv, June 2, 2008.

83. For these conversations with Richard Gundrey: field notes, Santa Fe, May 24, 2008, and April 2, 2007. See also Associated Press, "From Prison-Lifer to Priest, Former Principal, Murderer Believes He Has Been Rehabilitated," *Daily Journal* (Kankakee, Ill.) (February 18, 2002). For "white bread": Gundrey, Church of Antioch listserv, December 12, 2007.

84. Gundrey, interview.

85. J. Gordon Melton, "Preface," in *Independent Bishops: An International Directory*, ed. Gary L. Ward, Bertil Persson, and Alan Bain (Detroit: Apogee Books, 1990), pp. v–viii, at p. vii.

86. For the quotation, see Maude Petre, *Autobiography and Life of Father Tyrrell*, vol. 2 (London: E. Arnold, 1912), pp. 379–80. On the friendship between Tyrrell and Mathew, see Peter Anson, *Bishops at Large* (1964; Berkeley: Apocryphile Press, 2006), pp. 165, 175–76, 179.

87. Field notes, Antioch Convocation, October 21, 2006. Yonce, interview.

88. For the percentage of full-time independent Catholic priests: Independent Catholicism Survey, question 55. For examples of their professions: Independent Catholicism Survey, question 57.

89. For "stealth" priests: John Plummer, Independent Sacramental Movement listserv on Yahoo, December 14, 2006. For "gypsy church": Franzo King, African Orthodox Church archbishop and pastor of St. John Coltrane African Orthodox Church, interview, San Francisco, Calif., August 10, 2005. For the quotation of Bishop Diana Dale: Uwe Siemon-Netto, "New Leaders for Old Catholic Church," *Beliefnet*, August 7, 2001. For "love and appreciation," see Gundrey, "Seeing the Christ," pp. 76–77. Lemieux: field notes, Santa Fe, May 25, 2008.

90. Gundrey, Church of Antioch listserv, June 2, 2008.

91. Acts of the Apostles 8:9–24. Gundrey, Church of Antioch listserv, October 25, 2005.

92. For "very prevalent": Gundrey, Church of Antioch listserv, October 25, 2005. For "integrity," see Gundrey, "Seeing the Christ," p. 77.

93. Richard Marosi, "Beloved Mexican Priest Is Branded a Rogue," *Los Angeles Times*, December 21, 2009. Roberto Foss called attention to this news item on the Church of Antioch listserv, December 21, 2009. Omar Millán, "Vatican Ousts Beloved Priest for Defying Order," *SanDiegoRed.com*, January 12, 2012.

94. Gundrey, Church of Antioch listserv, October 25, 2005.

95. Gundrey, Church of Antioch listserv, June 14, 2006.

96. For "moved along": Gundrey, interview. Bishops were discussing aspects of the future leadership plan by 2005: field notes, Antioch Convocation, October 15, 2005.

97. Richard Gundrey, "Free House," Church of Antioch newsletter, April 2005, unpaginated, sixth page. Field notes, Antioch Convocation, October 15, 2005.

98. For this conversation with Richard: field notes, Santa Fe, April 9, 2007. On the hope to buy (or get donated) Loretto Chapel: field notes, Antioch Convocation, October 15, 2005.

99. For Richard's words: field notes, Santa Fe, April 8, 2007, and May 23, 2008.

100. Gundrey, Church of Antioch listserv, February 23, 2008; March 1, 2008; April 19, 2006. Field notes, Antioch Convocation, October 6, 2007.

101. Richard Gundrey, Church of Antioch listserv, July 1, 2008; Sweeley, interview.

102. Richard Gundrey, adding to Church of Antioch listserv thread of March 2007. Richard Gundrey, adding to Church of Antioch listserv thread of November 2007.

103. On "for the best": field notes, Santa Fe, May 24, 2008.

104. Foss, interview. Pischner, interview. Sweeley, interview.

105. Sweeley, interview.

106. J. A. Douglas, "Foreword," in Episcopi Vagantes *and the Anglican Church*, ed. Henry R. T. Brandreth (1947; Springfield, Mo.: St. Willibrord Press, 1987), p. xvi.

107. Eagar, interview. Sweeley, interview.

5. MIX AND MYSTICISM: EXPERIMENTING WITH US CATHOLICISM

1. Field notes, Church of Antioch, Los Angeles, November 23, 2007. Paula is not the real name of Roberto's colleague and I have occluded other identifying details to preserve her anonymity.

2. Field notes, Church of Antioch, southern California, November 24, 2007.

3. This whole section draws on my interview with Roberto Foss, Church of Antioch deacon, age forty-eight, Los Angeles, Calif., November 24, 2007; and field notes, southern California, November 21–25, 2007.

4. On the Catholic charismatic movement, see Susan A. Maurer, *The Spirit of Enthusiasm: A History of the Catholic Charismatic Renewal, 1967–2000* (Lanham, Md.: University Press of America, 2010).

5. On being a love consultant: field notes, Church of Antioch Convocation, Santa Fe, N.M., October 20, 2006. On the Dignity mass: Richard Gundrey, Church of Antioch newsletter, April 26, 2008, unpaginated, second page.

6. On the Yogi Bhajan homily: Jack Pischner, Church of Antioch seminarian, age sixty-two, interview, Salinas, Calif., October 7, 2007. On the World Parliament event: Richard Gundrey, Church of Antioch listserv, October 23, 2009.

7. The website of the Old Catholic Church (Province of the USA) had the most complete account of this meeting and subsequent events.

8. Björn Marcussen, "A Background to Professor Esser's Four Points," written after the Queens Village meeting, on the website of the Ecumenical Catholic Communion.

9. Bowdoin College scholar Elizabeth Pritchard's forthcoming book on TOCCUSA promises a rich ethnographic and historical narrative of this independent body. The working title is *Intimate Catholics*.

The announcement about the appointment of Esser as official liaison was posted on the website of TOCCUSA as of September 2013. The announcement was no longer posted as of October 4, 2014. According to Pritchard, Archbishop Vercammen recalled Esser as official liaison so that TOCCUSA might first develop its relationship with the Episcopal Church, but Esser has stayed on as a resource for TOCCUSA in an unofficial capacity. Elizabeth Pritchard, email to author, January 14, 2015.

10. I read discussions about implicit ultramontanism, possible self-hatred, and exclusion-by-intercommunion on two independent Catholic Yahoo groups, the Independent Sacramental Movement and the Autocephalous Sacramental Movement, between 2006 and 2009. During most of Richard's tenure, Bishop Mark Newman headed ecumenical activities for Antioch and told me about church guidelines for intercommunion agreements: Mark Elliott Newman, Church of Antioch bishop, age fifty-nine, interview, Phoenix, Ariz., April 13, 2009.

11. On the Independent Catholic Survey, 64 percent of Antioch respondents said they were formerly Roman Catholic or Eastern Catholic within the Roman communion (question 30). Jack Sweeley, Church of Antioch priest, age sixty-four, interview, Baltimore, Md., July 24, 2007. Bob Mitchell, Church of Antioch listserv, April 20, 2008. For Marian Bellus's words: field notes, Church of Antioch, Philadelphia, Pa., July 29.

12. On Sister Helen Prejean and the monk, see (respectively) Church of Antioch at Santa Fe Facebook announcement for January 25, 2015, and field notes, Church of Antioch Convocation, [midwestern city and state], September 11, 2009. On St. Vincent's: Richard Gundrey, Church of Antioch newsletter, April 26, 2008, unpaginated, first page.

13. Jim St. George, Church of Antioch listserv, August 19, 2007. An example of a similar event: on April 28, 2012, I attended an ordination anniversary and party for a Manhattan independent Catholic priest (not in the Church of Antioch). The mass was held in a Roman Catholic sanctuary with the approval of the parish's pastor, clearly a good friend. About two hundred gathered parishioners seemed unevenly aware that the feted priest is independent. Among places he works, as listed on his Silver Jubilee prayer card, are three Roman Catholic parishes and two independent Catholic churches.

I ran across two accounts of independent priests doing weddings in Roman churches with the pastor's permission: Paul Clemens, Church of Antioch listserv, November 8, 2007; and Robert Dittler, abbot-bishop, and Tom Dowling, priest, White-Robed Monks of Saint Benedict, interview, San Francisco, Calif., August 10, 2005.

The anecdote about chancery office referrals comes from one of my Antioch interviews.

14. I know of two instances in other jurisdictions in which independent Catholics reported being fired from Rome-affiliated jobs due to independent affiliation: one was mentioned on the Independent Sacramental Movement Yahoo listserv in April 2007, and the other on the Autocephalous Sacramental Movement Yahoo listserv in July 2008. In a slightly different instance, the adjunct professorship of Antioch priest Jim St. George at Chestnut Hill College in Philadelphia provoked a local media storm in 2011, when the college fired him after someone notified the institution that Father Jim is not a Roman priest and is married to his partner Sean. Chestnut Hill administrators said they were not aware of those commitments, while Father Jim is certainly "out" and publicly known as the pastor of an independent church. Eventually the parties resolved things "amicably," as quoted in Theresa Materson, "Gay Priest Settles with Chestnut Hill College," NBC10.com, March 21, 2011. For "jazzed": field notes, Antioch Convocation, October 20, 2006.

15. For Bishop Michael's request: field notes, Church of Antioch Convocation, Richmond, Va., October 16, 2005. Father Tom David is quoted in Chris Dovi, "Unconditional Faith: An Independent Catholic Community in Richmond Makes Acceptance the Foundation of Faith," RVA Magazine 1 (Spring 2010): 46–49, at p. 49. Roberto Foss, Church of Antioch listserv, January 15, 2009.

16. For "our sister church": Diana Phipps, Church of Antioch listserv, December 18, 2005.

17. On intercommunion: documentation of five agreements dated 2005–8 are located in Richard's Important Documents Book #1 (1987–2005), and Bishop Mark Newman sent me word of one more. These are not counting three intercommunion agreements that found the relationships between autocephalous Churches of Antioch in Argentina, Australia, and, as of November 2010, England (Mark Newman, Church of Antioch listserv, October 26, 2010, and email to author, June 6, 2015). On the Arizona independent collaboration and the Liberal Catholic Apostolic Church seminarian: field notes, Church of Antioch, Arizona (mostly Phoenix area), April 7, 9–12, 2009; Arizona Association of Independent Catholic Clergy, Directory of Arizona Independent Catholic Clergy, Seminarians, and Religious, March 29, 2009; and Arizona Association of Independent Catholic Clergy, Mission Statement/General Principles, no date. The latter two are short Word documents, both sent by Bishop Mark Newman, email to author, April 16, 2009.

18. On Father Ted: field notes, Church of Antioch, Baltimore, Md., July 23–24, 2007. On Monsignor Bowling: field notes, Church of Antioch, Harker Heights, Texas, June 15–16, 2007. On the Episcopal homilists: field notes, Church of Antioch Convocation, Salinas, Calif., October 6, 2007; and Bishop Jorge Eagar, email to author, January 25,

2015. On the substitute or interim gigs, sources are respectively: Linda Rounds-Nichols, Church of Antioch listserv, January 30, 2006; Deirdre Brousseau, Church of Antioch listserv, March 22, 2008; Michael Adams, Church of Antioch listserv, January 22, 2010; Richard Gundrey, "Supply Clergy," Church of Antioch newsletter, February 2006, unpaginated, second page; and field notes, Church of Antioch, Washington State, September 9–16, 2008.

19. On vows as a hermit and sarabite: field notes, Church of Antioch, Washington (mostly Seattle area), September 11, 2008; and Father Jay Nelson, Church of Antioch listserv, October 24, 2006. On Dick Gray's community: field notes, Church of Antioch, Ariz., April 7, 2009. On Lanzetta's keynote: Church of Antioch Convocation Schedule 2008 (October 30–November 3), listing Lanzetta for November 1 (I was not present for this Convocation but did receive registration materials). On Jeff Genung: Jeff Genung, Church of Antioch deacon, age forty-seven, interview, Austin, Tex., June 23, 2007; and field notes, Church of Antioch, Texas, June 23–24, 2007.

20. Jim Willems, Church of Antioch member, age sixty-three, interview, Ojai, Calif., November 25, 2007 (initiated by Anagarika Sri Munindra). Daniel Dangaran, Church of Antioch priest (later bishop), age fifty-three, interview, Santa Fe, N.M., April 5, 2007. Paul Clemens, photographs of chapel, Church of Antioch listserv, May 27, 2007. On Kemp: field notes, Ascension Alliance Convocation, August 20, 2011; Alan Kemp, "A Eucharistic Pooja," in *A Free Catholic Concise Liturgy and Other Useful Writings* (Gig Harbor, Wash.: Hermitage Desktop Press, 2015), pp. 113–36; and Alan Kemp, Ascension Alliance listserv, July 14, 2014. On Eagar: Jorge Eagar, Church of Antioch bishop, age sixty-three, interview, Tempe, Ariz., April 13, 2009; and field notes, Church of Antioch, Arizona, April 12, 2009.

21. For "non-sacramental," see Jim Willems, Church of Antioch listserv, February 16, 2010. For the rest: William Buehler, email to author, June 24, 2015; field notes, Ascension Alliance Convocation, Seattle, Wash., August 20; and Diana Phipps, Church of Antioch bishop, age sixty-three, interview, Fredericksburg, Tex., June 16, 2007.

22. PJ Johnston, "The Church on Armenian Street: Capuchin Friars, the British East India Company, and the Second Church of Colonial Madras," PhD diss., University of Iowa, May 2015.

23. PJ Johnston, email to author, September 4, 2012. I accessed the website in February 2005 but it was defunct within a few years.

24. On Burke, see J. Gordon Melton, *The Encyclopedia of American Religions*, 8th ed. (Detroit: Gale/Cengage, 2009), p. 723; and James Lewis, "Gnostic Orthodox Church of America," in *The Encyclopedia of Cults, Sects and New Religions*, 2nd ed. (Amherst, N.Y.: Prometheus Books, 2001), p. 360.

25. For "fringe": Genung, interview. For "way out there": Alan Kemp, Church of Antioch bishop, age fifty-eight, interview, Gig Harbor, Wash., October 10, 2008. Hamilton, interview. Pischner, interview.

26. Genung, interview. Clemens, interview. Field notes, Church of Antioch, Tex., June 20, 2007. Michael Adams, Church of Antioch bishop, age fifty, interview, Salinas, Calif.,

October 6, 2007. Doug Walker, Church of Antioch seminarian, age fifty-nine, interview, Santa Fe, N.M., April 10, 2007. Field notes, Church of Antioch Convocation, Salinas, Calif., October 5–8, 2007 (October 6). Willems, interview. Field notes, Church of Antioch, Ariz., April 8, 2009.

27. Adams, interview. Phipps, interview. Kemp, interview. Anonymous, Church of Antioch priest, age fifty-four, interview, [city], Wash., September 11, 2008. Claire Vincent (pseudonymized at interviewee's request), Church of Antioch seminarian, age forty-five, interview, Salinas, Calif., October 7, 2007.

28. As John Plummer wrote, independents consistently labored to bring "public, visible, esoteric churches . . . into being," hoping to incarnate the "esoteric Christian tradition in ecclesiastical expression": Plummer, *The Many Paths of the Independent Sacramental Movement* (Dallas: Newt Books, 2004), pp. 71, 97. Antiochians who expressed a wish for more appreciation of western mysticism include Genung, interview; Eagar, interview; and Mark Newman, field notes, Phoenix, Ariz., April 7, 2009.

29. Field notes, Antioch Convocation, October 15–16, 2005. "Mildred Joy Cowan Gulbenk," *Tennessean*, July 8, 2008. Jim Willems et al., *Guild for Mystical Praxis*, distributed at Antioch Convocation, [midwestern city and state], September 13, 2009.

30. On the attributed "ahistoricism" of practitioners of "metaphysical, mystical, and harmonial traditions," see Catherine Albanese, *A Republic of Mind and Spirit* (New Haven: Yale University Press, 2007), p. 8; and Courtney Bender, *The New Metaphysicals: Spirituality and the American Religious Imagination* (Chicago: University of Chicago Press, 2010), pp. 5–10. On the historical rather than theological emphasis of independent Catholicism, see Robert J. Caruso, *The Old Catholic Church* (Berkeley: Apocryphile Press, 2009), p. 97.

31. For the "experiential turn," see Ann Taves, *Religious Experience Reconsidered: A Building-Block Approach to the Study of Religion and Other Special Things* (Princeton: Princeton University Press, 2009), pp. 3–5. Thomas Hickey, *Independent Catholicism for the Third Millennium*, 3rd ed., ed. Alan Kemp (1989; Tacoma, Wash.: Ascension Desktop Press, 2002), pp. 41–42.

32. Lian Reed, Church of Antioch seminarian, age fifty-one, interview, Santa Fe, N.M., April 6, 2007.

33. On the progress of Spanish-language initiatives: Richard Gundrey, Church of Antioch newsletter, January 18, 2008, unpaginated, first page; June 5, 2008, unpaginated, first page; January 7, 2009, unpaginated, first page; and Eagar, interview.

34. On Trujillo and Granberry, see, respectively, the website of the American Catholic Communities and the Facebook page of the Walking in Faith International Worship Center. I talked to Bishop King on August 10, 2005, and attended St. John Coltrane on August 7, 2005. I also talked to leaders and members of the Imani Temple and attended mass at its cathedral at Maryland Street and C Street about ten times from 2001 to 2004. Sources include Clinton Anderson, deacon, interview, July 1, 2003; anonymous layperson, interview, June 24, 2003; Adrian Isaac Bayo, priest, interview, June 23, 2003; Bill Beaviers, layperson, interview, July 1, 2003; Robert Gibbs, seminarian, interview, June 24, 2003; Carlos Harvin, bishop, interview, July 3, 2003; Soyami

Stallings, Imani Temple First Lady, July 1, 2003, all in Washington, D.C.; field notes, Imani Temple, Washington, D.C., June 2001, May 2002, June–July 2003, and May–July 2004; field notes and archival research, Josephite Archives, Baltimore, Md., May 2002; and Bishop Glenn V. Jeanmarie et al., *Masumbu Ya Imani*, rev. ed. (c. 1989; Washington, D.C.: African-American Catholic Congregation, 1996). The latter serves as the Imani theological and constitutional text.

35. Willems, interview.

36. Pew Forum on Religion and Public Life, "U.S. Religious Landscape Survey: Religious Affiliation: Diverse and Dynamic," full report, February 2008, pp. 20–35. Richard Gundrey, Church of Antioch listserv, June 1, 2008.

37. Field notes, Antioch Convocation, October 15, 2005; and Antioch Convocation, October 21, 2006.

38. Richard Gundrey, compiler and editor, "A Brief History on the Origins and Faith of the Church of Antioch," October 2004, Church Archives CD, Document 7, p. 10. Other sources for Archbishop Richard's invocation of the Law of Attraction: field notes, Antioch Convocation, October 15, 2005; and Richard Gundrey, "Starting a Real Church and Keeping It Going," presentation at Sursum Corda II Conference, October 5–8, 2003, DVD by Jim Waters/Sanctus Media.

39. Richard Gundrey, Church of Antioch listserv, June 2, 2008. Kera Hamilton, Church of Antioch bishop, age fifty-seven, interview, Philadelphia, Pa., July 27, 2007.

40. Gundrey, Church of Antioch listserv, June 2, 2008. Other mentions of "Julie's book" in this capacity include Linda Rounds-Nichols, Church of Antioch bishop, age fifty-eight, interview, Salinas, Calif., October 7, 2007; field notes, Antioch Convocation, October 6, 2007; Linda Rounds-Nichols, Church of Antioch listserv, October 27, 2008; Ted Feldmann, Church of Antioch listserv, October 28, 2009; field notes, Church of Antioch Convocation, [Roman Catholic retreat center, midwestern city and state], October 26, 2014.

41. Field notes, Church of Antioch, Santa Fe, N.M., April 4, 2007.

42. Richard Gundrey, letter of resignation, November 17, 2008, sent to the church mailing list.

43. Official Church of Antioch numbers as of February 2008: seventy-five clergy and thirty-three registered churches or ministries in the United States. Gundrey, "Seeing the Christ," p. 72. Official numbers reported at Convocation two years earlier were sixty-seven clergy and twenty-eight churches or ministries in the United States. "Annual Report," distributed to the assembled, October 21, 2006. Ted Feldmann, Church of Antioch priest, age fifty-seven, interview, Baltimore, Md., July 23, 2007.

44. Becky Taylor, Church of Antioch seminarian, age fifty-six, interview, Richmond, Va., July 23, 2007.

45. Pischner, interview. Sweeley, interview. Carol Calvert, Church of Antioch priest, age fifty-seven, interview, Santa Fe, N.M., April 5, 2007. Walker, interview. Kemp, interview.

46. On the home addition: field notes, Santa Fe, April 9, 2007. For the reception: field notes, Antioch Convocation, September 10, 2009.

47. Field notes, Antioch Convocation, October 22, 2006.

48. Bob Ross, in interview of Archbishop Richard Gundrey, Santa Fe Public Radio KSFR, March 15, 2008. Calvert, interview.

49. Herman Spruit, "What Does It Take to Be a Bishop in Our Church?," August 3, 1981, Church Archives CD, Document 101.

6. SACRAMENTS AND SAINTS: HEARING A NEW CALL

1. Here and throughout this section, I draw on Kera Hamilton, Church of Antioch bishop, age fifty-seven, interview, Philadelphia, Pa., July 27, 2007.

2. Ibid. Field notes, Church of Antioch, Philadelphia, Pa., July 29, 2007.

3. Field notes, Church of Antioch Convocation, Santa Fe, N.M., October 20, 2006. The ex-Catholic population of the United States in 2008 was about 10 percent of the total US population, which would be 30 million people. Pew Forum on Religion and Public Life, "U.S. Religious Landscape Survey," 2008, full report, p. 7. Since about 34 percent of US Catholics live in the east, I surmise that about 34 percent of ex-Catholics also live in the east, which would be roughly ten million ex-Catholics. For the regional distribution of Catholics: William D'Antonio et al., *American Catholics Today* (Lanham, Md.: Rowman and Littlefield, 2007), p. 183. Here I used the D'Antonio study of 2007 and the Pew numbers from 2008 rather than updated numbers, since the time of my study is closer to 2007.

4. Here and throughout this section, I draw on JoEllen Werthman, Church of Antioch priest, age sixty-one, interview, Philadelphia, Pa., July 27, 2007.

5. Pope John Paul II's apostolic letter stating that the question of women in the priesthood is not "open to debate" is *Ordinatio sacerdotalis*, May 22, 1994.

6. Werthman, interview.

7. Field notes, Church of Antioch, Philadelphia, July 29, 2007.

8. St. Mary Magdalene Catholic Apostolic Church of Antioch, mass program, July 29, 2007. Code of Canon Law, cc. 924–25, in *The Code of Canon Law: Latin-English Edition* (Washington, D.C.: Canon Law Society of America, 1983).

9. Here and throughout this section, I draw on field notes, Church of Antioch, Philadelphia, July 29, 2007.

10. A number of parishioners mentioned these same words as the source of great solace, which have been spoken and printed in the mass programs at St. Mary Magdalene since 2001. In 2013 Pope Francis wrote something similar in *Evangelii gaudium*: "The Eucharist, although it is the fullness of sacramental life, is not a prize for the perfect but a powerful medicine and nourishment for the weak" (November 24, 2013, sec. 47). The idea of communion as "medicine" dates to the second-century Christian title given to the Eucharist, the "medicine of immortality." It is first written as such in Ignatius of Antioch's *Epistle to the Ephesians*, chapter 20 (c. 98–117 CE). See the relevant passage in *The Apostolic Fathers*, vol. 1, edited and translated by Bart Ehrman, Loeb Classical Library (Cambridge, Mass.: Harvard University Press, 2003), pp. 240–41.

11. "Open orders": Richard Gundrey, interview of Archbishop Richard Gundrey by Bob Ross, Santa Fe Public Radio KSFR, March 15, 2008. For "open to all humanity," see Kate McGraw, "A Community 'Open to All Humanity,'" *Albuquerque Journal–Santa Fe/North*, May 18, 2006. Roberto Foss, Church of Antioch deacon, age forty-eight, interview, Los Angeles, Calif., November 24, 2007.

12. For Episcopal acknowledgment of moral relationships apart from marriage, see Caroline Addington Hall, *A Thorn in the Flesh: How Gay Sexuality Is Changing the Episcopal Church* (Lanham, Md.: Rowman and Littlefield, 2013), p. 137.

13. Lian Reed, Church of Antioch seminarian, age fifty-one, interview, Santa Fe, N.M., April 6, 2007.

14. Claire Vincent (pseudonymized at interviewee's request), Church of Antioch seminarian, age forty-five, interview, Salinas, Calif., October 7, 2007.

15. Michael Adams, Church of Antioch bishop, age fifty, interview, Salinas, Calif., October 6, 2007.

16. Modern Roman canonical norms indicate that ordained men cannot marry, but married men can be ordained, for example, when married priests of Eastern churches or the Anglican communion are accepted as priests into the Roman church. Orthodox and Roman bishops cannot ever be married. Yet there is at least one instance in which a married independent Catholic bishop was accepted back into the Roman church and, still married, became a Roman bishop. Salomão Barbosa Ferraz had founded a "Free Catholic Church" and was consecrated a bishop by Carlos Duarte Costa of the Brazilian Catholic Apostolic Church. After Barbosa Ferraz's reconciliation with Rome, in 1963 Pope John XXIII named him a titular bishop. See Phyllis Zagano, *Women and Catholicism: Gender, Communion, and Authority* (New York: Palgrave Macmillan, 2011), p. 74.

Jeff Genung, Church of Antioch deacon, age forty-seven, interview, Austin, Tex., June 23, 2007. Ted Feldmann, Church of Antioch deacon, age fifty-seven, interview, Baltimore, Md., July 23, 2007.

17. For "You've done this before" and "You are a continuation": Hamilton, interview; Darleen Mitchell, in field notes, Church of Antioch Convocation, [midwestern city and state], September 12, 2009. Deirdre Brousseau, Church of Antioch listserv, September 21, 2006. Diana Phipps, Lian Reed, and Claire Vincent also cited warrant for ordination in past lives, in interviews or Convocation conversations.

18. Linda Rounds-Nichols, Church of Antioch listserv, November 1, 2013. Diana Phipps, Church of Antioch bishop, age sixty-three, interview, Fredericksburg, Tex., June 16, 2007. Field notes from 2007, not specified here in the interest of discretion.

19. Werthman, interview. Hamilton, interview.

20. Field notes, Church of Antioch, Philadelphia, July 29, 2007.

21. Ibid.

22. Ibid.

23. On the various collaborations: Kera Hamilton, Church of Antioch listserv, August 12, 2007, December 28, 2007, and March 23, 2008; JoEllen Werthman, telephone call with author, February 22, 2010. "St. Paul Episcopal Church to Host Food with Friends," *Bristol Pilot* (Bristol, Pa.), February 5, 2011.

24. Werthman, telephone call.

25. Hamilton, interview.

26. Congregation for Divine Worship and Discipline of the Sacrament, *Redemptionis Sacramentum*, section 104, April 23, 2004. "The Custom of Intinction," insert in mass program, St. Mary Magdalene, Fairless Hills, Pa., July 29, 2007.

27. Hamilton, interview.

28. States' composite religious affiliations are available at the website for the Pew Forum on Religion and Public Life, "U.S. Religious Landscape Survey," February 2008. In 2000 and 2004 the county of Richmond voted for Republican presidential candidate George W. Bush, and in 2008 it went for Barack Obama. This information is available from numerous sources.

29. On religious same-sex marriage ceremonies in the United States, see Jeff Wilson, "'All Beings Are Equally Embraced by Amida Buddha': Jodo Shinshu Buddhism and Same-Sex Marriage in the United States," *Journal of Global Buddhism* 13 (June 2012): 31–59; and Wilson, "'Which One of You Is the Bride?' Unitarian Universalism and Same-Sex Marriage in North America, 1957–1972," *Journal of Unitarian Universalist History* 35 (Spring 2012): 156–72. Wilson told me that his oral-historical research for these articles suggests that religious (including Catholic) same-sex marriages could have been performed even earlier, but more historical work remains to be done. Jeff Wilson, email to author, January 13, 2015.

30. Congregation for the Doctrine of the Faith, *Letter on the Pastoral Care of Homosexual Persons*, section 3, October 1, 1986. Jane Gross, "Suffering in Dignity and Exile," *New York Times*, December 20, 1988.

31. Timothy d'Arch Smith, *Love in Earnest: Some Notes on the Lives and Writings of English "Uranian" Poets from 1880–1930* (London: Routledge and Kegan Paul, 1970). Sheila Rowbotham, *Edward Carpenter: A Life of Liberty and Love* (London: Verso, 2009), pp. 150, 351. Gregory Tillett, *The Elder Brother: A Biography of Charles Webster Leadbeater* (London: Routledge and Kegan Paul, 1982), pp. 283, 997, as well as chapter 23.

32. Stuart Timmons, *The Trouble with Harry Hay: Founder of the Modern Gay Movement* (New York: Alyson, 1990), pp. 27–28.

33. Gustavo Gutiérrez, *A Theology of Liberation: History, Politics and Salvation*, rev. ed. (1973; New York: Orbis Books, 1988); it was originally published in Spanish in 1971. For more on Itkin, see Mark Sullivan and Ian Young, eds., *The Radical Bishop and Gay Consciousness: The Passion of Mikhail Itkin* (Brooklyn, N.Y.: Autonomedia, 2014), esp. pp. 59, 80, and 117. The Sullivan and Young volume reproduces Itkin's *Radical Jesus and Gay Consciousness*, 2nd ed. (pp. 58–60 and 70–145). It was first published as Mikhail Itkin, *The Radical Jesus and Gay Consciousness: Notes for a Theology of Gay Liberation*, 2nd ed. (Long Beach, Calif.: Communiversity West, 1972).

34. "Rev. George Augustine Hyde," profile, Lesbian, Gay, Bisexual, and Transgender Religious Archives Network. "Rev. George Augustine Hyde," oral history interview by J. Gordon Melton, Lesbian, Gay, Bisexual, and Transgender Religious Archives Network.

35. Ibid. Heather Rachelle White, "Proclaiming Liberation: The Historical Roots of LGBT Religious Organizing, 1946–1976," *Nova Religio: The Journal of Alternative and Emergent Religions* 11, no. 4 (May 2008): 102–19, at pp. 103–4, 113–15. On the Mattachine ad: Karl Pruter and J. Gordon Melton, *The Old Catholic Sourcebook* (New York: Garland, 1983), pp. 65–66, 77–80. See also Mark D. Jordan, *Recruiting Young Love: How Christians Talk About Homosexuality* (Chicago: University of Chicago Press, 2011), pp. 66–70.

36. Ronald Enroth and Gerald Jamison, *The Gay Church* (Grand Rapids, Mich.: William B. Eerdmans, 1974), pp. 102–4. See also Sullivan and Young, *Radical Bishop and Gay Consciousness*; and White, "Proclaiming Liberation." On Broshears, see Pruter and Melton, *Old Catholic Sourcebook*, p. 79; and "The Sexes: The Lavender Panthers," *Time*, October 8, 1973. "Bishop Michael Francis Augustine Itkin," profile, Lesbian, Gay, Bisexual, and Transgender Religious Archives Network. Jordan, *Recruiting Young Love*, pp. 104–5, 120.

37. "Rev. Robert Mary Clement," profile, Lesbian, Gay, Bisexual, and Transgender Religious Archives Network. For another oral-historical account of Clement, his partner John Noble Darcy, the Church of the Beloved Disciple, and their famous "church shop," Lavender Elephants, see the memoir by New York fashion photographer and socialite Patrick McMullan, "Stonewall and the Church of the Beloved Disciple," *PMc Blog*, June 20, 2009. Wilson, email to author.

38. On "a gay subset": Tom Dowling, in Robert Dittler, White-Robed Monks abbot, and Tom Dowling, White-Robed Monks priest, interview, San Francisco, Calif., August 10, 2005. Lester Kinsolving, "The Paper Priests," *San Francisco Examiner*, October 11, 1971, p. 33. Enroth and Jamison, *The Gay Church*, p. 5.

39. Independent Catholicism Survey, question 12: "Besides religious and spiritual affiliations, what organizations or social causes are a main part of your life, if any?" Fifty-one of 270 independent Catholic responses indicated involvement in advocacy for the LGBTQ community; the next most popular causes were the environment (14), professional organizations (12), human rights, children, and homelessness (11 each), and women's rights (9). On the poly-wedding jurisdiction: John Plummer, *The Many Paths of the Independent Sacramental Movement* (Dallas: Newt Books, 2004), p. 94.

40. Tom Gallub, Church of Antioch deacon, age sixty-three, interview, Richmond, Va., July 21 and 22, 2007.

41. Here and throughout this section, I draw on Gallub, interview.

42. Ibid. Field notes, Church of Antioch, Richmond, Va., July 21–22, 2007. Chris Dovi, "Unconditional Faith: An Independent Catholic Community in Richmond Makes Acceptance the Foundation of Faith," *RVA Magazine* 1 (Spring 2010): 46–49.

43. Gallub, interview.

44. Ibid. Field notes, Church of Antioch, Richmond, July 21–22, 2007.

45. Gallub, interview.

46. Ibid. Field notes, Church of Antioch, Richmond, July 22, 2007.

47. Gallub, interview.

48. Anonymous, Church of Antioch priest, age fifty-four, interview, September 11, 2008. Field notes, Church of Antioch, Santa Fe, N.M., April 11, 2007.

49. Richard Gundrey, Church of Antioch listserv, January 18, 2008. Field notes, Church of Antioch, Santa Fe, April 11, 2007. Reed, interview.

50. Foss, interview.

51. Feldmann, interview.

52. Vincent, interview. Mark Elliott Newman, Church of Antioch bishop, age fifty-nine, interview, Phoenix, Ariz., April 13, 2009.

53. Feldmann, interview. Foss, interview. Werthman, interview. Jack Pischner, Church of Antioch seminarian, age sixty-two, interview, Salinas, Calif., October 7, 2007.

54. Church of Antioch listserv discussion, November 2006. Field notes, Antioch Convocation, September 13, 2009.

55. Field notes, Antioch Convocation, October 19, 2006.

56. "Reverend Uly Harrison Gooch: Obituary," *Salisbury Post* (Salisbury, N.C.), October 21, 2006.

57. Here and throughout this section, I draw on Thomas David Siebert, Church of Antioch priest, age fifty-two, interview, Richmond, Va., July 22, 2007.

58. Siebert, interview. Dovi, "Unconditional Faith," p. 49.

59. Siebert, interview. Tom David Siebert, email to author, March 3, 2009.

60. Siebert, interview.

61. Patsy Grubbs, Church of Antioch listserv, March 23, 2008.

CONCLUSION: ALL CATHOLICS

1. JoEllen Werthman, email to author, August 24, 2013.

2. Michael Adams, email to author, February 10, 2011.

3. On Richard's activities: Richard Gundrey, message forwarded to the Ascension Alliance listserv by Alan Kemp, September 22, 2013. On the new ministry: Alan Kemp, Ascension Alliance listserv, October 25, 2012.

4. Alan Kemp, Ascension Alliance listserv, June 3, 2014. Mark Elliott Newman, Church of Antioch listserv, June 4, 2014.

5. On Meri's funeral: Alan Kemp, Ascension Alliance listserv, June 21 and 27, 2014; and Mark Elliott Newman, Church of Antioch listserv, June 23, 2014.

6. Pew Research Center, "America's Changing Religious Landscape," full report, May 12, 2015, p. 21. Lawrence S. Cunningham, *An Introduction to Catholicism* (Cambridge: Cambridge University Press, 2009), p. 23.

7. Cunningham, *An Introduction to Catholicism*, p. 8; Mark D. Jordan, *The Silence of Sodom: Homosexuality in Modern Catholicism* (Chicago: University of Chicago Press, 2000), p. 1.

8. Dena Ross, "Sinéad O'Connor's Act of Love," *Beliefnet*, June 27, 2007.

9. Manuel Vásquez, presentation at session "Critical Catholic Studies" sponsored by the Roman Catholic Studies Group, American Academy of Religion Annual Meeting,

Baltimore, Md., November 23, 2013. Others who propose a Wittgensteinian "family resemblance" approach to defining Catholicism include independent scholar-bishop John Plummer; Elizabeth Pritchard, author of a forthcoming book on the Old Catholic Church USA; and Ludger Viefhues-Bailey, who identifies "conduits of discourse" to define evangelicalism: Viefhues-Bailey, *Between a Man and a Woman? Why Conservatives Oppose Same-Sex Marriage* (New York: Columbia University Press, 2010), pp. 4–6.

10. Though I doubt he was the first, Victor Conzemius used the word "anti-Romanism" to describe some US Polish Catholics in his discussion of Old Catholic outposts in the United States: Victor Conzemius, "Catholicism: Old and Roman," *Journal of Ecumenical Studies* (Summer 1967): 426–45, at pp. 436–37.

11. My suggestion that Catholic splits are human rather than Protestant comes from reading F. B. Welbourn on African Independent Churches, or AICs, Christian groups also known for splitting and often explained as imitative "of white America." Instead, Welbourn writes, maybe human institutions just always break and branch. F. B. Welbourn, *East African Rebels: A Study of Some Independent Churches* (London: SCM Press, 1961), pp. 168–69.

12. Michael Adams, Church of Antioch bishop, age fifty, interview, Salinas, Calif., October 6, 2007. The phrase "the centre cannot hold" comes from the poem "The Second Coming," by W. B. Yeats (1919).

13. Marian Ronan, "What Would Dorothy Do?," *An American Catholic on the Margins* blog, June 2, 2014.

14. J. A. Douglas, "Foreword," in *Episcopi Vagantes and the Anglican Church*, ed. Henry R. T. Brandreth (1947; Springfield, Mo.: St. Willibrord Press, 1987), pp. ix–xix, at p. xiv. Society for the Propagation of Christian Knowledge, "The History of the Old Catholic Movement," *Church Quarterly Review* 19, no. 37 (October 1884): 130–59, at pp. 151, 158–59.

15. Alan Bain, *"Bishops Irregular": An International Directory of Independent Bishops* (Bristol, UK: A. M. Bain, 1985), pp. 11–13. Independent Catholicism Survey, question 26.

16. Independent Catholicism Survey, question 27.

17. Bain, *"Bishops Irregular,"* pp. 11–13.

18. Jim Willems, Church of Antioch listserv, February 16, 2010.

19. Jeff Genung, Church of Antioch deacon, age forty-seven, interview, Austin, Tex., June 23, 2007. Frank Bugge, Church of Antioch listserv, July 6, 2003. This post and several of Archbishop Frank's emails on the same topic are collected as "Female Lines of Apostolic Succession," Church of Antioch Archives CD, Document 38.

20. Kera Hamilton, Church of Antioch bishop, age fifty-seven, interview, Philadelphia, Pa., July 27, 2007.

21. Pope Francis, *Evangelii gaudium*, November 24, 2013. Rachel Donadio, "On Gay Priests, Pope Francis Asks, 'Who Am I to Judge?,'" *New York Times*, July 29, 2013. For

"the people's pope," see Howard Chua-Eoan and Elizabeth Dias, "Pope Francis, The People's Pope," *Time*, December 11, 2013.

22. For 90 percent: David Masci, "Pope Francis's Popularity Extends Beyond Catholics," Pew Research Center, March 13, 2015. On meeting with the widow: Chua-Eoan and Dias, "Pope Francis." (The bishop and concelebrator in question are Jerónimo Podestá and Clelia Luro.) On Old Catholics: "Pope's Address to Old Catholic Bishops' Conference of the Union of Utrecht," *Zenit*, October 30, 2014. On outreach to the Society of St. Pius X: "Letter of His Holiness Pope Francis According to Which an Indulgence Is Granted to the Faithful on the Occasion of the Extraordinary Jubilee of Mercy," September 1, 2015.

23. For "son of the Church": Antonio Spadaro, "A Big Heart Open to God," interview with Pope Francis, *America*, September 30, 2013.

24. Peter Manseau, "What It Means to Be Catholic Now," *New York Times*, March 10, 2014.

25. Ibid. Peter Manseau, *Vows: The Story of a Priest, a Nun, and Their Son* (New York: Free Press/Simon and Schuster, 2005).

26. Here and in this section, I draw on field notes, Church of Antioch Convocation, Richmond, Va., October 14–17, 2005.

PRIMARY SOURCES

INTERVIEWS: CHURCH OF ANTIOCH

Adams, Michael. Church of Antioch bishop, age fifty. Interview, Salinas, Calif., October 6, 2007.

Anonymous. Church of Antioch priest, age fifty-four. Interview, September 11, 2008.

Anonymous. Church of Antioch priest, age sixty-two. Interview, April 8, 2009.

Bowling, Weldon. Church of Antioch priest, age seventy-six. Interview, Harker Heights, Tex., June 15, 2007.

Brousseau, Deirdre. Church of Antioch priest, age fifty-seven. Interview, Salinas, Calif., October 7, 2007.

Calvert, Carol. Church of Antioch priest, age fifty-seven. Interview, Santa Fe, N.M., April 5, 2007.

Clemens, Paul. Church of Antioch bishop, age sixty-three. Interview, Salinas, Calif., October 8, 2007.

Dangaran, Daniel. Church of Antioch priest (later bishop), age fifty-three. Interview, Santa Fe, N.M., April 5, 2007.

Eagar, Jorge. Church of Antioch bishop, age sixty-three. Interview, Tempe, Ariz., April 13, 2009.

Feldmann, Theodore. Church of Antioch deacon (later priest), age fifty-seven. Interview, Baltimore, Md., July 23, 2007.

Foss, Roberto. Church of Antioch deacon, age forty-eight. Interview, Los Angeles, Calif., November 24, 2007.

Gallub, Thomas. Church of Antioch deacon, age sixty-three. Interview, Richmond, Va., July 21 and 22, 2007.

Genung, Jeffrey. Church of Antioch deacon, age forty-seven. Interview, Austin, Tex., June 23, 2007.

Gundrey, Richard. Church of Antioch archbishop and presiding patriarch, age seventy-one. Interview, Santa Fe, N.M., May 28, 2005.

Hamilton, Kera. Church of Antioch bishop, age fifty-seven. Interview, Philadelphia, Pa., July 27, 2007.

Kemp, Alan. Church of Antioch bishop, age fifty-eight. Interview, Gig Harbor, Wash., October 10, 2008.

Molina, Liza. Church of Antioch deacon, age forty. Interview, Santa Fe, N.M., May 27, 2008.

Newman, Mark Elliot. Church of Antioch bishop, age fifty-nine. Interview, Phoenix, Ariz., April 13, 2009.

Phipps, Diana. Church of Antioch bishop, age sixty-three. Interview, Fredericksburg, Tex., June 16, 2007.

Pischner, Jack. Church of Antioch seminarian, age sixty-two. Interview, Salinas, Calif., October 7, 2007.

Reed, Lian. Church of Antioch seminarian, age fifty-one. Interview, Santa Fe, N.M., April 6, 2007.

Rounds-Nichols, Linda. Church of Antioch priest, age fifty-eight. Interview, Salinas, Calif., October 7, 2007.

Siebert, Thomas David. Church of Antioch priest, age fifty-two. Interview, Richmond, Va., July 22, 2007.

Spruit, Meri Louise. Church of Antioch matriarch emerita, age eighty-one. Interview, Marina, Calif., October 8, 2007.

St. George, James. Church of Antioch deacon, age forty. Interview, Fairless Hills, Pa., July 27, 2007.

Sweeley, Jack. Church of Antioch priest, age sixty-four. Interview, Baltimore, Md., July 24, 2007.

Taylor, Becky. Church of Antioch seminarian, age fifty-six. Interview, Richmond, Va., July 23, 2007.

Vincent, Claire (pseudonymized name). Church of Antioch seminarian, age forty-five. Interview, Salinas, Calif., October 7, 2007.

Walker, Douglas. Church of Antioch seminarian, age fifty-nine. Interview, Santa Fe, N.M., April 10, 2007.

Werthman, JoEllen. Church of Antioch priest, age sixty-one. Interview, Philadelphia, Pa., July 27, 2007.

Willems, James R. Church of Antioch lay leader, age sixty-three. Interview, Ojai, Calif., November 25, 2007.

Yonce, Sara. Church of Antioch priest, age sixty-five. Interview, Montgomery, Tex., June 19, 2007.

INTERVIEWS: OTHER INDEPENDENT JURISDICTIONS

Anderson, Clinton. Deacon, African-American Catholic Congregation (Imani Temple). Interview, Washington, D.C., July 1, 2003.

Anonymous. Bishop, Catholic Apostolic National Church, formerly Catholic Apostolic Church in North America, formerly Old Catholic Church of the United States. Telephone interview, October 9, 2004.

Anonymous. Layperson, African-American Catholic Congregation (Imani Temple). Interview, Washington, D.C., June 24, 2003.

Anonymous. Priest, Liberal Catholic Church, Province of the USA. Interview, [city], N.M., May 30, 2005.

Babauta, Ken. Priest, White-Robed Monks of St. Benedict. Telephone interview, August 9, 2005.

Bayo, Adrian Isaac. Priest, African-American Catholic Congregation (Imani Temple). Interview, Washington, D.C., June 23, 2003.

Beaviers, Bill. Lay leader, African-American Catholic Congregation (Imani Temple). Interview, Washington, D.C., July 1, 2003.

Dittler, Robert. Abbot, White-Robed Monks of St. Benedict. Interview, San Francisco, Calif., August 10, 2005.

Dowling, Tom. Priest, White-Robed Monks of St. Benedict. Interview, San Francisco, Calif., August 10, 2005.

Gibbons, Robert. Seminarian, African-American Catholic Congregation (Imani Temple). Interview, Washington, D.C., June 24, 2003.

Harvin, Carlos. Bishop, African-American Catholic Congregation (Imani Temple). Interview, Washington, D.C., July 3, 2003.

Jenkins, Scott. Priest, Ecumenical Catholic Communion. Telephone interview, August 20, 2008.

King, Franzo. Archbishop, African Orthodox Church. San Francisco, Calif., August 10, 2005.

Mapplebeckpalmer, Richard. Priest, White-Robed Monks of St. Benedict. Interview, San Francisco, Calif., August 9, 2005.

FIELD TRIPS

2001–2004. African-American Catholic Congregation (Imani Temple), Washington, D.C.

May 28–30, 2005. Church of Antioch, Santa Fe, N.M.

August 7 and 10, 2005. St. John Will-I-AM Coltrane African Orthodox Church, San Francisco, Calif.

August 9–10, 2005. White-Robed Monks of St. Benedict, San Francisco, Calif.

October 14–17, 2005. Church of Antioch Convocation, Richmond, Va.

October 19–22, 2006. Church of Antioch Convocation, Santa Fe, N.M.

November 3–5, 2006. Call to Action National Conference, Milwaukee, Wis.

April 2–11, 2007. Church of Antioch, Santa Fe, N.M.

June 15–24, 2007. Church of Antioch, Tex. (Harker Heights, Fredericksburg, Austin, Houston).

July 21–22, 2007. Church of Antioch, Richmond, Va.

July 23–24, 2007. Church of Antioch, Baltimore, Md.

July 27–29, 2007. Church of Antioch, Philadelphia, Pa.

October 5–8, 2007. Church of Antioch Convocation, Salinas, Calif.

November 21–26, 2007. Church of Antioch, southern California (Los Angeles and Ojai).

May 23–29, 2008. Church of Antioch, Santa Fe, N.M.

July 18–20, 2008. Joint Conference of Federation of Christian Ministries, CORPUS, Women's Ordination Conference, and Roman Catholic Womenpriests, Boston, Mass.

September 9–16, 2008. Church of Antioch, Wash. (mostly Seattle area).

November 7–9, 2008. Call to Action National Conference, Milwaukee, Wis.

April 7–14, 2009. Church of Antioch, Ariz. (mostly Phoenix area).

May 15–17, 2009. Intentional Eucharistic Communities Conference, Chevy Chase, Md.

September 10–14, 2009. Church of Antioch Convocation, [Roman Catholic retreat center, midwestern city and state].

August 19–21, 2011. Ascension Alliance Convocation, Seattle, Wash.

October 16, 2011. Shabazz African Orthodox Church, Brooklyn, N.Y.

October 20–24, 2011. Church of Antioch Convocation, [Roman Catholic retreat center, midwestern city and state].

April 28, 2012. Mass and party for anniversary of ordination of independent priest, [Roman Catholic church, New York, N.Y.].

August 22–25, 2014. Ascension Alliance Convocation, Tahlequah, Okla.

October 23–27, 2014. Church of Antioch Convocation, [Roman Catholic retreat center, midwestern city and state].

PRIVATE LISTSERVS

Ascension Alliance private listserv, 2010–2016.

Autocephalous Sacramental Movement Yahoo group, 2008–2009.

Church of Antioch private listserv, 2005–2016.

Independent Sacramental Movement Yahoo group, 2006–2013.

New York City Independent Catholic/Old Catholic Yahoo group, 2006–2016.

ARCHIVES VISITED OR CONSULTED

Archives, Church of Antioch, Santa Fe, N.M. Church Archives CD. Available as permitted by the patriarch or matriarch of the Church of Antioch or the presiding bishop of Ascension Alliance.

Archives, Episcopal Diocese of Fond-du-Lac, Appleton, Wis.

Archives, Imani Temple, Washington, D.C.

Archives, Science of Mind, Golden, Colo.

Archives, Society of St. Joseph of the Sacred Heart (Josephites), Baltimore, Md.

J. Gordon Melton American Religions Collection, University of California at Santa Barbara Library, Santa Barbara, Calif.

Library of Congress, Washington, D.C.

Rare Books and Special Collections, Hesburgh Library, University of Notre Dame, Notre Dame, Ind.

Full bibliographic information for all print, visual, and audio primary and secondary sources can be found in the endnotes of this book. The same information, sometimes with a link to the source on the Internet, is available on the Columbia University Press website (cup.columbia.edu). Also at the website is a bibliographic essay. Please visit the web page for *The Other Catholics*.

INDEX

Note: Page numbers in italics refer to figures. Those followed by *n* refer to notes, with note number.